How to Do Everything with Windows® XP Digital Media

How to Do *Everything* with Windows® XP Digital Media

Curt Simmons

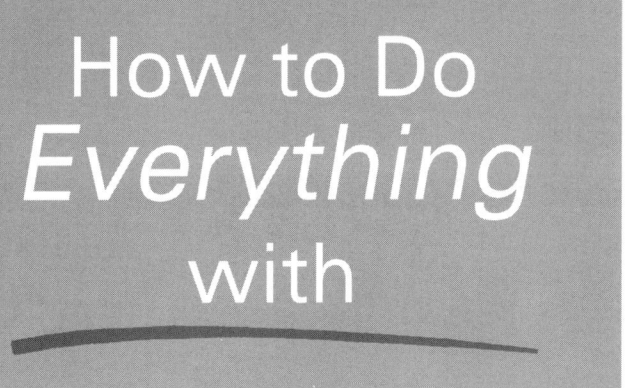

CHESHIRE LIBRARIES	
H J	21/04/2004
006.7	£16.99
GT	

McGraw-Hill/Osborne

New York Chicago San Francisco Lisbon
London Madrid Mexico City Milan New Delhi
San Juan Seoul Singapore Sydney Toronto

*The **McGraw·Hill** Companies*

McGraw-Hill/Osborne
2100 Powell Street, 10th Floor
Emeryville, California 94608
U.S.A.

To arrange bulk purchase discounts for sales promotions, premiums, or fund-raisers, please contact **McGraw-Hill**/Osborne at the above address. For information on translations or book distributors outside the U.S.A., please see the International Contact Information page immediately following the index of this book.

How to Do Everything with Windows® XP Digital Media

Copyright © 2004 by The McGraw-Hill Companies. All rights reserved. Printed in the United States of America. Except as permitted under the Copyright Act of 1976, no part of this publication may be reproduced or distributed in any form or by any means, or stored in a database or retrieval system, without the prior written permission of the publisher, with the exception that the program listings may be entered, stored, and executed in a computer system, but they may not be reproduced for publication.

1234567890 FGR FGR 019876543

ISBN 0-07-225342-8

Publisher:	Brandon A. Nordin
Vice President &	
Associate Publisher	Scott Rogers
Acquisitions Editor	Megg Morin
Project Editors	Emily K. Wolman, LeeAnn Pickrell
Acquisitions Coordinator	Athena Honore
Technical Editor	Will Kelly
Copy Editor	Emily K. Wolman
Proofreader	Susie Elkind
Indexer	James Minkin
Composition	Apollo Publishing Services
Series Design	Mickey Galicia
Cover Series Design	Dodie Shoemaker
Cover Illustration	Wil Voss

This book was composed with Corel VENTURA™ Publisher.

Information has been obtained by **McGraw-Hill**/Osborne from sources believed to be reliable. However, because of the possibility of human or mechanical error by our sources, **McGraw-Hill**/Osborne, or others, **McGraw-Hill**/Osborne does not guarantee the accuracy, adequacy, or completeness of any information and is not responsible for any errors or omissions or the results obtained from the use of such information.

About the Author

Curt Simmons is a freelance author, technical trainer, Windows guru, and lover of digital technology. Curt is the author of more than thirty computing books on a variety of topics, including the bestseller *How To Do Everything with Windows XP* and *How To Do Everything with Photoshop Album*. When he is not writing and using digital media, Curt spends time with his wife and daughters. Visit Curt at www.curtsimmons.com.

Contents at a Glance

Part I	**Get into the Groove with the Music You Never Want to Be Without**	
1	Create a CD with Your Favorite Tunes for Someone You Love	3
2	Spin Your Face: Put Your Smile on a Custom CD Label	21
3	Become an Internet Radio DJ	41
4	Customize Windows Media Player	53

Part II	**Create Fun Things with Your Digital Photos**	
5	Organize Your Memories: Make Sure You Can Find Photos When You Need Them	73
6	Print Perfect Digital Photos of Any Size— Every Time!	99
7	Make a Printed Photo Album So You Can Take Your Loved Ones with You	117
8	Turn Your Photo Memories into a Slide Show	127
9	Make Photo Stories with Your Digital Photos	143

Part III	**Be in the Movies!**	
10	Create Your Own Birthday or Wedding Video	165
11	Make a Scary Movie!	181
12	Step Back in Time and Create Movies That Look Like the Old Days	197
13	Build a Custom Video Sound Track	209
14	Put Your Movie on a CD for Cannes, and More!	227

Part IV		**Become a Digital Maniac!**	
	15	Monitor Your House with a Webcam	245
	16	Use Your Vacation Video to Make a Video Screen Saver	257
	17	Wake Up to Windows XP: Turn Your Computer into an Alarm Clock	265
	18	Turn Your Computer into a Jukebox (and Back Again)	277
	19	Digitize Your Old Cassettes, 8-Tracks, and Records	295
	A	Get to Know Windows Movie Maker 2	313
	B	More Inexpensive and Fun Digital Software	327
		Index	329

Contents

	Acknowledgments	xv
	Introduction	xvii
PART I	**Get into the Groove with the Music You Never Want to Be Without**	
CHAPTER 1	**Create a CD with Your Favorite Tunes for Someone You Love**	**3**
	Get Ready to Make Your CD	4
	Rip Songs to Windows Media Player	6
	Make Sure the Ripping Goes As Planned	7
	Rip Songs from a CD	8
	Organize Your Songs into a Playlist	13
	Burn Your CD	15
	More Great Ideas	19
CHAPTER 2	**Spin Your Face: Put Your Smile on a Custom CD Label**	**21**
	Gather Your Materials	22
	Plan Your Label	23
	Create Your CD Label with Plus! CD Label Maker	24
	Start the Label Maker and Choose CD or Playlist	24
	Choose a Template	25
	Design Your CD Label	27
	Print Your Label	34
	Create Your Jewel Case Label with Plus! CD Label Maker	37
	More Great Ideas	39
CHAPTER 3	**Become an Internet Radio DJ**	**41**
	Get Familiar with Internet Radio	42
	Find the Stations You Want	45
	Browse Existing Categories	45
	Perform a Basic Search	45
	Listen to Internet Radio	47
	Create My Stations	50
	More Great Ideas	51

CHAPTER 4	**Customize Windows Media Player**	**53**
	Adjust the Now Playing Area	54
	Color Chooser	58
	Cross Fading and Auto Volume Leveling	59
	Graphic Equalizer	59
	Media Link for E-Mail	59
	Play Speed Settings	59
	Quiet Mode	60
	SRS WOW Effects	60
	Video Settings	61
	Work with Visualizations	61
	Get More Visualizations	62
	Modify Visualizations' Behavior	62
	Choose Skins	64
	Work with Plug-Ins	68
	Use Plus! Speaker Enhancement	69
	More Great Ideas	70
PART II	**Create Fun Things with Your Digital Photos**	
CHAPTER 5	**Organize Your Memories: Make Sure You Can Find Photos When You Need Them**	**73**
	Get to Know Photo File Types	74
	Name Photos	78
	View Photos	79
	Create a Folder Structure That Works	85
	Back Up Photos	87
	Use Windows XP Backup	87
	Store Photos on the Web	92
	More Great Ideas	96
CHAPTER 6	**Print Perfect Digital Photos of Any Size— Every Time!**	**99**
	Understand PPR—The Basics of Quality Photo Printing	100
	Printers	101
	Paper	102
	Photo Resolution	103
	Print Your Photos	106
	Order Prints Online	108
	Other Printing Options	113
	More Great Ideas	115
CHAPTER 7	**Make a Printed Photo Album So You Can Take Your Loved Ones with You**	**117**
	Create a Photo Album Manually	118
	Use a Photo Album Program	120

Contents **xi**

	Get a Photo Book Printed	124
	More Great Ideas	126
CHAPTER 8	**Turn Your Photo Memories into a Slide Show**	**127**
	Get the HTML Slide Show Wizard PowerToy	128
	Understand What the HTML Slide Show Wizard Does	129
	Create a Slide Show	130
	Cull Your Photos	130
	Use the Slide Show Wizard	132
	View Your Slide Show	139
	Share Your Slide Show	140
	More Great Ideas	142
CHAPTER 9	**Make Photo Stories with Your Digital Photos**	**143**
	Understand What Plus! Photo Story Does	144
	Get Ready to Use Plus! Photo Story	145
	Gather Your Photos	145
	Decide About Narration	145
	Pick Your Background Music	146
	Create Your Photo Story	147
	Start the Plus! Photo Story Wizard	147
	Choose and Organize Your Photos	148
	Record Your Story	150
	Create a Title Page	157
	Choose Background Music	159
	Choose Quality Settings and Save Your Story	160
	More Great Ideas	161
PART III	**Be in the Movies!**	
CHAPTER 10	**Create Your Own Birthday or Wedding Video**	**165**
	Get Ready to Create a Birthday or Wedding Video	166
	Identify Your Goal	166
	Gather Your Film and Photos	167
	Plan the Movie Flow	168
	Import Video and Photos into Movie Maker	168
	Organize Your Footage	169
	Create a Title Page	170
	Assemble Your Movie	174
	Add Transitions	176
	Add Special Effects	178
	More Great Ideas	179
CHAPTER 11	**Make a Scary Movie!**	**181**
	Explore Scary Movie Variations	182
	A Real Scary Movie	182

	A Scary Movie Spoof	183
	Real-Life Horror Spoofs	183
	Halloween with the Kids	183
	Know What Makes a Scary Movie Scary	183
	Visual Scares	183
	Sound Scares	184
	The Element of Surprise	185
	Situational Tension	185
	Blood and Gore	185
	Plan Your Scary Movie	185
	Create Summary Statements	186
	Create a Storyboard	186
	Write the Script	187
	Film Your Scary Movie	188
	Assemble Your Scary Movie in Movie Maker	188
	Import Your Video	188
	Create, Trim, and Combine Your Clips	189
	Drag Clips to the Storyboard in Correct Order	189
	Create a Title Page and End Credits	189
	Add Transitions and Effects	189
	Add Your Sound Track	194
	Save Your Movie	194
	More Great Ideas	194
CHAPTER 12	**Step Back in Time and Create Movies That Look Like the Old Days**	**197**
	Why Old Movies Are Fun (and Why You Should Make One)	198
	Understand Old-Movie Basics	199
	Make Your Old Movie	200
	Import Your Movie	200
	Remove the Movie Sound Track	200
	Turn the Movie to Black and White	201
	Add Aging Effects	203
	Create Cue Cards Between Clips	205
	Save and Use Your Movie	207
	More Great Ideas	207
CHAPTER 13	**Build a Custom Video Sound Track**	**209**
	Know the Basics: Sound Tracks 101	210
	Sound and Movie Maker	211
	How You Should Use Sound in Your Movie	211
	Plan Your Sound Track	212
	Mute the Original Movie Sound Track	214

	Record Dialogue	218
	Use Background Music	222
	Have Fun with Other Sound Effects	225
	More Great Ideas	225
CHAPTER 14	**Put Your Movie on a CD for Cannes, and More!**	**227**
	Decide What to Do with Your Movie	228
	Save Your Movie to Your Computer	229
	Save Your Movie to a CD	233
	Send Your Movie Over E-Mail	236
	Send Your Movie to the Web	239
	Save Your Movie to a DV Camera	240
	More Great Ideas	241
PART IV	**Become a Digital Maniac!**	
CHAPTER 15	**Monitor Your House with a Webcam**	**245**
	Get the Stuff You Need	246
	Understand How Timershot Works	248
	Set Up Timershot	249
	Frequency of Pictures	251
	Photo Sizes	251
	File Location	251
	Where to Save	252
	Review Your Photos	253
	More Great Ideas	256
CHAPTER 16	**Use Your Vacation Video to Make a Video Screen Saver**	**257**
	Get the Windows XP Video Screen Saver PowerToy	258
	Choose a Video File Format	259
	Set Up Your Video Screen Saver	261
	Use a Playlist As a Screen Saver	264
	More Great Ideas	264
CHAPTER 17	**Wake Up to Windows XP: Turn Your Computer into an Alarm Clock**	**265**
	Start the Alarm Clock	266
	Create a Wake-Up Alarm	269
	Create a Weekly or Monthly Alarm	270
	Manage Alarms	272
	Change, Delete, or Turn Off an Alarm	273
	Use Cool and Cruel Options	274
	More Great Ideas	276

How to Do Everything with Windows XP Digital Media

CHAPTER 18	**Turn Your Computer into a Jukebox (and Back Again)**	**277**
	What Is Party Mode for Windows Media Player?	278
	Get Ready to Use Party Mode	279
	Set Up Party Mode	284
	Privacy Option	285
	Now Playing Options	286
	Marquee Options	287
	Skin Option	289
	Use Party Mode	290
	Stop the Party	293
	More Great Ideas	294
CHAPTER 19	**Digitize Your Old Cassettes, 8-Tracks, and Records**	**295**
	Connect Your Player to Your Computer	296
	Check Out the Hardware Requirements	297
	Connect a Stereo	298
	Connect a Record Player	300
	Connect a Cassette or Reel-to-Reel Player	300
	Digitize Your Music	300
	Test Your Input	301
	Record Your Music	302
	Review, Modify, and Delete Tracks	304
	Clean Tracks	307
	Set Content-Protection Options	308
	Select Quality Settings and Save Tracks	308
	More Great Ideas	311
APPENDIX A	**Get to Know Windows Movie Maker 2**	**313**
	What Movie Maker 2 Can Do for You	314
	Get Ready to Use Windows Movie Maker	316
	Get Video into Windows Movie Maker	317
	Check Out the Movie Maker Interface	318
	Record and Import Video	320
	Work with Collections and Clips	322
	Make Movies	323
	Split Clips	323
	Combine Clips	323
	Get Familiar with the Workspace	324
	Create a Storyboard	324
	Trim Clips	325
	Add Audio Files to Your Movies	326
APPENDIX B	**More Inexpensive and Fun Digital Software**	**327**
	Index	**329**

Acknowledgments

Thanks to Megg Morin for the idea and the vision—it was great working with you, as always. Also, a big thanks to Will Kelly for a fine technical review, and to Emily Wolman for crossing all of the *t*s and dotting the *i*s. Finally, thanks to Susie Elkind for her eagle eyes on this book, and thanks to my family for their support.

Introduction

Digital, digital, digital—you hear the word all the time. Everything from digital music to digital video to digital photos and much more. We are truly living in a digital world! If you are reading this book, the odds are quite good that digital technology has already impacted you in some way. Maybe you own a digital camera or a digital video camcorder. Maybe you love using music with your computer and you want to do even more. The great news is that your Windows XP computer has all of the power and features you need for your digital life, and many more are waiting in a collection of free Microsoft PowerToys and inexpensive Plus! packs.

That's why I wrote this book. *How to Do Everything with Windows XP Digital Media* is your one-stop shop for all things digital. But hey, I didn't just write a book about digital technology. Instead, I wrote a book of fun digital projects that you can do on your Windows XP computer. Armed with this book and a little creativity, you are about to find out just how far Windows XP can take you into the digital world. For example, how would you like to…

- Create personalized music CDs
- Make personalized CD labels
- Become an Internet radio DJ
- Make Windows Media Player your own
- Make digital photos easier to use on Windows XP
- Print perfect digital photos
- Make printed photo albums
- Make digital photo slide shows
- Create wedding or birthday videos

- Make scary movies
- Make movies look like the old days
- Create custom movie sound tracks
- Monitor your house with a webcam
- Turn Windows XP into an alarm clock
- Turn Windows XP into a jukebox
- Digitize your old cassettes and records

You can do all of these things and more in this book. You'll get creative with Windows XP digital media and learn how to make fun products and do fun things.

I've written this book in an easy to read, step-by-step manner. All you need to know before you start using this book is how to turn on your computer and how to use your keyboard and mouse. If you have that down, you're ready to get started!

All the books in this series include special features that call out certain bits of information to make them easily accessible. Such information can be found under the following headings:

- **How to…** A boxed section giving instructions on how to perform a specific task
- **Did You Know?** A boxed section that provides background information or explores a topic related to the main text
- **Note** Supplemental information
- **Caution** Something to watch out for
- **Tip** A time-saving alternative
- **Spin** A tip that applies to digital music
- **Roll Film** A tip that applies to digital video
- **Picture This** A tip that applies to digital pictures

So, let's have some fun with Windows XP digital media! And let me know how your projects come out; I would love to hear from you. You can reach me at curt_simmons@hotmail.com and at www.curtsimmons.com.

Part I

Get into the Groove with the Music You Never Want to Be Without

Chapter 1

Create a CD with Your Favorite Tunes for Someone You Love

How to...

- Rip songs to Windows Media Player
- Create playlists
- Burn CDs

Ah, those romantic love CDs. You see them advertised on late-night television: "A collection of your favorite and memorable hits all combined in a two-CD, 48-track pack, all for only $19.95!" You think, "Sure, but half of the songs I don't know, and $19.95 is kind of steep for a rehash of old songs." And you're right! Why buy CDs that have mixes of your favorite music when you can create them yourself on Windows XP?

With Windows XP's Media Player, you can copy songs from other CDs, mix them up, and then burn your own CD with only the songs you want, in the order you want. Pull out those old love songs, those favorite hits from the '40s, '80s, or '90s, or your child's favorite songs and mix them up on one convenient CD. As you can imagine, there are many different uses for the custom CDs you can create on Windows XP, and in this chapter, you'll see how to make the personalized CD you want—from start to finish!

What You'll Need

For your custom CD project, you'll use Windows Media Player, which is already built into your Windows XP Home or Professional operating system. Your computer must be outfitted with a CD burner (see your computer's documentation to find out if you have one), and you'll need a standard CD-R disc. You can buy all kinds of CD-R brands (and even colors) at any computer or department store. It's a good idea to buy a CD-R disc that has at least 700MB of storage space, or one that is around 80 minutes in length. This is a standard size, so practically any CD-R disc you buy will work just fine.

Get Ready to Make Your CD

Windows Media Player gives you everything you need to copy songs from various CDs, organize those songs, and then create your own CD with the songs you want. To make sure you are up-to-speed with the current cool lingo, the process of copying

CHAPTER 1: Create a CD with Your Favorite Tunes for Someone You Love 5

a song from a CD to Media Player is called *ripping,* while the process of creating your own CD is called *burning.* So with Windows Media Player, you rip the songs you want to Media Player, organize them, burn them to your own CD, and voila! You have a custom CD.

The good news is Windows Media Player is ready for this project without any special setup or installation from you. However, before you proceed with your project, there are two items you should check out. First, you should be running the most current version of Media Player. This will ensure that you get the best performance and that you have all of the features available that this chapter covers. At the time of writing, the current Media Player is version 9. To see what version of Media Player you're using, click Start | All Programs | Windows Media Player. Then, click Help | About Windows Media Player. The dialog box that appears will tell you what version you're running.

If you are not running version 9, you can download and install it on your computer free of charge from Microsoft. Just go to www.microsoft.com/mediaplayer, choose version 9 to download, and follow the instructions as they appear on your screen. You can also get the latest version of Media Player by visiting the Windows Update site at http://windowsupdate.microsoft.com.

The second thing you'll need to do is decide what songs you want to rip to Media Player. Before you begin working with your computer, sit down with a piece of paper and write down the songs you want to use on your personal CD.

Did you know?

Windows Media Player 9

One thing is for sure: Software never stops changing. Windows Media Player is no exception to this rule. It has expanded from its old Windows 98 days, when Media Player was nothing more than a simple utility used to play media, to Media Player 9 —a full-fledged, grown-up media player, replete with all kinds of bells and whistles.

As a practice, you should use the latest version of Media Player, as Microsoft releases versions from time to time. Why, you might ask? With each rebirth of Media Player, you get new features, a better interface, and simply more to do! Media Player updates are free, so be sure to take advantage of them as they are released.

Decide the order of those songs at this time so you'll have a working list to go by. Depending on the CD you're creating, think carefully about song order. If your CD includes both fast and slow songs, you may want to mix them up so that not all slow songs are grouped together and not all fast songs are grouped together. Or you may want to think in terms of theme. Here are some examples:

- If you're making a love CD for that special someone, consider putting songs in the order of your life. For example, put a few songs you both loved when you first met followed by some songs from later in your relationship. If you have been with that special someone for years, you'll have a lot of material to pick from.

- If you're making a CD for a relative, such as a parent, brother, or sister, choose songs that are especially meaningful to different times of your lives. For example, make a CD for your brother or sister that has a few tunes you both loved as kids, them some tunes from your adolescent years, and finally some favorites from college. This trip down memory lane is sure to be a hit!

- Make a CD for your child's high school graduation. You could call it the "Songs of Your Life" and include some toddler tunes, preadolescent tunes, and favorite teenager tunes. Be sure to include music that has special family meaning or brings to mind fond family memories.

As you can see, you have lots to think about, so always begin by constructing your CD list on paper before you begin. Once you're happy with your list, round up all of the CDs that have the various songs you'll need. Now you're ready to begin ripping those songs.

 *You may be thinking, "This sounds great, but a lot of my favorite songs are on old 8-tracks, vinyl records, and cassettes. What do I do now?" The good news is you can get a tool from Microsoft that will let you hook up your stereo to your Windows XP computer and record those analog tapes and records into Windows Media Player. Media Player can even digitize and clean them up before you burn them to a CD! See Chapter 19 to find out more.*

Rip Songs to Windows Media Player

Once you decide what songs you want on your custom CD, your next task is to rip all of them. Again, ripping just means that you copy the songs you want from various CDs to Windows Media Player, where you can organize and burn them to your own CD. The following sections show you what to do.

Make Sure the Ripping Goes As Planned

Before you rip any songs, spend a couple of minutes reading this section and checking out Media Player, just to make sure the ripping process happens as it should and as you want. Underneath the surface of Media Player are a few settings that determine how ripping works, so let's take a look at these and make sure that everything is in order for your ripping session.

To do so, just open Windows Media Player and click Tools | Options. This opens the Options dialog box, a place where you can determine various settings for Media Player. If you click the Copy Music tab (see Figure 1-1), you see there are a few settings that determine how Media Player rips music. The odds are quite good that there is nothing you need to configure here, but the following list details the options, just in case you need to make any changes:

- ■ **Copy Music to This Location** Windows Media Player stores any music that you rip in the My Music folder, which is found in My Documents. This location is fine, but if you want your songs in a different folder, click the Change button and choose a different folder. Unless you have a specific reason for changing it, though, it's recommended that you simply leave it as it is. Also, you can click the File Name button and change the name of the song file when it is ripped. By default, Media Player saves the song by the song's name, which is probably what you want anyway.

- ■ **Format** Use this drop-down list box to save songs either in Windows Media Audio format or as MP3 files. MP3 files provide more compression than Windows Media files, but Windows Media files provide better quality. In short, MP3 files are used primarily on the Internet, because their file size is small for downloading. However, the quality always suffers. Since you are ripping the songs so you can burn them to a CD, leave the format option as Windows Media. This will give you crystal-clear audio quality.

- ■ **Copy Protect Music** Select this option when you are ripping copy-protected music—audio that requires a license key in order to play. Windows Media Player can rip copy-protected music and store your license key so that you can listen to it. For this project, you are not using copy-protected music, so don't select this check box.

- ■ **Copy CD When Inserted** Select this option to start the copy (ripping) process automatically when you insert a music CD. If you select this check box, the entire CD is copied; therefore, don't use it for this project, since you'll want only certain tracks from certain CDs.

- **Eject CD When Copying Is Completed** Select this option to eject the CD from the CD drive automatically when copying is finished. For this project, you may use this feature.

- **Audio Quality** Select this option to actually compress song files so that they don't take up as much room on your computer. For example, if you are ripping songs to store in Media Library just so you can listen to them on your computer, you can choose a setting on the slider bar between Smallest Size and Best Quality. However, since you want to burn your songs to a new CD for this project, you want the best quality you can get, so move the slider bar to Best Quality.

When you are done with these settings, just click OK. This will take you back to the Windows Media Player interface.

Rip Songs from a CD

So now you have your collection of CDs with your favorite songs noted on a piece of paper, and you're ready to get going. First things first: You don't have to rip the

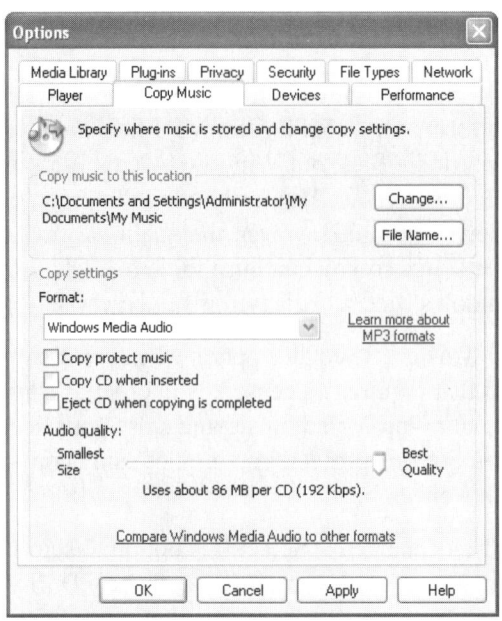

FIGURE 1-1 The Copy Music tab enables you to customize how Media Player rips songs.

CHAPTER 1: Create a CD with Your Favorite Tunes for Someone You Love

songs in the order you want to burn them on your custom CD. You'll organize your songs later, so all you have to do right now is make sure you rip the songs you want. Follow these steps to rip songs from a CD:

1. Connect to the Internet. (You'll see why in just a moment).
2. Open Windows Media Player.
3. Insert the CD from which you want to rip a song or songs in your CD-ROM drive.
4. In Windows Media Player, click the Copy From CD button on the left side of the Windows Media Player interface. Note that Media Player knows the names of the songs on the CD. It uses the Internet to gather this information, so if you don't see the song names here, just make sure you are connected to the Internet, then click the Find Album Info button so that Media Player can gather the information.

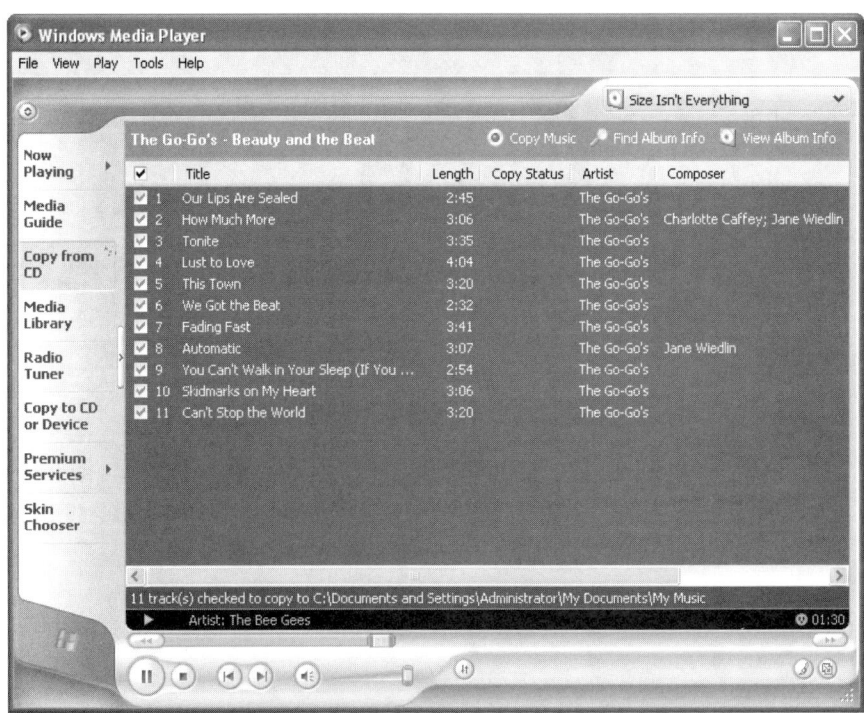

10 How to Do Everything with Windows XP Digital Media

5. A check box appears next to each song on the CD. If the check box is selected, Media Player will copy the song. So review the CD song list and clear the check boxes beside songs you do not want to copy. For example, in this illustration, I want to copy only three songs from this CD:

6. After selecting the songs that you want to copy, click the Copy Music button. Media Player begins ripping your selected songs, as shown next, and the songs that are copied to your computer will show up in your Media Library.

CHAPTER 1: Create a CD with Your Favorite Tunes for Someone You Love

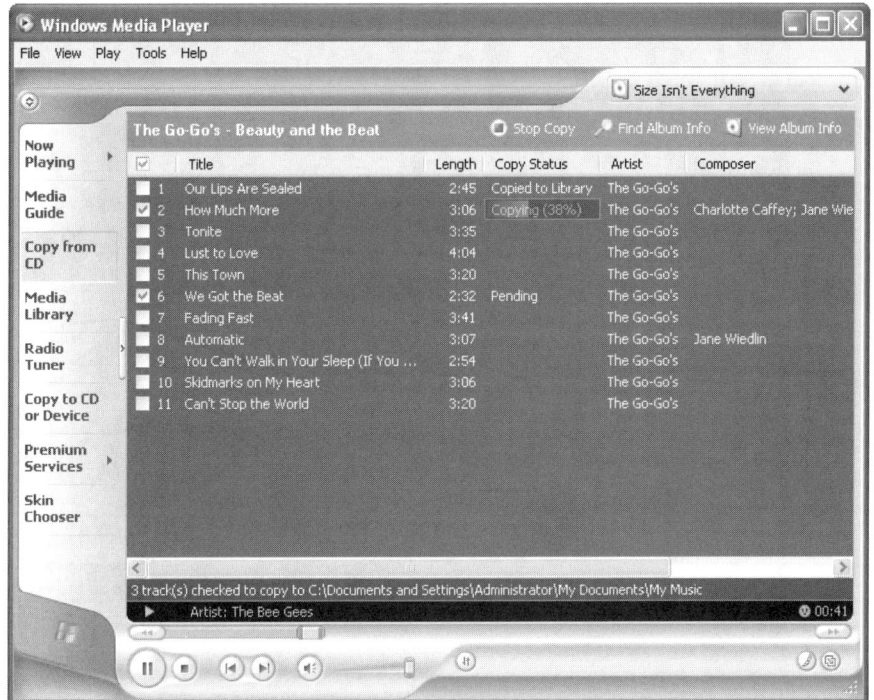

7. Repeat this process for each CD that has a song or songs you want to copy.

Once you copy all of your songs, you can see the copied songs in the Media Library. In Windows Media Player, click the Media Library button (on the left side of the interface), and then click All Music | Album (see Figure 1-2). You can view all of the titles of the CDs from which you copied songs, and you can see the songs copied from each CD by simply clicking a CD name. Now that you have your songs in Media Player, you are ready to organize them!

12 How to Do Everything with Windows XP Digital Media

FIGURE 1-2 Your ripped music appears in the Media Library

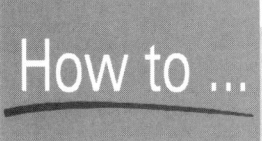 **Get Songs from the Internet**

Suppose that you don't have all of the CDs that contain some of the favorite songs you want to include on your custom CD. You don't want to buy a whole CD just to get the single song, but you are willing to pay a small fee and download the song from the Internet. Once you do, it belongs to you just as if you purchased a CD. So how do you then get that downloaded song into Windows Media Player? You can import it to the Media Library so that you can use it just as you would any other song that's stored there.

In Windows Media Player, click the Media Library button, then click File | All to Media Library | Add File or Playlist. Then, you can browse for the song you downloaded and select it, and it will be added to the Media Library.

If you are interested in downloading songs, check out www.mp3.com or www.buymusic.com to get started.

Organize Your Songs into a Playlist

You can organize any collection of songs in Windows Media Player by creating a *playlist,* which is nothing more than a simple list of some songs you have selected in the Media Library. You can put any song in your Media Library on a playlist and organize the songs the way you want, and Media Player will keep your custom playlist in the Media Library, just as it would albums, videos, or anything else you put there.

When you create a playlist, you decide what songs from what albums should go on the playlist and their order. Then, you can listen to the playlist on your computer anytime you like, or you can burn the song list to your own custom CD.

Creating a playlist in Media Player is quite easy, so grab your custom CD's song list, and let's get started. Simply follow these steps to create a playlist:

1. In Media Player, click the Media Library button to open the Media Library.

2. In the Media Library, click Playlists | New Playlist.

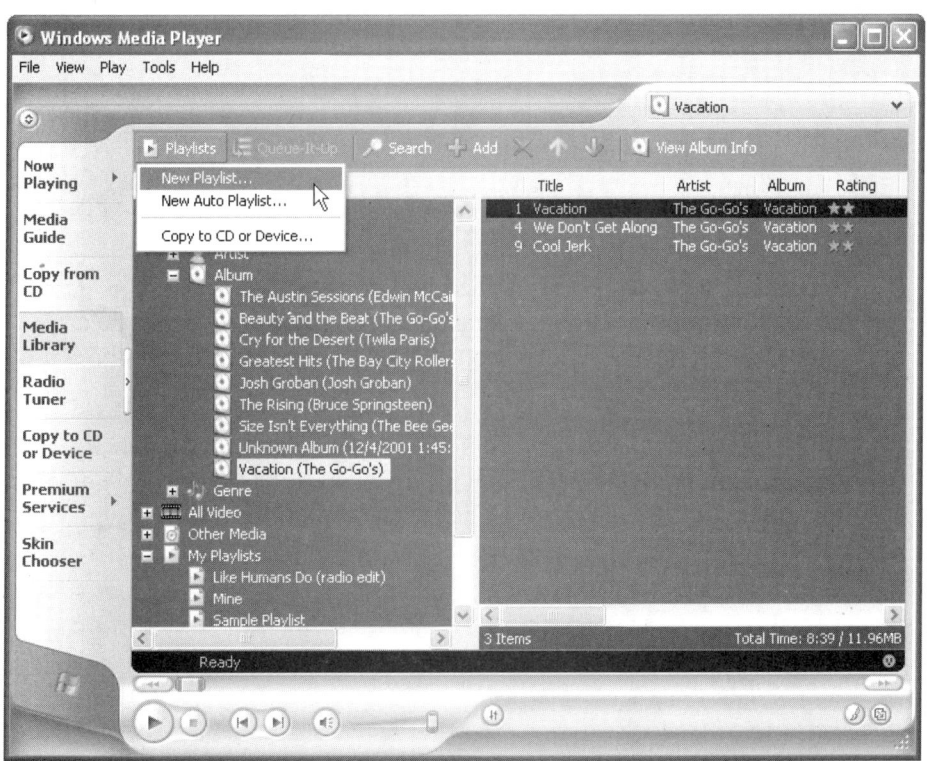

14 How to Do Everything with Windows XP Digital Media

3. In the New Playlist window that appears, click the album titles in the left pane to reveal the songs you have ripped. Then, simply click a song to add it to the new playlist, shown in the right pane. Don't worry about the order of the songs at this time; just move around through your albums and click the songs you want to include.

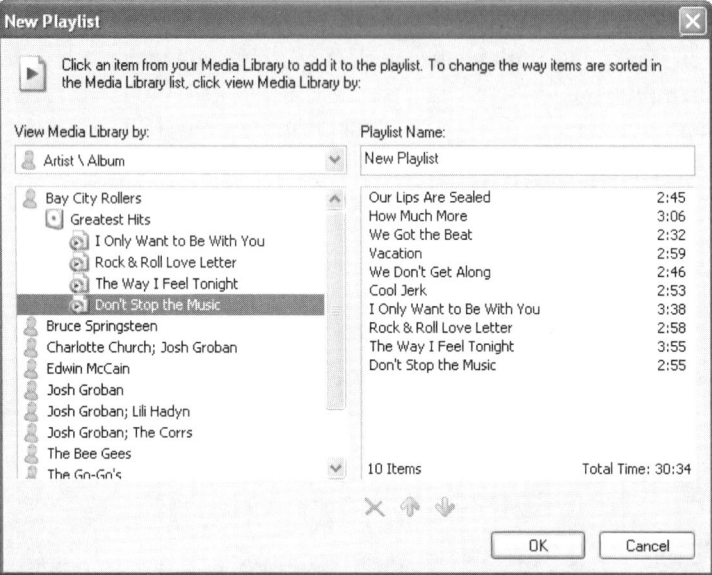

4. Once all of your songs are on the playlist, enter a new name in the Playlist Name text box. Use a descriptive name; in my project, since I'm creating a CD of retro songs for my sister, I'll call the playlist Angie's Songs.

5. Adjust the order of your songs. To do so, select a song on the playlist. You'll see the up and down arrow buttons come to life at the bottom of the dialog box. Click the arrows to move the song up or down in the list.

6. Repeat step 5 for the other songs until you have a list order that you like.

7. When you're done, just click OK. The playlist now appears in your Media Library.

Burn Your CD

Okay, your songs are ripped, and the playlist is in the order you want, so the only thing left to do now is burn your CD! Once you do, you'll have your custom CD, all ready to give to your loved one or friend.

So, is there anything else you need to do before burning the CD? Not really, but you should understand the three types of CDs that Windows Media Player can create:

- **Audio CDs**   Audio CDs contain music. You can play them on PCs and in standard home and car CD players, or any other CD player for that matter. Windows Media Player automatically places two seconds of silence between each track, so you'll have a standard-sounding CD. It doesn't matter what file formats have been used for your music in Media Player; all of the file formats—such as Windows Media, .wav, MP3, and so forth—are converted to .cda files, which are standard music files that any CD player can read. This is the option you want for your project.

- **Data CDs** Data CDs are designed to hold all kinds of data, such as music, movies, pictures, documents, spreadsheets, and so on. Windows Media Player can also create data CDs for when, for example, you want to back up files or folders, or share them with someone else. However, though most PCs can read data CDs, standard CD players can't. Therefore, do not create data CDs when you want to share music with other people.

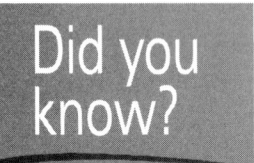

A Word About "CD Music" Discs

If you stroll into your favorite department store on a mission to buy some burnable CDs, you are likely to face an avalanche of options. You'll find CDs from different manufacturers, all touting a bunch of features or options. You'll also find a lot of price differences. So what do you need for your project? Here's the skinny:

- **CD-R** CD-R discs are writeable discs. You burn them one time, and that is it. After that, the CD is "closed" and can't be burned to again. This is the kind of CD you must use for your music CD project.

- **CD Music** CD Music discs are nothing more than CD-R discs, just with different packaging. They are exactly the same as CD-R discs and, in many cases, a bit more expensive. Skip the flashy advertising and save yourself a few bucks—buy standard CD-R discs.

- **CD-RW** CD-RW discs can be written to over and over again, much like a floppy disk. They cost more than CD-Rs and are great for data storage, but you don't need them to burn music to a CD. Go with the less expensive CD-R discs—they're all you need for your music CD project.

CHAPTER 1: Create a CD with Your Favorite Tunes for Someone You Love

■ **HighMAT** This file format is used to create audio CDs for portable devices. The format uses MP3 files so that file sizes are smaller in nature. As with data CDs, HighMAT CDs do not play on standard CD players, so do not choose this option for your project.

Now that you know a few things about the kinds of CDs you can create, you are ready to actually burn your project onto a CD. To do so, follow these steps:

1. Open Windows Media Player.
2. Click the Copy To CD Or Device button on the left side of the interface.
3. In the Items To Copy section of the window, click the drop-down menu, and choose the playlist you created. For example, in this illustration, I'm selecting the Angie's Songs playlist that I created earlier:

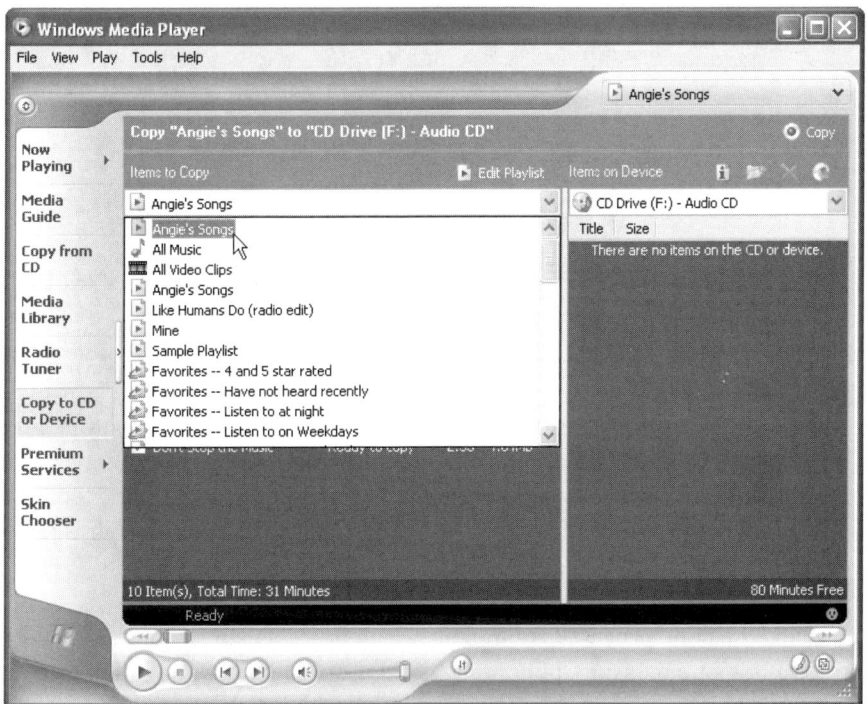

4. Insert a CD-R disc into your computer's CD-RW drive.

5. On the right side of the interface under Items On Device, click the drop-down menu and choose Audio CD. This option may already be selected for you, but check to make sure.

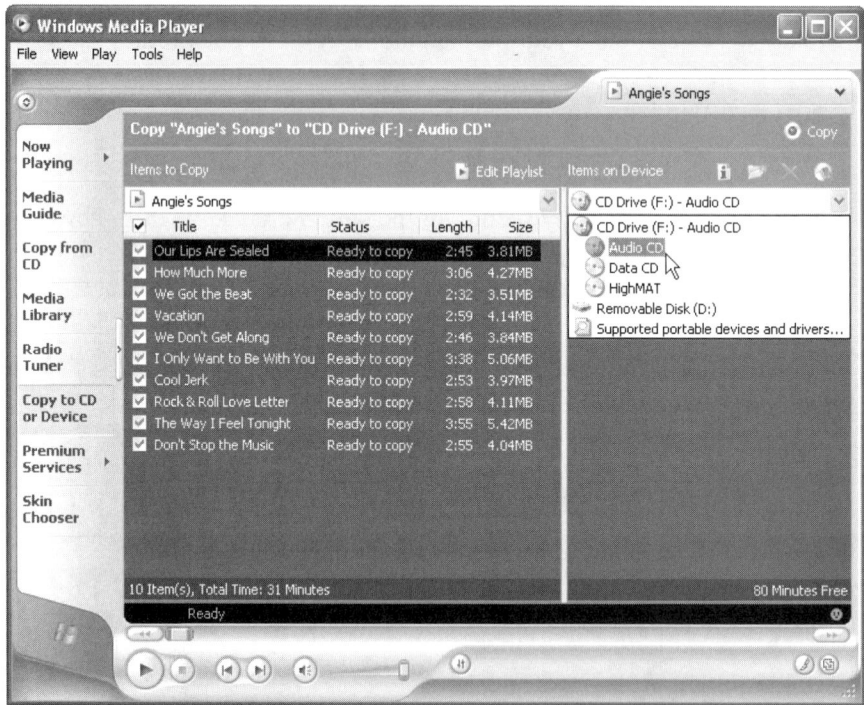

6. Now you are ready to burn your CD. Just click the Copy button, above the Items On Device section of the window. Windows Media Player converts all of your songs to the standard CD format so you can play the disc on any CD player. Once the conversion takes place, the copy (or burn) process begins. This may take some time, so take a break while you wait.

Once the copy process is complete, eject your CD, and you're done with your project! For safe measure, pop the CD into any CD player and listen to it, just to make sure there are no problems before you give it to a friend.

CHAPTER 1: Create a CD with Your Favorite Tunes for Someone You Love

> **SPIN** *Want to make your CD extra special? Add a personalized label to it! See Chapter 2 to learn how. You can also use jewel cases, the plastic holders used to house CDs. Some CD-R discs are sold in a stack without jewel cases, so you might want to pick up a package of empty jewel cases so you can store your CD project safely.*

More Great Ideas

As you think about creating personal CDs for those you love, here are a few more ideas:

- The next time you throw a bash, create a custom playlist and burn a CD of your favorite music to play at the party on your home stereo. Then, as guests are leaving, give them a copy of the CD as a memento. This idea also works great for your kids' birthday parties, holiday gatherings, anniversary celebrations, and so on.

- If your computer is equipped with a microphone, record your kids singing some songs. Then, import those files into the Media Library and burn them on a CD to share with grandparents and other relatives.

- Send your parents on a romantic getaway weekend, and create a CD of relaxing, classical music selections for their trip!

Chapter 2

Spin Your Face: Put Your Smile on a Custom CD Label

How to...

- Prepare to make CD labels
- Use Microsoft Plus! CD Label Maker to create custom CD labels and jewel case labels

Hey, let's face it: Creating personal CDs is loads of fun, but looking at those generic CD faces and jewel case inserts screams boredom. Even if you buy those spiffy blank CDs with cool colors, they are still...well, generic. The good news is that you don't have to stand for those boring CD-R discs and cases—you can make your own CD labels and put them on your custom CDs! The even better news is that the process is much easier than you might think. You can even use your own custom digital photos on the labels so your face can spin happily on a CD.

The great thing about creating a custom CD label and/or insert is individuality. None of us is a robot, and none of us likes our custom CDs to look like something that's mass-produced in a factory. So with just a bit of work and a bunch of creativity on your part, you can make your CDs unique and fun. In this chapter, you'll tackle a CD labeling project that will help you make any custom CD truly your own.

What You'll Need

For your custom CD project, you'll need to purchase two inexpensive items. First, the CD label–making software isn't on Windows XP, but it's available as an add-on pack called Microsoft Plus! Digital Media Edition. You'll also need some CD labels. Since both of these are custom items, see the "Gather Your Materials" section to learn more.

Gather Your Materials

Often, after operating systems like Windows XP are released, companies such as Microsoft produce add-on software for the operating system. Sometimes the software is free, as you'll see in some projects later in this book, and sometimes it is not, as in the case of the CD label maker. For this project, you'll need a Microsoft product called Microsoft Plus! Digital Media Edition. The Plus! CD contains the label-making tool and several other helpful software tools that you'll use in projects throughout this book. You can get Microsoft Plus! Digital Media Edition at most computer and department stores for around $20. It's also available online at stores such as www.amazon.com and www.circuitcity.com.

Once you buy the Microsoft Plus! Digital Media CD, just insert it into your computer's CD-ROM and follow the simple instructions that appear. After installing the label maker, you can access it by clicking Start | All Programs | Microsoft Plus! Digital Media Edition | Plus! CD Label Maker.

SPIN *The Plus! Digital Media Edition software may also be available in Start | All Programs | Accessories | Entertainment.*

The second thing you'll need is a pack of CD labels. One pack includes labels for your CD, the jewel case spine, and even the jewel case insert. They are adhesive labels and are designed to be printed directly on your inkjet or laser printer. They are similar to photo printing paper, except they are peel-off adhesive labels.

You can find CD label packs at most computer and department stores (look in the section where CD-R discs are sold). You can buy packs of 20 to 100 labels, typically from about $9 to $20 for the pack, depending on what you want. Most major brands—A-1, APLI, Avery, Fellowes, Memorex, and more—work just fine, and the label-making software has many templates you can choose that will match up to the labels that you buy.

Plan Your Label

Like many projects in life, your CD labels should begin with a pencil and a piece of paper. Sit down for a few moments and think about why you want the CD label. What do you want it to convey? Do you simply want a custom label for the actual CD itself? Do you plan on creating a jewel case insert, complete with song information? The choice is completely yours, and the Plus! CD Label Maker can help you make what you want.

Once you have the basic idea laid out, create a basic sketch of your label. Think about titles and basic text you would like to see on the CD. Also, if you want to use a custom background, you can use any digital photo or other graphics file you want. For those of you who are into photo editing and graphics, you can take a program such as Photoshop Elements and use its photo editing and paint tools to create your own custom background. It's all up to you, but here are some quick background tips as you plan, and I'll mention some more issues later in the chapter:

- The CD label can work with most graphic file formats, such as JPEG, TIFF, GIF, and BMP. When in doubt, JPEG always seems to work great.

- Try to make the background match the CD content. You want your background picture or graphic to go with the style of music and the mood of your CD. In other words, think of the label as an extension of the CD's content; it is the first thing people will see when they look at your CD, so make the graphic count.

- Keep in mind that the background will have to conform to a round CD with a hole in the middle. That may not be a problem, depending on your graphic, or it may remove someone's face, depending on the photo. The point is that you'll have to experiment a bit to get the background graphic to look the way you want. You'll see exactly what I'm talking about later in the chapter.

Once you have a good idea and a sketch of what you want in your CD label project, you are ready to start creating your CD label. The rest of this chapter shows you how to create your project. First, we'll take a look at creating CD labels, then we'll see how to make CD jewel case inserts.

Create Your CD Label with Plus! CD Label Maker

The Plus! CD Label Maker is simply a wizard that walks you through a series of steps, from selecting a template to printing the label. There are several different issues and items you need to consider in each step, however, so the next sections look at each step in turn. You may want to read over these sections before you fire up the wizard, or you can start the wizard and simply follow along—the choice is yours.

Start the Label Maker and Choose CD or Playlist

You can launch the Plus! CD Label Maker by clicking Start | All Programs | Microsoft Plus! Digital Media Edition | Plus! CD Label Maker. The wizard jumps to life. Click Next on the Welcome screen, and you're ready to get started.

The first wizard step prompts you to choose a CD or playlist for the CD label (see Figure 2-1). The wizard checks your computer's CD drive(s) for any music CDs, and it also pulls up any playlists from Windows Media Player. In the left column of the wizard window, just click the CD or playlist for which you are creating a label, and the contents of the CD or playlist appear in the right pane. You wonder, though, "Why do I need this step if I'm only creating a label for the CD itself?" In reality, you probably don't, but Label Maker wants to gather this information in case you make a label for your jewel case insert. If you are making a jewel case insert, you can put the song list on it, which is rather cool. Now, don't worry if the song list isn't exactly right or if you want to do some editing. As you'll

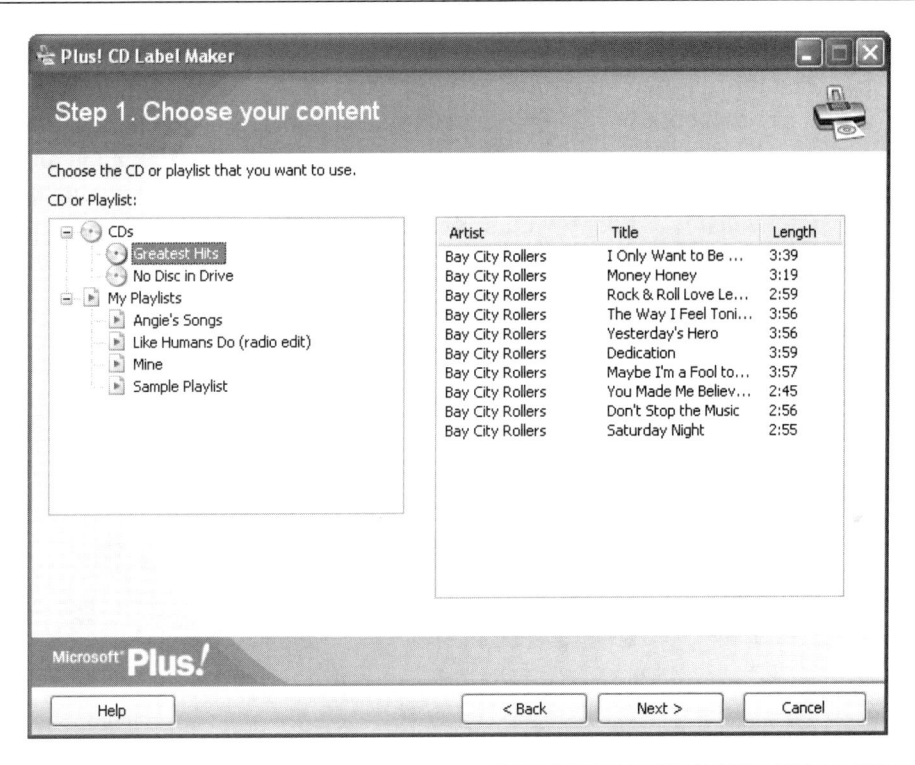

FIGURE 2-1 Choose a CD or playlist for the label.

see in the "Design Your CD Label" section later in this chapter, you can easily change it later in the wizard if you are actually creating a jewel case insert. Once you are happy with your selection here, just click Next to continue.

Choose a Template

The Plus! CD Label Maker uses templates in order to print your CD labels correctly. Simply put, the most popular and common label manufacturers are listed in the left pane of the wizard's second step, along with different product names and numbers. For example, in Figure 2-2, I am using a Fellowes Neato CD label.

When scrolling through the list of templates to find the CD label product you bought, you'll probably notice that there are several versions of the same product. No problem. Just look on the outside package of your CD labels for a product number, generally in one of the corners on the packaging. Then look for this product number in the templates list. As you can see, my product number is 99943, so I have selected that option. A sample of my CD template appears on the right side of the screen, as you can see in Figure 2-2.

Now, what do you do if your product is not listed in the templates list? What if you find the product but can't find the actual product number? Don't worry; the odds are very good that an existing template will work just fine. Pull out one of your printable CD label pages and check it out. Then, click through the templates and look for one that is similar to yours. Keep in mind that if you select a template on the left side of the wizard, a sample of it appears on the right side. Try to get as close a match as possible, and you should have fine results.

There are two more quick items to mention here. First, the Paper Section drop-down list box may be enabled, depending on the template you are using. If enabled, you'll see Upper and Lower options. This option appears if there are multiple print areas on your label paper. For example, in Figure 2-2, my label page has two labels,

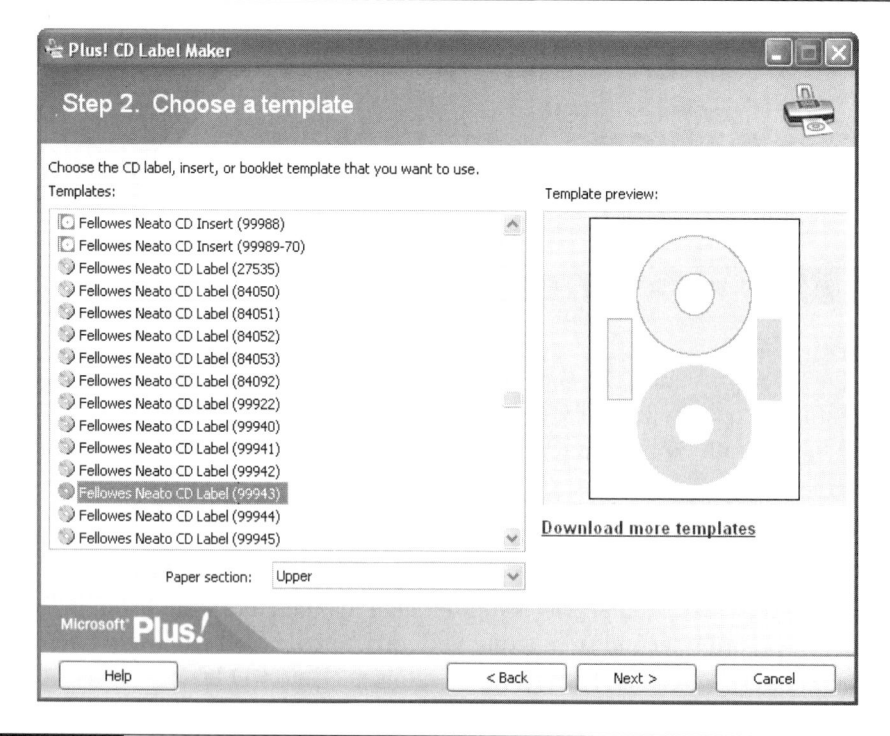

FIGURE 2-2 Choose a CD label template.

> **Did you know?**
>
> ## Duplicating Labels
>
> Unfortunately, you can't make a label duplicate on the same page. In other words, if you have a label page that provides two labels, you can't print the same label content on both at the same time. You'll have to run the page back through your printer and use the Paper Section menu to change the print section location. Of course, this is a bummer if you are trying to make multiple copies of the same label, since you'll have to run each page through twice.
>
> If you are connected to the Internet, you can also click the Download More Templates link. This will connect to you to www.microsoft.com, where you can see if any additional label templates are available. At the time of this writing, there are no new labels, but you can certainly check from time to time to make sure you have the latest templates. Click Next when you are ready to continue.

so I use the Upper or Lower option to tell the wizard to which label I want to print. Later, I can create a second label using the lower label if I want.

Design Your CD Label

Now comes the fun part! At this stage of the wizard, you get to design your CD label. First of all, familiarize yourself with the interface (see Figure 2-3). You have a sample label and a tab for that label. Depending on the template you chose, you may have more than one label and more than one tab. For example, in Figure 2-3, my template can print both the label for the CD and the label for the jewel case spine. You can click either label to select the one you want to design, and this will automatically jump you to the correct tab so you can design the label, or you can just click the tab to get there directly. The point is that if you have more than one label printing according to your template, you have a design tab for each option on your template.

For each CD label, you can create a title and a footer, and you can choose a different background (or no background at all). Note that the wizard gives you a default template, which is green with some music notes on it. You are free to use that one if you don't want to use your own background; the choice is completely yours.

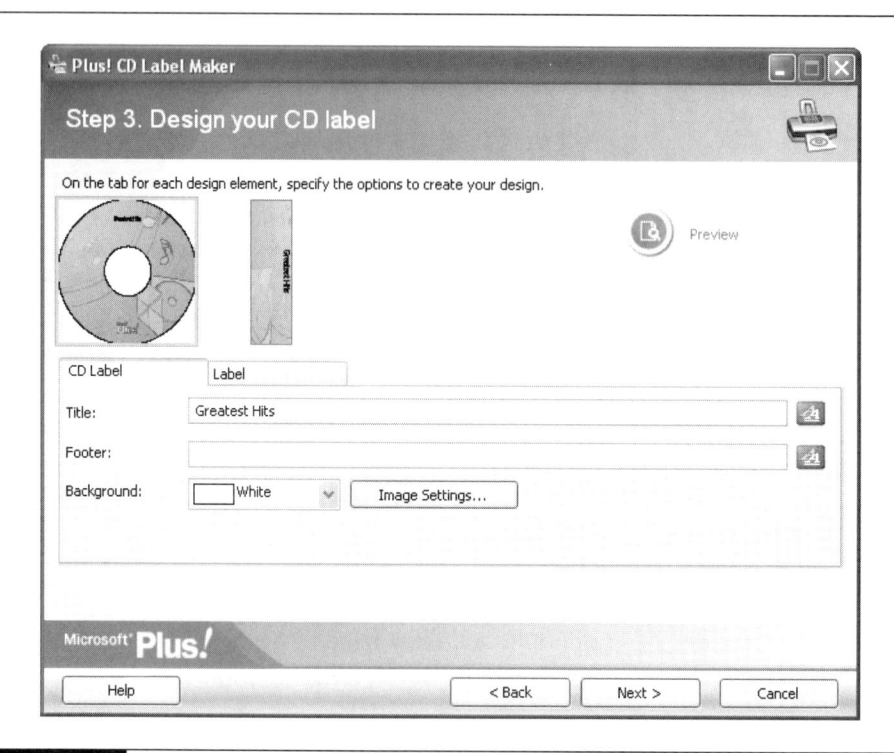

FIGURE 2-3 Each CD label has an individual design tab.

Create Text

First things first: Type the title text and footer text into the provided text boxes on the tab. Keep in mind that the title and footer titles have to actually fit on the CD label, so try to keep the info short and sweet. When you're done, click the formatting button (it looks like a double A) at the end of the text box. This opens a Font dialog box (see Figure 2-4) in which you can select the font, style, and color for your text. As you are working with these options, however, do refer to the sketch you made earlier. Keep in mind the background you want to use, and make sure that the colors and fonts look good with the background, or that the background doesn't overpower and wash out your text.

After you make your font selections, click OK. This takes you back to the wizard. In the upper-right corner of the page, click the Preview button to see a

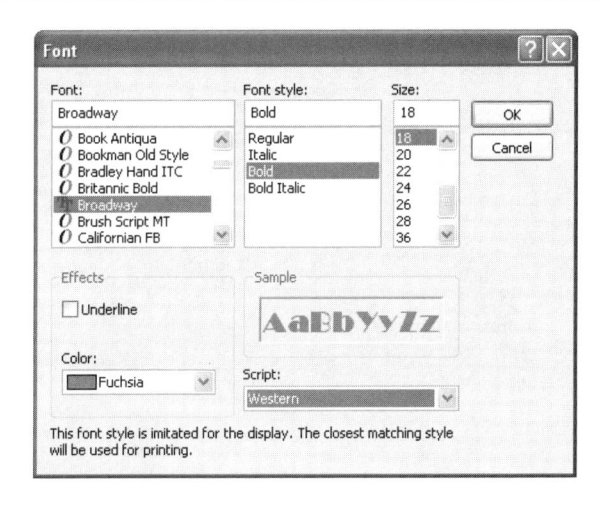

CHAPTER 2: Spin Your Face: Put Your Smile on a Custom CD Label   29

FIGURE 2-4   Use the Font dialog box to customize your text.

sample of how your text will look when it is printed. You can use the Zoom drop-down list box to adjust the size of the preview so you can see it easily (see Figure 2-5).

Of course, you may not like what you see. Maybe the font is too big, or perhaps the colors look bad. No problem—just go back to the Font dialog box and make any changes you like. You may need to go through several cycles of text formatting and previewing before you get things just how you want them. Follow this same process for the footer; if you don't want a footer, just leave the text field blank.

SPIN *Here's a helpful idea: The background you choose greatly affects the text style and color. Usually what I do is create my text, then move on to the background. Once I have the background just right, I go back to my text and make final adjustments.*

Create a Background

Now you are ready to work on your background. As I mentioned earlier, you can use any digital photo or graphics file for your background, as long as it is saved in a

FIGURE 2-5 Use the Preview window to see how your label will look when it's printed. Use the Zoom drop-down list box to adjust the preview size for easy viewing.

standard graphics file format, such as JPEG. You can also just use the default green background, or you can choose a solid background color. Here's how you do it:

1. On the wizard selection page, click the Image Settings button.
2. If you don't want to use a background image, in the Background Image Settings dialog box that opens, select the Do Not Use Image radio button and click OK. This returns you to the main wizard page. Click Next to proceed since you do not want a background image, and skip to the next section of this chapter.

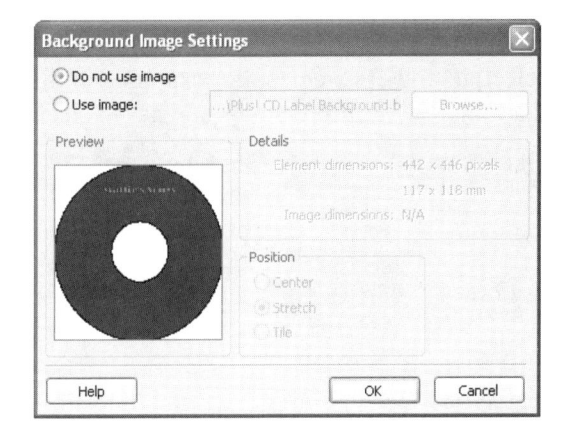

CHAPTER 2: Spin Your Face: Put Your Smile on a Custom CD Label 31

3. If you want to use a background image, use the Background drop-down menu to choose a background color. If you select None, you get a plain-colored label without an image.

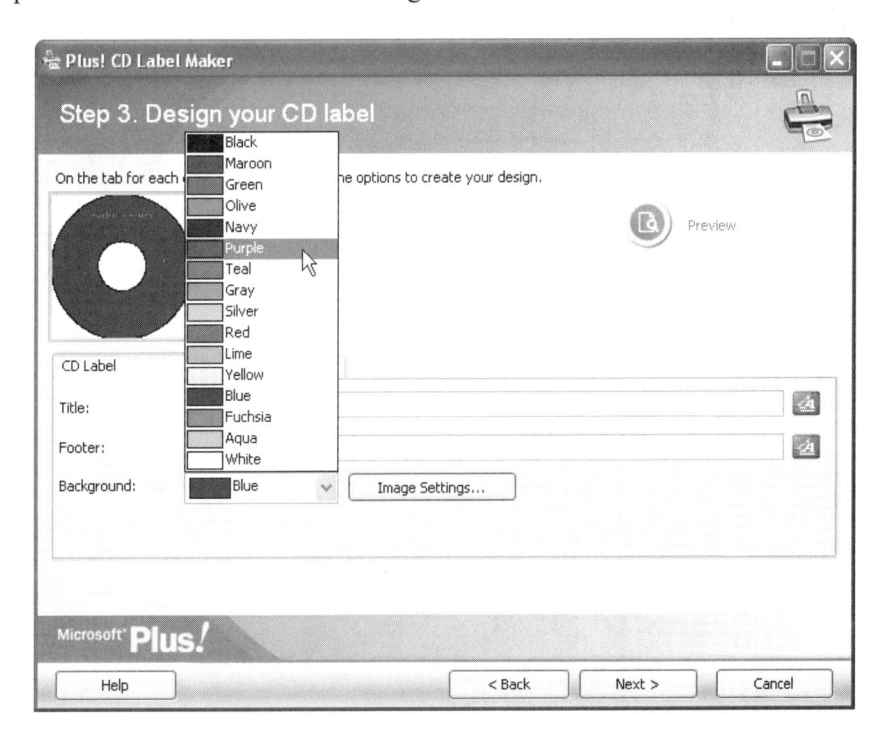

4. In the Background Image Settings dialog box, click the Use Image button, and then click the Browse button. This takes you to a standard Open window, with My Pictures being the default folder. In other words, Windows is trying

to help you find the image you want. Just browse around and locate the image, select, it, and click Open. For example, in this illustration, I have accessed a folder of vacation photos and have selected the photo I want:

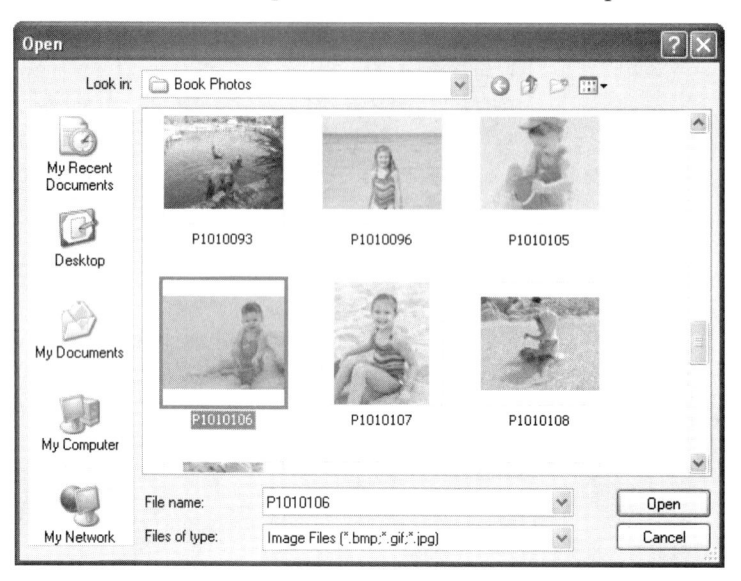

TIP *As you open folders, do you see only icons and not preview thumbnails, as shown in the previous illustration? To change that, just click the View Menu button in the upper-right corner of the window and click Thumbnails in the menu that appears.*

5. Return to the Background Image Settings dialog box. You can see a sample of your image on the label:

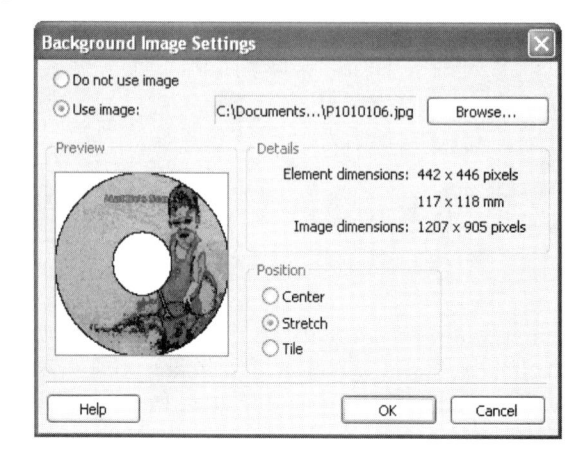

CHAPTER 2: Spin Your Face: Put Your Smile on a Custom CD Label   **33**

The image will be very grainy and maybe even distorted-looking here, but don't worry—it won't come out that way when you print it. Notice the Center, Stretch, and Tile radio buttons; use these options if your image is not large enough to cover the whole label, such as in the case of a graphics file or wallpaper you might want to use. Click these radio buttons to determine how you want the wizard to apply the background. If you are using a digital photo, there is nothing you need to do here.

6. Click OK when you are done. This returns you to the wizard.

7. Click the Preview button to see your background and text. Note that your background will still look grainy and somewhat distorted, and that's fine. At this time, you may want to return to the Font dialog box and adjust your text so that it looks better with your background selection.

8. Once you're happy with your background selection and text, click Next to move forward with the wizard.

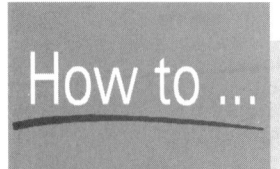

How to ... Solve Problems with Backgrounds

The background feature is cool and fun, but it can be a source of headaches. After all, you have to allow the CD hole to come out of the middle of the graphic. What can you do, then, if you have a favorite photo, but the CD label hole seems to wreck the whole image? If you have an image-editing program, such as Photoshop or Photoshop Elements, there are a few things you can try:

- By cropping or removing unnecessary portions of the photo, you may change the perspective enough so that the CD hole falls on a less important part of the photo. In previous examples of my daughter on the beach, I actually cropped the photo so that it had more of a rectangle appearance, putting my daughter on the far right side of the photo and extending the beach to the left. This placed her on the left side of the CD label instead of in the middle. Be sure to make a copy of your photo before cropping and working with it so that you don't inadvertently destroy the original.

- Copy and paste the parts of the photo that you want onto a generic background in Photoshop or Photoshop Elements to get the right perspective and location of the objects on the document file.

- Create a collage of several photos, leaving a hole in the center for the CD hole. This will give you a fun, festive CD label.

Obviously, you'll have to know a few things about Photoshop, Photoshop Elements, or a related graphics program to try these options, but if you are not working with digital photos and photo editing, you should be! There is a whole creative world awaiting you with digital photography, and there are scores of books on digital photography and specific editing applications. Consider checking out *Get Creative! The Digital Photo Idea Book* (McGraw-Hill/Osborne, 2003) to get you started with fun projects.

Print Your Label

Now you are ready for the last step: printing your label! The final wizard screen (see Figure 2-6) allows you to choose the printer you want to print to and the number of copies.

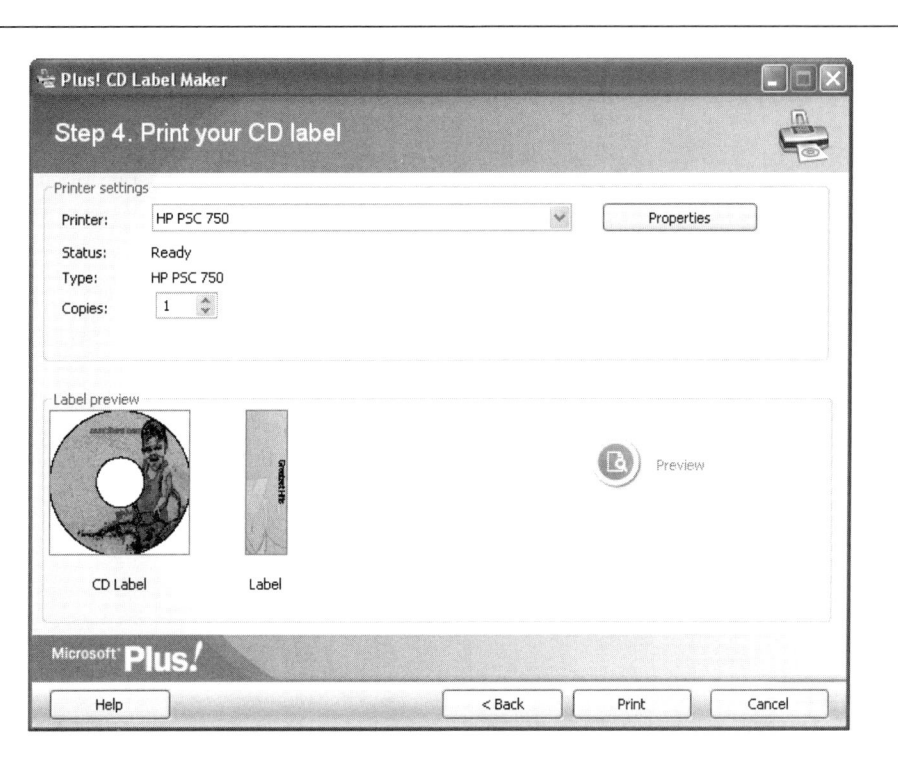

CHAPTER 2: Spin Your Face: Put Your Smile on a Custom CD Label

FIGURE 2-6 Choose the printer and number of copies.

But wait! Before clicking the Print button, you may need to click Properties and tell your printer what you are doing. Your printer responds only to the instructions you send it, and it may not know that you are printing a graphic on photo-quality paper (which is what your CD label is made out of). So click the Properties button to open a dialog box (see Figure 2-7) in which you tell your printer what kind of paper is being used and the quality at which it should print. This dialog box may vary a bit, depending on your printer, but the point is that you should tell your printer what you are doing. You may not have a CD Labels selection as a printer source, but just find something similar, or choose the Specialty Paper option.

Now you are ready to print your label for the first time. Insert the label paper into your printer and click Print. A final window appears, asking what you want to do next (such as print another copy, exit, print a jewel case insert, etc.).

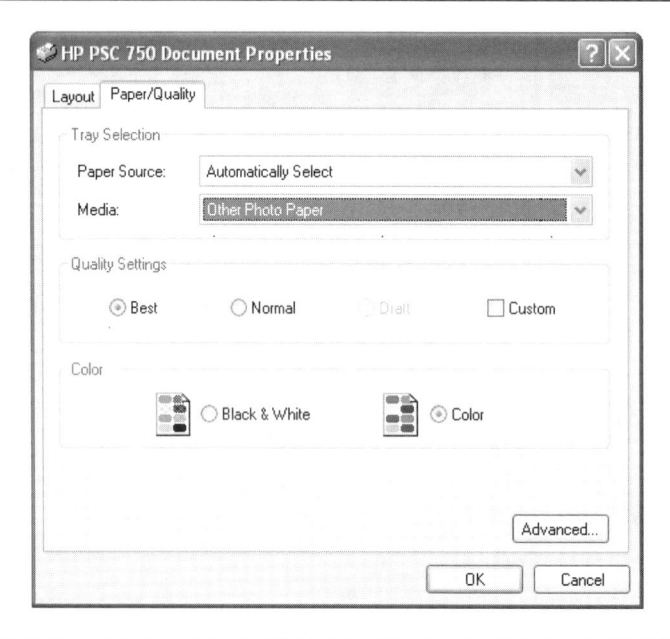

FIGURE 2-7 Tell your printer what you are printing.

At last, your label is printed in all of its glory! But before you stick it on a CD, here are a couple of quick tips:

- Make sure the label is completely dry! The ink may still be wet when it comes out of the printer, so wait about five minutes before you touch the label.

- If you have a double label sheet, don't peel the printed label off until you print the second label. Run the label sheet back through your printer and print the second label. If you take the first label off, the printer will most likely jam up the paper on your second print run.

- Are you making a bunch of copies? You can get a CD label applicator, which is a little device that holds your label and applies it exactly to your CD. These applicators are inexpensive and available at most places where CD label paper is sold, and they can be real time-savers.

Create Your Jewel Case Label with Plus! CD Label Maker

Just as you can use the Plus! CD Label Maker to create a CD label, you can also create a custom jewel case insert. For the most part, the process of creating the insert is exactly the same as for a label. You buy the jewel case insert label paper, select the correct template using the wizard, and then configure the text and background as you like. Generally, the jewel case label allows you to create a front and back insert card, which you fold in half and put in the jewel case. You can add your own background image as usual and manage the titles, fonts, and so forth.

> **TIP** *You have to pay some attention to the CD-R disk jewel cases you buy. Some are very thin and really don't allow room for a spine label.*

By default, your song list will appear on the insert. The cool thing is you can directly edit the song-list text without changing anything directly on the CD. For example, the first song on the CD might be "When I Fall In Love." You could leave the title and add your own text in parentheses, such as "'When I Fall In Love' (This was the first song we danced to)." This editing feature is really cool if you want to customize your song list and add in your own text or comments for your personalized CD.

Just go to step 3 in the wizard and click the Edit button, next to the Track List drop-down list box (see Figure 2-8).

A simple dialog box (see Figure 2-9) appears where you can directly edit the track list however you like. Just make any changes you want (there's no built-in spell-checker, so watch your spelling!) and click OK.

> **SPIN** *Don't want a track list, such as on the CD insert cover? No problem—just use the drop-down menu on the step 3 wizard page and choose None.*

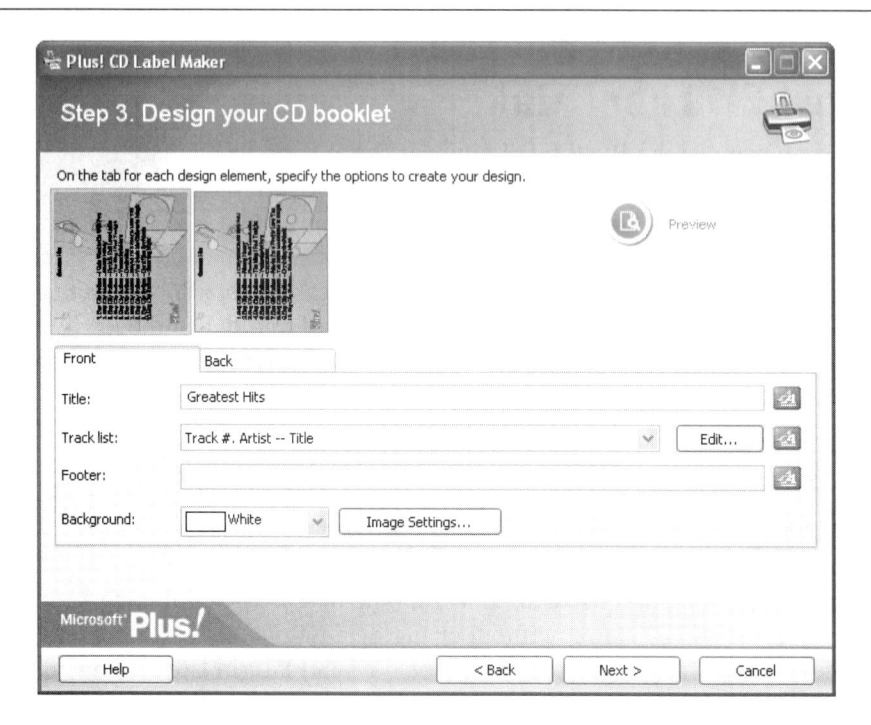

FIGURE 2-8 Go to step 3 and click Edit, next to the Track List drop-down list box.

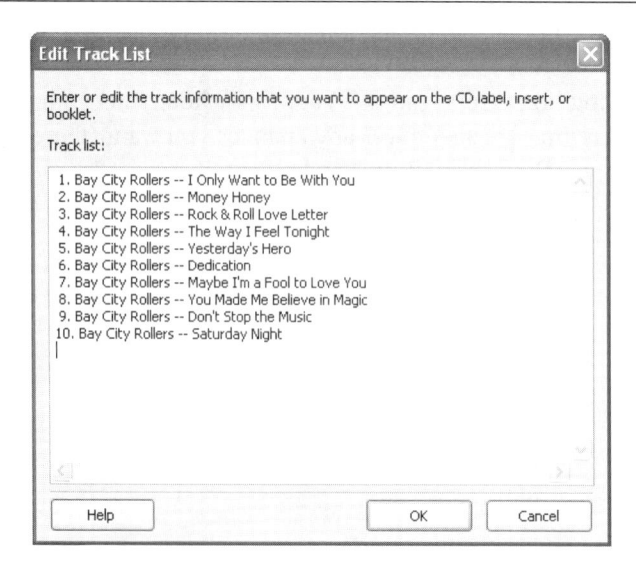

FIGURE 2-9 Edit the track list however you like.

More Great Ideas

As you are thinking about CD labels, here are some fun ideas you might try:

- If you are getting married, create a CD of music that will be played at the reception. Then, create personalized CD labels that have a photo of you and your future spouse on the label. Give the CDs to your wedding guests as mementos.

- At your child's birthday party, create CDs using music from it. During the party, take some digital photos of your child, then have a friend use one to create the CD labels. Quickly put them on the CDs you have already made, then hand them out as a party favor.

- Feeling creative and wacky? With a digital camera, have someone take a close-up of your face with your mouth open. Then, use the photo on the CD label, with the CD hole in your open mouth. I told you it was wacky!

Chapter 3

Become an Internet Radio DJ

How to...

- Familiarize yourself with Internet radio
- Find the stations you want
- Create custom stations lists

Internet radio is one of those fun things we can easily fall in love with. Why not? After all, you're not limited by location! You can listen to Internet stations that are local to your area or that are physically located on the other side of the country—or the world. The cool thing is that Internet radio has grown in popularity during the past few years, so there are hundreds and hundreds of stations to choose from, no matter what musical style or genre you prefer. In fact, most major radio stations today provide an Internet version so you can listen whenever you like.

But that's not all (yes, I sound like a salesman here): With Internet radio and Windows Media Player, you can create your own station list so you can always access directly the radio stations you love. You can completely customize your station presets and find new radio stations on the Internet at any time. In this chapter, you'll see how to use Internet radio and how to become your own Internet DJ.

What You'll Need

To become an Internet DJ, all you need is Windows Media Player and a connection to the Internet. Frankly, Internet radio works much better if you have a broadband Internet connection. See the upcoming "Internet Radio and Broadband Internet" box to learn more.

Get Familiar with Internet Radio

Internet radio is built directly into Windows Media Player, so all you have to do is make a few clicks to access the Internet radio interface. Just click Start | All Programs | Windows Media Player. When Media Player opens, click the Radio Tuner button on the left side of the interface to view the basic Radio Tuner (see Figure 3-1).

Luckily, Media Player's Internet radio feature is probably one of the easiest interfaces you'll ever work with, because it contains only two basic parts: a place to keep track of your stations and a place to find stations. As you can see in Figure 3-1, the left side of the Radio Tuner contains three options:

CHAPTER 3: Become an Internet Radio DJ   43

- **Featured Stations** These common and popular stations are placed in the Radio Tuner by default, giving you a variety of music.

- **My Stations** This option enables you to become your own Internet radio DJ. As you locate stations you like, add them your My Stations list so you can easily move from one preferred station to the next. You'll see how to use this feature in the "Create My Stations" section later in this chapter.

- **Recently Played Stations** This helpful feature lists all the stations you have recently played. For example, you may find a really cool station but forget to add it to your My Stations list. In this case, instead of having to search for it from scratch, all you have to do is look at the Recently Played Stations list to find the station again.

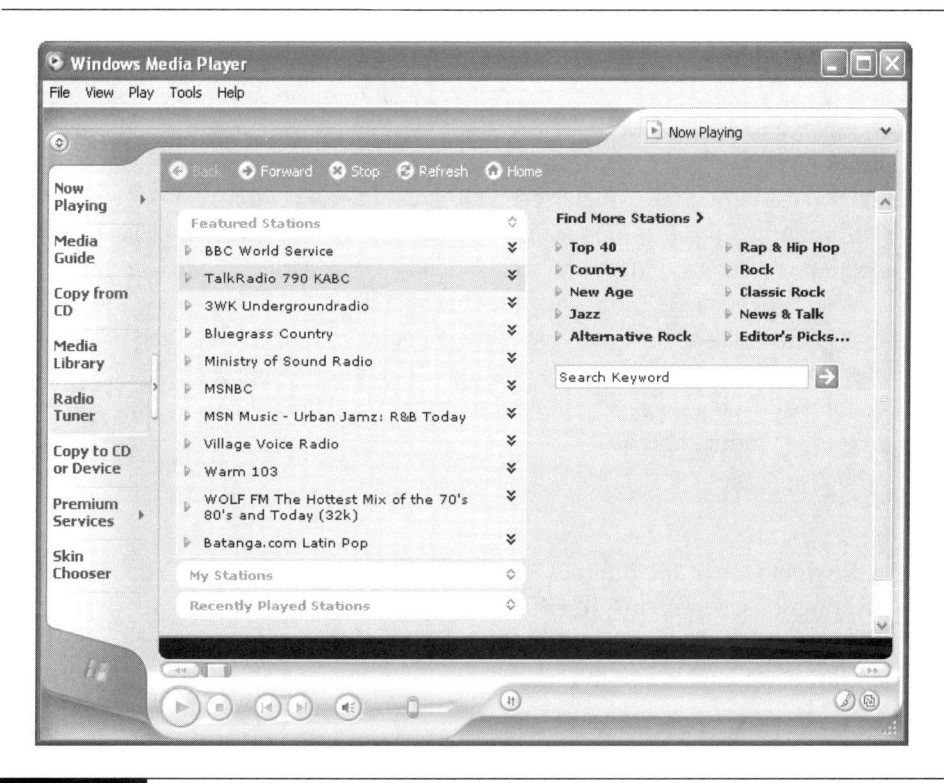

FIGURE 3-1 Windows Media Player's Radio Tuner

> **Did you know?**
>
> ## Internet Radio and Broadband Internet
>
> Without diving into a land of techno-babble that you don't care for anyway, there are a couple of things you need to know about Internet radio. First of all, there are two basic kinds of Internet connections: broadband and dial-up. Dial-up connections use a modem that connects to a standard telephone line. When you want to access the Internet, your computer dials an access number, and you connect to an Internet server. From that point, you are able to get e-mail, surf the Web, download programs and files, and, yes, listen to Internet radio. The problem, though, is that dial-up connections have a maximum connection speed of 56Kbps (with a real top connection speed of about 48Kbps due to telephone regulations). That's not very fast for Internet radio.
>
> Internet radio sends music to your computer through a process called *streaming*. The sound is streamed from the Internet in a constant line of data that your computer reads and plays back to you as music. Unfortunately, Internet radio may (and probably will) stream music to your computer faster than your modem connection can keep up with. The end result is gaps in the download streaming, making your Internet radio experience choppy and intermittent.
>
> The solution? I'm afraid there isn't one except to upgrade to a broadband connection. This is a connection type—such as DSL, cable, or satellite—that uses much faster transmission speeds. These kinds of connections are more expensive than dial-up, but you'll love them once you move to the land of "fast-moving data." Check your phone book for companies in your area that may provide broadband service if you are interested in stepping up your Internet speed a few hundred notches.

On the right side of the Internet Radio Tuner is a search feature. You can click through common categories—Top 40, Country, Jazz, Rock, and so forth—to see a listing of possible stations, or you can search for a different category or particular station. You'll see how to use the search feature in the next section.

Find the Stations You Want

The greatest task in becoming an Internet radio DJ is finding stations that you really love. To help find them, you can use some quick and easy Windows Media Player search features. Once you start finding potential stations, you'll have to spend some time listening to them to see if you really like them or not. This is all part of the fun, however, because it can be really exciting to discover a new station that you enjoy listening to.

There are three basic ways to find stations using the Radio Tuner:

- Browse existing categories.
- Perform a basic search.
- Perform an advanced search.

Browse Existing Categories

The easiest way to find a new station is to browse the existing categories you see on the right side of the Radio Tuner interface. If you click one of the categories, the Radio Tuner interface changes to a search page (see Figure 3-2) that shows all of the possible stations Radio Tuner finds in the selected category. You also have your standard search options that remain on the left side of the page.

SPIN *You must be connected to the Internet to view these options.*

If you don't like what you see, just click the Back button to return to the main interface. Then you can choose another category to view.

Perform a Basic Search

If you don't find what you're after in the existing categories, or if you just want to do more searching on your own, you have a quick and easy search option you can use. First, click a category to get to the main search window (refer to Figure 3-2). Notice on the left side of the page that you can browse other categories by genre. If you click the drop-down menu, you'll see a long list of possible music categories. Just click a category, and a possible listing of stations appears on the right side of the interface. Radio Tuner is simply doing the searching for you as you click a category. Under the Search dialog box, you can further refine your search by entering any desired search information. You can make it more specific to a certain genre of music,

46 How to Do Everything with Windows XP Digital Media

FIGURE 3-2   Click an existing category to view all of the stations that Radio Tuner finds in that category.

or you can even enter a station name or call sign to see if you can find the station. Just enter your search request and click the green search (arrow) button.

Finally, you can also search for radio stations in your area by entering your zip code (see Figure 3-3). This is helpful if you want to find a local station for which you can't think of the name or call sign, or if you want to find stations within a particular zip code where you don't live. For example, you might live in L.A. but want to explore stations in New York City.

SPIN   *This feature works for U.S. zip codes only.*

FIGURE 3-3 Use the Zip Code text box to search for stations by zip code.

Listen to Internet Radio

Once you have found the radio station you want to listen to, the fun begins when you actually listen to it. There are two ways in which you can hear a station once you find it: Some stations allow you to play them directly from within Media Player, while others require that you jump to the station's web site to play it. Some sites want to charge you for "premium services" or ad-free listening. You can check these out if you like, but I recommend that you stick with the free sites. After all, there are tons of them, so why should you pay for radio at all?

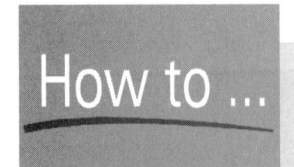

How to... Perform an Advanced Search

An advanced search is simply a standard search that gives you more options. As you can see in Figure 3-3, there is a Use Advanced Search link option under the Zip Code text box. Simply click this link to access additional parameters—such as genre, language, country or region, state (U.S.), speed, band, and keywords—you can use for searching (see Figure 3-4). These search options allow you to be more specific in your search, and you can use a combination of searches to try and find the station you are looking for. Just choose your search options and click the Search button.

CHAPTER 3: Become an Internet Radio DJ 49

When you find a station through searching or browsing, just click the station to play it. As you can see in Figure 3-4, some radio stations allow you either to play the station directly or to visit the web site. To play the station directly, just click the Play button.

However, some stations don't give you the option to play them directly. As you can see in Figure 3-5, you must click Visit Website to Play to access the station's web site and play the station. Some stations begin playing automatically once you open them; other sites give you some options to choose exactly what station you want to hear; still other sites lead you through a myriad of advertisements and features before you can play the station. Just navigate through the web site as you would any other web site to actually play the station.

FIGURE 3-4 Click the Play button to start playing the station.

FIGURE 3-5 Some stations require that you access their web sites before you can play them.

Create My Stations

All right, now that you found and are listening to stations, you are bound to come across some that you really love. This is where you get to start playing Internet DJ: You can select the stations that you like and put them in your My Stations list. After that, all you have to do is access My Stations to immediately hear your favorite stations. When you find a station you like, click the Add to My Stations link (see Figure 3-6).

When you click this option, the link changes to Added to My Stations, letting you know that you have added the station to your station list. Once you have added stations to My Stations, you can return to the main Radio Tuner interface (click the Back button or the Home button) and click My Stations to view a listing of your stations (see Figure 3-7). If you click a station, you can play it, visit the station's web site, or remove it from the My Stations list. Also notice that you can use the

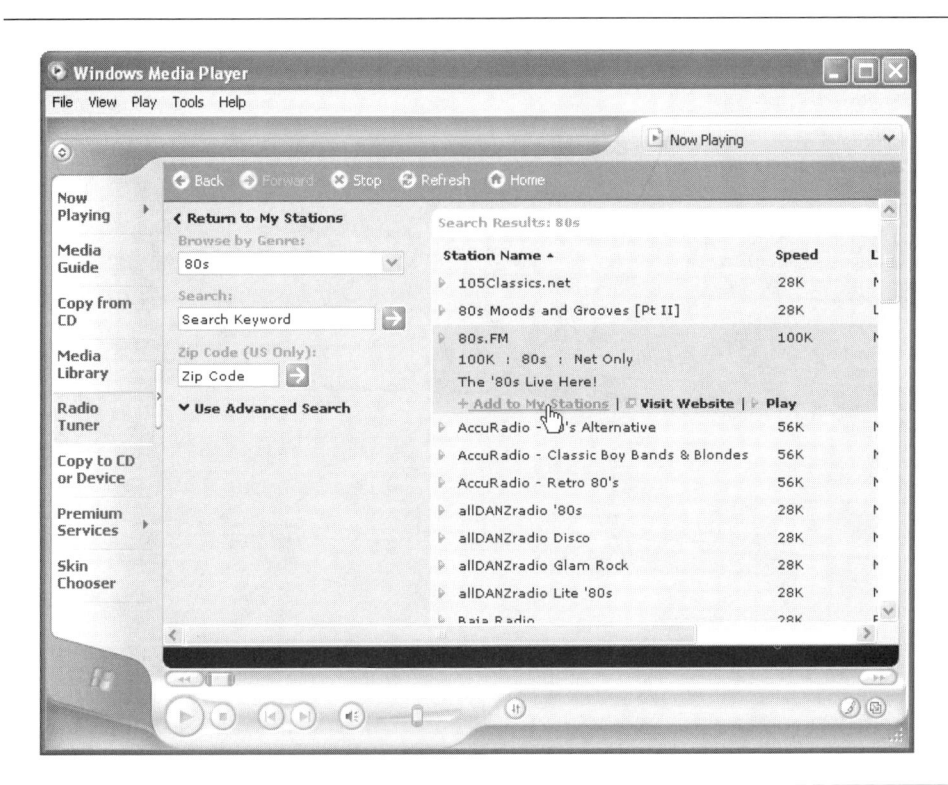

FIGURE 3-6 To save a favorite station to My Stations, you can click the Add to My Stations link.

up and down arrows to move the station within the My Stations list, enabling you to easily organize your stations so that your most popular stations are listed first. Now you can access your favorite stations quickly and click around the Internet radio!

More Great Ideas

Internet radio is a fun and simple-to-use feature of Windows Media Player. Here are few more ideas you might like:

- Remember to use the Recently Played Stations feature. As you are looking for new stations, play a series of different ones you might like. You can then go to Recently Played Stations, gather up the winners, and quickly add them to My Stations. This feature allows you to focus on listening rather than adding stations, which you can do later.

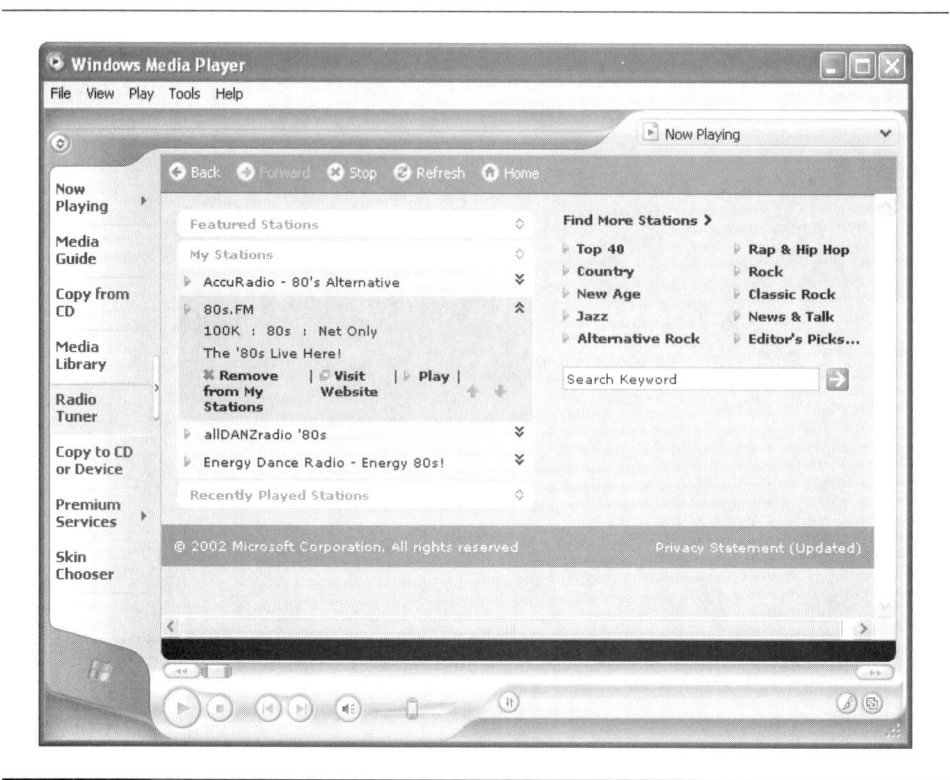

FIGURE 3-7 Use My Stations to become your own Internet radio DJ.

- Gather a mix of stations for different events. For example, you might want a classical station, a rock station, a '70s station, and so forth. When you entertain, you'll have a collection of radio stations for any event. Having a dinner party? Tune in to your classical station. Are friends over for a relaxing visit? Turn up your '70s station. You get the picture—just find stations you can quickly use for a variety of purposes.

- Keep your My Stations list neat and tidy. Always remove stations that you no longer listen to, and use the organizational arrows to arrange your stations. You may want to list them in order of popularity or by genre. There is no right or wrong way to do it; just make My Stations readily usable so you can find what you're after at any given moment.

Chapter 4
Customize Windows Media Player

How to...

- Configure the Now Playing area
- Use visualizations
- Get a new skin
- Use plug-ins and Microsoft Plus! Speaker Enhancement

Windows Media Player works great just the way it is. After all, you have a standard interface that plays media and is easy to use. However, just saying the words "standard interface" is enough to put you to sleep. Who wants a standard interface? Why not something more interesting, more exciting, and more tailored to your personality?

The good news is you can have just that. Windows Media Player doesn't leave you with just a default interface: You can change it in a number of ways. Using visualizations, skins, and other features, you can certainly make Windows Media Player look like something that is completely your own. In this chapter, you'll customize Windows Media Player to your personality and general sense of style.

What You'll Need

To customize Windows Media Player, all you need is Media Player and a connection to the Internet. You may want some additional software for further customization, but I'll tell you about that as we go.

Adjust the Now Playing Area

One of the first things you can do to customize Windows Media Player is make some changes to the Now Playing area (see Figure 4-1), which simply shows you what Media Player is playing at the moment—a CD, something from the Media Library, a movie, etc. There are several things you can do with the Now Playing area so that it works the way you want it to, but before we jump into those items, let's take a quick look at the buttons and controls that are available to you by default.

CHAPTER 4: Customize Windows Media Player   55

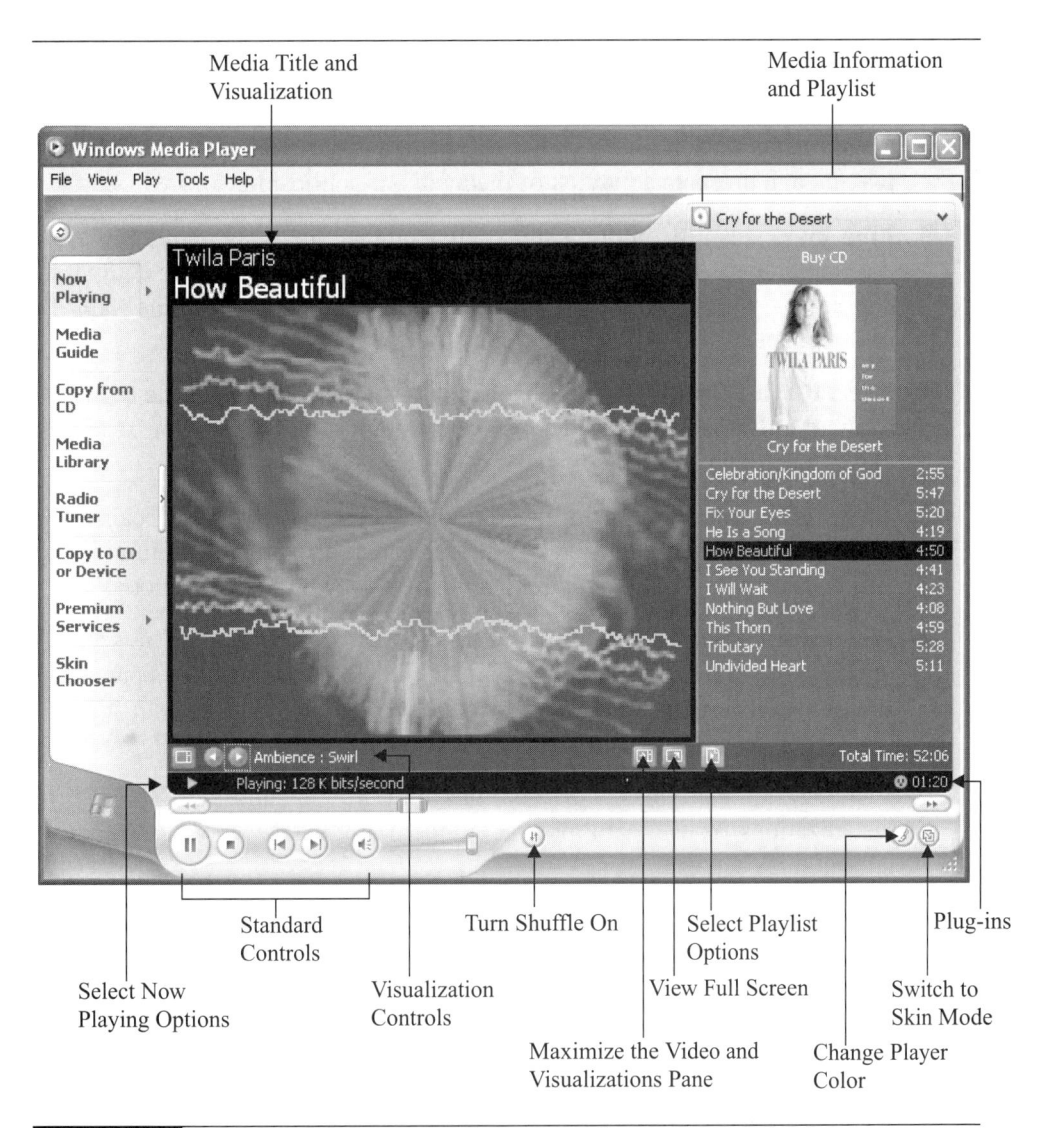

FIGURE 4-1   You can customize the Windows Media Player Now Playing area.

In Figure 4-1, I've added some callouts to the buttons and portions of the Now Playing area:

- **Media Title and Visualization**   This area of the window is used to display media. If you are playing music, you'll see a title and a visualization running (which you'll read more about in the "Work with Visualizations" section later in this chapter); if you are playing a movie, it will play in this window.

- **Media Information and Playlist**   This area shows you what you are playing and presents a playlist of the media, if applicable.

- **Plug-ins**   This little button simply tells you that plug-ins are running in the background. You may not see this button, depending on your computer. A plug-in—which you'll learn more about in "Work with Plug-Ins" later in this chapter—is a small program that works with Media Player.

- **Select Playlist Options**   This button allows you to make immediate changes to a currently used playlist. It's really just a quick way to reorganize a playlist from the Now Playing area.

- **View Full Screen**   This helpful option enables you to view your visualization or current movie playing full screen. This is a quick and cool feature; if you use it, just press ESC on your keyboard to leave full screen mode.

- **Maximize Video/Visualizations**   If you don't want to use the full screen option, just click this button to maximize the video/visualizations pane. Basically, this option removes the Media Information and Playlist pane so that your movie or visualization can have the full window (see Figure 4-2).

- **Visualization controls**   These buttons allow you to choose different visualizations. You'll learn more about them in "Work with Visualizations" later in this chapter.

- **Select Now Playing Options**   This feature provides a number of different options for customizing the Now Playing area. We'll explore those features in just a moment.

- **Switch To Skin Mode**   This feature allows you to switch to a skin mode. You'll see how to use skins in the "Choose Skins" section later in this chapter.

- **Change Player Color**   This option slowly starts changing the color of Windows Media Player. The good news is you have another color control option, which gives you more direct control; you'll see this later in this section.

- **Turn Shuffle On**   When using music, this feature allows Media Player to shuffle the songs and play them in random order.

- **Standard controls**   Use these to switch between songs, adjust the volume, play, pause, and so on.

CHAPTER 4: Customize Windows Media Player

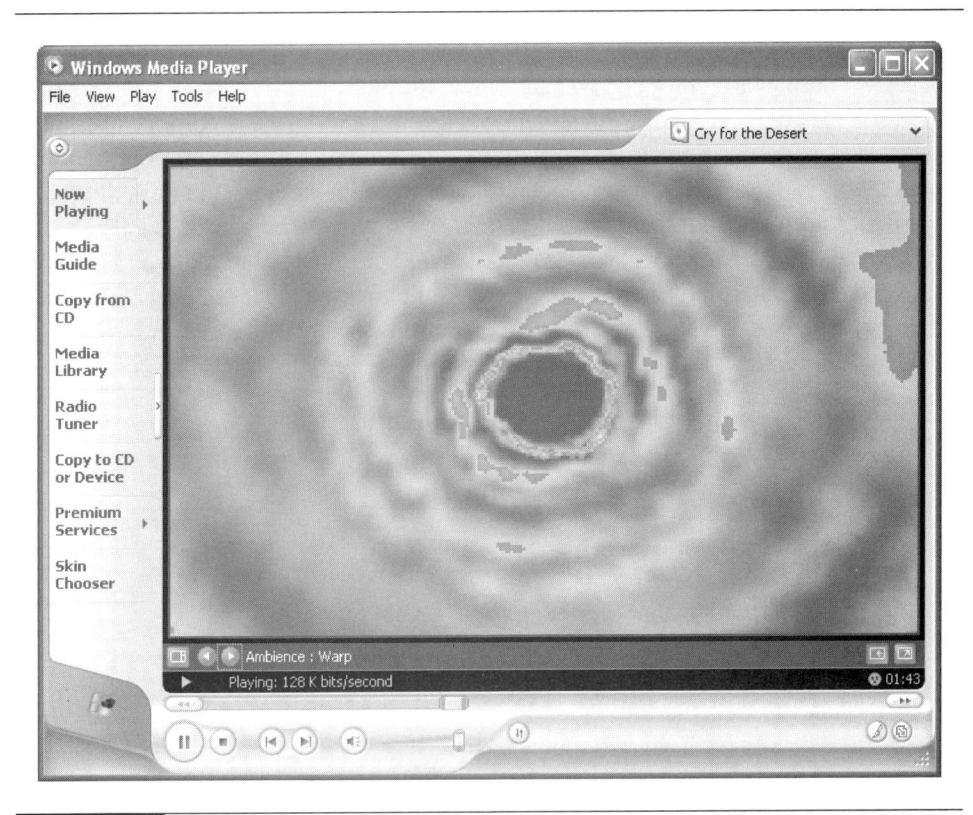

FIGURE 4-2 Click the Maximize button to view your video or visualization in the whole window.

As you can see, with just these basic controls, you can do several different things to make the Now Playing area look the way you want. However, there are even more options! First of all, you can click View | Now Playing Options and see a menu of items that you may use in Media Player. Four items are selected by default, but you can turn them on and off at will. For example, you can choose to show or hide the title, playlist, resize bars, and media information. Try turning these features on and off to see the changes in Media Player.

A second, and more interesting, thing you can do is configure some Now Playing effects. If you click Select Now Playing Options | Enhancements | Show Enhancements or click View | Enhancements | Show Enhancements, you have access to several different control features that you'll probably find fun and useful. Once you click Show Enhancements, a small window appears in the Now Playing area where you can click through the enhancements and configure them as you like. The following sections discuss these enhancements in more detail.

Color Chooser

Your first option is the color chooser, as shown in Figure 4-3. With this feature, you can move the Hue and Saturation slider bars around to adjust the color of Media Player. Use the Saturation slider bar to adjust the boldness of the color option you choose. This is a great way to turn Media Player from the default Windows blue to any other color you want, even bright yellow or hot pink. The choice is entirely yours, so just move the slider bars around as you like. Also, note that you have the option to use black as the background color by clicking the provided check box, and if things get really ugly, just click the Reset button to take Media Player back to its default blue color. Click the arrow button in the left corner of the Enhancements window to move on to the next enhancement.

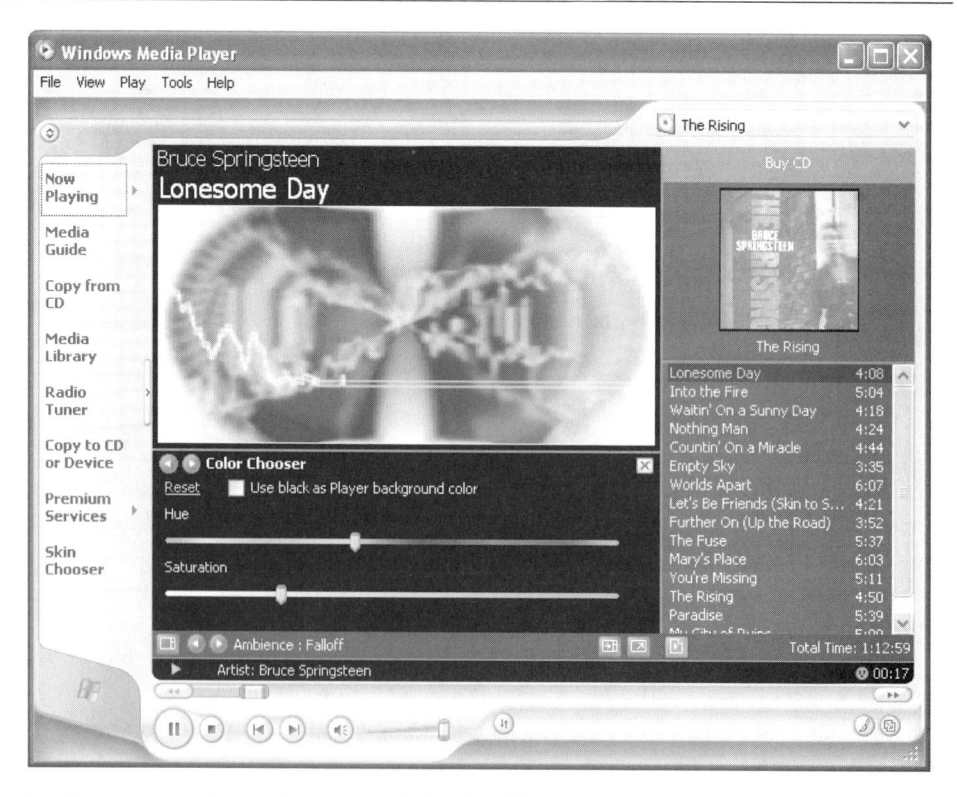

FIGURE 4-3   Use the Hue and Saturation slider bars to change the color of Windows Media Player.

Cross Fading and Auto Volume Leveling

If you clicked the Next arrow after choosing a color, you arrive at settings for Cross Fading and Auto Volume Leveling. (You can also click View | Enhancements | Cross Fading And Auto Volume Leveling.) First, you see an option to turn on Auto Volume leveling. This feature attempts to correct volume problems for some media by leveling the volume so that there are no volume surges. This a "fix" feature and not one you should turn on unless you are having specific volume control problems with a certain media.

The next option, which is very cool, is a cross-fading feature. When you are playing a CD or playlist, you can adjust this cross-fade option so that songs fade into each other by the number of seconds you choose. This simple option adds a nice element to your music so there are no pauses between songs. Try it out—I bet you'll like it! Click the arrow button in the left corner of the Enhancements window to move on to the next enhancement.

Graphic Equalizer

Get more control over the sound of your music with the handy graphic equalizer, shown in Figure 4-4. As you can see, the feature works just like a regular stereo equalizer in that you can adjust the bass, treble, and so on. You can also click the Custom button and select a style of music (pop, rock, country, etc.), and the equalizer will attempt to adjust itself for you. If you get into trouble, notice the reset button that you can click to put everything back to the default settings.

Media Link for E-Mail

If you are listening to media on the Internet, you can use this option to automatically create a media link in an e-mail message so you can let someone else know about the link. Just click View | Enhancements | Media Link For E-Mail. You'll see an option where you can send the media link. Just click the option, and the link will appear in an empty e-mail message, using your computer's default e-mail program. Note that the media link option doesn't work if you are listening to music or watching movies on your local computer; it works only for stuff you are using on the Internet.

Play Speed Settings

This slider bar is an odd yet sort of interesting option that allows you to slow down or speed up music you're listening to. The default, normal setting is 1.0. This feature can be helpful if music or a movie seems to drag a bit, or if you just want to have some fun and slow down or speed up the music or movie.

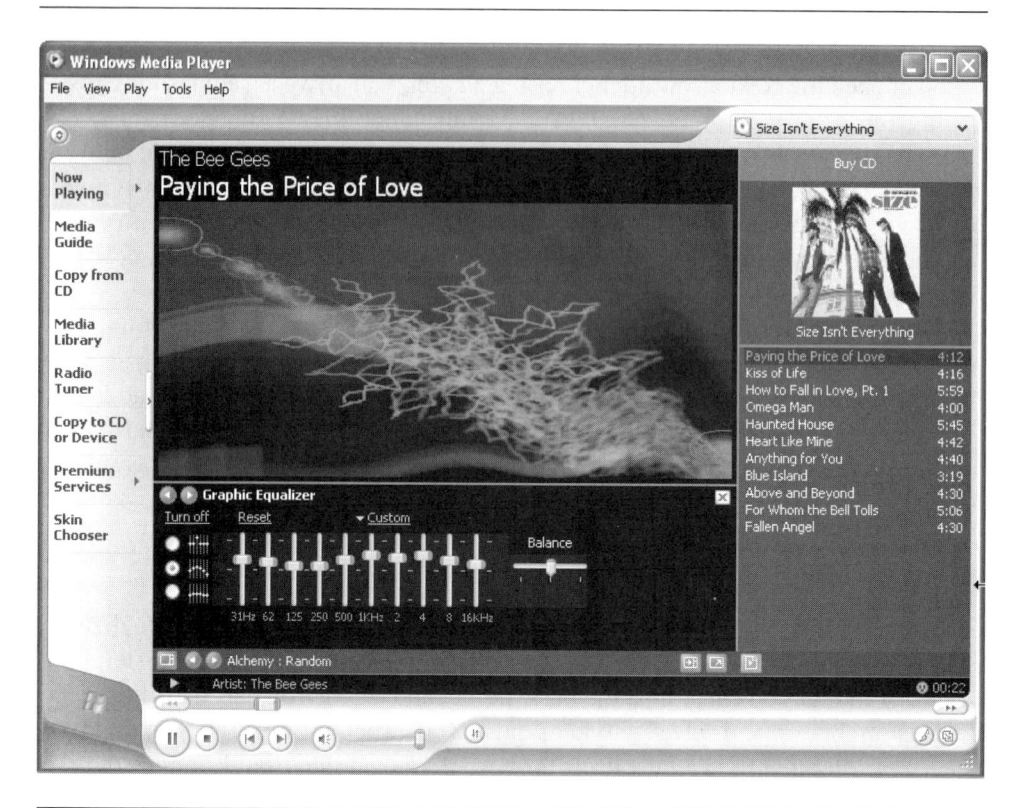

FIGURE 4-4 Use the graphic equalizer to adjust the quality of your music.

Quiet Mode

Quiet Mode is a feature that allows you to control the difference between the loudest and softest sounds when you play audio. You may want to reduce this difference, which is called the *audio dynamic range,* when watching movies at night or when listening to music with headphones. Turning on Quiet Mode keeps the sound level more uniform, avoiding great swings in audio volume.

SRS WOW Effects

SRS (surround sound) WOW Effects provide a more full range of sound to your speakers, giving you better bass tones and the overall feel of full stereo. You should turn on this feature and use the slider bars to adjust the effects until they sound pleasing to you.

CHAPTER 4: Customize Windows Media Player   61

Video Settings

Use the Video Settings option to adjust the color qualities and saturation of video in order to make the video look the best it can. Just remember this option is available when you watch video, as you may need to adjust it from time to time.

Work with Visualizations

Visualizations are just little Windows Media Player plug-ins, or small programs, that are designed to work with Media Player. In a nutshell, they don't do anything but provide entertainment when you listen to music. The visualizations move to the beat of the music, and if you choose to go to full screen mode, they simply make your monitor display dance to the beat of the music.

To use visualizations, click View | Visualizations. As you can see in Figure 4-5, you can choose to not use a visualization, or you can point to a category and see a pop-out menu of available visualizations. Just click a visualization to use it.

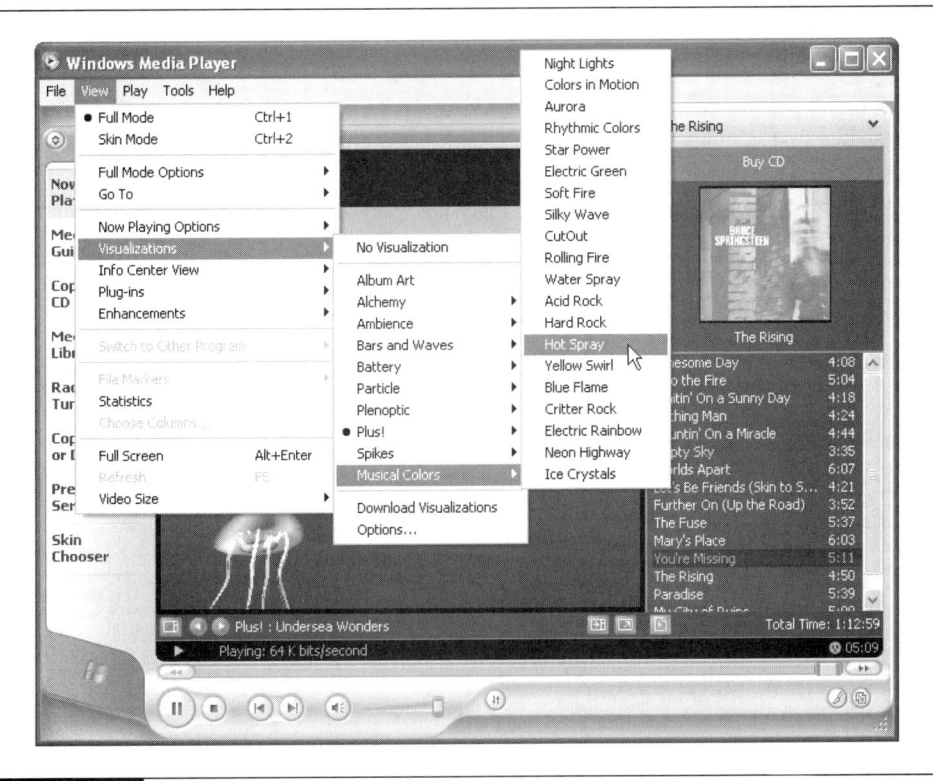

FIGURE 4-5   Choosing a visualization

TIP: *You can shuffle between visualizations by clicking the selection buttons on the Now Playing area once you have turned on visualizations for use. You can also choose the Random option so that you see a combination of different visualizations.*

Aside from choosing a provided visualization, there are two other actions you can take: Get more visualizations or configure existing visualizations to behave differently, if possible.

Get More Visualizations

First of all, you can get more visualizations by connecting to the Internet and then clicking View | Visualizations | Download Visualizations. This takes you to www.windowsmedia.com, where you can download more visualizations as they become available. There are several cool options, many of them developed by third parties, so the site is certainly worth a look. At the time of this writing, there is even a visualization that enables you to use your digital photos for the visualization. Just follow the instructions for downloading, and the visualization will automatically install and be available on Windows Media Player.

You can also acquire a few more visualizations by purchasing and installing the Microsoft Plus! Windows XP software, which is available for purchase. This software gives you only a few more visualizations, however.

To get still more visualizations, simply search the Web for "Windows Media Player 9 Visualizations." You can find web sites that contain a number of visualizations that you can download and install. Try www.wmplugins.com to get you started. Naturally, these sites are not guaranteed to provide plug-ins that actually work, so proceed at your own risk.

Modify Visualizations' Behavior

Some visualizations allow you to adjust how they work, such as the speed at which they run or the resolution. Normally, you don't have to do anything with these settings, but you can check them out if you are curious. Click View | Visualizations | Options to access the Plug-ins tab, which has the Visualization option selected by default (see Figure 4-6). You can select a visualization and click the Properties button; if there is anything that can be adjusted, you'll be able make the changes in a small dialog box that appears.

CHAPTER 4: Customize Windows Media Player   63

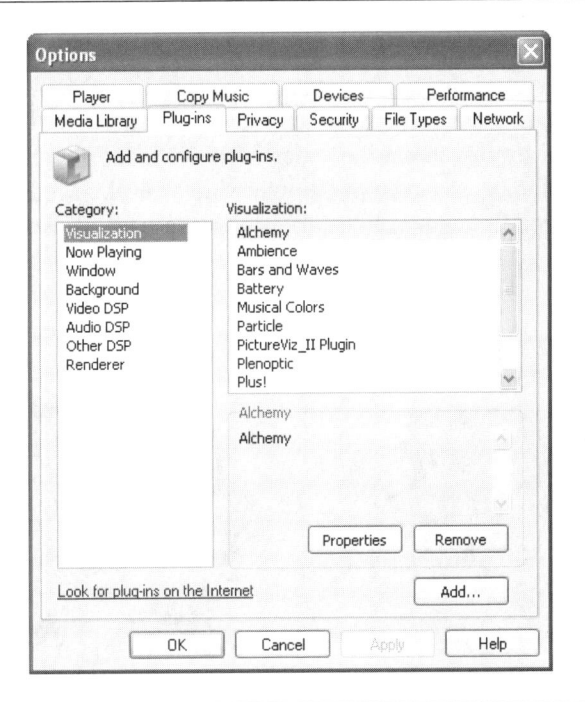

FIGURE 4-6   Adjust visualizations on the Plug-ins tab.

How to ... Remove a Visualization

So, let's say you get download-happy and download a whole bunch of visualizations. That's fine, but what happens if, later, you decide you want to get rid of some of them? After all, too many visualizations tend to junk up your menu items, and they take up storage space on your computer. If you are not really using all of your visualizations, it's a good idea to lose them. How? The process is easy, although not directly intuitive. Click View | Visualizations | Options to open the Plug-ins tab with Visualizations selected in the Category pane. In the right pane, locate the visualization that you want to uninstall and click the Remove button. A warning message appears asking if you are sure. Just click Yes, and the visualization will be removed from your computer.

Choose Skins

Skins are probably one of the coolest features of Windows Media Player, simply for the fact that you can virtually make Windows Media Player look any way that you want. A skin is simply an overlay interface for Media Player that changes the way Media Player looks. For example, how would you like Media Player to look like the top of someone's head, or like a toothy grin, as you can see in the following illustrations?

Interested? I thought so. First things first. You need to understand that Media Player has two modes: Normal and Skin. In Normal mode, you see the typical interface that we have used so far in this chapter. When you switch to Skin mode, you see whatever skin you select for Media Player to use. There are many default skins available in Windows Media Player, and you can get more from the Internet or by purchasing and installing Microsoft Plus! Windows XP.

So, to get started using skins, you first need to select a skin for Media Player to use. Follow these steps:

1. In Media Player, click the Skin Chooser button on the left side of the interface.

2. Click through the list of skins on the left side of the window. You'll see a sample of how the skin looks on the right side of the window:

CHAPTER 4: Customize Windows Media Player   65

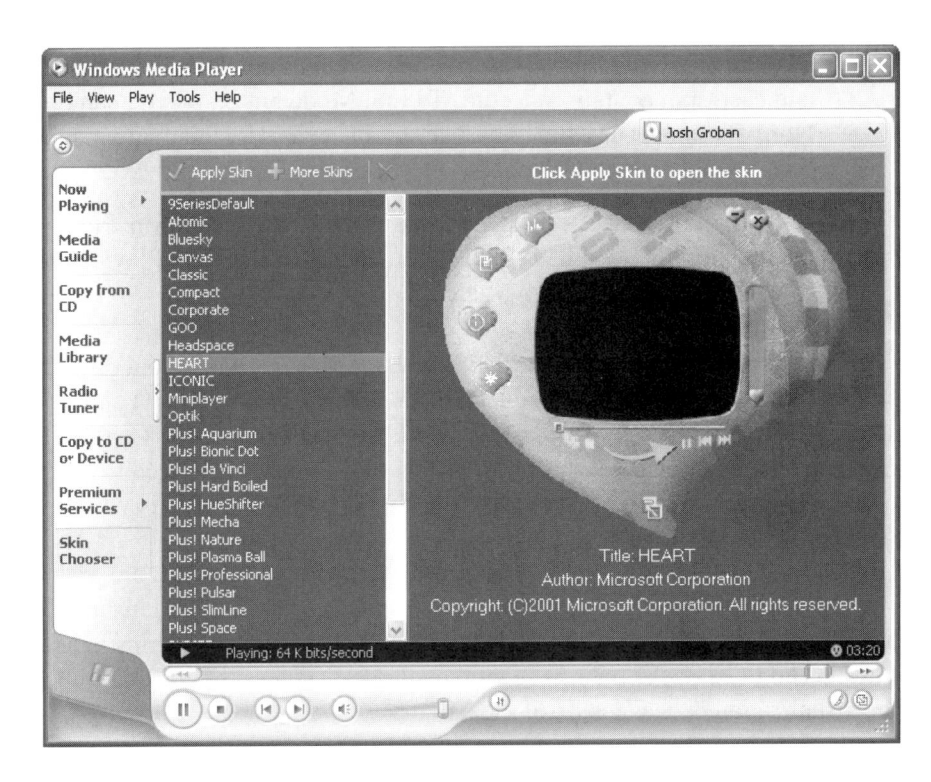

3. Once you find a skin you like, click the Apply Skin button. Media Player now goes to Skin mode:

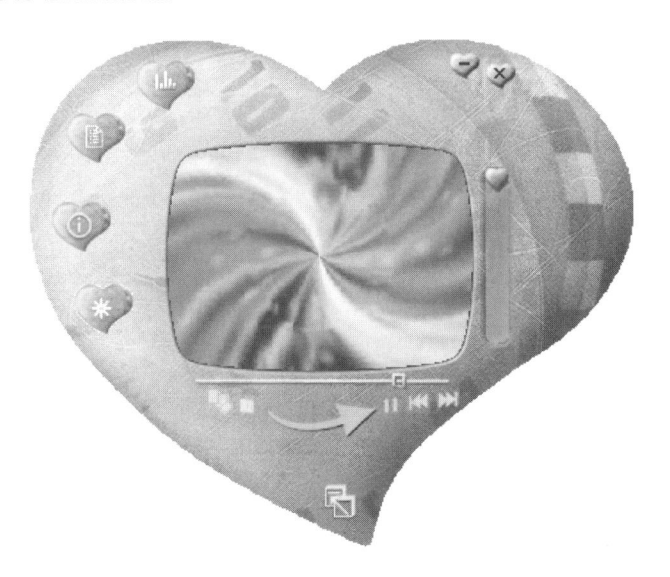

The skin has the primary buttons you need to use the Media Player interface, and each skin contains a Return To Full Mode button so you can go back to Normal mode at any time you like. In this example, this button is located at the very bottom tip of the heart interface.

4. You can go to Skin mode at any time when you are in Normal mode by clicking the Switch To Skin Mode button on the Now Playing area, or by clicking View | Skin Mode.

At any time, you can return to the Skin Chooser and change to a different skin; simply click a different skin and click Apply Skin. It's that easy! The more you use skins, the more you are likely to enjoy them. However, some skins are easier to use than others due to the size of the button controls, so you'll need to spend some time experimenting with different skins to find one that really suits you (no pun intended).

So, what happens if you really love skins and you want more? No problem. As with visualizations, you can get more skins by purchasing and installing the Microsoft Plus! Windows XP software, which will install more skins in Media Player. The Plus! pack contains several cool ones, such as the Plasma Ball, where the visualization dances inside of the ball:

If you prefer to get free skins, just go to the Skin Chooser and click the More Skins button. Assuming you are connected to the Internet, the Skin Chooser opens a web browser and connects to http://Windowsmedia.com, where you can download skins just as you can download visualizations. Just look through the options and choose to download the skin. The skin will be added to Media Player automatically once you install it and will be available on the Skin Chooser pane with the other skins. As you can imagine, the download site has everything from movie skins (such as Tomb Raider) to other fun skins (such as Elvis):

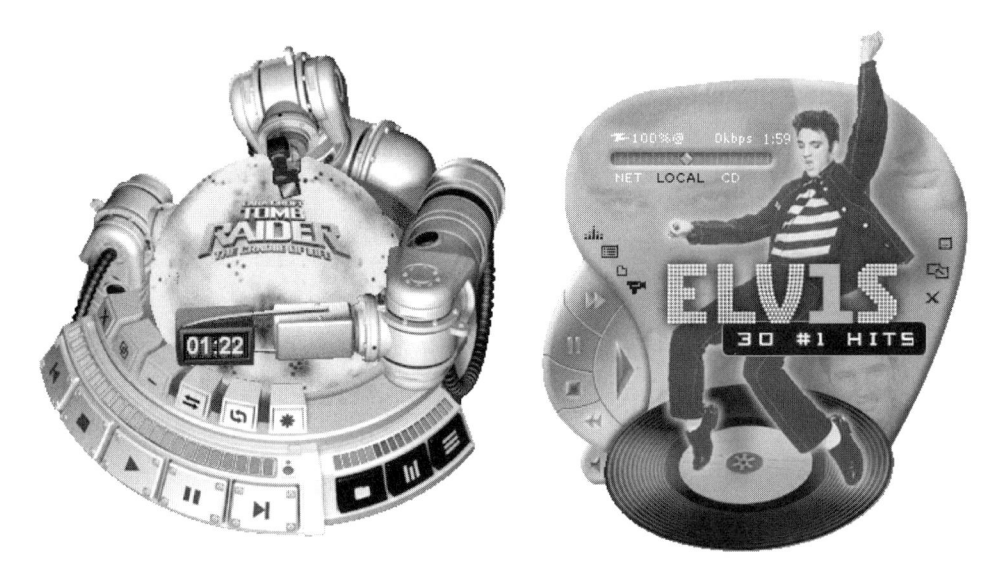

Naturally, you can download even more skins from the Internet. Check out www.theskinsfactory.com to get started.

Did you know? Accessing Premium Services

Windows Media Player includes an option called Premium Services, which is available in the list of buttons on the left side of the interface. As you can see in the following screen, the Premium Services feature enables you to subscribe to music and movie servers, where you can stream media to Media Player and watch it. This option works great if you don't mind both paying a monthly fee for the service and watching movies or dealing with all of your music within Media Player. Each service has a free trial option, but you do have to surrender your credit card number, then cancel out of the free trial. Also, note that the movie option may contain pornographic films, depending on the package you choose to purchase. So, if you have children or teens around the house, they could easily access the porn movies without your consent.

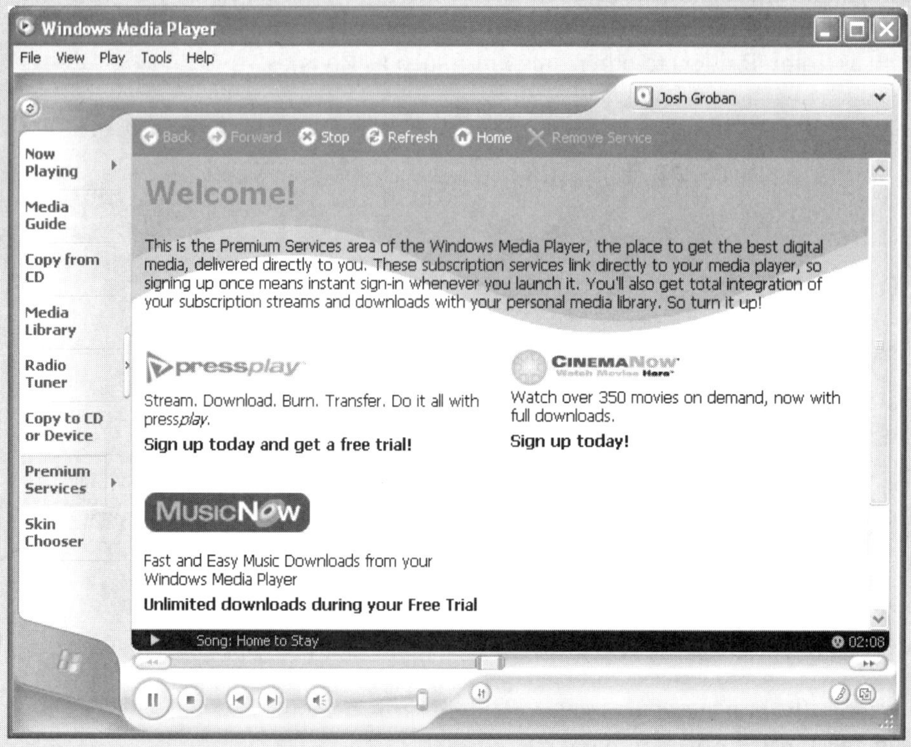

The good news about these services is they automatically log you on when you open Media Player, so you can access the services easily. The bad news is you have to pay for them, and if you are using a dial-up connection, you are not likely to get the streaming quality you want, especially on the movie side of things.

Work with Plug-Ins

As I've mentioned a couple of times in this chapter, Windows Media Player can use *plug-ins,* which are small programs designed to work within Media Player. Some common examples are visualizations and skins. However, there are also other plug-in features that can give Media Player more options. For example, if you install the Microsoft Plus! packs, they will add some plug-ins to Media Player so that some software features—such as Plus! Alarm Clock, which we'll explore later in Chapter 17—can interact with Media Player.

You can easily manage, remove, or add plug-ins using the Plug-ins tab of the Options dialog box (refer to Figure 4-6), available by clicking Tools | Options in Media Player. A helpful feature of this tab is you can click a link to access http://Windowsmedia.com, where you can see what additional plug-ins are available that you might want to install.

Use Plus! Speaker Enhancement

If you have Microsoft Plus! Windows XP, there is one additional feature you should install that can help your speakers sound better when you use Windows Media Player. This tool, called Plus! Speaker Enhancement, enables you to tell Media Player what brand and type of speakers you are using. It then uses a profile to configure Media Player for the best sound option for those speakers. Just open Microsoft Plus! and install the speaker enhancement software; then, in Media Player, click Tools | Plus! Speaker Enhancement | Configure Speakers. A simple dialog box opens (see Figure 4-7) in which you can choose the brand and model of your speakers.

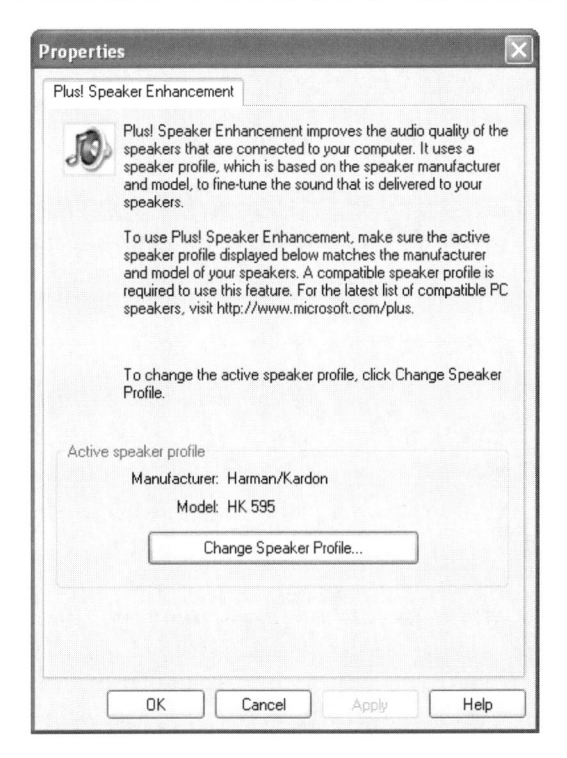

FIGURE 4-7 Choosing the brand and model of your speakers

Just click the Change Speaker Profile button, select your brand and model of speakers, and then click OK twice. Once you are done, click Tools | Plus! Speaker Enhancement | Enable to turn on the feature. That's all there is to it!

More Great Ideas

The customization options for Media Player give you several ways to make Media Player your own. Here are a few more quick suggestions:

- Spend some time playing around with the Now Playing interface. This will give you a great way to see all of the options available so that Now Playing looks and works the way you want it to.

- Get on the Internet and check out those skins and visualizations! There are many different options to choose from, and new ones are added all the time. If you are a Terminator 3 fan, be sure to check out the T3 skin at www.skinz.org. Very cool!

- Check out the available plug-ins at http://Windowsmedia.com. Some of them seem a bit dull, but there are several useful ones, especially those that make MP3 files easier to use and work within Windows Media Player.

Part II

Create Fun Things with Your Digital Photos

Chapter 5

Organize Your Memories: Make Sure You Can Find Photos When You Need Them

How to...

- Understand photo file types
- Name and store your photos
- Organize photo folders
- Back up photos

Raise your hand if you have boxes of old photos stuck in your closet, stuck here and there in a disorganized way. I thought so. Let's face it: Finding time to put pictures in a photo album and keep them nice and neat is a time-consuming task. Digital photography promises us an easier way to take care of photos, but if you are like me, your computer just as easily becomes a digital photo-storage closet— a place where you put your digital photos and then spend hours trying to find them when you need them.

The good news for us all is simple: We don't have to manage digital photos this way! With just a tiny bit of effort, you can make your Windows XP computer become a virtual storage closet of sorts—a place where you put your digital photos, where they are easy to use, and where they're easy to find. Sound too good to be true? It's not, and the best news of all is Windows XP has everything you need built right into the operating system. You just have to know how to use the features and how to store your digital photos in an effective way. In this chapter, you'll take a crash course on how to store your memories effectively so you can find them easily, and how to back up your photos so that you never lose those precious moments that you caught with your digital camera.

What You'll Need

For this project, you already have everything you need. So simply get your Windows XP Professional or Windows XP Home Edition computer up and running, and you'll be all set.

Get to Know Photo File Types

All someone has to do is say the word "files," and you suddenly feel like you are sinking to the bottom of the ocean, as if a wave of boring technical jargon is about to pass over you. Relax. I'm not going to go technical on you, but if you want to store your photos effectively, there are some fundamental things you need to understand. One of those things is file types.

Any piece of data that you store on your computer is saved as a file of some kind. You can think of your computer's hard drive as a big filing cabinet inside of which files are created and stored in different folders. Digital pictures, spreadsheets, word processing documents—you name it—are all stored as files.

In fact, your computer's entire operating system is made up of different files that work together. Files on your computer reside in different folders, and they appear as icons in your computer's folders. Figure 5-1 shows you some different files on a computer, which are in the user's My Documents folder. You can see some Word documents, photos, a web document (HTML), and other items; all of these items are considered files.

So, all data on your computer is stored in a file format. Files have individual names that distinguish them from one another, and those names must be unique (this is why you cannot name two different digital photos with the same name and store them in the same folder). However, there are different kinds of files on your computer, and you can even create different kinds of files from your digital photos—and this is where things can get a bit complicated. So let's start at the beginning.

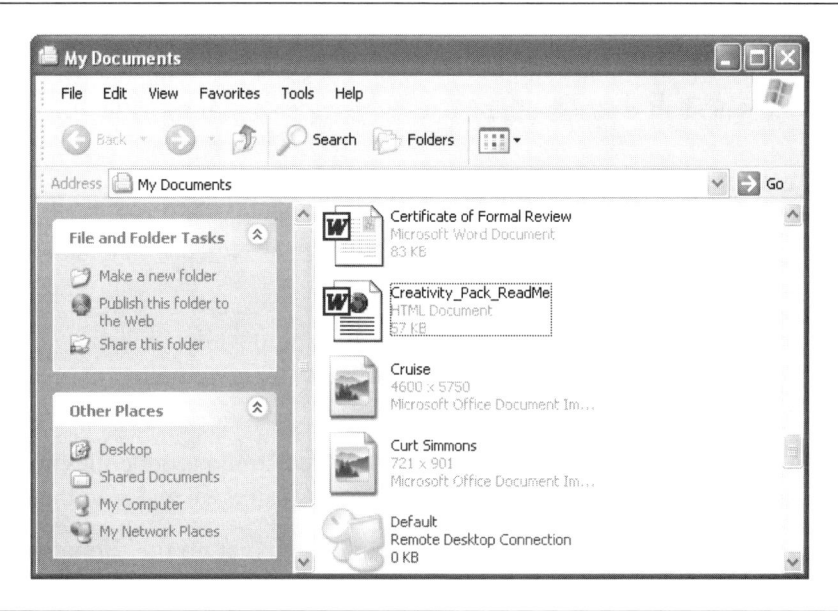

FIGURE 5-1 Files are represented by icons on your computer.

Different programs can open and read different kinds of files, depending on what the program is designed to do. Different programs also create different kinds of files. Some programs can read and save only one type of file, and some programs read and save another. Some programs read many different types of files but can save in only one type, while others read and save many types. Ugh, see how confusing it can all become?

Here's an easy way to look at it: Programs are written to do certain jobs. They do some jobs well, others not so well, and some not at all. For example, your photo-editing software is great at editing photos, but it probably does not provide great painting capabilities, nor does it help you create spreadsheets at all. The program is created to do certain jobs and to read and create files pertaining to those jobs. That is why you have different programs on your computer and why you have different types of files.

So here's the deal: In order to open and take a look at a file on your computer, the computer must have an application that understands and can read the file. If there is no program that can open and read it, you'll get some kind of error message. How does a program recognize the file? That occurs through the use of an extension. Each file on your computer has an extension that identifies it as a certain kind of file. The extension follows the name of the file. For example, let's say you have a digital photo named *vacation* that was saved as a JPEG file. The actual name of the file is vacation.jpg. When you double-click the file to open it, your computer looks for programs that can open JPEG files and uses the default one to open it.

There are many, many different file types because there are many different programs, but here are a few common ones with which you may be familiar:

- **Text (.txt)**   Text files are simple files that contain only text. Many different programs can open text files, including all word-processing applications and even other applications, such as Notepad in Windows.

- **Acrobat Reader (.pdf)**   Acrobat Reader files are often found on the Internet and on different installation CDs as product documentation. You must have Adobe Acrobat Reader installed on your computer to open a PDF file.

- **Word (.doc)**   Microsoft Word documents are stored as .doc files. Word and some other word-processing applications can open and read them.

- **JPEG (.jpg or .jpeg)**   JPEG files are common picture file formats used on the Internet.

These are just a few of the many different examples of files that you can use. Remember: All files have a file extension that identifies the file type, and a program must be able to recognize and open the file for you to use it on your computer. So, if different programs open and read different kinds of files, then how can you share pictures with others or post them on the Internet? In reality, there are a few picture file formats that are standardized so that, basically, all computers have programs that can read them. Your digital photo-editing software enables you to save your photos in a variety of formats, including the software's own format. For example, if you are using Photoshop Elements (visit www.adobe.com), you can save your photos as Photoshop Elements (PDD) files, but only computers that have Photoshop Elements or another program that read PDD files can open them. The editing software's internal file format is great while you are working on the photos, but it may not be the best choice for storing and using them.

So, if your editing software's file format is not the best, what should you use, and what are your options? First, a one-minute history lesson: When the Internet first came on the scene back in the '90s, web pages contained only text. Later, however, pictures and graphics were added. The problem is that pictures and graphics must use some kind of standard format that all computers can read. Otherwise, you would try to download a page, and the picture would not appear because your computer cannot read it. So a bunch of early Internet folks developed some picture and graphics standards, and now all PCs and Macintosh computers are equipped to read those file formats.

There are additional standards that are also useful to use for pictures you want to print that may not be used on all computers. Regardless, you should get familiar with these basic types of picture formats. You'll see them again and again, and you will use several of them, including the following:

- **JPEG** These files were first developed by the Joint Photographic Experts Group. JPEG (pronounced JAY-peg) photos encompass most every photo and graphic you see on the Internet. In fact, every photo you have seen in this course is a JPEG file. Why? There are a few important reasons:
  - All computers can read JPEG files. JPEG is a standard, and all of today's computers contain software that can read JPEG, including web browsers such as Internet Explorer and Netscape. You can e-JPEG pictures to anyone, and they can be opened and viewed easily. JPEG is also the standard file format used by webcams, digital cameras, camera-enabled PDAs, and other common devices (including those cool camera phones).

- JPEG files are small. They don't use a lot of disk space, but they typically keep the picture looking good.

- JPEG files are considered *lossy* files. This means that a lot of the inner-workings of the photo are discarded to give you a small file size, but the picture stays intact (at least, what you can see of it, anyway). In other words, a pixel contains data about all colors, but the JPEG formats discards the pixel information that is not actually used in the photo.

- GIF (Graphics Interchange Format) files are also commonly used on the Internet. They are similar to JPEGs and are often used for animated graphics. The good thing about GIF images is that you can reduce their size and color and still keep the image looking pretty good. So if you need a photo to be really small in size, GIF may be a good choice.

- **TIF (or TIFF)**   Tagged Image File is a standard file format that is used extensively, but for the opposite reasons than why a JPEG or GIF is used. TIF files save every pixel exactly as it is without trying to reduce the image size. For this reason, you get very high resolution, but the file size is large. TIF images are great to use for photos that you want to print in order to get high resolution, but they are not good for e-mail or Internet posting because they can be huge (often over 1MB, which would take someone with a dial-up modem about 20 minutes to download). Both Windows and Macintosh computers can read TIF files.

- **BMP**   Bitmap files are used on a Windows operating system, but they're not that great to use for print or e-mail purposes due to large file size and potential quality loss. You can still use them on Windows, and they are great for wallpaper. But I recommend that you stick with JPEG or TIF files, depending on what you want to do. By the way, newer Macintosh systems can also open and work with bitmap files.

What kind of picture file formats are used most often? JPEG and TIF. Your camera probably takes photos directly in the JPEG format, and it may be able to take TIF format photos as well.

Name Photos

Now that we have gotten the idea of file types out of the way, your first task for organizing your photographic memories is to name them. When you download photos from your camera, the first thing you probably notice is that they have names such as 125365448B.jpg. Right, that's helpful. So, what you want to do when you have downloaded photos is rename them to something descriptive and helpful. This way, when you are looking for photos later, you'll be able to find them easily, by name. In Windows XP, all you have to do to rename a photo is right-click it and click Rename. Then, you can just type a new name. Here are some quick tips on how to name your photo files:

- Use something descriptive. CancunTrip.jpg works much better than 1254685.jpg.

- Keep it short. A filename is simply that—a name—so don't make the name an entire sentence about the photo.

- Don't abbreviate the title too much. If you can't make sense of the title, it doesn't do you any good, so whatever you do, just make sure it makes sense to you.

- For a collection of photos, you may want to number them, such as Wedding14.jpg. This is helpful, but you'll still have to look around to find the specific photo. Still, if you keep the collection in one folder on your computer, that won't be too hard (see "Create a Folder Structure That Works" later in this chapter).

View Photos

Once you download your photos to your Windows XP computer, you can begin using them in any way you want. Before doing so, it's a good idea to find out what is available to you and how you can view and manage your photos. Windows XP is rather flexible and gives you several different options that you'll find helpful.

Keep in mind that you can organize photos however you want. This means that you can download all of your photos to a single folder, or you can create multiple folders and move them around as you like. Your photos may be downloaded to the My Pictures folder by default, and that's fine. However, note that the My Pictures folder doesn't have any magical organizational powers—it is simply a folder like any folder on Windows XP. I often organize my photos into various folders so I can look through them more easily. I typically organize them by event (vacation, birthdays, holidays, etc.), but you can create any kind of system you want. People who take a lot of digital photos often create a new folder for each month and put all of the photos for that month in one folder. There is no right or wrong approach, of course, but you'll want to decide on an organization method that works best for you. After all, there is nothing worse than taking a great digital photo and then not being able to find it on your computer!

TIP *If you happen to be using Adobe's Photoshop Album software to manage your digital photos, check out* How to Do Everything with Photoshop Album *(McGraw-Hill/Osborne, 2003).*

Once you open a folder that has photos stored in it, you are ready to begin using the photos. As you can see in Figure 5-2, a folder containing photos has a Picture Tasks box that gives you several options, as a well as a typical File and Folder Tasks option that can also be helpful. We'll explore the features you see here in upcoming chapters, but I do want to point out a few direct features here. First of all, it's a good idea to view the View menu to choose a viewing option that works well for you. Figure 5-2 show the Thumbnails view, which enables you to see the actual photo along with the filename.

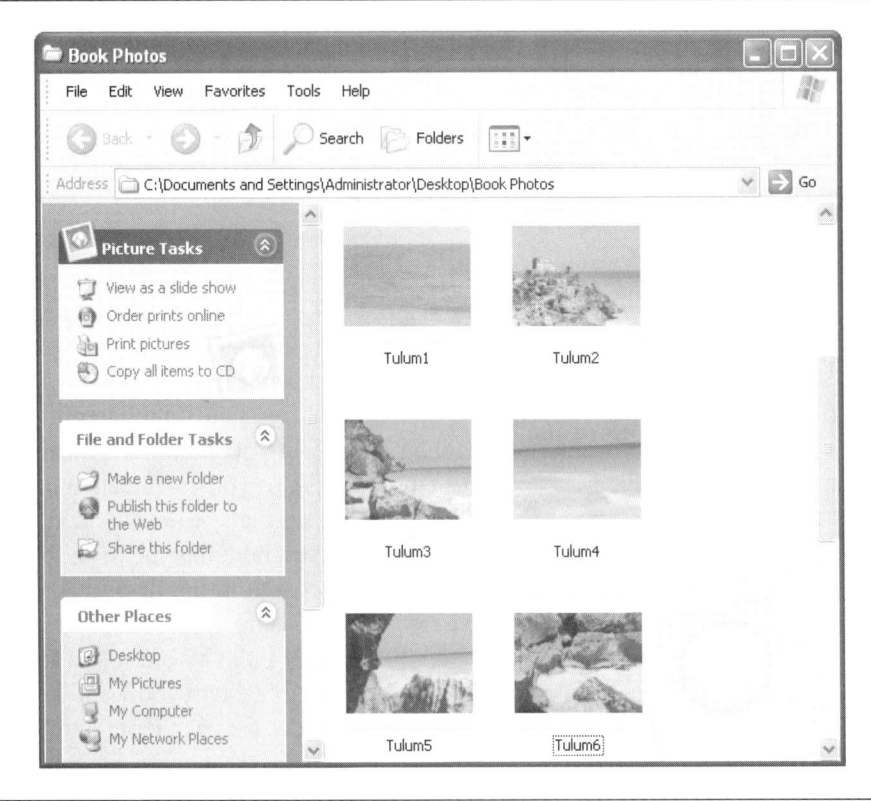

FIGURE 5-2 Folders with photos give you several management tasks.

The View menu contains these options:

- **Filmstrip** This option presents your photos in a filmstrip fashion. You can select a photo and see a bigger image of it as well as use the controls to simply click through all of your photos. You also have controls that enable you to directly rotate an image. The Filmstrip view (see Figure 5-3) is really helpful if you want to get a good look at your photos.

- **Thumbnails** The Thumbnails view gives you small photo views (shown in Figure 5-2). This is a good way to see photos and filenames at the same time.

- **Tiles** The Tiles option gives you icons (not photos themselves), filenames, image sizes, and image file types (JPEG, TIF, etc.).

- **Icons** This option gives you smaller icons with only the filenames.

FIGURE 5-3 Filmstrip view shows you individual photos within a folder.

- **List** This option gives you even smaller icons with only the filenames. This view is useful to see a listing of photo filenames.

- **Details** This option is the same as List, but it gives you more information—such as size, type, date modified, etc.—about each photo (see Figure 5-4).

Aside from these basic viewing options, you also have quick access to some features by simply right-clicking a photo; this opens the basic contextual menu that appears when you right-click just about anything, but you also see some specific options that are useful in managing photos:

- **Preview** This opens the photo in Windows Picture and Fax Viewer. Windows Picture and Fax Viewer is not an image-editing program, but

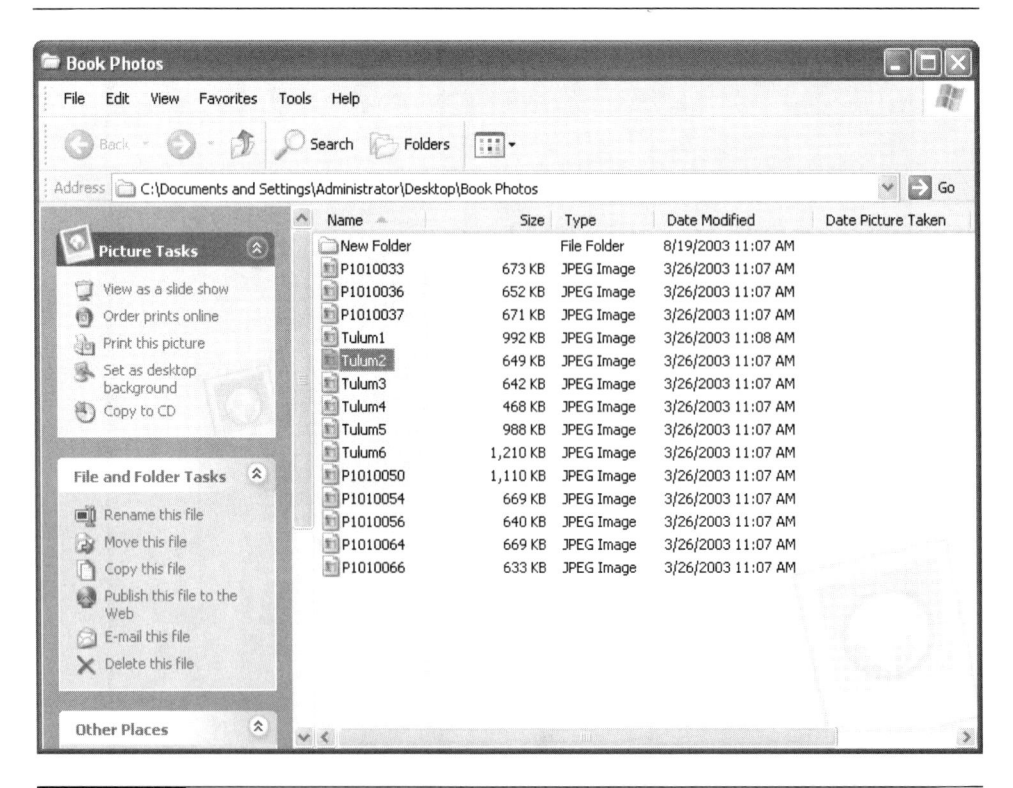

FIGURE 5-4   Use the Details view to get more information about your photos.

as you can see by the buttons at the bottom of the viewer, you can look through photo collections; view different sizes; see a slide show; zoom in or out; rotate, delete, print, or save a photo; or open the image in whatever default image editor you have installed on your computer.

- **Edit** This option opens the photo in your computer's default image-editing program. This might be Microsoft Paint, Photoshop, Photoshop Elements, Paint Shop Pro, or another program that you currently have installed.

- **Print** This action opens a photo-printing wizard. You can find out more about using this wizard in Chapter 6.

- **Resize Pictures** This option opens a quick and handy Resize Pictures dialog box. You can resize the photo, which creates a copy in a different size (your original photo is not tampered with, so don't worry). This helpful feature enables you to resize the photo quickly to meet whatever need you have. Click the Advanced button to enter a custom size. (The Advanced button then turns into the Basic button.)

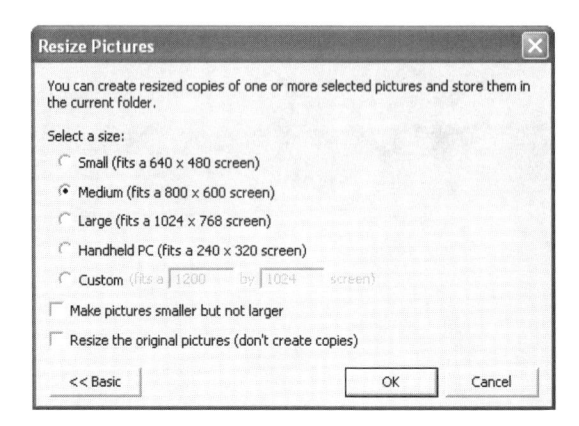

- **Rotate** These options enable you to rotate your photo quickly.
- **Set As Desktop Background** This option immediately sets the photo as your desktop background, which keeps you from having to wade through Display properties to make the change.

> **TIP** *You can also set a photo as the desktop background by selecting it in a folder and clicking the Set As Desktop Background option found in the Picture Tasks box.*

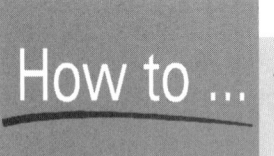

How to ... View Your Photos as a Slide Show

Windows XP has a built-in "slide show" feature that you can use to view the photos in a folder as a slide show. In the folder, just click the View As A Slideshow option that appears in the Picture Tasks box. Your photos will come to life as a full screen, automatically advancing slideshow. However, if you move your mouse, you'll see options to manually advance or back up during the slideshow:

You can also stop the slideshow with the manual controls, or just press the ESC key on your keyboard.

Create a Folder Structure That Works

Your best friend for finding digital photos is a folder. Windows XP and most other modern computer operating systems use folders to organize and store files. As mentioned earlier, think of your computer as a filing cabinet and files as the papers in the filing cabinet. Just as you would not want to throw hundreds of pieces of paper in a filing cabinet and expect to find them easily, the same goes for your computer. To be blunt, the biggest mistake most digital photography enthusiasts make is putting all of their digital photos in one folder. That may work fine at first, but over time, that folder grows to a hundred photos, then a few hundred, then even more. Before long, you have problems finding what you need.

Just as you would use a filing cabinet to organize papers, you should get in the habit of putting photos in folders in a way that has meaning to you, and doing so

How to Do Everything with Windows XP Digital Media

when you download them from your camera. You can create as many folders on your computer as you like and name them as you want (just right-click them and click Rename to rename them). You can also make any number of subfolders within a folder as needed. Here are a few quick tips to get your "digital closet" organized:

- Organize photos in folders by events. For example, you might have a Thanksgiving 2003 folder, a Carl's Birthday 2003 folder, a Vacation to Colorado 2003 folder, and so own. Be specific, and use the date and year when necessary.

- If you are really wild about digital photography and you take a bunch of photos each month, you may want to organize photos and files by the month and year. Just name the folders October 2003, November 2003, and so on.

- If necessary, consider creating subfolders in the main folder to further organize your photos. For example, I use this tactic for vacations. Recently, I took my family on a cruise and shot over 400 digital photos. To make them easy to find, I created a main folder for the cruise, and then created different subfolders to hold my photos according to different portions of the trip, as you can see in Figure 5-5.

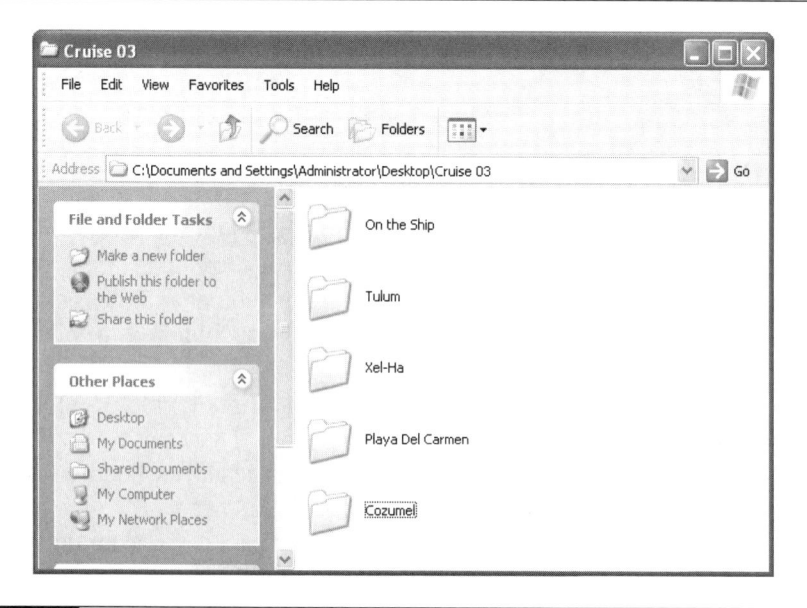

FIGURE 5-5   Subfolders can help you manage main folders that contain a lot of photos.

- Be careful with subfolders. While they are helpful, too many of them become more confusing than useful. If you find yourself creating a bunch of subfolders but putting only a couple of pictures in each one, step back and think about your folder structure. Try to find more generic subfolder headings so that you store more photos.

> **TIP** *Some people print thumbnail images of all photos in any given folder, and then keep the hard copy for quick reference. See Chapter 6 to learn how.*

Back Up Photos

You have memories; you have photos. So, what happens if your computer decides to die and the computer's hard disk implodes? You lose all of those photos, and they cannot be recovered. Yikes! That's an event none of us wants to experience, but it happens to people every single day. So, what you need to do is make backup copies of your photos. When you make a backup, you store the backup copies in a location off of your hard drive, such as on a CD, a disk drive of some kind, or even on another computer. There are two additional resources I want to mention that can help you keep your photos backed up: Windows XP Backup and the Web.

> **CAUTION** *I cannot stress enough the importance of backing up your photos. Read on, and then make a point to develop an effective, regular backup plan of your own to make sure your photos are always safe and sound.*

Use Windows XP Backup

If you are using Windows XP Professional, you have Backup software built right into your operating system. If you are using Windows XP Home edition, you can also get the software—it's hiding on your installation CD-ROM. Using Windows Backup, you can effectively back up everything on your computer if you like; in the event of a catastrophic failure, you can put everything back in place, not just your photos.

First things first: If you are a Windows XP Home Edition user, you'll have to install the backup software; Windows XP Professional editions have the software installed already. Home users, follow these steps to install Windows Backup:

1. Insert your installation CD into the Windows XP Home computer's CD-ROM drive.

2. Click Start | My Computer.

3. Right-click the CD-ROM drive and click Browse.

4. On the CD, in \valueadd\msft\ntbackup, double-click the backup.msi file to install the backup wizard.

Once backup is installed, you're ready to start using it. The following steps walk you through a backup session using Windows XP Professional's Backup; Home users should see the same screens:

1. Click Start | All Programs | Accessories | System Tools | Backup to start the Backup Utility Wizard. Notice that on the Welcome screen, you have the option to use Advanced mode. Don't use Advanced mode until you have more experience using the Backup wizard.

2. Click Next to continue using the wizard.

3. In the Select An Option window, you can choose to perform a backup or restore files. Select the Back Up Files And Settings radio button, and then click Next.

4. In the next window, you can choose to back up everything on your computer, certain drives and files, or everyone's files and settings. Make a selection and click Next.

CHAPTER 5: Organize Your Memories 89

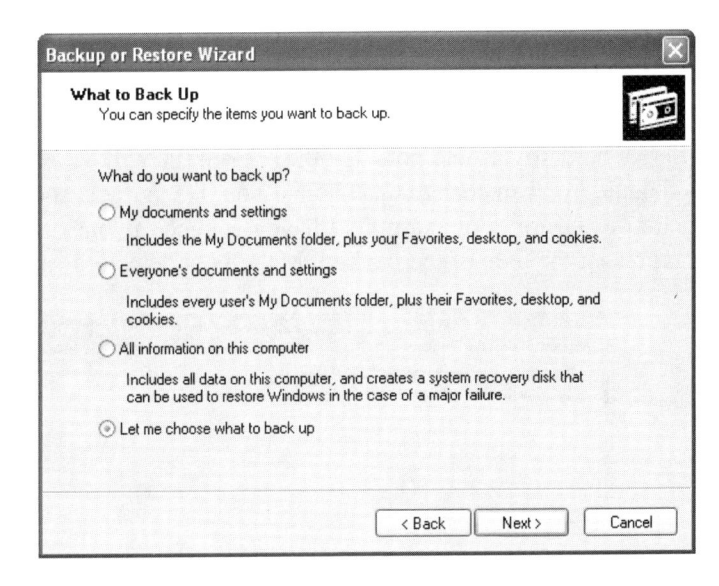

5. If you chose to back up selected files, an Explorer-type window appears in which you can select the drives, folders, or even specific files that you want to back up. Click the check boxes for the items you want to back up. As you can see in the following illustration, I am going to back up the My Documents folder. Make your selections and click Next.

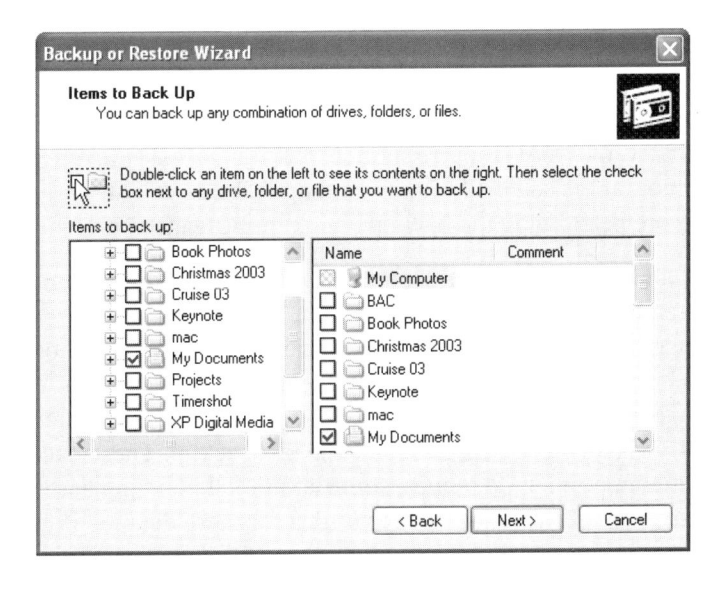

6. Choose the location where you want to store the backup file. Use the Browse button to select a removable media drive or even a network location. If your computer has multiple hard drives, you can even save the backup file to a different hard drive. Also note that the backup file will be named backup.bkf by default. You can change this name if you like, but you should not change the .bkf extension. For example, I have renamed my backup file 0912.bkf to represent the date of the backup. Make your selections and click Next.

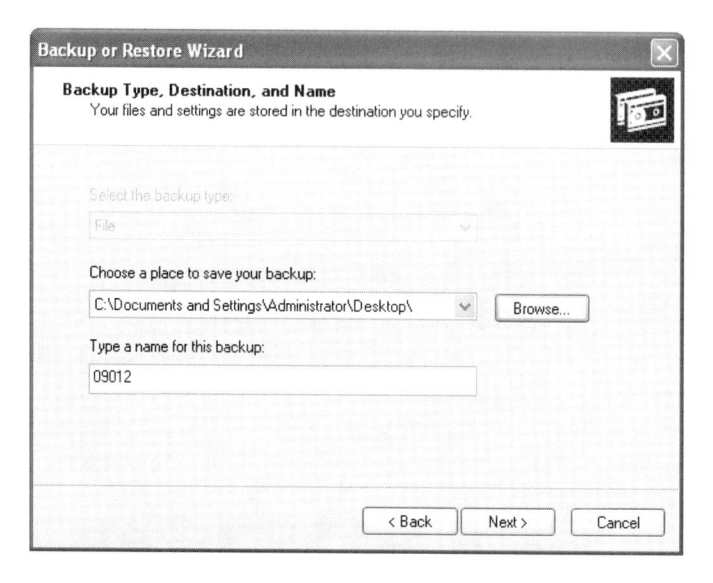

7. In the completion window, you can click Finish to start the backup job. However, before doing so, notice that you have an Advanced button. This option offers some additional backup features you may want to consider before performing the backup. Click the Advanced button.

8. In the Type Of Backup window, you see a drop-down menu that allows you to choose a backup type. By default, a typical backup is *normal,* which means a backup file is created. However, you can also choose other types of backup options such as *incremental,* which backs up files only if they have not been backed up previously, and *differential,* which backs up files only if they have changed since the last backup. These backup options, while important, do require some additional planning and study on your part. See the Windows XP Help files for more detailed information about these options. Make any desired selections and click Next.

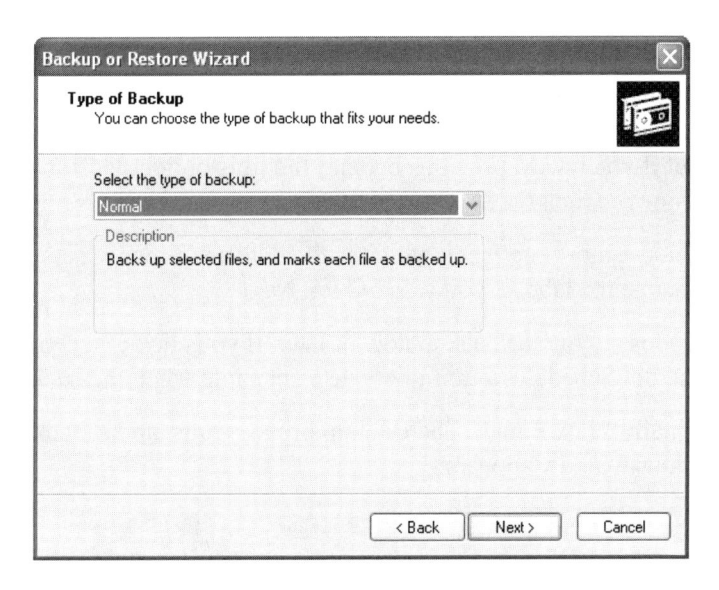

9. The next window, How To Back Up, asks if you want Windows XP to verify data once it has been backed up, which is a good idea. You can also opt to use compression if it is available on the storage device. Finally, you can choose to disable Volume Snapshot, which allows Windows XP to save files even if they are in use at the time of the backup. Make any desired selections and click Next.

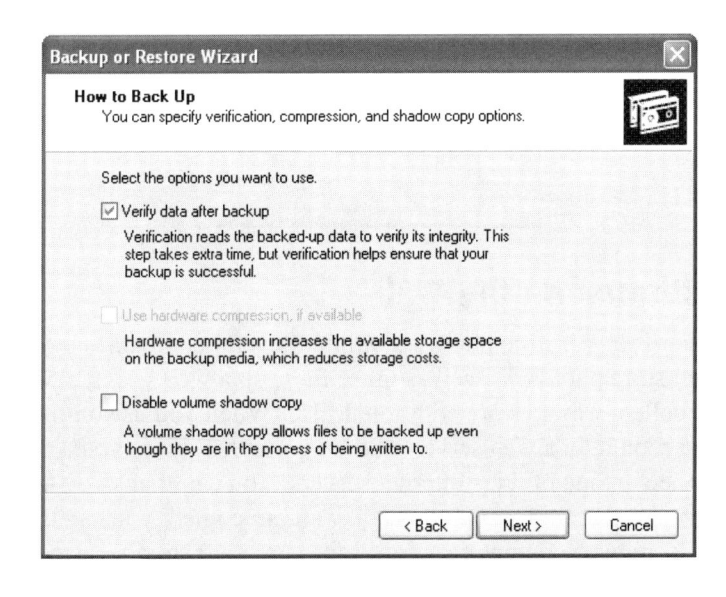

10. In the Backup Options window, you can choose either to replace an existing backup file that might exist in the same location or to append the new backup file to the old one. Be default, the append option is selected, but if you have a previous backup file, this option doesn't apply to you anyway. Click Next.

11. Choose a backup label, which is the date and time by default. You can change the label if you want. Click Next.

12. Choose to run the backup now or later. If you click Later, you'll need to click the Set Schedule button to create a schedule when the backup should run.

13. Finally, click Finish. The Backup process runs, and a Backup Progress status window appears:

Store Photos on the Web

Another cool way to store photos is online. Several companies offer online storage, so you can store photos, as well as other files, on a web site. It's private and fast, and an excellent way to store additional files. When you use online storage, you set up an account on a web server. The web site then gives you a certain amount of disk space on one of their Internet servers. You can then copy any files you want to the web site for storage. Once you have them copied, you can then delete the originals from your computer so you'll free up more storage space. Or, if you want to use the Web as a backup (as opposed to a storage) option, simply copy your files to the online storage center and keep the originals on your computer. In the end,

CHAPTER 5: Organize Your Memories

you have your files on a web server on the Internet, and you can access them from any computer using any web browser. Since you have an account password, your files are safe and sound, sitting on the Web.

CAUTION *Remember that your photos are not fault-tolerant unless you have two copies stored in two different places. Online storage is great for backup, but keep in mind that to have effective backup, you must have two copies in two separate locations. Do not depend solely on the web site to keep your photos safe. Even web servers crash!*

Did you know?

The Safety of Online Storage

If you like the idea of online storage yet you feel a little uneasy about it, don't worry—that feeling is normal. Let me answer a few common questions and worries about web storage:

- *Are my photos safe?* Yes. Theft can happen anywhere, even from your own computer. Web servers user a number of security features, and if you stick with a major storage site (some of which are discussed later in this chapter), your photos are just as safe stored on the Web as they are stored on your local PC.

- *What if the site goes out of business?* Will they delete my photos? Web sites that store data are responsible. Should the site need to go down or stop business, they will let you know in advance so you can download your photos back to your computer.

- *If I copy my photos to the web site and delete them from my computer, are they completely safe?* No. If you want to ensure that you have a safe backup plan, you need to have at least two copies of the same data in different locations. I use online storage, but I also burn photos to a CD. This way, I have two different locations where the photos are stored.

- *Can I get my photos from another computer?* Yes. You can download your photos using a web browser (along with your username and password) from any computer.

- *Are all sites free?* No. Some sites charge, and some will give you a trial membership before you decide to buy.

If online storage sounds like a great solution for your storage and photo-backup headaches, you'll want to check out some of the sites that offer this feature. Keep in mind that online storage is only a storage location. This is not the place to create online photo albums or share photos with people online. Storage sites are designed just to hold your photos, not view them. However, you may give out your site password and username to a trusted friend so he or she can download your photos. The way you use online storage is up to you, but just remember these sites are here for storage.

So, what sites can you access? There are several. I'm not going to list them all, but I want to point you in the direction of a few good ones I'm aware of or have used. This does not mean that sites that aren't listed here are not good—I just don't have any experience with them.

XDrive

XDrive (www.xdrive.com), shown in Figure 5-6, provides data backup for both individuals and corporations. If you are a Plus user, you can even download a utility

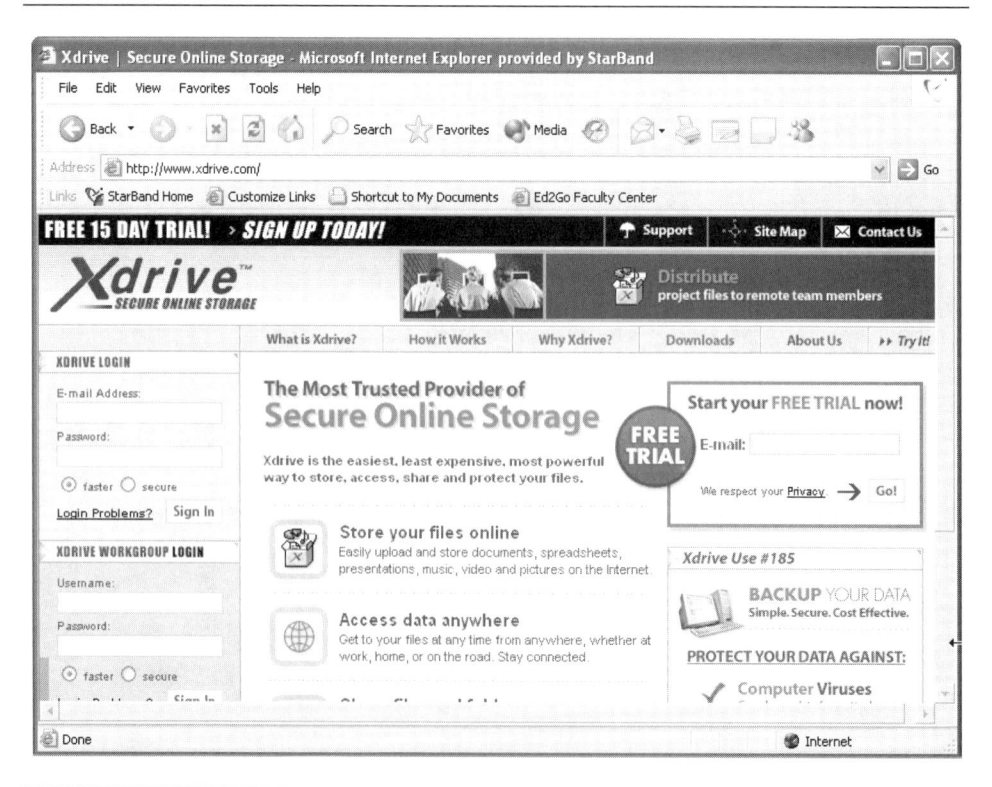

FIGURE 5-6 XDrive.com

that will make XDrive look like the photos are residing on your local computer instead of on the Internet. This site is not free, but it is worth the investment. You can get a 15-day trial membership, but after that, a 75MB storage account will cost you $4.95 a month. You even get up to a 1GB account for $49.95 a month, which is a lot of storage. Overall, the site is great, as is XDrive's quality of service.

ImageStation

ImageStation (www.imagestation.com), which is owned by Sony, provides a hybrid site for creating photo albums and ordering prints. It's meant to be a one-in-all site, and it works well. You simply set up an account and upload your photos. Your photos stay on the site as long as your account is active. You can then order prints directly from the site, since your images are already stored. If you are looking for a one-site-fits-all approach, check out this one; if you want more flexibility with online storage, try one of the other sites.

GlobeDesk

GlobeDesk (www.globedesk.com), shown in Figure 5-7, is another online storage facility. You can also get a free trial account here, but the service will cost after your 15-day trial membership. The cost is very reasonable for keeping your photos safe: 100MB of storage space is only $4.95 a month (you can get up to 10GB for $350 a month, if you are serious about storage space).

Streamload

Streamload (www.streamload.com) is a bit different from the others in that it offers a flat fee of $4.95 per month for practically unlimited storage. If you have music and video files, they can even be streamed directly from the site, which can be a cool feature if you have a web page and want to offer streaming media. Like other sites, you can set up a free account and try it out for 15 days.

MyDocsOnline

MyDocsOnline (www.mydocsonline.com) provides storage and sharing for files (including photos) and backup options. They host a personal and enterprise edition, so home users like you and me can use the service. 50MB will cost you from $9.95 every three months to 1GB for $109.95 every three months. Overall, this is a good site with a number of features you may enjoy.

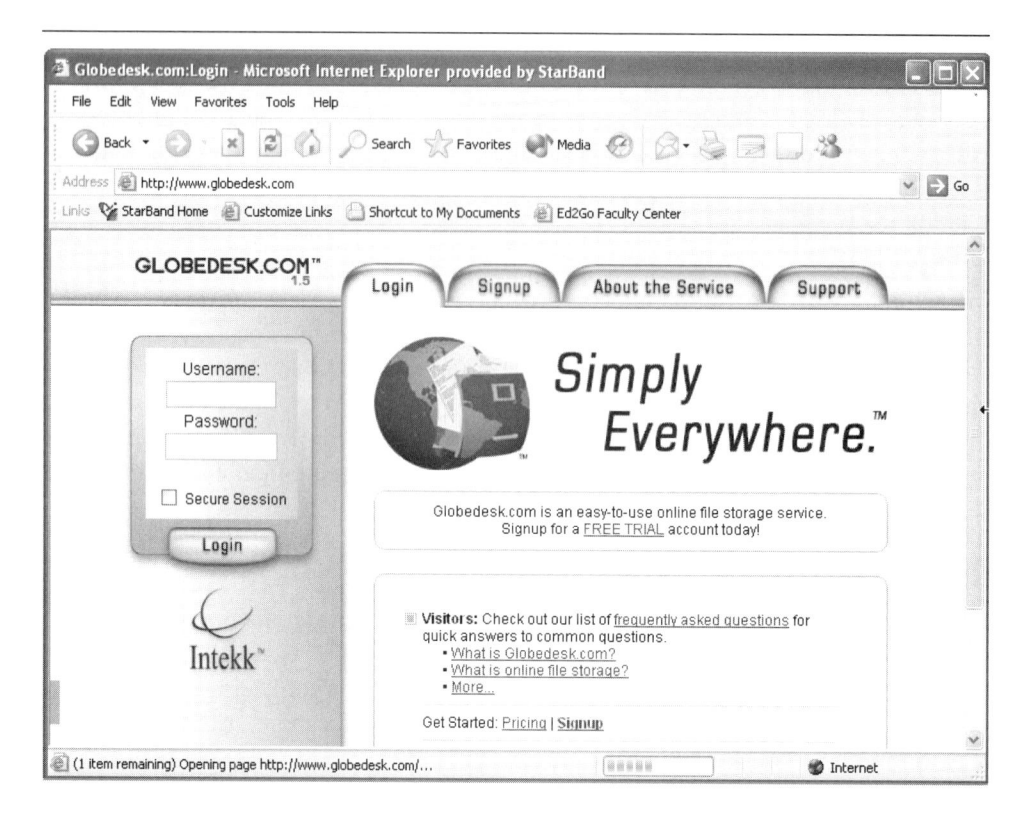

FIGURE 5-7 GlobeDesk.com

iBackup

iBackup (www.ibackup.com) is a cool backup site. Using their tools, you can even schedule file backups from your computer at specified times, automatically. You can also use their tools to see your drive on their web site, as if the drive was local on your computer. You can get a free trial, and then 50MB of storage space costs only $3 per month. Not a bad deal!

More Great Ideas

Windows XP gives you everything you need to store and manage your digital photos in an easy and effective way. Here are a few more ideas to consider:

CHAPTER 5: Organize Your Memories

- Your digital camera software may give you a way to store digital photos on your computer. You should check out the software to see what it offers, but don't limit yourself to it. You can still move your photos around and create folders for them as you like.

- Don't forget to make copies of your photos and store them on a CD. This is an easy way to back up your photos. However, keep in mind that CDs are easily scratched and don't last forever, so you might consider making two copies, or using a combination of storage methods—such as backup and online backup—for safety.

- Always use the View menu in a folder that holds photos so you can see actual images instead of icons. This will make your work much easier.

- Can't find a photo? If you know the photo's filename, just click Start | Search, and then use Windows XP's easy Search feature to find the photo.

Chapter 6

Print Perfect Digital Photos of Any Size— Every Time!

How to...

- Use your printer to print perfect photos
- Use the Web and other resources for printing

I'm sure you probably do not need to read this chapter. After all, printing digital photos so that they come out perfectly every time is one of the easiest things to do. Yeah, right! In fact, printing quality photos is one of the most aggravating things you are likely to do with your digital photos, and printing them at the size you want can be an even bigger nightmare. How can you take a standard digital photo and make it print as a frame-quality 4×6? Can you take any digital photo and print a quality 8×10? If you have done some experimenting with digital photo printing, you have probably wasted plenty of paper and turned a few of your hairs gray in the process.

However, digital-photo printing doesn't have to be a nightmare. Armed with the right information and the right tools—which Windows XP provides—you should be able to print quality photos in the sizes you want, assuming you have a decent printer. To put this problem in its grave once and for all, this chapter shows exactly how to master the art of quality photo printing, so let's get started.

What You'll Need

For this project, you'll need some digital photos, some photo-quality printer paper, and a good printer.

Understand PPR—The Basics of Quality Photo Printing

No, "PPR" isn't some technical term you'll have to memorize. Actually, it's an abbreviation I like to use when I talk about quality printing. As you think about quality photo printing, there are three items you must always keep in mind (and understand):

- Printers
- Paper
- Resolution of the photo you want to print

Having the right combination of these three elements—printer, paper and resolution (PPR)—will guarantee that you get great prints of your digital photos every time. The following sections take a look at PPR and help you understand what you need to know.

Printers

The two most common printers on the market today are laser printers and inkjet printers. In fact, I'll bet that virtually all of you use one or the other, with most of you using inkjet printers. That's good news, because an inkjet printer is you best choice for printing photos.

The first printer I bought was an old, ridiculously simple dot-matrix printer. When I bought my first Macintosh, I decided to go for bust and buy a black-and-white laser printer. The quality and the price were awesome, but of course, it did not print in color.

A laser printer works a lot like a copy machine. Using the print job, your computer sends an image of the print job to the printer. Next, the printer charges the job electronically onto a piece of paper. The laser printer's toner cartridge then places toner on the electronically charged portions of the paper. Finally, the toner is burned onto the paper, giving a crisp, clear print job.

You can buy a black-and-white laser printer from a number of manufacturers for around $200 to $500. The problem is that a color laser printer will cost you around $1,000, and quite possibly more for a really good model. For this reason, color laser printers are not as popular for photo printing. Also, prints from a laser printer tend to have a glare and simply do not look as good as inkjet-printer prints.

Thus, the most popular kind of printer on the market today is the inkjet printer. Inkjet printers read the color pixels of a photo, or even text, and basically spray fine beads of color onto the paper to re-create the picture. The process is complicated such that each bead retains its own boundaries yet combines with the other beads to create a stunning picture. Inkjet printers are more reasonable than laser printers, costing from about $100 to $500. The good news is that printer manufacturers are very in-tune with our need to print photos, and even a basic $100 inkjet printer will print good-quality photos.

Most printer companies produce inkjet printers, and you'll find a number of models from popular brands such as HP, Epson, Lexmark, and Canon. For a standard, high-quality inkjet printer, you can expect to pay around $200 or so, depending on the features that you want. It is helpful to buy a printer that specifically advertises itself as a "photo printer." I have an Epson Stylus Photo 820 printer (that cost only $99), and it prints fantastic photos. I also have an HP PSC 720 (about $250) that does a fine job, as well.

> **NOTE** *In case you are wondering, Canon calls their inkjet brand "Bubblejet," but it's the same thing.*

So what kind of printer do you really need? That depends on several factors. Obviously, the more money you have to work with, the more options you have. However, you don't have to spend a lot of money on a printer to make great high-quality prints. If you want to print only photos (and a bunch of them), use an inkjet printer. If you want to have two good printers for text and photo printing, use text on a laser printer and photos on an inkjet. If you do both (like me), just get a good inkjet printer.

As you shop for a printer, keep these points in mind:

- **Usage** Always keep your photo-usage needs in the forefront of your mind when you are looking for a printer. Don't let the salesperson distract you from your original intentions.

- **Resolution** The printer you are using must support high resolution to print photos well. For laser printers, you need a model that supports at least 600dpi. Inkjet printers should support at least 1440dpi. Most of them today support more than this anyway, so you don't have to worry a lot about the printer's resolution values.

- **Size** Most standard printers can print only up to 8×10 pictures because of the paper size restriction. If you want to print larger photos, such as 11×17, you need to buy a wide-format printer that can support paper sizes this large.

Paper

Do you want to know a digital-photo–printing secret? Then, here it is: Paper is everything. In fact, I'll go so far as to say that paper is more important than the printer. Do you find that hard to believe? I once did, too, until I bought photo-quality paper and saw the difference. In fact, if you are using a standard inkjet printer, you can produce great-quality print photos as long as you invest a little of your hard-earned money on the right paper for the job. Sure, you can produce prints on plain printer paper, but what is the point if you do not get photo-quality prints? Plain copy paper tends to absorb the ink from the inkjet printer, which gives you fuzzy, dull-looking prints.

CHAPTER 6: Print Perfect Digital Photos of Any Size— Every Time!

So, what do you need? There are myriad paper types for many different printing jobs, and it seems that printer manufacturers like to produce more types of paper than is really necessary. And by the time you see five different brands of the same thing, it can all get confusing. Basically, though, photo-quality paper is all the same—the trick is that you have to find what photo paper seems to work best with your printer. You'll find glossy photo paper, which works better than plain photo paper and gives your prints that 35mm feel. Glossy photo paper has a slick print side that is able to hold the color of the printing process more finely. Some paper brands allow you to print on only one side of the paper, while some brands are double-sided.

So which paper should you use? In the end, you'll need to experiment with some different kinds of photo paper and see which one looks best with your printer. The paper brands do tend to look different, depending on the printer, and I suggest you start with the same paper brand as your printer brand. For example, if you are using an HP printer, you may have the best luck with HP photo paper. No matter which way you go, photo paper is expensive—around $7 to $12 for 20 sheets—but you'll need to spend the money to get the quality you want. You can buy photo paper at any department store, computer store, or office store (and many other places), and be sure to watch for sales!

And, if you are wondering, I use just standard glossy photo paper. I mainly use an HP printer, so I often opt for HP paper, but I have had comparable results with most other brands that you see in the stores. I'm not picky, and my printer doesn't seem to be either, but you may want to experiment and find the paper that works best for your printer.

Photo Resolution

In the digital photography world, resolution is one of those words that keeps coming back to haunt you. The concept of resolution can be difficult to understand at first, and what resolution is needed where can be dizzying. First things first: A digital photo is made up of pixels. A pixel is basically a dot of color. One by one, these tiny dots of color are pushed against each other to create the picture you see before you. The more pixels there are, the higher the resolution of your photo; similarly, the fewer pixels there are, the lower the resolution. If the pixel count isn't high enough, the pixels are stretched to fit the size of the photo you want, creating jagged lines and other print-quality problems.

Your digital camera can probably shoot photos at different resolutions, depending on the model. For example, you may notice that your camera can shoot 1024×768 or 1600×1200. These values represent the vertical and horizontal pixel values. A 1024×768 photo contains 786,432 pixels (1024×768 = 786,432). A 1600×1200 photo contains 1,920,000 pixels (1600×1200 = 1,920,000), also called 1.9 megapixels. In short, the more pixels that reside in a photo, the larger the size at which you can print them.

In terms of shooting pictures with your camera and printing your pictures, at which resolution do you need to shoot? That all depends on the photo size that you want to print. If you want to print larger photos, such as 5×7s or 8×10s, you'll need to shoot at a higher resolution so that the pixel count is high enough for your printer to reproduce images of this size.

> **TIP** *No software can give you more pixels in a photo. Some software products can use a method that basically copies pixels and tries to extend them, but in reality, a software program cannot make your photo "bigger." It can reduce the number of pixels by cropping the photo, but once you shoot the photo with your camera, the photo is stuck at whatever resolution at which you shot the photo. So, it's very important that you think about how you are going to use your pictures in terms of printing when you are choosing the resolution settings on your camera.*

You may think, "Well, then, I'll just shoot everything at the highest resolution possible." Yes, you can do that, but also keep in mind that high-resolution photos are big in terms of bytes. A typical memory card may be able to hold 30 or 40 300KB images, but may hold only two or three high-resolution images (each can be several megabytes in size), so resolution is always a trade-off between file size and what you want to do. If you know that you like to print a lot of 5×7 photos or 8×10 photos, you'll need to shoot at higher resolutions.

So, exactly what resolution do you need to shoot at? Table 6-1 lists some general guidelines of the minimum resolutions you need. As you can see, the larger print size you want, the larger picture you need to shoot in terms of resolution.

As a final thought, keep in mind that higher resolution values are needed when printing larger photos. Study your camera settings, consider your printing habits, and then shoot at resolutions that are generally right for your needs.

As you read this section, you may discover that your camera can't shoot at a resolution that is high enough to print even a good 8×10 photo. Well, lower resolution cameras don't provide enough resolution, so if printing 8×10s is really important to you, it is probably time to think about buying a new camera.

Did you know?

Getting to Know DPI

Photo printing is confusing, often due to the combination of terms used. You may hear about *pixels* when you talk about photos, but you'll see *DPI,* or *dots per inch,* when you talk about printers. DPI is a resolution value used with printers. The value represents the number of ink dots that can be used per inch in the photo. Once again, you are back to the resolution of the photo; it's just that printers express resolution in dots rather than pixels. Loosely, dots and pixels are the same thing, but what does this really mean to you? All this means is that in order for a printer to re-create an image effectively, your photos need to meet a certain DPI value—generally around 250.

If you keep your mind set on pixels and resolution in your photos, you really don't have to worry about DPI—your photos will turn out great. But if you are curious, you can figure the DPI of a photo by dividing the size photo you want to print by a photo's resolution. For example, let's say you have a 2048×1536 resolution photo. You want to print the photo as a 5×7. To figure the DPI, divide the height by the photo size. In this example, divide 2048 by 7, which equals 292. (Digital photos are measured in width by height, whereas printed photos are measured in height by width; this is why you divide 2048 by 7.) Since you need around 250dpi to get a good quality print, a value of 292 tells you that you are good to go.

The main thing you need to know about DPI is that high-resolution photos print well with medium to high DPI settings on your printer. If you are trying to print a low-resolution photo, use a lower DPI setting. I know this may not make sense, but higher DPI settings often make low-resolution photos look worse, so keep this in mind if you are trying to squeeze the best printing power out of a low-resolution photo.

Print Size	Photo Resolution
Small prints or for computer-screen viewing	640×480
4×6 prints	1024×768
5×7 prints	1280×1024 (1 megapixel)
8×10 prints	1600×1200 (2 megapixels)

TABLE 6-1   Print Size and Photo Resolution

Print Your Photos

In order to effectively print photos at the size and quality you want, you need some software. There, I said it—the secret is out. Without some software to help you, it is very difficult to control the print size and really get what you want. That's no problem, though, because you have Windows XP. Windows XP's Photo Printing Wizard is designed to fix this problem once and for all, so once you're sure you have the right PPR, you should be able to easily print the photos you want at the sizes you want any time. Follow these steps to use the Photo Printing Wizard:

1. In the folder that contains the photos you want to print, click the Print Pictures option in the Pictures Tasks box. You can also right-click any photo and click Print, or select multiple photos by CTRL-clicking them, then right-clicking them and clicking Print.

2. When the Photo Printing Wizard appears, click Next.

3. In the Picture Selection window, select the photos you want to print by clicking the check mark in the corner of each photo. If you choose to print only one photo by right-clicking it, you can just move on by clicking Next. Clear the check boxes next to any photos that you do not want to print. Click Next when you are done.

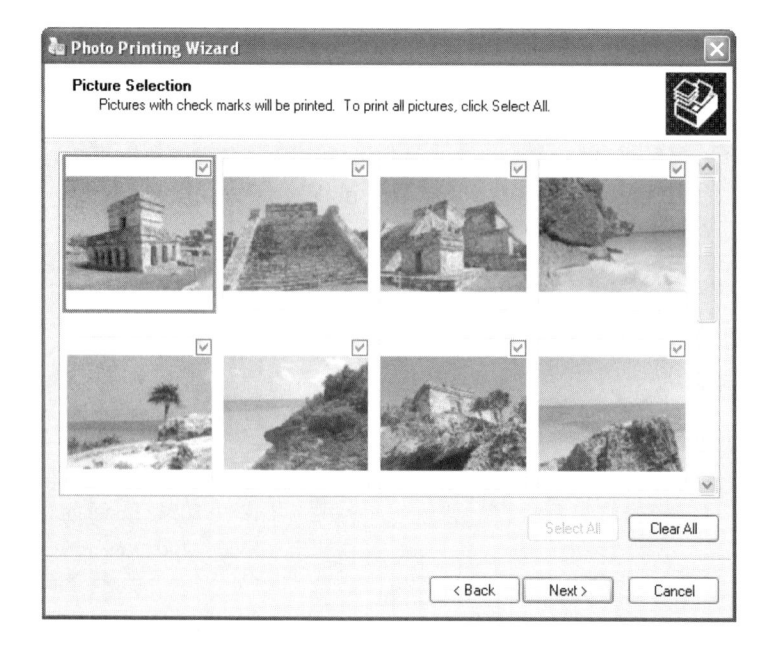

CHAPTER 6: Print Perfect Digital Photos of Any Size— Every Time! **107**

4. In the Printing Options window, use the drop-down menu if necessary to select the printer, and then click the Printing Preferences button.

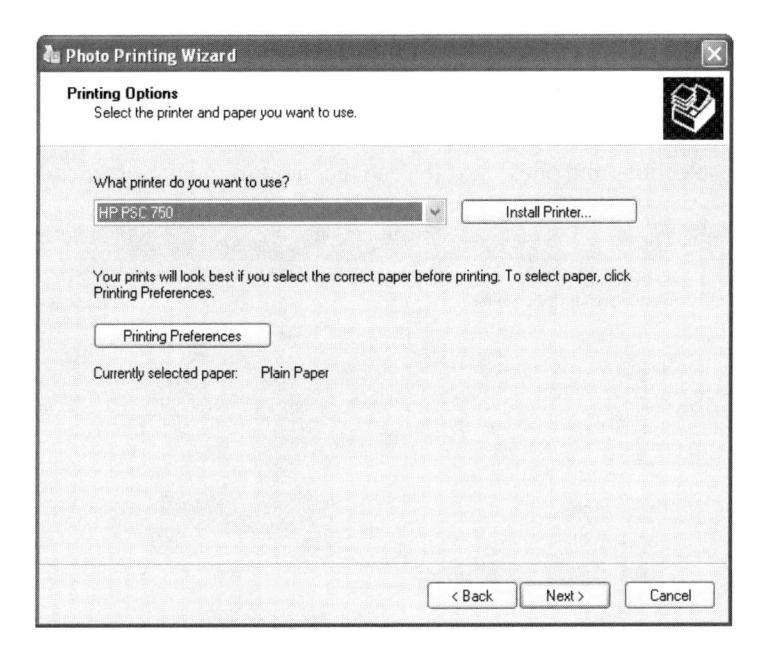

5. In the properties dialog box that appears, make your paper, color, and quality selections. Make sure you choose a photo paper from the Media drop-down menu. When you are done, click OK. This returns you to the Printing Options window.

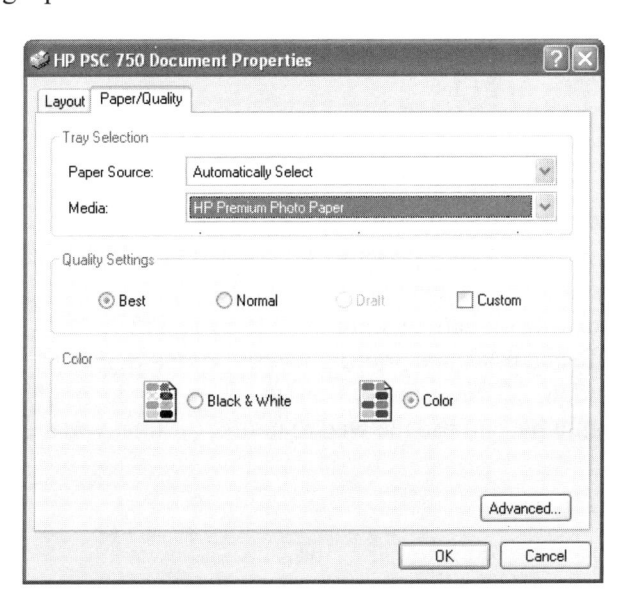

6. Click Next.

7. In the Layout Selection window that appears, choose what you want to print. Your layout options including full-page, contact sheets, and a variety of sizes. As you can see in the following illustration, I am printing three 4×6 photos on a single page. Each photo is printed only once unless you use the Number Of Times To Use Each Picture option and change the value. Make your selections and click Next to send the pictures to the printer and print them.

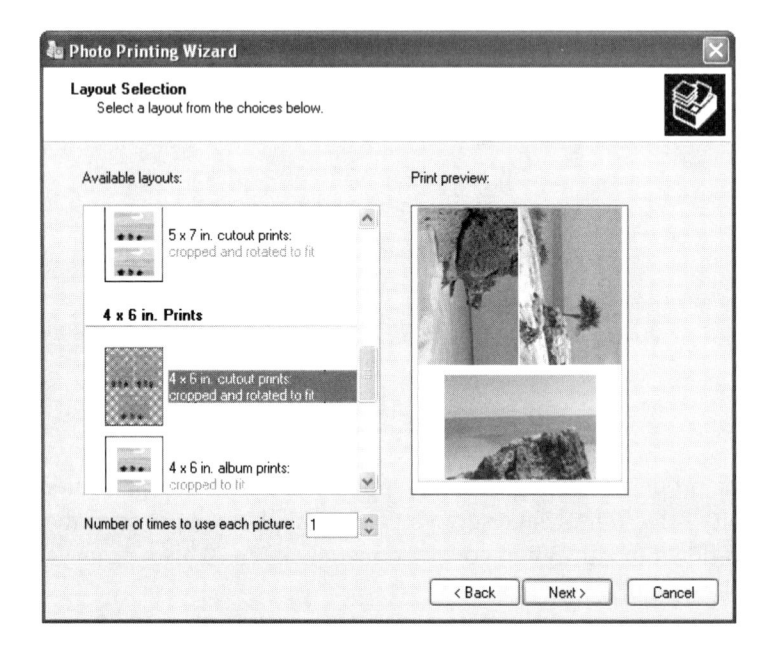

8. Click Finish.

Order Prints Online

So, you don't like to waste your paper and ink; in fact, you would rather someone else do the work for you. That's certainly no crime. One of the great things about digital photos is you can print them on your home computer's printer with awesome quality, or you can upload them to an Internet store and have them do it for you. The process is safe and easy, and you'll get your printed digital photos in the mail in a few days. Windows XP provides a wizard to help you order prints online. Keep in mind that you do not have to use the wizard to order prints; you are free to simply

CHAPTER 6: Print Perfect Digital Photos of Any Size— Every Time!

How to ... Print a Contact Sheet

If you took a look at Chapter 5, I mentioned that some people store digital photos in different folders and then print a contact sheet of all the photos in the folder for easy perusing. You can do that easily with the Photo Printing Wizard. Just open the desired folder containing the photos, and then click the Print Photos option in the Picture Tasks dialog box. The wizard appears, with all of the photos from the folder selected. Continue through the wizard and choose the contact sheet option. This will print thumbnail images of all of the photos on a sheet (or sheets, if necessary) of paper for your records. It's fast and easy!

access any web site that provides prints and follow the site's instructions, but you may find the wizard helpful, especially if this is the first time you are ordering prints.

If you are wondering about from which sites you should order prints, keep in mind that there are many to choose from (just search for "photo printers" on any search engine, such as www.msn.com), but I can recommend some reputable printers. This list is not exclusive, but I have personally dealt with the following companies and got quality results and service:

- www.snapfish.com
- www.ofoto.com
- www.photoworks.com
- www.clubphoto.com

If you want to order prints online using Windows XP's wizard, just follow these steps:

1. Connect to the Internet.
2. Open the desired folder where your photos reside and, in the Picture Tasks dialog box, click Order Prints Online. The Online Print Ordering Wizard appears.
3. Click Next on the Welcome screen.

4. In the Change Your Picture Selection window, choose the photos you want to order by selecting the check box beside each one. Simply clear the check box of any photo that you do not want to order.

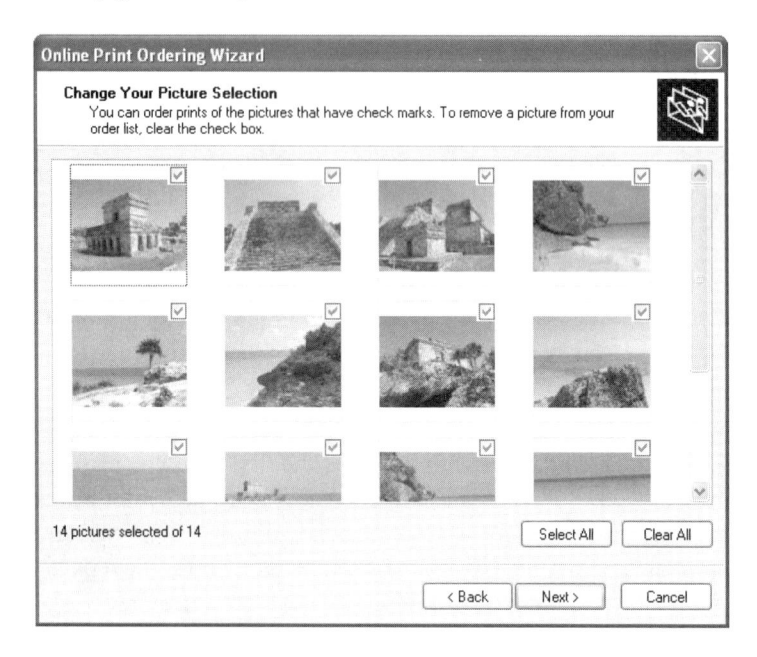

5. Click Next. The wizard connects to the Internet and downloads information. This may take a few moments depending on the speed of your connection.

6. In the selection window that appears, select the photo company from which you want to order, and then click Next.

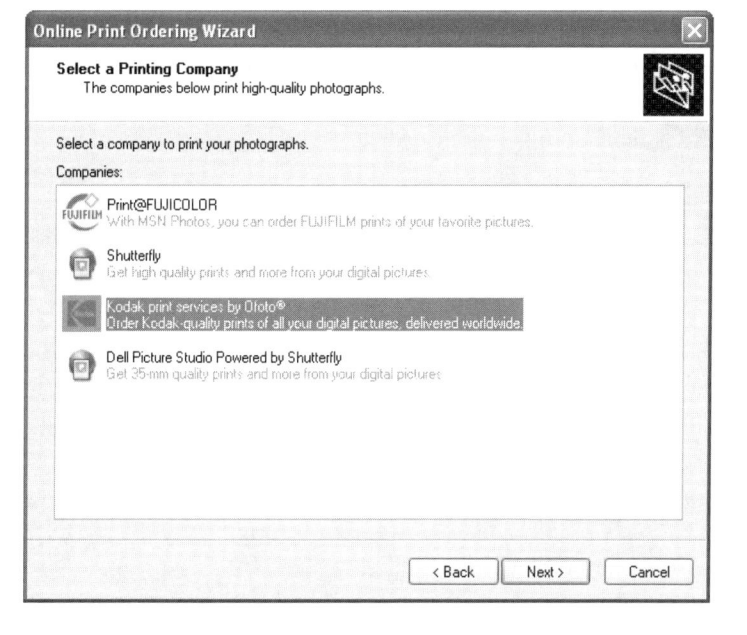

CHAPTER 6: Print Perfect Digital Photos of Any Size— Every Time! 111

7. The wizard downloads and displays ordering information from the company that you selected. For each print that you want, use the ordering window to select the number of prints, the size, and so forth. When you're done, scroll to the bottom of the window to see your subtotal and click Next.

8. Depending on the company you selected, you then move through a series of windows where you establish an account and provide your credit card and shipping information. This process is safe, so follow the remainder of the wizard screens to place your order.

How to ... Publish Photos on the Web

Aside from printing photos on paper, how about having some more fun with them? Using Windows XP, you can easily prepare and put photos on the Internet so that friends and family can see them. You can create your own web sites using web-authoring programs, or you can create accounts on sites that essentially allow you to create a home page by walking through an online wizard. You can also use Windows XP's Web Publishing Wizard to share your photos online. This option creates an account in MSN Groups, where you can post your photos and enable other people to see them.

Naturally, there are a lot of options for creating web sites and showing pictures online. Some sites allow you to create online photo albums quickly and easily, so Windows XP's Web Publishing Wizard certainly isn't your only option. If you want to use the Web Publishing Wizard, just click the option to Publish The Selected Items To The Web in the File And Folder Tasks box, found in the folder with your photos. If you want to check out other options for sharing your photos online and creating a web site online, check out the following links:

- Geocities.yahoo.com
- www.mayfamily.com
- www.topcities.com
- picturecenter.kodak.com
- photos.msn.com
- photos.yahoo.com
- www.clubphoto.com
- www.snapfish.com
- www.webshots.com

TIP *If you don't want to hassle with the Internet, some other great options are just outside your front door. Most photo-processing centers, including those in department stores, will print your digital photos now, but you have to take the digital photos to them. Simply burn your photos to a CD (see Chapter 5), stroll up to the photo-processing counter, and say, "I'd like to have these developed, please." You'll decide what you want, just as you would do with film, and you'll be on your way!*

Other Printing Options

Sure, the Windows XP Photo Printing Wizard is great, but it may not do everything you want. Maybe you need different picture packages, or maybe you want different combinations by the page. The Photo Printing Wizard gives you the basics of what you'll probably need, but if not, you need to turn to another program. Generally, image-editing programs—such as Photoshop Elements, Photoshop Album, Paint Shop Pro, and many others—give you print options within those programs. Just check out their help files to learn more. If you are a digital photography enthusiast, you probably have some image-editing software, and there you probably have some additional printing power and flexibility at your fingertips.

Did you know? About E-mailing Photos

Consider this scenario: You take a high-resolution photo of your pet cat. The photo is a 2-megapixel TIFF file, which comes out to around 4MB in size. The photo is great for printing, but you also want to e-mail the photo to your friends. If you try to send the 4MB photo, you'll likely go gray before it ever reaches your recipients.

Unless you have broadband service such as DSL or cable and all your recipients also have broadband service, you never want to e-mail something that large to anyone. Even if you can get it sent, most likely your recipients' e-mail servers would reject the photo for being too big. So, the problem is simply this: You need high-resolution photos for printing, and you also need copies of those photos in a low-resolution JPEG format for sending in e-mails.

In the past, that meant you had to use an image-editing program to alter your original file and skinny it down. No longer—Windows XP can do this translation process for you with just a few clicks. Here's what you do:

1. In the folder where your pictures are stored, select the photo you want to e-mail. You can select multiple photos by CTRL-clicking them. Then, either click the E-Mail The Selected Items option found in the File And Folder Tasks box, or just right-click the photo(s) and click Send To | Mail Recipient.

2. In the Send Pictures Via E-Mail window, choose the option to make your pictures smaller. If you click the Show More Options link (which becomes Show Fewer Options once you click it, as shown here), you see that you can determine the size that you want to make the pictures. Make your selections and click OK.

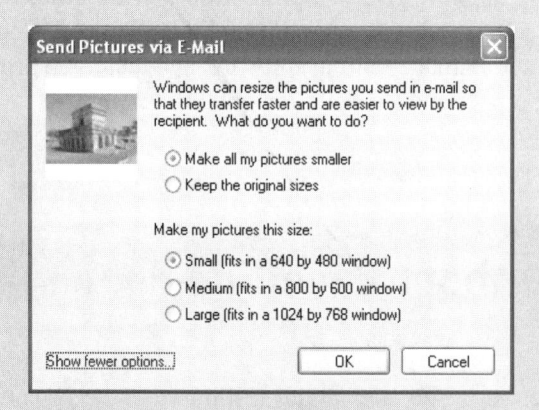

3. Windows XP prepares your images and puts them in an empty e-mail message using your default e-mail program. You can then enter the desired addresses, type a message, and click Send to send your photos.

If you love free software from the Internet, I am pleased to recommend IrFanview, a free image-viewing and -printing utility you can download from www.irfanview.com (it's less than 1MB, so the download is doable, even with a dial-up connection). The software, as you can see in Figure 6-1, is designed to show you pictures and

FIGURE 6-1 IrFanview is a fun and free image-viewing and -printing utility.

enable you to work with them at a basic level. You can easily perform basic photo-editing options, and you can print photos using a number of different print options.

More Great Ideas

Quality printing is one of the major features you want for digital photography. Here are a few more ideas to get you on your way:

- Unless you are printing an 8×10, try to print multiple photos on the same page in order to conserve paper—and money.

- Photo printing burns a lot of ink cartridges, so watch for ink sales. Some photo-printer companies offer discounts if you buy several at one time from their web sites, so check around for the best deals.

- Make sure you try different kinds of photo-printing paper. Some varieties may work better with your particular printer. Also, see your printer documentation for suggestions.

- Remember that you may be able to do more with a photo-editing program. For example, in Photoshop Elements, you can create a photo collage, complete with text and a background, and print it. So, check out your software (get a good software package if you don't have one) and have some fun!

Chapter 7

Make a Printed Photo Album So You Can Take Your Loved Ones with You

How to…

- Create photo albums manually
- Use other software options to create photo albums
- Print photo books

Sure, let's face it: Digital photos are great, and you can do all kinds of cool things with them. But there's nothing quite like a printed photo album that you can show to someone or take along with you to the office. You love your digital photos from your trip to France, but showing them to people is a bit problematic without an album of printed pictures.

In this chapter, we'll consider a few different ideas for creating a photo album. Windows XP doesn't give you any direct photo album software, and there are no Microsoft downloads or goodies that directly create photo albums for you. However, with a little creativity, you can manually create one, or you can get some additional software that can do it for you. Also, you can have a book of your digital photos printed by an Internet company!

What You'll Need

To create a printed photo album, you'll need some different software, which I'll point out how to get as we move forward. You should also have Internet access for the projects in this chapter.

Create a Photo Album Manually

In reality, you have everything you need to create a photo album using Windows XP. After all, all you really have to do is print your photo pages, punch holes in them, and bind them in any kind of three-ring binder. In the end, you get a way to transport photos around in a printed and easy-to-view format.

If you are going to create a printed photo album this way, begin by choosing all of the photos you want to include in the album. Like any photo collection project, try to cull the ones that are duplicates or just don't look that great. The great thing about digital photography is you can take as many pictures as your camera's memory card can hold, then you can delete the ones that aren't perfect.

Next, to create the printed album, gather up some photo-quality paper. If you are not familiar with printing photos, see Chapter 6 to learn how to manage photo printing on Windows XP.

CHAPTER 7: Make a Printed Photo Album So You Can Take Your Loved Ones with You 119

Once you have your photos and your paper, follow these steps to print the photo pages:

1. Select the photos you want to print, right-click them, and click Print. You can also click the Print option in the Picture Tasks box in the folder that holds the pictures.

2. The Photo Printing Wizard begins automatically. Click Next on the welcome screen.

3. In the Picture Selection screen, make sure the photos you want to print are selected, and then click Next.

TIP *If the photos are not in the order you want, cancel the wizard and return to the folder that contains the photos. You can reorganize your photos there, then choose to print again.*

4. In the Printing Options window, choose the printer you want to print to and the paper type you are using (if this is confusing to you, see Chapter 6 for details.).

5. In the Layout Selection window, choose a print option that you like. The 4×6 Album Prints template and the 3.5×5 Cutouts option (as shown here) work well for album pages.

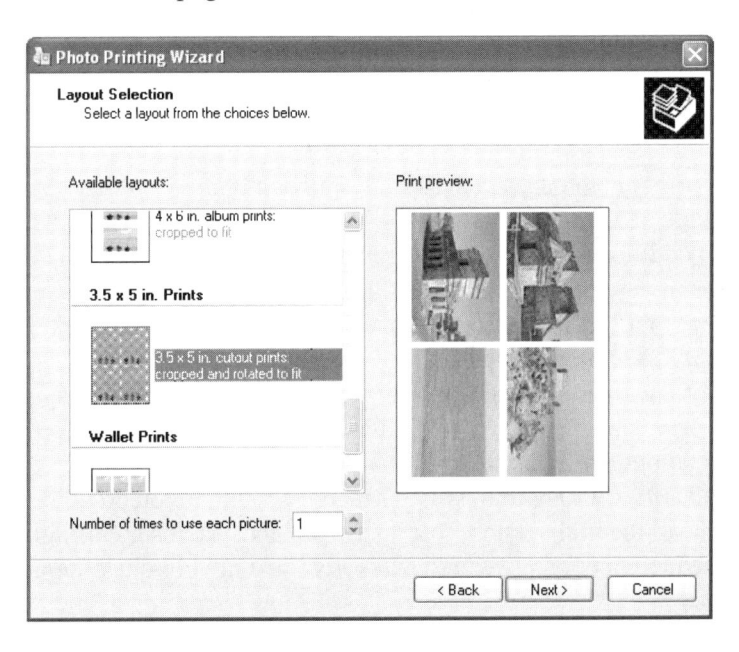

6. Click Next to start the printing of your photo pages.

How to ... Use a Standard Photo Album

As you are working with photos and making photo albums, keep in mind that you are free to use a standard photo album, just as you would with typical film prints. All you need to do is print the sizes you want and cut them out for your album. Or, just take your photos on a CD to a local photo-processing center and have them print standard sized prints for you—let them do the work!

As your photo pages are printing, remove each page from the printer when it is complete and lay it on a flat surface to dry—do not allow the photo pages to stack up in the printer tray, or they may stick together.

At this point, you can use the print pages in your album, or even cut out the photos and put them in a standard photo album that you buy. If you choose to use the printed pages in your album, put a blank piece of plain printer paper between each page to ensure that the photos don't stick to each other.

TIP *For more fun, consider decorating the outside of the album using glitter pens, glue-on sequins, paint, fabric pens, and other common items you can find at any art store.*

Use a Photo Album Program

You can print photo pages using Windows XP's Photo Printing Wizard but, of course, the wizard doesn't give you a lot of options. The good news is there are plenty of additional software packages that can come to your rescue. Popular printing software packages, such as Print Shop (visit www.broderbund.com), work great, but I'm going to introduce you to a cool printing package designed specifically to print album pages.

PhotoSlate, made by ACD, is easy to use and works great. Using this software, you can print album pages, cards, calendars, and other helpful print products using your digital photos. You can buy the software for around $30, but you can also download a free 30-day trial, which I recommend that you do before you buy it. To download the trial version, just visit www.acdsystems.com/English/Products/FotoSlate/index.htm. Once you download it, just double-click the installation icon

CHAPTER 7: Make a Printed Photo Album So You Can Take Your Loved Ones with You   **121**

to install the software. Follow the instructions provided. You'll have to get an installation key that the company will e-mail to you, so just follow the simple instructions that appear. Once you download the software and open it, you'll see a blank work area (see Figure 7-1).

As you can see, the interface is rather simple. The following steps walk you through the process of creating a photo album page:

1. Open the FotoSlate software using the Start menu (Click Start | All Programs | ACD Systems | ACD FotoSlate), or double-click the shortcut icon that appears on your desktop.

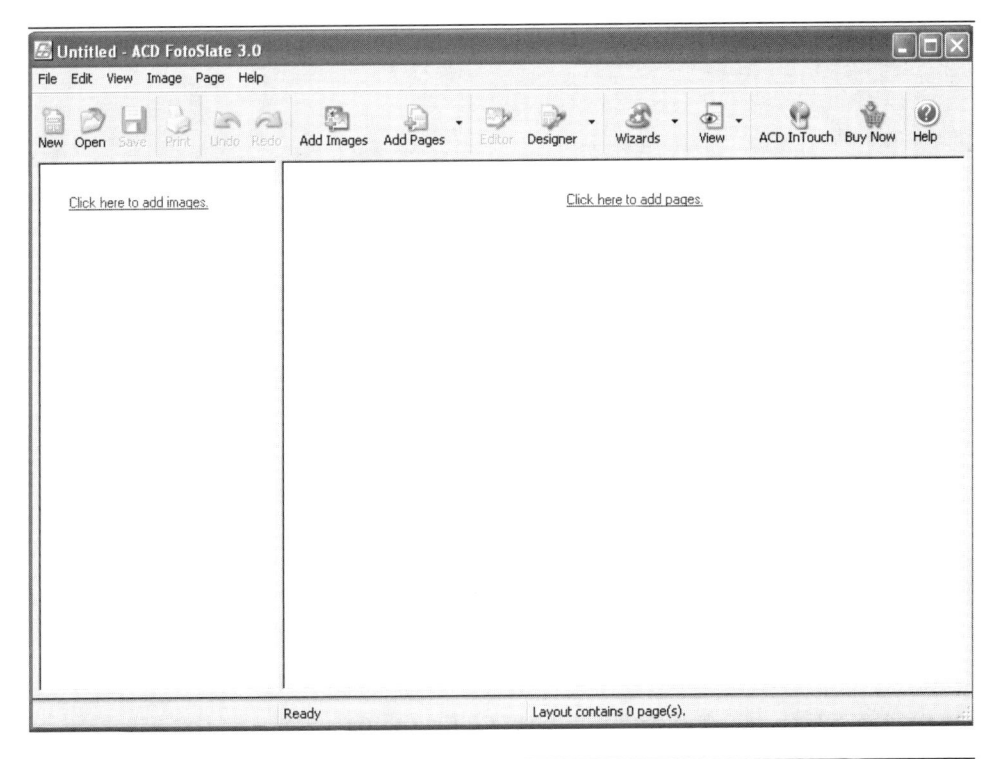

FIGURE 7-1 FotoSlate software

2. Click the Click Here To Add Images link in the left column.

3. In the browse window that appears, locate the photos you want to use. In the Available Images area, you see the photos that are available for selection. Just drag the photos that you want to use for this print job to the Chosen Images pane on the bottom of the screen.

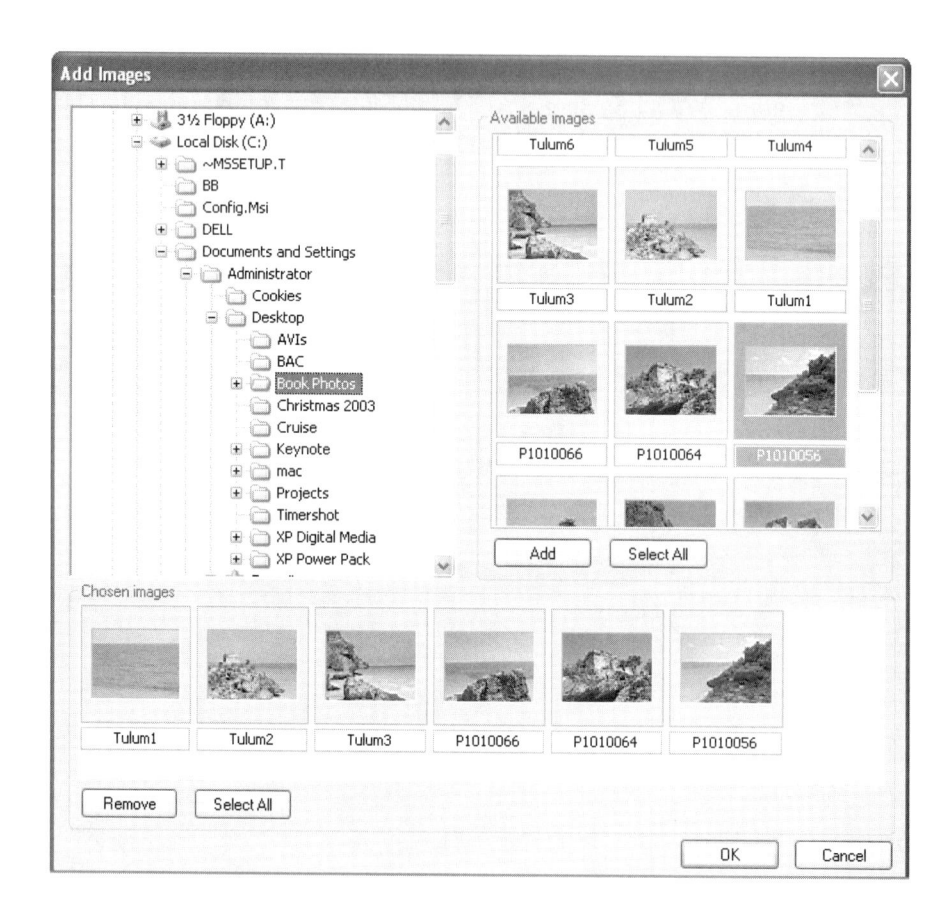

4. Click OK. The photos now appear on the main page.

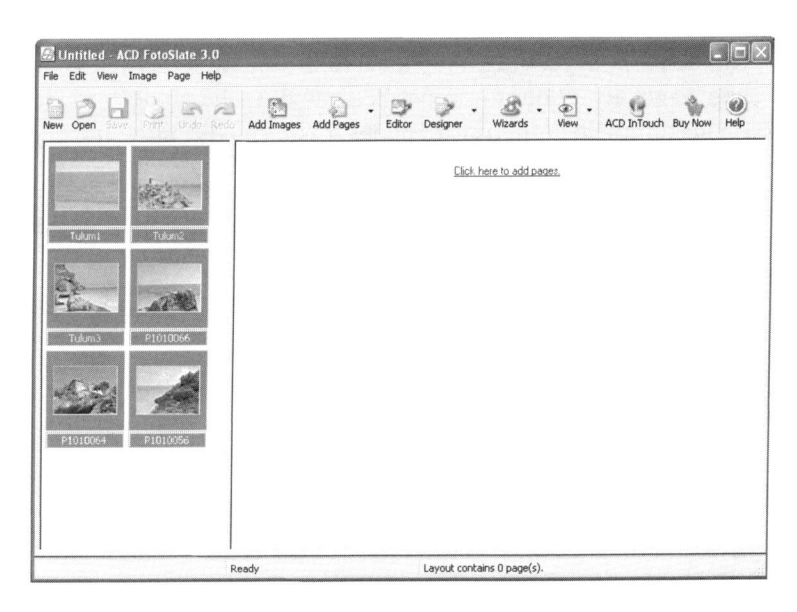

CHAPTER 7: Make a Printed Photo Album So You Can Take Your Loved Ones with You   **123**

5. Click the Click Here To Add Pages link in the right pane.

6. In the Add Pages window that appears, choose between Landscape and Portrait folders (on the left side). Then, find a template you want (on the right side), drag it to the bottom window, and click OK.

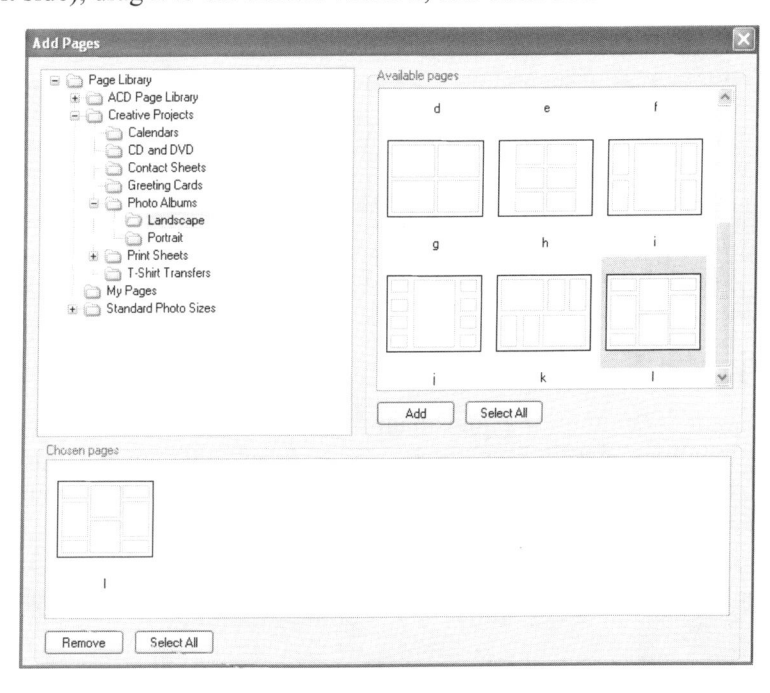

7. On the main page, drag the photos to the location on the template where you want each photo to reside. You can drag the photos around and around on the template until you are happy. (You can use the same photo more than once if you like).

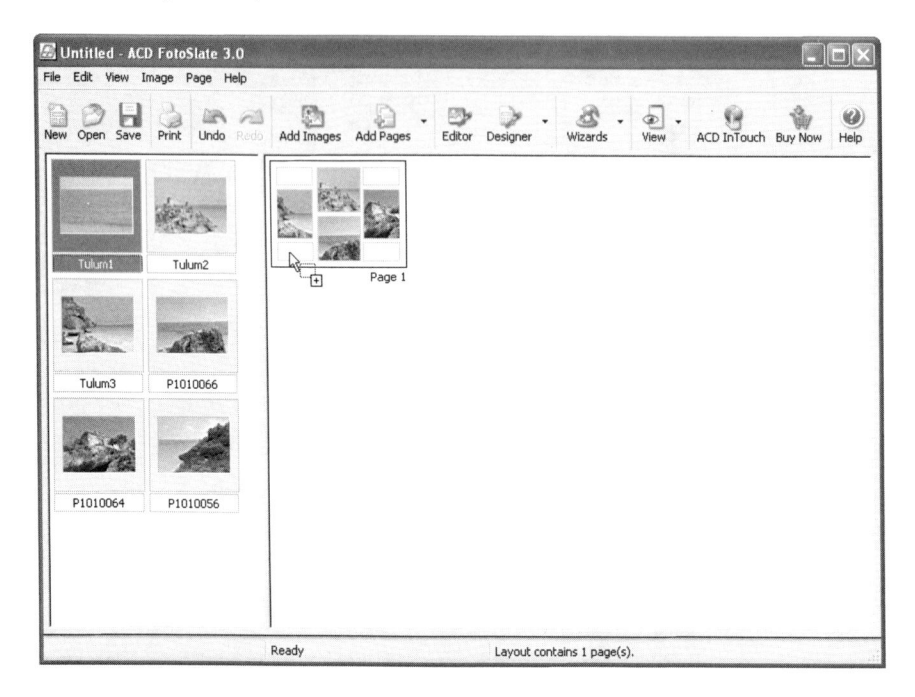

8. When you are ready, just click the Print button to print your page.

> **TIP** *Using the FotoSlate software, you can also create custom pages so that they look however you like. Just click Designer | Create Page and follow the instructions that appear.*

Get a Photo Book Printed

If you want the ultimate in photo albums, why not have a book of your photos professionally printed and sent to you? When I took my wife and kids on our first cruise, I came back with an armload of photos, and I wanted something I could put on a bookshelf to remember the trip forever. Guess what? For around $50, I had a 10-page, cloth-hardback book made and sent to me. It's an item that will never end up in a garage sale, and it makes a perfect gift for those special occasions!

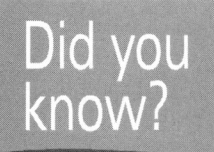

CHAPTER 7: Make a Printed Photo Album So You Can Take Your Loved Ones with You

Did you know?

Other Fun and Cool Options

While this chapter focuses on printing photo album pages, there are many software programs that help you create electronic photo albums that you can view on your computer and share with people on a web site, send through e-mail, burn to a CD, and so forth. You can download trial versions of the following products, which you'll find fun and creative:

- **ReaGallery Pro** This easy-to-use software allows you to create a number of photo galleries and online albums. You can get a trial version at www.reasoft.com/products/reagallery, and the real version will cost you around $40.

- **JAlbum** This web-album generator is free, and gives you a quick and easy way to make HTML albums. Check it out at www.datadosen.se/jalbum.

- **FlipAlbum** This fun and easy software creates an HTML book that you actually flip through with your mouse. The software costs $30, and you can get a free trial at www.flipalbum.com.

- **3-D Album** This option creates a 3-D album that looks really cool. The software will cost you around $40, and you can learn more about it at www.3d-album.com.

A few different Internet companies provide this service, but I recommend MyPublisher (www.mypublisher.com), only because I have had books created by them in the past. If you visit the MyPublisher web site (see Figure 7-2), you can find out about specific pricing and policies, get an overview of the service, and create your book by starting a new account, uploading your photos, and ordering the book you want—it's that easy! You can also include captions with your photos.

TIP *If you happen to be using Adobe's Photoshop Album, you can create your book directly within Photoshop Album and upload it to MyPublisher. See* How to Do Everything with Photoshop Album *(McGraw-Hill/Osborne, 2003) to learn more.*

FIGURE 7-2 MyPublisher.com

More Great Ideas

As you can imagine, there are a number ways to use printed photo albums and a printed book, such as:

- Create a photo album of your last trip, a memorable occasion, or any other photo collections you want to show off.

- Use the FotoSlate software to create all kinds of printing pages—many of them are suitable for framing.

- Photo books make the perfect gift for $50 or less! Consider having one printed to remember extra special events, such as weddings, the birth of a baby, a retirement party, a special wedding anniversary, or a great family vacation!

Chapter 8
Turn Your Photo Memories into a Slide Show

How to...

- Gather your photos for slide shows
- Create slide shows with the HTML Slide Show Wizard
- View and share your slide show

Digital photos are so much fun to take and use, but wouldn't it be great if you had an easy and cool way to share those digital photos with other people? Wouldn't it be nice if you could easily create a photo slide show that anyone using any computer could watch, or you could even put on your web site?

No problem! Using a Windows XP PowerToy that is free to download, you can create a slide show with your photos. The slide show is an HTML slide show that any web browser, such as Internet Explorer or Netscape, running on any computer can watch! Put it on the Web, a disk, or a CD, or e-mail it to friends and family—you can do all of this simply and quickly, and this chapter shows you how!

What You'll Need

To create your slideshow, you need the HTML Slide Show Wizard PowerToy that is available for free download from www.microsoft.com. Keep reading to find out how to get and use it.

Get the HTML Slide Show Wizard PowerToy

The HTML Slide Show Wizard is a free, easy-to-get PowerToy download from Microsoft. Just open your web browser and go to www.microsoft.com/windowsxp/pro/downloads/powertoys.asp. In the list of PowerToys, locate the HTML Slide Show Wizard (htmlgen.exe) and click the link to start the download (see Figure 8-1). The download is a little over 700Kb, so if you are using a dial-up connection, the download may take a few minutes, but you should be able to complete the download in a reasonable amount of time (probably ten minutes or so, depending on your connection speed). You can choose to download the .exe file to your desktop, then simply double-click the downloaded icon to install it. Once you have installed the HTML Slide Show Wizard, you can find it in Start | All Programs | PowerToys for Windows XP | HTML Slide Show Wizard.

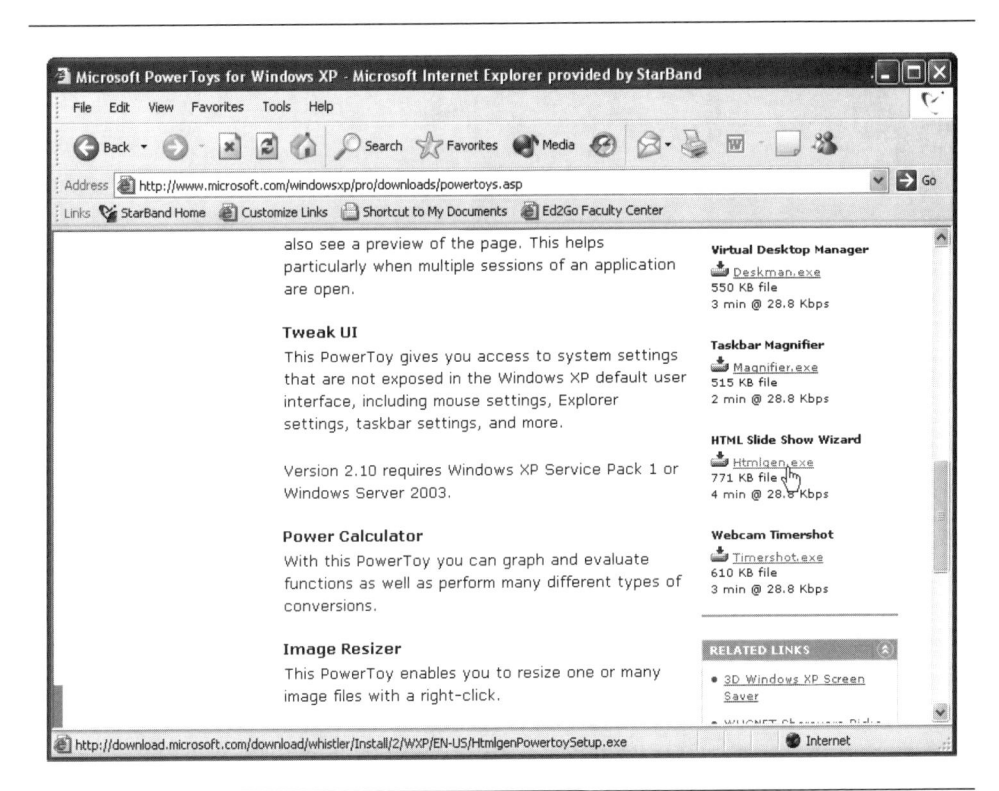

FIGURE 8-1 Downloading the htmlgen.exe file to your computer

Understand What the HTML Slide Show Wizard Does

In brief, the HTML Slide Show Wizard takes your photos and creates a spiffy HTML slide show presentation that can be viewed in any web browser. Now, if you have that sinking feeling because I am talking about HTML, don't worry—you don't have to really know anything about HTML in order to use the HTML Slide Show Wizard. However, as a point a reference, let's get a few techie things straight before we proceed. First of all, HTML (which stands for Hypertext Markup Language) is the computer language used on the Internet. Basically, all web pages are HTML pages. The job of your browser, such as Internet Explorer, is to download the HTML, interpret it, and display the web page to you. HTML is a standard

> **Did you know?**
>
> ## Don't Worry About Your Photos...
>
> As you are working with the HTML Slide Show Wizard, you may think, "Wait a minute! Is this thing taking my photos and moving them around?" You can relax. The wizard creates copies of any photos that you choose to use in it. So, your original photos stay safe and sound in their folders or wherever you have them stored. If you put your slide show on a CD or e-mail it to someone (or post it on the Web), again, your original photos are not moved or tampered with in any way—only the copies are used. The point is this: Your original photos are safe and secure, so you can relax and have fun!

language; all computer operating systems can read HTML because they all contain web browsers, a program that interprets HTML.

What does this mean to you? Simply this: You can create a photo slide show using the HTML Slide Show Wizard that anyone on any computer using any basic web browser can see. You don't have to worry about operating systems, software, or other technical nightmares. You simply create your slide show, distribute it however you want, and your friends and family will be able view it using any PC or Mac. That's the great thing about this little tool!

When you use the wizard to create a slide show, copies of your photos are organized and put into a folder. Then, the wizard creates an HTML page so you can view the slide show. All you have to do is double-click the HTML page to open it, and your photos will come to life in a slide show in all its glory!

Create a Slide Show

All right, now it's time to get things moving and actually create your HTML slide show. The following sections walk you through what to do.

Cull Your Photos

The first step in creating your slide show is deciding what photos you are going to include. To make your life easier, I recommend that you create a folder and put all of the photos you want to use in your slide show in that folder. This option step will just make using the wizard easy, because you'll be able to grab all of the photos from one location.

CHAPTER 8: Turn Your Photo Memories into a Slide Show

PICTURE THIS *Your camera software may make folders for you by default. In this case, you don't need to do anything except enjoy your photos, since the software is doing the work. However, many people choose not to use the software; often, camera software does not give you the flexibility you need. Since Windows XP can automatically detect your camera and download the pictures without the help of your camera software, you may wish to uninstall the camera software and do things manually, which will give you more control over the download process and where the photos are stored.*

So, what photos should you include in a slide show? That may seem like an easy question, but you may have some planning to do. For example, in my slide show, I'm going to use a bunch of photos from a cruise to Mexico. Now, I have several hundred digital photos, so do I want to include them all? No, the slide show will be way too long, so I'll have to do some culling so that I include only the best photos possible.

How can you cull your photos? Well, a good eagle eye and a good dose of common sense will help, but here are some additional pointers:

- Watch for quality. Don't use any photos that have problems such as brightness, contrast, focus, and other photography issues. The only exception is if you have only one not-so-good photo of an item that must be included, such as an older photo that you have scanned.

- Show a progression of events. In most cases, there is some kind of progression of events in a slide show. For example, if you create a slide show of your child's birthday party, the natural way to organize it and share it with others would be for it to move from the beginning to the end of the party. If you go on vacation, arrange the photos in the order of the trip to portray a natural sense of the vacation. Obviously, some slide shows—such as those showing products or random photos, such as landscapes—do not work as well using a progression of events. But even then, always think, "Where is my slide show leading the viewer?" This will help you focus on a logical order for your photos.

- Avoid duplicates. It's easy to have too many photos in a slide show that are duplicates. By duplicates, I mean photos that are too similar. For example, let's say you took a vacation to the Grand Canyon. You may have 50 photos of the Grand Canyon that you would like to put in the slide show, but you'll need to look carefully at those photos and try to use photos that are distinct. Viewers become quickly bored with a slide show if the photos are too similar.

- Consider the mood and theme. As you plan your slide show, think about the mood and theme of the photos. Are the photos a celebration, family fun, somber and thought provoking…?

■ Look for contrast. Slide shows work better when photos are unique, so try to make the slide show diverse and fun to view.

Use the Slide Show Wizard

Now that you know what photos you want to use, you are ready to use the wizard to create your HTML slide show. First things first: Fire up the wizard by clicking Start | All Programs | PowerToys for Windows XP | HTML Slide Show Wizard. The wizard appears with a typical welcome page, telling you what the slide show can do. Click Next to get going.

Select Your Photos

The first thing you need to do with the wizard is add the images you want to use in the slide show, and then organize them. Note that you can add photos individually, or you can add a whole folder at one time. This is why I recommended that you put all of the photos you want to use in one folder. As you can see, the step will save you some time.

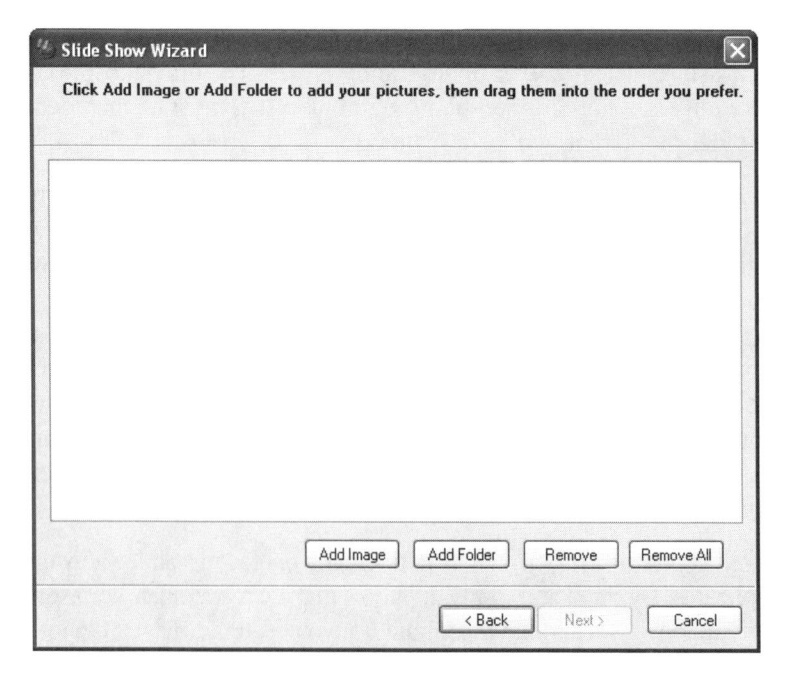

So, to gather your photos, click the appropriate button (Add Image or Add Folder). This will open a typical browse dialog box in which you can find the photos or the folder, depending on which button you have clicked. Just choose the photo or folder and click OK; the images appear in the wizard.

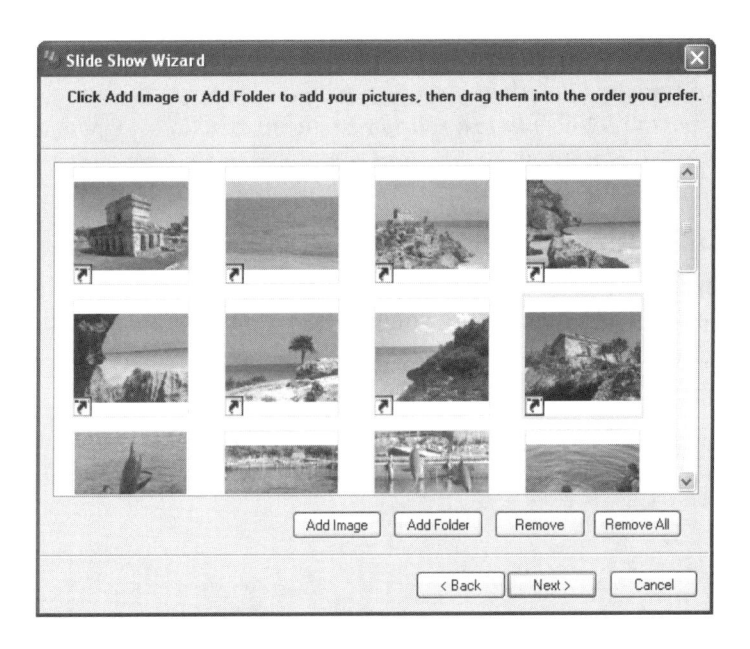

CHAPTER 8: Turn Your Photo Memories into a Slide Show   **133**

Now, you can once again cull your photos. If you need to remove one (or all of them), just select the photo and click the Remove button. Also, you can organize your photos by simply dragging them around as needed, as you can see in the following illustration. The list of photos you see here (reading left to right) is the order the photos will appear in your slide show, so look at the organization carefully and critically.

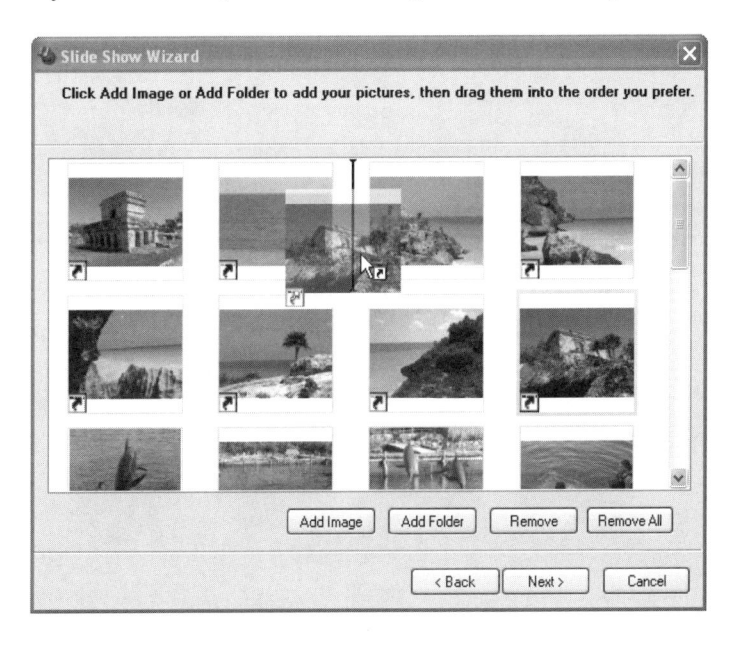

PICTURE THIS *Once again, you can remove photos from your collection here, but this doesn't remove the photo from the original location on your computer. So, feel free to remove photos, reorganize them, or whatever you need to do; your original photos are safe and sound on your computer.*

Choose Slide Show Options

Once you have your photos organized, click Next to continue the wizard. As you can see in the following illustration, you have several things to do on this page of slide show settings, so let's carefully consider your options and take a look at some examples.

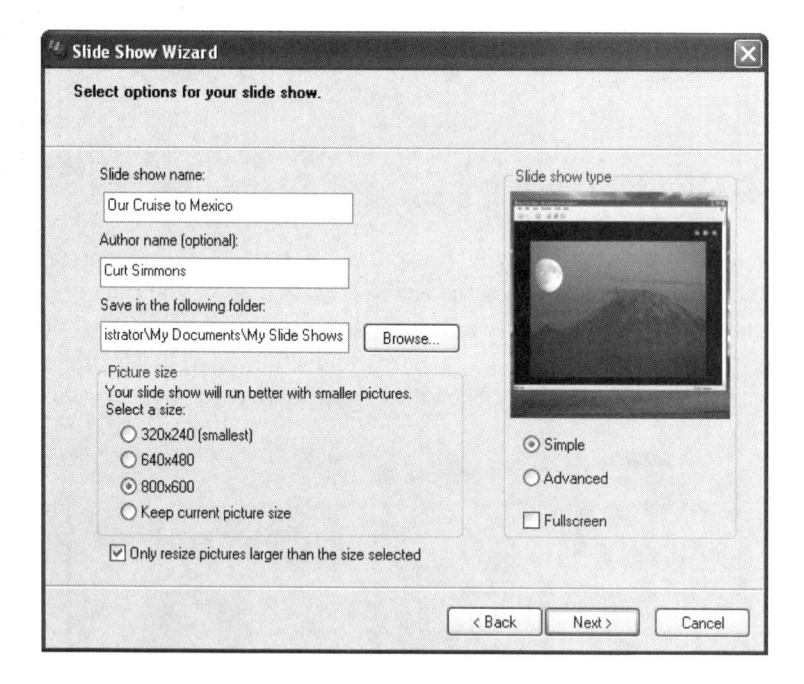

The first thing you need to do is name your slide show and, optionally, put your name in the Author Name dialog box. Use something short and descriptive for the title, such as "Our Trip to Montana" instead of "Slide Show." Also, you don't have to put an author name at all, if you don't want any attention drawn to yourself.

CHAPTER 8: Turn Your Photo Memories into a Slide Show   135

The next item allows you to tell the wizard where to save the slide show. By default, the slide show is saved under your user account in My Documents/My Slideshows. This location is fine, but if you want to put it somewhere else, click the Browse button and choose a new location, or type the location path directly into the dialog box, if you are a little tech-savvy.

The next item is the picture size. You have the following options (but as a general rule, I recommend the 640×480 or 800×600 size):

- **320×240** (smallest)   This size makes your pictures small, but the design works great if you are e-mailing the slide show to people, because the photos are small and don't take up a lot of space. So, if you want to e-mail your photos, consider using this size. If you do, your slide show will look like this:

- **640×480** This is a good general size for most purposes, including putting your slide show on the Web or e-mailing it to people. This illustration shows you an example:

- **800×600** This size is getting a bit large for e-mail and the Web, but it works great for burning your slide show to a CD or looking at on your own computer.

> **TIP** *There doesn't appear to be a lot of difference between 640×480 and 800×600. However, the 800×600 photos may look sharper when viewed, although they are larger in terms of file size.*

- **Keep Current Picture Size** This option keeps the original size of the photo, whatever it may be. This setting is fine, but if you have really large pictures, the view may have to scroll around to see it all.

CHAPTER 8: Turn Your Photo Memories into a Slide Show

PICTURE THIS *Notice the check box that appears under the size options in the wizard. This check box resizes a photo only when it is larger than the selected size. In other words, it doesn't make a photo larger than its original size, because this would cause you to lose quality. I suggest you keep this check box selected.*

The last option you have is to choose a type of slide show. You have two options: Simple and Advanced. The Simple slide show gives you a standard slide show, such as what you have seen in the previous illustrations. The Advanced option allows viewers to see the slide show in three different ways:

- **Slide Show** This is a standard slide show option with backward and forward control buttons.

- **Filmstrip** This view shows the selected photo (in a smaller format) but gives a small selection option or each image, offering the viewer a quick way to see your slide show.

- **Previews** This option enables the viewer to see all of your photos at one time. Viewers can click a photo to change the view to Filmstrip.

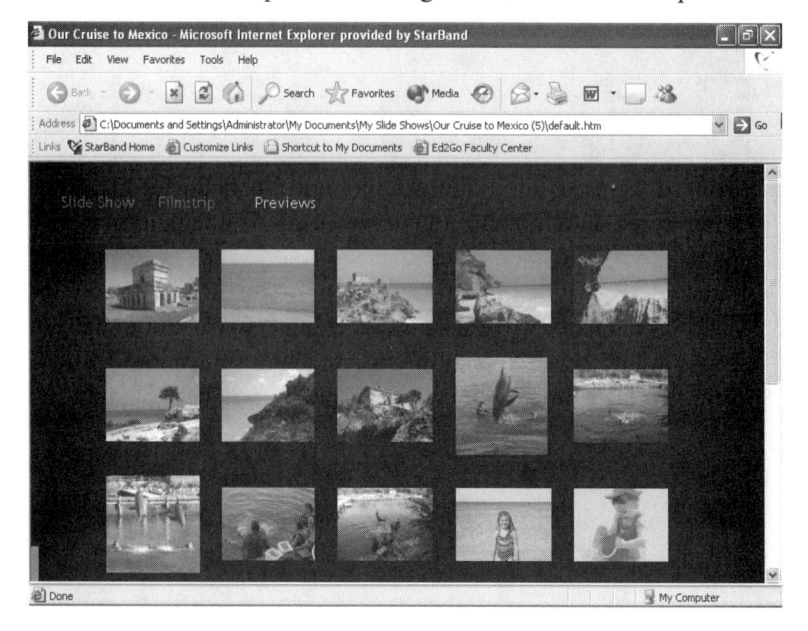

CHAPTER 8: Turn Your Photo Memories into a Slide Show 139

Finally, notice the Fullscreen check box. This option removes the browser window and displays the slide show on the whole computer screen, as shown below. This is a nice option that you may want to use for your slide slow. Note that this option works for either the Simple or the Advanced slide show.

When you're done, just click Next and voila! Your slide show is created. On the final wizard screen, you see an option to view your slide show if you like, or click Finish to complete the wizard.

View Your Slide Show

Once you are done creating your slide show, you can quickly and easily view by going to the folder where it is stored (depending on where you chose to store the slide show, such as in My Documents/My Slideshows). To view the slide show, just double-click its folder and you'll see a default.htm file in the folder. You also see a couple of other folders that hold the slide show information and photos. All you have to do is double-click the default.htm file to start the slide show, as shown in Figure 8-2. This is what any person who views the slide show must do to start it.

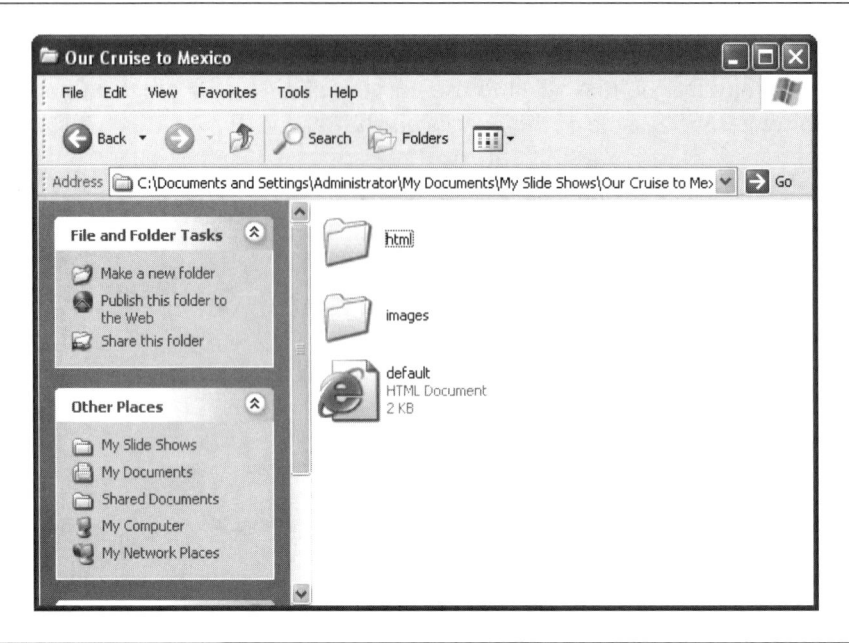

FIGURE 8-2 Viewing your slide show

When you are watching the slide show, just use the Play, Back, and Forward controls to move around within the show. That's all there is to it.

PICTURE THIS *If you choose the Play option, the slide show displays each photo for five seconds. Unfortunately, you can't edit the time allotment given.*

Share Your Slide Show

Now that your slide show is complete, all you have to do is share it. You can do that in a few fun ways, such as through e-mail, by posting it to a web site, or burning it to a CD or other disk. You can share your slide show as you would any other file, but here are a couple of notes to keep in mind:

- If you e-mail the slide show, you must e-mail the entire folder, which includes the default.htm file and the two content folders. However, you can compress the entire folder before you e-mail it. When you send the compressed folder to people, make sure you tell them to open it, then double-click the default.htm file to watch the slide show.

- If you burn the slide show to a CD, the same rules apply. You must copy the whole folder, and tell your viewers to open it from the CD and double-click the default.html to watch the show.

- If you upload the slide show to a web page, you must upload the whole folder, and you cannot change the name of the default.htm file. It is beyond the scope of this book to explore web-site creation and rules, but if you have a web site, you understand what to do. Just link to the show within the web site by linking to the default.htm file. However, you can change the name of the main folder to something less cumbersome and Web-friendly if you like.

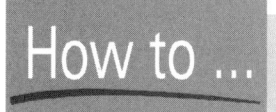

How to ... Get Another Slide Show Tool

When you downloaded the HTML Slide Show Wizard from the PowerToys web page, you may have noticed another slide show download called CD Slide Show Generator. This little utility doesn't give you a wizard or anything to work with, but what it does do is simply add an autorun file to any CD of photos that you burn. Then, when someone on another computer opens your CD, they automatically run the photos as a slide show. This tool works only for CD burning and doesn't give you as much flexibility as the HTML Slide Show Wizard, which you can also put on a CD. For this reason, I recommend you cut down on the clutter in your life and just stick with the HTML Slide Show Wizard for making digital-photo slide shows.

More Great Ideas

Here are a few fun ideas to consider:

- Make slide shows of family holidays and get-togethers, and then share them over e-mail, or burn CDs and give them away.
- Make a slide show of birthday parties. They are fun to watch and great to keep as mementos.
- Have a business? Use the HTML Slide Show Wizard to create a quick and easy slide show concerning your business and products. This feature works great on web sites as a tour about your business or company.

PICTURE THIS *Did you like this project but found yourself wanting a bit more? No problem—check out Chapter 9 for free and cool ways to make slide show movies!*

Chapter 9

Make Photo Stories with Your Digital Photos

How to...

- Organize photo stories
- Make and use photo stories

Photos are most often thought of as static. We look at them, smile, and put them away. However, with digital photography, you have so many other fun options that it might be difficult to contain your enthusiasm. As you saw in Chapter 8, you can easily turn your photos into slide shows, but how would you like something a bit more fun? How about turning your digital photos into a movie?

Now, before you start worrying about costs, you don't have to buy any hardware or additional software if you have Microsoft Plus! Digital Media Edition. In reality, what you make is a slide show that has motion effects, and you can even narrate the slide show and set it to music. Once you are done, the movie slide show is saved as a Windows Media Player file and stored in your Media Player library. You can then view it any time you want and even burn it to a CD or put it on the Web. The software is called Plus! Photo Story, and it is one of the software options available in Start | All Programs | Microsoft Plus! Digital Media Edition. It's easy and a lot of fun, and in this chapter, you'll see how to create this project!

What You'll Need

For this project, you'll need Microsoft Plus! Digital Media Edition, which can be purchased for $20 or less at most computer stores or online, or downloaded for free if you have a broadband Internet connection. See Chapter 2 for details on getting and installing this software.

Understand What Plus! Photo Story Does

Plus! Photo Story is just another slide show program. It takes your photos, allows you to organize them, and then runs them as a slide show. The difference between this and any other slide show software, however, is that Photo Story uses a panning feature that makes your photos drift in and out and into each other. It's a soft but effective movement (many screensavers use this approach). Additionally, you can narrate the photo story (assuming you have a microphone connected to your computer) as well as add background music taken directly from songs stored in your Media

Library. The end result is a very smooth slide show that looks great, has sound, and is lots of fun to watch.

I can hear the wheels in your head turning, and I know you are thinking about all of the great uses for Photo Story—and you're right. Birthday parties, graduation photos, your parents' anniversary party, holiday and vacation stories—essentially any collection of photos will work well in Photo Story!

> **NOTE** *As mentioned many times in the previous chapter, Photo Story doesn't do anything to your original photos. Rather, it makes copies of the photos you choose to use in the slide show. So you can relax—your original photos are safe and sound on your computer. Photo Story doesn't tamper with them in any way.*

Get Ready to Use Plus! Photo Story

There are a few things you need to do before you use Photo Story. Don't worry, this won't turn into a bunch of work, but you'll need to decide what you want to include in the photo story and get everything ready before you begin working with the software.

Gather Your Photos

First of all, you'll have to decide what photos are going to be used in your photo story. That sounds easy enough, but you'll need to take a hard look at your collection of photos and cull them down so that your photo story doesn't last for three hours and consume all of the disk space on your computer. Chapter 8 talked a bit about choosing photos and what works well in any slide show, so refer to that chapter and then choose the photos you'll include in the photo story (you might want to put them in one folder; doing so is also explained in Chapter 8). Once you are done, it's time to start thinking about narration.

Decide About Narration

If you have a microphone connected to your computer, you can record narration for each photo. The photo story will display each photo until the narration is finished, and then move on to the next photo. The cool thing is you simply record the narration for each photo at a time, rather than having to narrate the entire story at once and try to avoid making mistakes, lest you have to rerecord the entire thing.

So, what should you do first to narrate your photo story? Most of us aren't that great at speaking off the cuff. For casual conversation, that's fine, but your best bet is to write yourself a script. Take a look at each photo, and write a few sentences that you want to mention about it. Here are some tips to help you write your script:

- Keep it short. A couple of sentences are usually enough. Remember, you are showing only one photo during the narration, so if the narration is too long, viewers become bored quickly.

- Keep it fun. Try to say some interesting things about the particular photo. Rather than saying, "And here we are again at the Grand Canyon," say, "When we first saw the Grand Canyon, we were amazed by its size." Again, keep it interesting, and try to say something that's photo-specific.

- Don't repeat yourself. You may have several photos about the same thing, but you should say something specific and unique about each one—avoid generalities.

- As you are preparing your script, read the narration you write out loud. Many times, things we write down just don't sound as good when we read them aloud. Test your script and make changes as necessary. Remember to talk to your viewers in a conversational tone—don't talk *at* them.

- As you prepare, keep in mind that although Photo Story enables you to narrate each photo, you don't have to narrate every single photo. You can include narration for some photos and not others. Also, you can use background music with your photos and narration as well.

TIP *Concerning your microphone, you may need to make some test runs to get the quality you want. Your PC microphone acts a lot like any other microphone, so if you put it too close to your mouth, you'll get popping noises. It is better to move it away from your mouth a bit and talk more loudly. By the way, you might consider purchasing a headset microphone, which you can find at any computer store for around $30. If you plan on doing some great mic work, the hands-free option can certainly help!*

Pick Your Background Music

Photo Story enables you to put background music in your story if you like. The background music plays along with your story and even behind your narration, if you choose to use narration. So, at this time, you need to pick the song you want to use. In so doing, you must adhere to two limitations:

- You can use only one song. If your story is longer than the song, then the song will play again.

- You can use songs in the WMA, MP3, or WAV formats. This is a snap because anything you copy from a CD is copied into Media Player in the WMA format, and virtually all files that you might download from the Web come in MP3 or WAV format. The easiest thing to do is simply import all music into Windows Media Player, from where you can insert it into your story.

As you are thinking about background music, it is important to think about the mood of your photo story. For example, don't use a rock and roll song for a nostalgic, sentimental photo story. Think about the overall look and feel of the story, and find music that matches its mood and theme.

Create Your Photo Story

All right, now that you have chosen your pictures, picked your background music, and scripted your narration (if you want to include narration), you are ready to start the Plus! Photo Story Wizard and assemble your photo story. For the most part, the wizard is easy to use, but there are several options you need to know about; I'll discuss those as you move forward through the wizard.

Start the Plus! Photo Story Wizard

You can start the wizard by clicking Start | All Programs | Microsoft Plus! Digital Media Edition | Plus! Photo Story. You may also be able to access Photo Story by clicking Start | All Programs | Accessories | Entertainment | Plus! Photo Story, depending on how your system installed Microsoft Plus! Digital Media Edition.

Once you start the wizard, you see a welcome screen (see Figure 9-1). Notice that you can begin a story, open an existing story, configure your microphone, or access Photo Story Help. We'll explore all of these additional issues in this chapter, so go ahead and click the Begin A Story button.

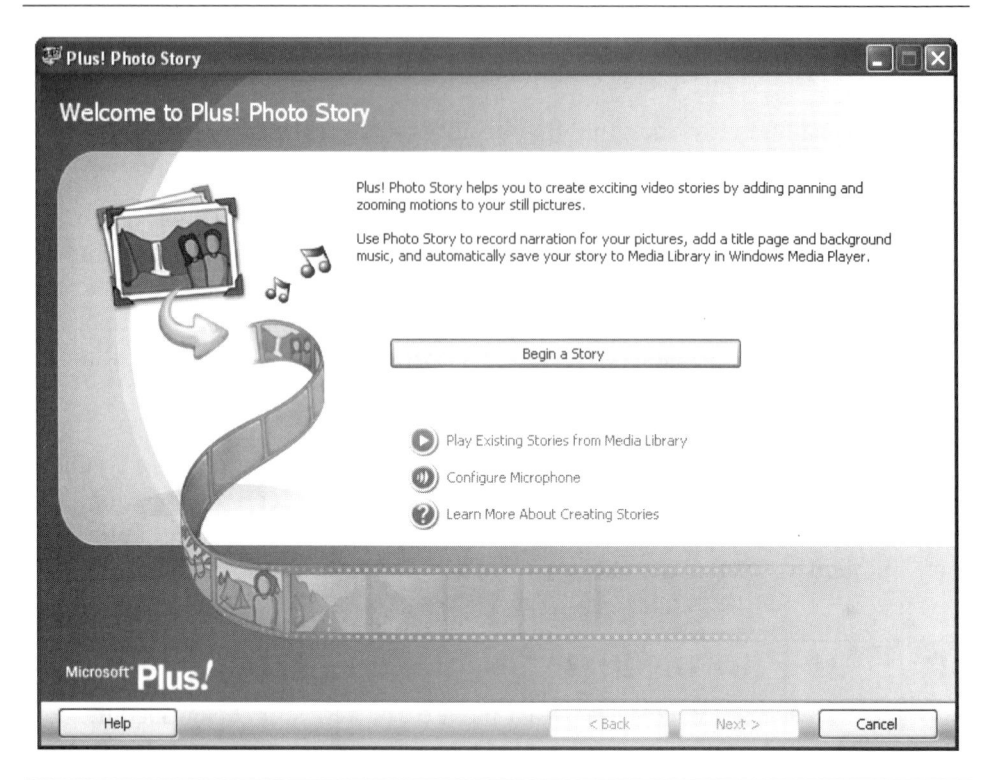

FIGURE 9-1 Starting Plus! Photo Story

Choose and Organize Your Photos

The next wizard screen (shown in Figure 9-2) enables you to choose and organize the photos you will include in the photo story.

The first thing you want to do is select the photos you will include in the story. To do so, click the Import Pictures button. In the standard Open window that appears, you can browse for your photos. Simply select them (you can select multiple photos by CTRL-clicking them) and click the Open button. This will import the photos into Photo Story. Again, keep in mind that Photo Story makes copies of your photos; it doesn't do anything with your originals.

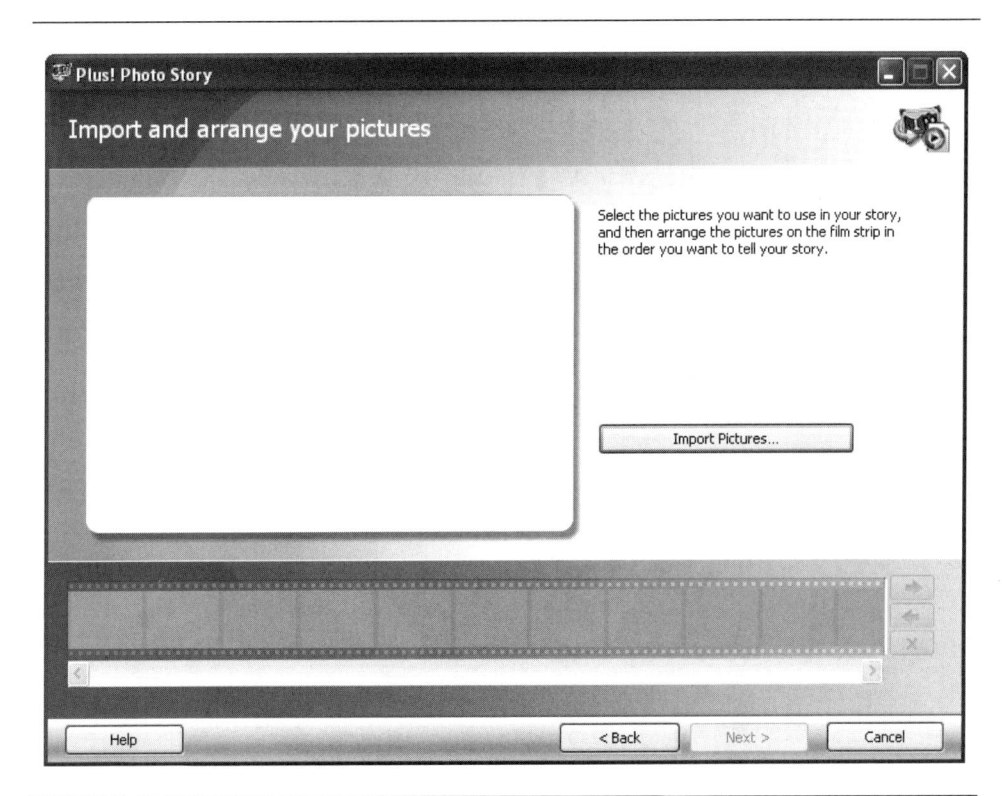

CHAPTER 9: Make Photo Stories with Your Digital Photos

FIGURE 9-2 Photo Story enables you to choose your photos and organize them.

Once you import the photos, they appear on the filmstrip at the bottom of the window. If you select a photo, you can see it in the preview window. Use the arrows next to the filmstrip to click through your photos and look at them, or just click any photo on the filmstrip to see it enlarged, as shown in Figure 9-3.

As you can see in Figure 9-3, there are a Delete (X) button and two arrow buttons next to the filmstrip. If you decide you don't want to include a photo, just select it on the filmstrip and click the Delete button. This will remove the photo from the story (but doesn't remove the original photo from your computer). Also, you can move a photo around on the filmstrip by selecting it and using the arrow buttons. With this feature, you can change the order of your photos on the filmstrip until

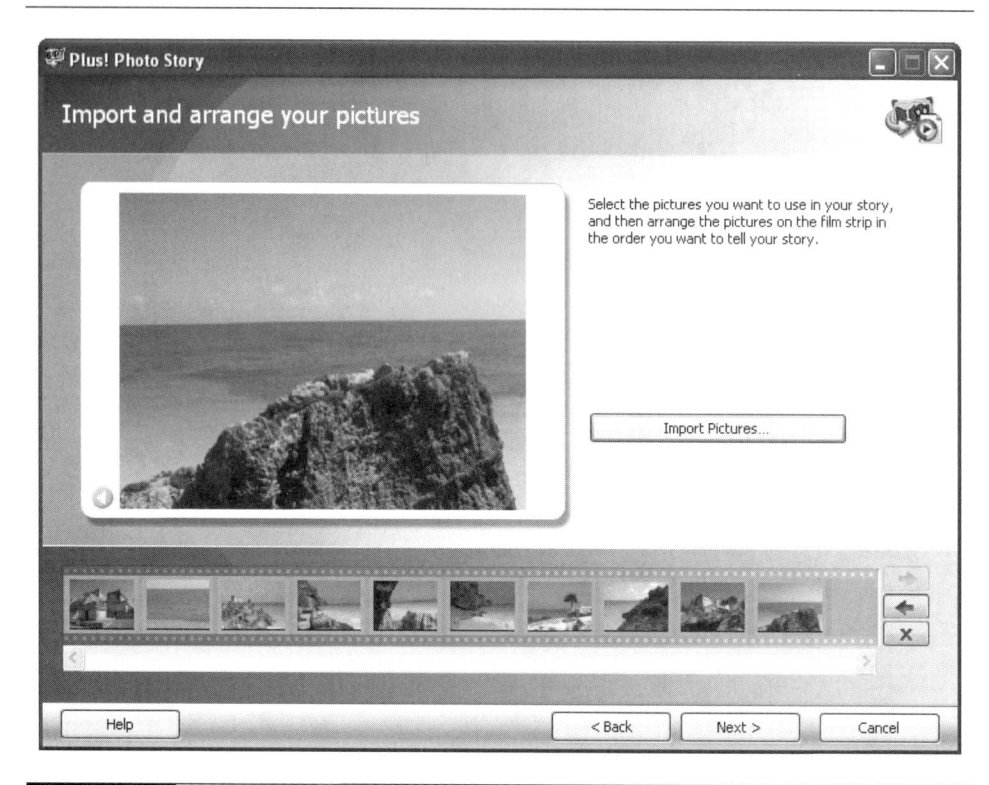

FIGURE 9-3 Viewing your photos in Photo Story

everything is in order, just the way you want. If you prefer, you can bypass the arrow keys and just click-and-drag photos around on the filmstrip to reorganize them.

No matter how you choose to do it, take a close look at your photos. Delete any that you do not absolutely want to include in your photo story, and organize the ones you do to your liking. Once you are done, click through the photos on the preview window so you can look at everything in order. When you are happy with the order, click Next to proceed.

Record Your Story

Once you choose and organize your photos, you come to the Record Your Story screen (see Figure 9-4). This screen allows you to record narration, make changes

CHAPTER 9: Make Photo Stories with Your Digital Photos   **151**

FIGURE 9-4   Recording your story

in the panning effects that are built into Photo Story, and adjust the amount of time that non-narrated photos are displayed.

To clarify things a bit for you, here are a few basic rules that this part of the wizard uses:

- You can narrate all photos, some photos, or no photos, depending on what you want to do. Narrated photos are displayed in the story for the length of the narration.

- Photo Story uses panning effects to make photos look as though they are moving. Photo Story does this automatically, but you can easily change the default panning action for a specific photo as you like.

- By default, non-narrated photos are displayed for five seconds in the story. However, you can change this duration if you want.

Narrating Your Story

To narrate your story, the first thing you need to do is make sure your microphone is plugged into your computer and working. Refer to your computer documentation for any help in setting up your microphone. To test your microphone so that you record effective narration, follow these steps:

1. Click the Configure Microphone link on the Plus! Photo Story Wizard. The Sound Test Hardware Wizard appears.

2. Click Next on the welcome screen. The Testing Sound Hardware page appears.

3. Allow the test to complete, and then click the Next button. If no microphone is detected, the test will tell you so.

4. On the Microphone Test window, follow the instructions and read the passage to test your microphone. You should see activity on the bar indicator. If the volume doesn't seem loud enough, click the Volume button to increase it. Click Next to continue.

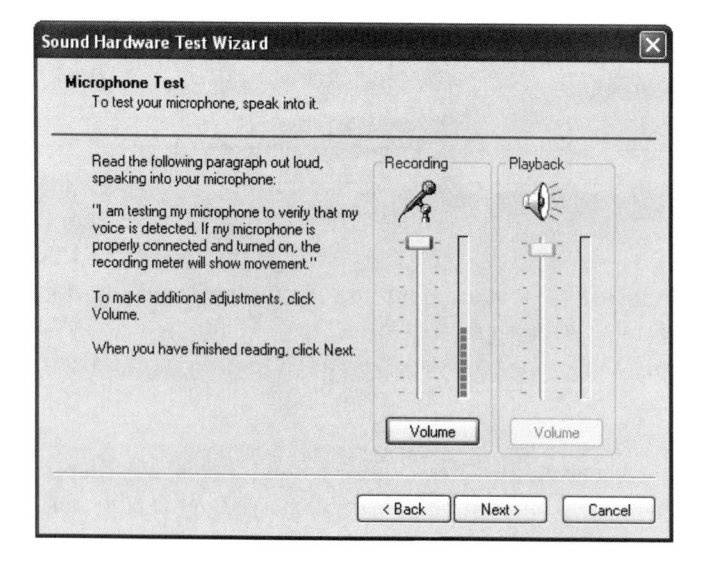

5. The next wizard screen enables you to check your voice with your speakers. You should be able to hear your voice through your computer speakers. Run the test (it is the same passage as in step 4) and listen for the results, then click Next.

6. Click Finish.

CHAPTER 9: Make Photo Stories with Your Digital Photos

Now you are ready to record your story. You can do so in one of two ways:

- You can record the narration for each photo, one at a time. This enables you to record the narration and stop. If you don't like the narration, you can simply change it.

- If you feel more confident, you can record the entire story at once and simply walk through each photo. Each photo retains its own narration, so you can still fix narration on individual photos if you like.

Either way, when you're ready to record, grab your script and follow these steps:

1. Make sure everything is quiet around you and get ready. You may want to read a bit of your script to get your voice warmed up.

2. Select the photo on the filmstrip that you want to start with. You may want to start with the first photo in order to avoid confusion.

3. Press the Record button on the wizard screen. The indicator shows you that it is recording, as shown below. As you speak, you can move your mouse to the area of the photo you are talking about. The Photo Wizard uses your mouse to determine the panning style needed for the photo (in order to make sure that what you are pointing to doesn't pan out of the photo; you can find out more about panning in the next section).

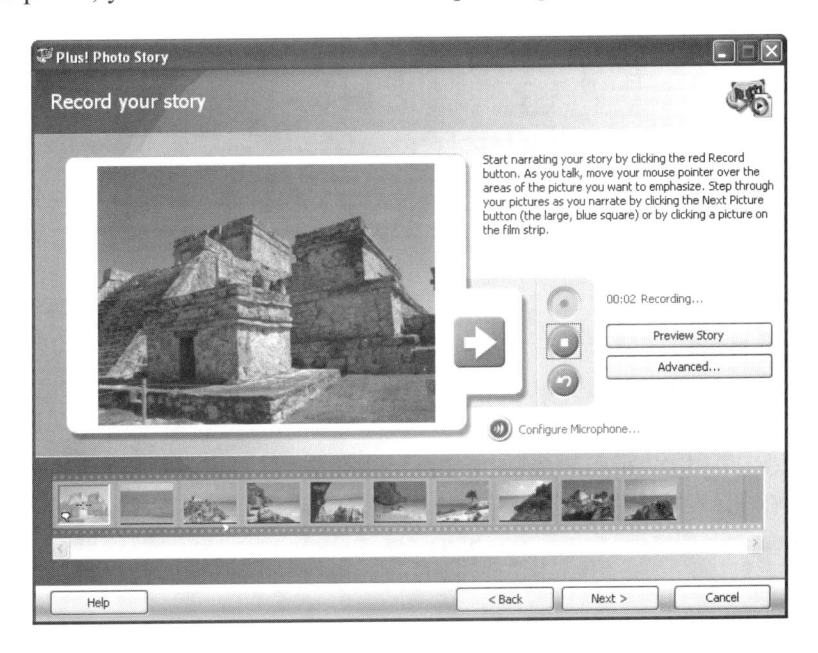

4. If you are recording your whole story, click the big blue arrow beside the preview window on the wizard to go to the next photo. Simply begin talking again when the next photo appears in the window.

5. If you want to record each photo individually, or if you've reached the end of your story, click the Stop button (the round button with the square in it) to stop recording. At this point, you can select a photo and reset it (by clicking the button with the curved arrow on it) so you can record the narration again. Also here, notice that the filmstrip timeline now displays the time for each photo and icon, noting that the photo has narration.

TIP *The great thing about the narration feature is that it is so forgiving. If you make a mistake, just click the photo you want to fix, click the Reset button, and record your narration again for that particular photo.*

Use Advanced Options

Photo Story uses its own panning functions in the story. However, for certain photos, you may not like the way Photo Story is panning them (you can see how the panning looks by clicking the Preview Story button on the Record Your Story wizard page).

CHAPTER 9: Make Photo Stories with Your Digital Photos 155

So, you can simply change what Photo Story is doing with the panning by choosing a different panning pattern.

1. To do so, select the photo in question on the filmstrip and click the Advanced button. This opens the Advanced Options window (see Figure 9-5).

2. Select the Control Pans And Zooms Manually check box, which enables the radio button options you can use. Select one of the pan/zoom options for the start and ending points of the motion, then click the Preview Motion button to see how it will look in your story.

3. If you don't like what you see, try other options until you are happy with the results, then just click OK.

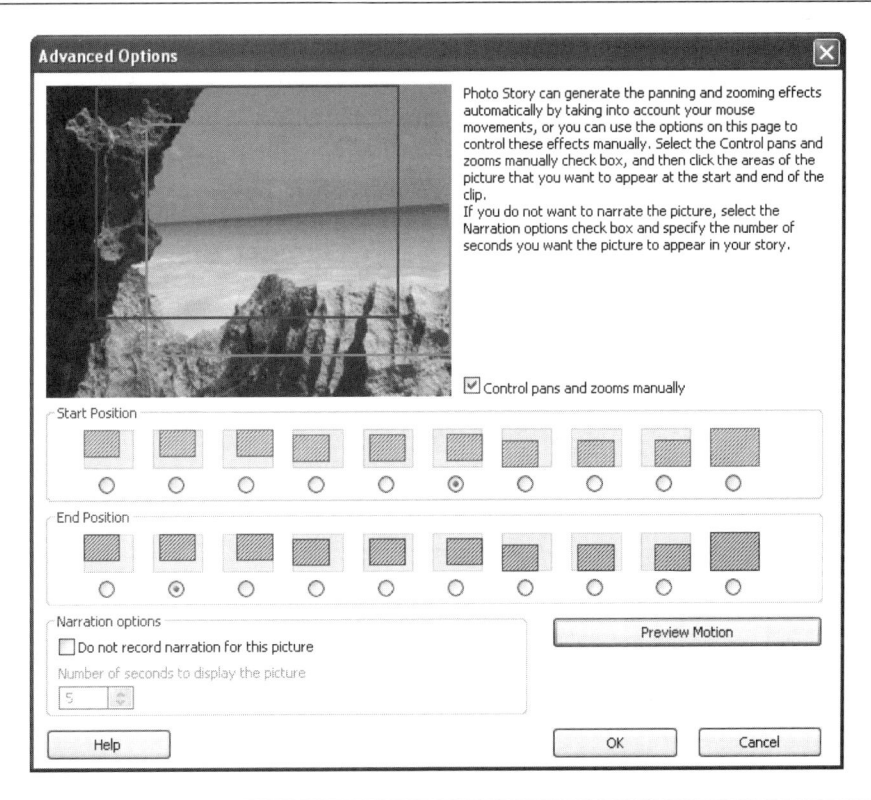

FIGURE 9-5   You can change the panning feature with Advanced Options.

How to ... Change the Display Time of Non-Narrated Photos

Narrated photos are displayed for the duration of the narration on that particular photo. However, photos that are not narrated are displayed for five seconds. You can change this behavior by selecting the photo on the filmstrip and clicking the Advanced button. This takes you, once again, to the Advanced Options window. On this window, select the Do Not Record Narration For This Picture check box, and then choose the number of seconds you want to display the photo. Keep in mind that five seconds is the default. Generally, five to ten seconds is a good choice. Be careful of going over ten seconds for a non-narrated photo because your story will start to get boring; if you do, make sure you have a logical reason for doing so. When you are done, click Next to advance to the next wizard page.

NOTE *Unfortunately, you can't select multiple photos and change the timing all at once; you'll have to change them one at a time.*

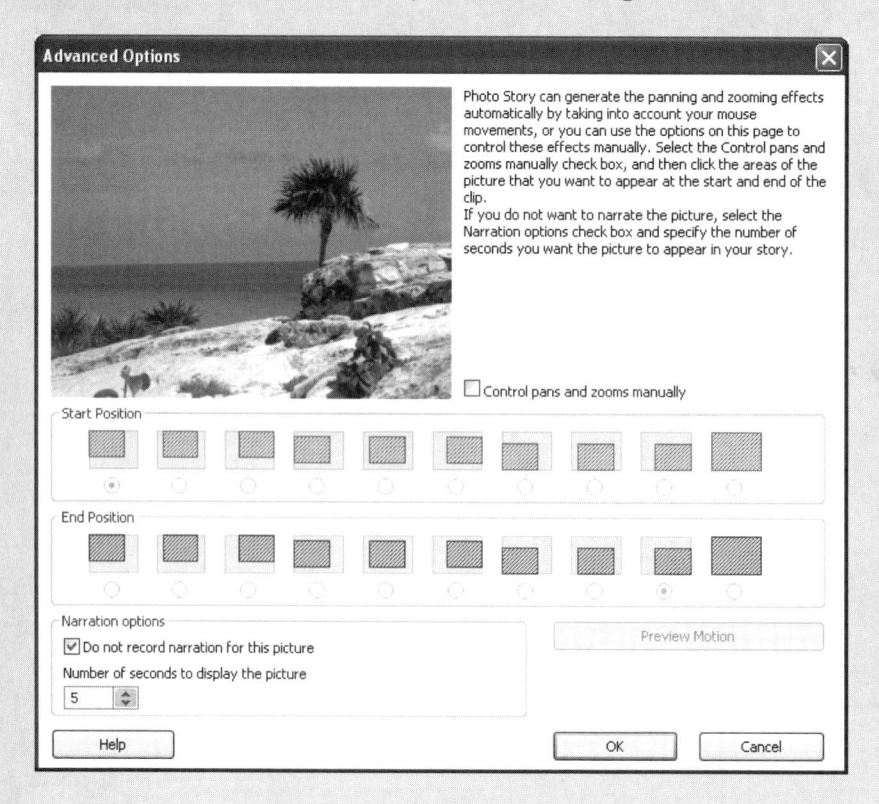

CHAPTER 9: Make Photo Stories with Your Digital Photos   **157**

Once you return to the main window, notice that the photo on the filmstrip now has an icon noting that you have made manual panning selections for that photo, as you can see in the selected photo in the following illustration:

Create a Title Page

The next wizard screen allows you to create a title page for your Photo Story. This can be fun and cool, and the available options are rather straightforward, as you can see in Figure 9-6.

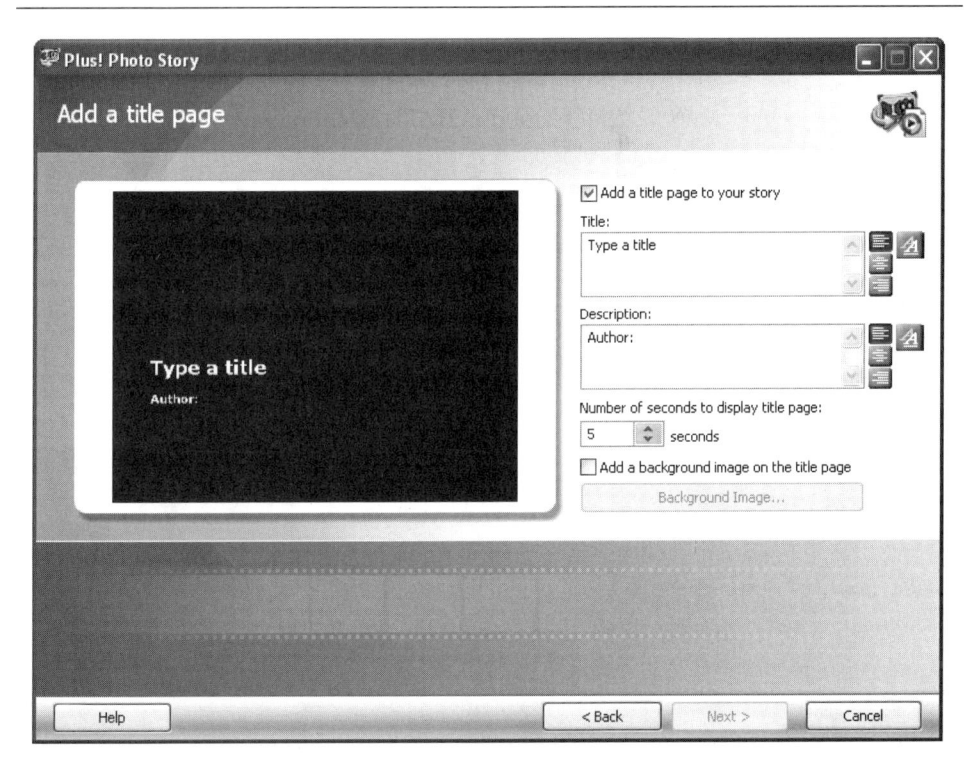

FIGURE 9-6 Creating a title

On this page, you can do the following:

- **Choose to have a title page.** If you don't want one, just clear the Add A Title Page To Your Story check box and click the Next button to move on.
- **Create a title.** Type your title text and use the positioning and font buttons to format the title to look the way you want.
- **Enter the author's name.** If you don't want to include any author, just leave the Description dialog box blank.
- **Choose the number of seconds to display the title page.** Five seconds is the default and is long enough.
- **Use a background image.** Select the Add A Background Image On The Title Page check box and click the Background Image button to choose an image from your computer.

As you can see, these options are easy, so experiment and have fun. Here's a sample title page I created:

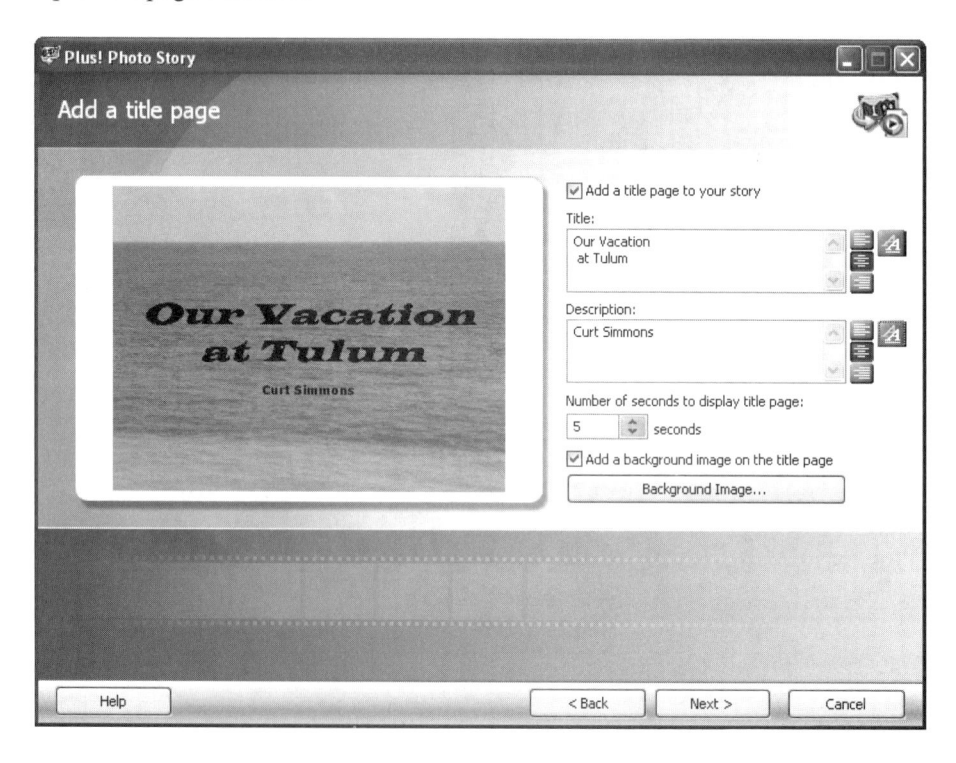

TIP *Don't forget to try different fonts and colors with your title text. Just use the Fonts button to choose these options.*

When you are done, click Next to move to the next wizard page.

Choose Background Music

In the next step of the wizard, you can choose to include background music if you like. Just select the check box to include music and click Browse. This will take you to your Windows Media Player library to choose a song, but keep in mind that you can use any song as long as it's in the WMA, MP3, or WAV format. You can also use the slider bar to determine how loud the music plays, which is important if the music will play behind narration (err on the side of softer instead of louder).

PICTURE THIS *Music that has been copy-protected in Windows Media Player cannot be used in Photo Story.*

Use Other Items on This Wizard Page

Notice that all photos with no specified duration are displayed for five seconds. You can change this value if you like, but don't make them display for too long, or your Photo Story will drag a bit when people watch it.

To review your whole story, click the Preview button; you'll see a small preview window in which you can watch your Photo Story.

Take a hard look to see if everything works well. If there is something you don't like, click the Back button to return to previous screens to fix it. If you like what you see, click Next to continue.

Choose Quality Settings and Save Your Story

After previewing your photo story, you come to the Quality Settings And Saving window, shown in Figure 9-7.

You can adjust video and audio quality for best and "better." Unless you are using the photo story as a post on a web site, stick with the best quality options. Also, if you are using quality profiles in Windows Media Player, you can also click the Advanced button and choose a profile option (which most of us don't use, so don't worry about it.)

Finally, type in a filename for your Photo Story. Notice that the story is saved in the WMA format. You can't change this, and it means that only Windows Media Player 9 is able to play the Photo Story. Click Next to save your story. You can then view the story in Windows Media Player or create another story. If you choose to view the story, Windows Media Player jumps to life and plays the Photo Story.

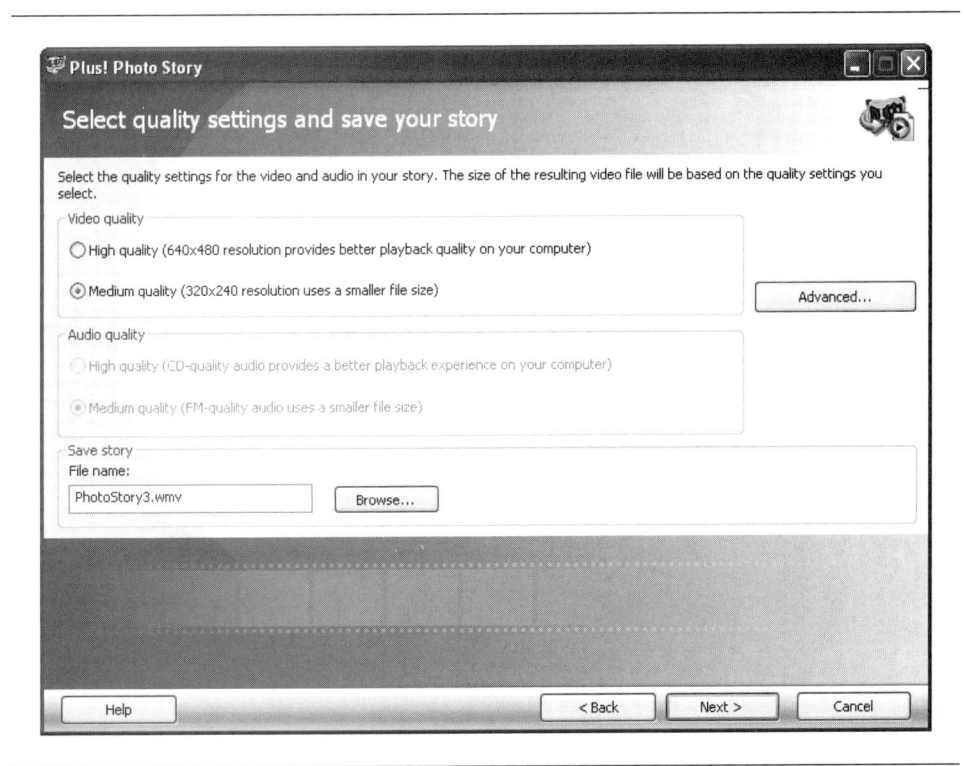

CHAPTER 9: Make Photo Stories with Your Digital Photos   161

FIGURE 9-7   Choosing quality settings and saving your story

More Great Ideas

As you might imagine, you can do all kinds of things with Plus! Photo Story. Here are a few ideas for you:

- Create family photo stories for holidays and special occasions—they are great keepsakes.
- Make a fun photo story for a surprise party or birthday—don't forget to include those embarrassing photos!
- Make a photo story to remember and narrate a trip or vacation.
- Share your photo story. You can e-mail it to friends or burn it to a CD. Just remember that anyone who wants to watch the photo story must be using Windows Media Player 9, which is a free download from www.microsoft.com.

Part III
Be in the Movies!

Chapter 10

Create Your Own Birthday or Wedding Video

How to…

- Plan birthday or wedding videos
- Use Movie Maker to create your movies

Let's face it, birthday and wedding videos are two of the greatest reasons to own a camcorder, along with vacations and holidays. We love capturing those special memories, and we love looking back at them and remembering those bygone days. As a kid, I remember sitting in my parents' living room and watching a reel-to-reel projector of silent, Super 8 video footage.

The great news is that technology gives us an easy way to capture great video these days, and Windows Movie Maker gives you great ways to edit that footage and create your own custom videos of weddings, birthdays, vacations, and other special events. In this chapter, you'll see how to take your wedding or video footage and use Movie Maker to create something special.

What You'll Need

For this project, you'll need Microsoft Windows Movie Maker 2. If your system has Microsoft Movie Maker 1, visit www.microsoft.com/windowsxp for more information about downloading Movie Maker 2. You'll also need some wedding or birthday video and/or photos.

Get Ready to Create a Birthday or Wedding Video

Like most projects, whether digital or otherwise, your first action should involve some prep work. No, prep work is never as much fun as actually playing with software, but it can certainly help you get ready to create your project and ensure that your end result is what you have in mind.

Identify Your Goal

First of all, stop for a moment and think about the actual product you want to produce. Think about the wedding or birthday event. What do you really want to capture in your movie? What are the things you really want to remember? The truth is that a wedding or birthday video is really just an entertaining record of what happened. As with any event, you have dull moments mixed with the exciting moments that you'll remember forever. Think about a special occasion, such as the birth of a child or a vacation of your dreams. Can you remember every single thing that happened? No, of course not, but what you do remember are noteworthy items—things that are exciting and fun to remember. So, your first step in creating an effective birthday or wedding video is to identify the things you really want to remember, the things you want to watch over and over again. Jot down those ideas on a piece of paper, and then start compiling the materials.

Gather Your Film and Photos

Your next task is to determine what film and photos you'll include in your movie. More than likely, you took camcorder film during the wedding or birthday party. You may also have a bunch of photos and, especially in the case of a wedding, you may have video film from other people as well. You'll need to spend some time taking a look at all of the film and photos and thinking about what you want to actually include in the movie. You may have a lot to choose from, in which case you'll need to do some culling in order to make the film look great.

First of all, I recommend that you mix film footage and photos in your movie. The combination of film and still photos looks really cool, especially considering the nostalgic content of your movie. Movies show action, but still shots freeze action in a moment of time. Your movie will look really nice if you mix and match the two elements.

So, what should you include? To figure that out, you'll need to sit down and watch your video footage. Take a piece of paper and note the "scenes" that you want to include in your movie. Using Windows Movie Maker, you'll be able to edit out the boring sections of tape, so you'll need to wade through it all and decide what should be kept and what shouldn't. In many cases, especially with a wedding, you may have two or three hours of video footage recorded that you want to get condensed down to half an hour or so, or maybe even less. Your first step is to simply watch the video and make some decisions about what should or should not be included.

Next, look through your photos. Naturally, all photos will have to be digitized, so if you have regular print photos you want to include, you'll need to scan those and create digital files so you can work with them in Movie Maker. Of course, include only the best photos. Weed out any photos that are not exactly right or that do not convey the meaning and feel you're after. Movie making is a subjective art, so let your own sense of style guide you. Make sure you review the photos carefully and cull any photos that are very similar. Each photo should be unique and add to the quality of your movie.

Plan the Movie Flow

Movie "flow" refers to the series of events that shape the movie. This includes video clips and still photos that are inserted in the movie. The flow of a movie makes it interesting and helps keep the audience's attention.

How do you create good flow? The first issue is simply variety. Mix up the film and photo footage. In other words, do not group all of your still photos into one place in the movie; mix them up with the video to create more variation.

The second issue is story flow. Since birthdays and weddings show a progression of events, I strongly recommend that you create your movie showing this progression. In other words, show the beginning of the wedding or birthday party, and move naturally to the end of the event. The same advice goes for vacations: Start with footage and film from the beginning of the vacation, and then move through the vacation until it's over. If you were creating a video of some nature scenery, a mixture would be fine. But remember, your wedding and birthday video tells a story, so you want to convey that story in chronological order when you create your movie.

Once you have thought through these issues and have gathered up all of your film clips and photos, you are ready to create your movie.

Import Video and Photos into Movie Maker

Your first task is to import all of your film and photos into Windows Movie Maker, creating a new Movie Maker project. This task involves direct importing of film using a digital camera, indirect importing of film using a capture device for analog camcorders, and using the Import Pictures option under Movie Tasks (see Figure 10-1). I assume here that you already know how to import film and photos into Movie Maker, but if you don't, relax: This book contains a special appendix just to get you up to speed if you have never used Movie Maker before. If you are a Movie Maker novice, stop what you are doing and read Appendix A. You'll need several of the skills explored in there for this project, so don't go any further in this chapter until you read Appendix A and know how to maneuver around Movie Maker.

If you already know the basics of using Movie Maker, go ahead and import all of your video footage and still photos at this time. You don't have to worry about importing the items in any particular order—we'll organize and assemble the movie in a bit. For now, just get everything imported into Movie Maker.

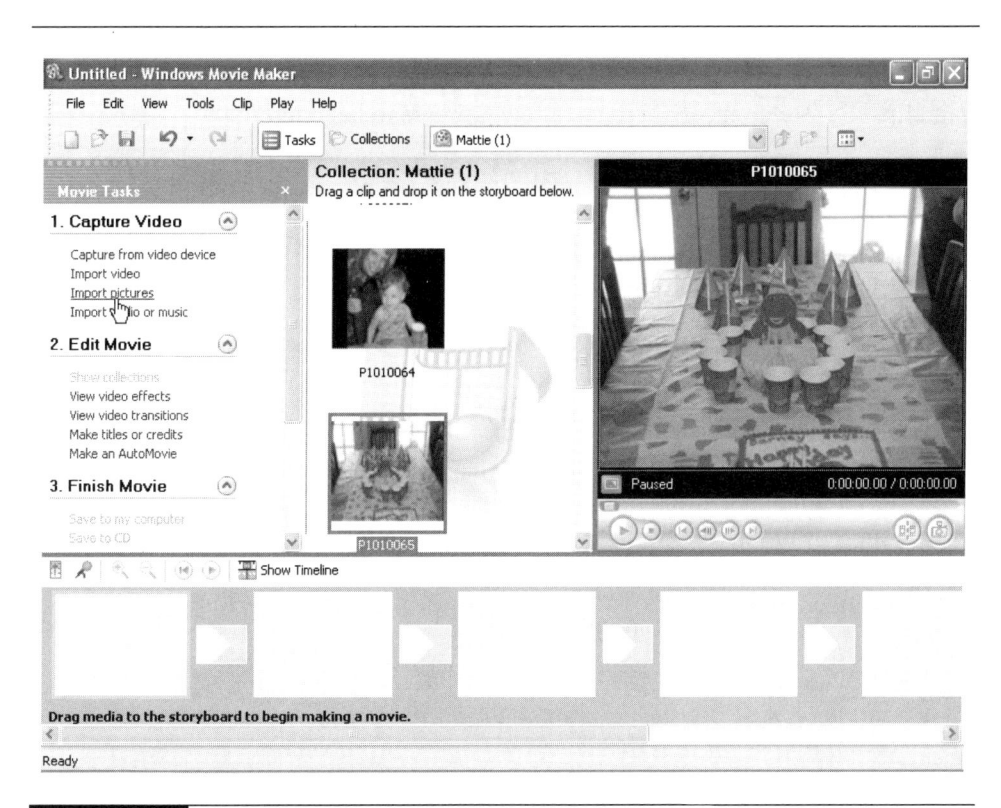

CHAPTER 10: Create Your Own Birthday or Wedding Video   **169**

FIGURE 10-1 You can easily import photos using the Movie Tasks option.

Organize Your Footage

Your next step is to organize your film footage. This doesn't mean that you assemble your movie yet, but you actually trim and split movie clips as needed. Since we all end up with miles of boring or uninteresting footage at any birthday party or wedding, you'll probably need to hone that footage down a bit and edit out the boring parts, as mentioned earlier. You can do that by trimming your video clips that have been imported. Likewise, you may have an imported video clip that contains two different scenes of action. In this case, you may want to split the clip into two pieces so that you can easily organize the movie in the way that you want.

Now, if all of this talk about trimming and splitting clips seems like foreign gibberish to you, then go to Appendix A, where you can learn how to trim and split clips. Before doing so, here are a few pointers to keep in mind:

- Trim clips so that you lose any boring scenes or parts of your video that simply didn't come out well. If Uncle Bob walked in front of the camera and the lens recorded his ear canal for two minutes, then you might want to trim out that part.

- Split clips that contain two different scenes. Try to get your clips down to a scene-by-scene basis. No, don't split them up into forty 20-second clips, but try to split them based on action.

- Name the clips something descriptive. "Clip 44" doesn't tell you much, but "Wedding processional" does. The names are not used in the actual movie, but they are used to keep you organized as you create the movie, so name the clips something descriptive so that they don't become a confusing sea of video pieces.

Movie Maker 2 doesn't contain any photo-editing capabilities, so if some of your photos need some cropping or other cleanup, you'll need to do that in a photo-editing application such as Photoshop Elements 2 or Adobe's Photoshop Album before you use them in Movie Maker.

Create a Title Page

Wedding and birthday videos look great with a title page, which makes your movie look professional and gives it that touch of class that looks so nice. The great thing about Movie Maker 2 is that it can help you create a title page easily and actually insert it into your movie for you. Follow these steps to create a title page:

1. In Movie Maker, click the Make Titles Or Credits link under Edit Movie, found in Picture Tasks.

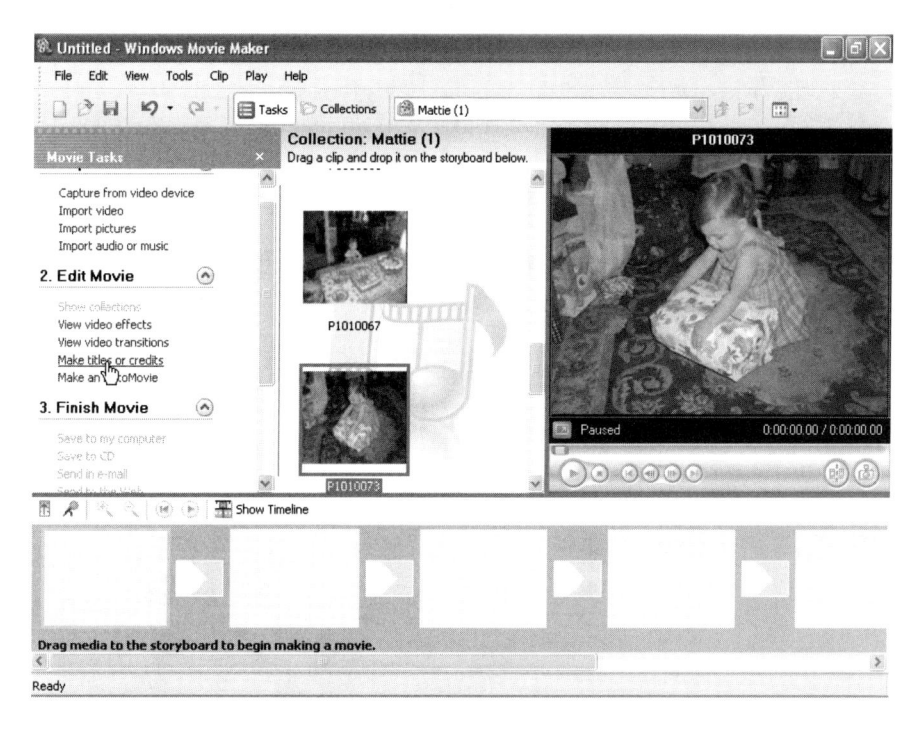

CHAPTER 10: Create Your Own Birthday or Wedding Video   171

2. The Picture Tasks box changes so that you can choose where you want to insert the title or credits. Click the option to create a title at the beginning of the movie.

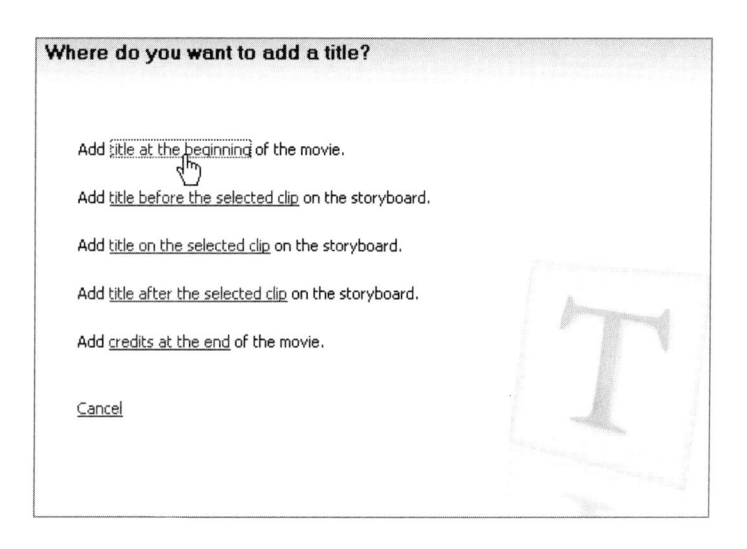

3. Two boxes appear in which you can enter title-page text. The first box is the primary title, and the second box gives you a subtitle. Simply type your text into these boxes, and it will appear in the preview window. Keep in mind that Movie Maker doesn't provide any spell checking, so watch your spelling.

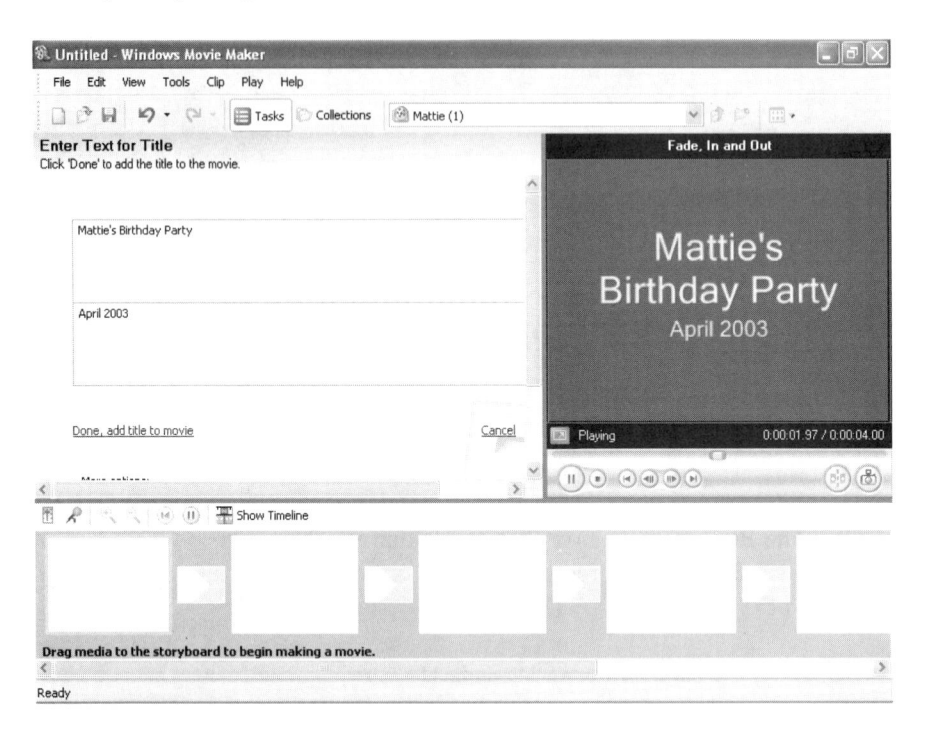

4. Scroll down under Enter Text For Title and you'll see more options where you can change the text animation or font and colors. Of course, if you are happy with the basic outcome of the title page, you don't have to use these options, but you might want to see what is available to you. If you click Title Animation, the window changes and presents a bunch of text animation options from which you can choose. Just scroll through the list, and you'll see a sample of each animation in the preview window; then just select the

CHAPTER 10: Create Your Own Birthday or Wedding Video 173

one you want to use. When you are finished, click the Done, Add Title To Movie link to return to the main title page.

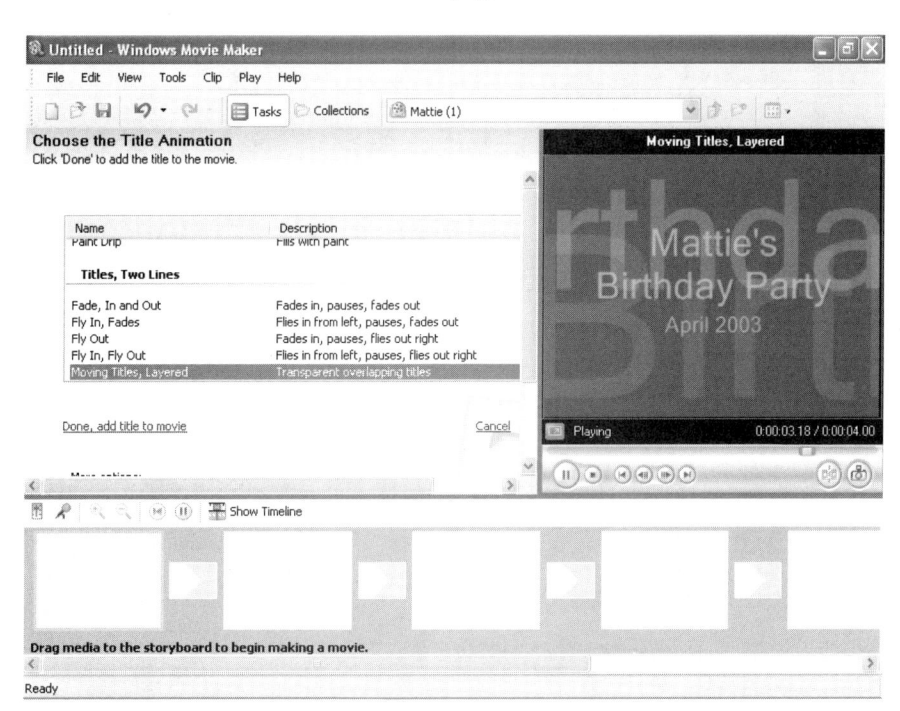

TIP *A lot of the animation features are fun, but make sure they match the style and tone of your movie and are easy to read.*

5. Click the Change Text Font And Color option. The window changes to offer a font and text-color feature that you can use to change the font and color in any way you like. Once again, make sure the font and colors you choose match the style and tone of your movie, and make sure they match.

Use your creative judgment here, but err on the side of conservative if you are in doubt.

6. When you are finished selecting fonts and colors, click Done, Add Title To Movie. The title is added to the first block on your storyboard.

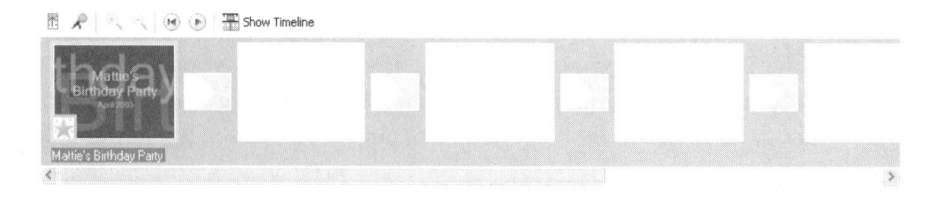

Assemble Your Movie

Now it's time to assemble your video. In the lower Movie Maker pane, click the Storyboard button so that you are in Storyboard mode. Then, simply drag the

CHAPTER 10: Create Your Own Birthday or Wedding Video   **175**

How to ... Make Your Own Title Pages

Movie Maker's title page feature is cool and easy, but you are limited by Movie Maker's options. In fact, you can design your own title page in any graphics program and simply import it into Movie Maker as a JPEG image. For example, use a program (such as Photoshop Elements) to make a collage of a few photos, and paint a title page or use the art features to create the titling. Then, simply save the collage as a JPEG image and import it into your movie. Since the collage is simply a photo (as far as Movie Maker is concerned), just drag it to the first location on the storyboard. As you can imagine, if you are graphics-program–savvy, you can create all kinds of cool title pages for your movie!

clips and photos to the storyboard in the order that you want. Keep in mind that the storyboard is the actual order of your movie, so drag items to the storyboard in the order in which they should appear in your movie. Of course, you can change the order of items on the storyboard just by dragging them around, but try to get the order right the first time to cut down on confusion. Refer to your notes and ideas about your movie, and then simply drag the clips and photos to the storyboard as needed, as shown in Figure 10-2.

FIGURE 10-2   Drag your clips and photos to the storyboard in the correct order.

Add Transitions

Transitions are simply visual effects that move you from one movie clip or photo in the storyboard to the next. Without transitions, Movie Maker simply jumps to the next clip or photo. The transition, then, adds a visual effect to the movement from one item to the next, giving your movie a more professional, or "softer," look. Transitions are great, and I highly recommend that you work with them and use them in your wedding or birthday movie.

Before we take a look at adding transitions, let's consider a few issues. First of all, Movie Maker gives you a good set of transition options, and if you have installed the Microsoft Plus! Pack for Windows XP, you'll get some more as well. It is easy to fall into Happy Transition Land when you are working with transitions. They are cool and fun, and you may feel the urge to use as many different transitions as possible in your movie. Avoid this feeling: A great variety of transitions tends to give the movie a choppy look rather than a smooth movement from scene to scene. As such, especially for wedding or birthday video, I typically recommend that you stick with just two or three different transitions. Don't use a different transition for each scene change; this approach usually doesn't come out well.

Second, you need to be aware that each transition is different. Some are smooth and nice looking, while others are bolder. You need to match the feel of your movie with the transitions. In other words, if you are creating a wedding video, softer, smoother transitions look better than something bold and bouncy. You want the transition to add an element of class to your video, but the transitions should not capture an undue amount of attention. After all, transitions are just that—transitions, not the actual movie.

Finally, concerning transitions and photos, you need to think about timing. By default, photos are shown for five seconds. When you add a transition, the transition takes up some of those five seconds on the photo. However, you can switch to timeline view and extend the amount of time the photo is shown. See Appendix A to learn more about timeline view.

So, once you are ready to add transitions, you can do so quickly and easily. Just follow these steps:

1. In the Movie Tasks pane under Edit Movie, click the View Video Transitions link. The transitions appear in the clips area.

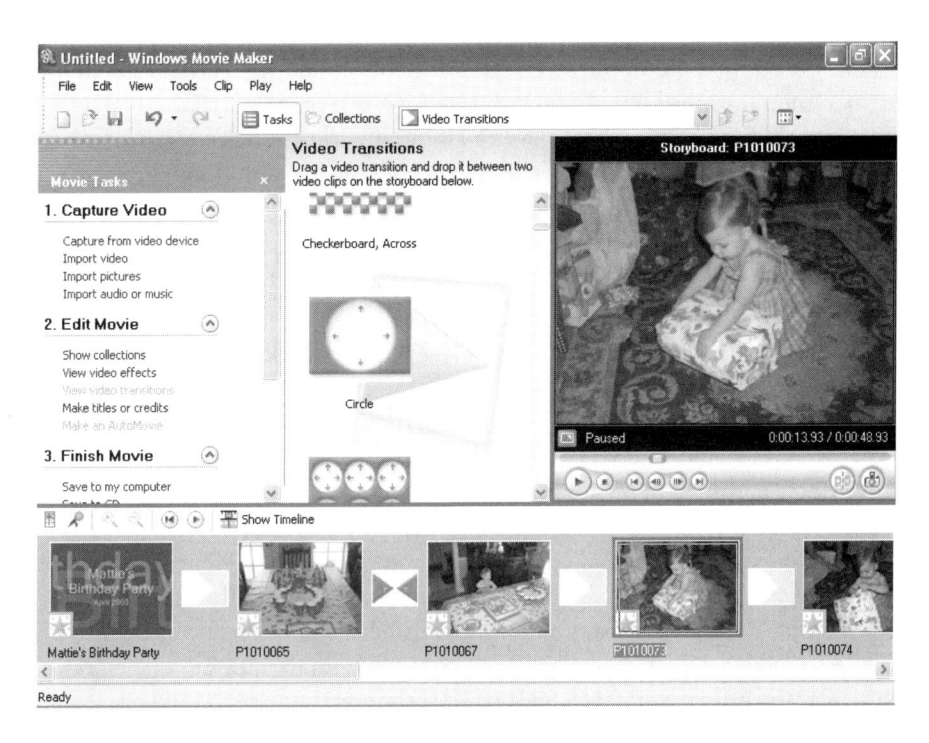

CHAPTER 10: Create Your Own Birthday or Wedding Video   177

2. Select the transition you think you might like, and then click Play on the view monitor. You'll see a sample of the transition action. Work through the transitions and try them out, noting the ones you like. Remember, keep in mind the theme and the mood of your movie, and look for transitions that work well with your movie.

3. When you are ready, simply drag the desired transition to the transition box that appears between each photo or movie clip on your storyboard. Repeat this process to fill in the transitions boxes as you like.

4. When you are done, select your title page, and then click Play in the monitor area so that you can watch your movie so far. If you decide that you don't like a particular transition, just right-click it on the storyboard and click Delete. Then, simply drag a new transition in its place.

Add Special Effects

Movie Maker 2 includes some special effects that you might want to add to your wedding or birthday video. Basically, these work in the same manner as a transition. If you have installed the Microsoft Plus! Pack for Windows XP, you'll have additional effects available to you, and you should periodically check www.microsoft.com/windowsxp for additional Movie Maker effects you can download for free.

Effects simply add some kind of visual interest to a clip or photo. Naturally, not all of them will look good with a wedding or birthday video, but you might find some that greatly enhance a clip or photo. For photos, for example, you might want to try the "ease in" or "ease out" effect, which gives the still photo some movement. For video clips, you might consider turning one or more into black and white for added effect. The choice is completely up to you, but once again, make sure that the effect you use actually complements the feel and tone of your movie.

To add effects, just follow these steps:

1. In Movie Tasks, under Edit Movie, click View Video Effects. The effects appear in the clips area.

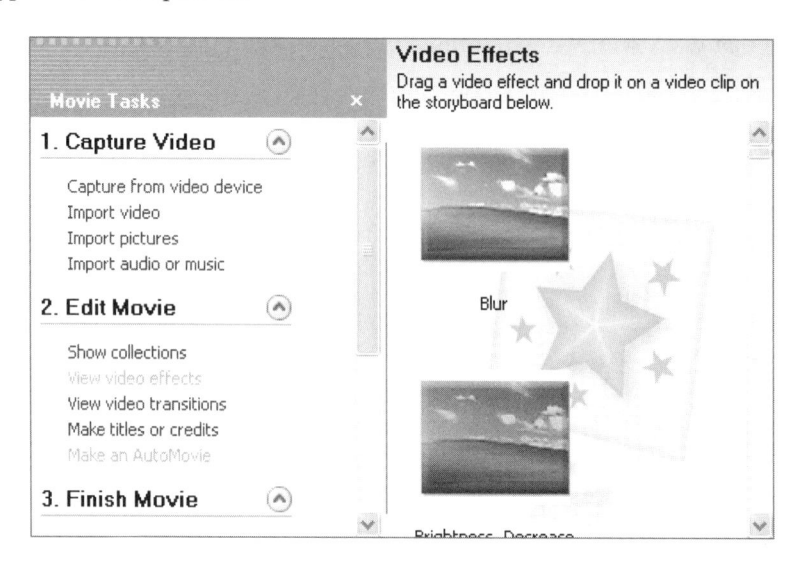

2. Look through the effects, choose one, and click Play in the monitor window to execute it.

3. If you find effects that you want to use, simply drag them to the star that appears on the lower-left corner of each clip or photo in the storyboard.

4. When you are done, click Play in the monitor area to watch your movie. Keep a critical eye on the effects and make sure they look good with your movie. To remove an effect, simply right-click the star on the clip or photo and click Delete.

NOTE *As you might imagine, a wedding or birthday movie works great with background music and narration. There are a number of cool things you can do concerning the sound track, and they're organized in Chapter 13, so refer to that chapter to learn more about adding sound to your project. Also, Movie Maker gives you several saving options, so you can use your movie in a way you like. See Chapter 14 to learn more about those features.*

More Great Ideas

As you might imagine, you can do all kinds of things with Movie Maker. Here are a few ideas for you:

- Create vacation movies that highlight fun times on family trips.
- Create a "remember when" movie that mixes up old family movies and photos.
- Make a fun movie about your kids or grandkids that you can show at a birthday party.
- Make your own movie about you and your special someone to show at your wedding rehearsal dinner.

And you can do even more! See Chapters 11 and 12 for additional fun movie ideas.

Chapter 11

Make a Scary Movie!

How to...

- Learn the basics of scary movies
- Plan scary movies
- Create scary movies with Movie Maker

When I was a kid, there was nothing I liked more than to get together with a group of my cousins and watch the scariest, goriest movie we could possibly get our hands on. As a creative youngster, there was something incredibly cool about being scared out of my mind by something I knew was not real, but yet looked so real. How did they do it?

In truth, making a scary movie with Windows XP's Movie Maker is not different from other movies that you create, but in order to create an effective scary movie, there are some important elements of scary movies you'll need to include. The great news is you can create your raw footage with your camera, and then use Movie Maker to add all of the effects you might want.

What You'll Need

To create your scary movie, you'll need Windows Movie Maker 2. If you are using Windows Movie Maker 1, you can get Windows Movie Maker 2 as a free download from www.microsoft.com/windowsxp.

Explore Scary Movie Variations

Now, as you are reading this chapter, you may think, "A scary movie is not for me, so I'm going to move on to something else." You are free to do that, of course, but before you do, let's consider a few variations of the scary movie, and maybe you'll find at least one way in which you can have some fun with them.

A Real Scary Movie

At the top of the list is an actual scary movie. This involves you writing a script and finding actors in your friends and family. The purpose of your movie is to provide a story about something scary and use costumes, props, and some Movie Maker magic to actually create a movie that is fun—and scary!—to watch.

A Scary Movie Spoof

Here's a fun one to do. Watch your favorite scary movie, and then write a script that is a spoof (or a comical rip-off) of the movie. Gather some friends and family to act in and film the movie, and then use Movie Maker to put it together. With a little creativity, the spoofs can be really fun, and great to show at your next party.

Real-Life Horror Spoofs

Another fun idea is take a common event, such as a birthday or family reunion, and then use Movie Maker to add horror effects to the movie. You end up with a movie that is hilarious to watch! (Try creating "The Nightmare at Christmas" from a family Christmas gathering. These almost always end up quite funny!)

Halloween with the Kids

If you have children, I'm quite certain that Halloween is a big camcorder night, as it is around our house. Instead of just keeping that footage as it is, put it in Movie Maker and add some fun effects and scary music to it. You'll end with a fun night to remember, but your added effects will make the movie an even better keepsake.

Know What Makes a Scary Movie Scary

In order to make a scary movie, you'll have to understand what makes a movie scary in the first place. This isn't hard, but watching a movie uses your senses of sight and sound, so you'll want to include both of those when you create your movie. Here are some things you should keep in mind at all times:

Visual Scares

Of course, the base portion of any movie is the visual appeal; in the case of a scary movie, the movie has to be visually frightening. This can come across in a few different ways, depending on the kind of scary movie you are creating. If you are creating a true horror flick, your use of masks, makeup, costumes, and the setting creates visually scary situations. This could include a vampire in a graveyard, a ghost in a haunted house, or any other kind of visual fright. In a horror movie, you create a fictional situation that is at least somewhat believable. Your movie audience puts aside reality and buys into the fantasy for a time.

However, what if you want to create a movie about a real-life serial murderer instead of an actual horror movie? These psychology thrillers are often very scary, and the scare comes about through the creepy presentation of the main character and the other characters' responses to him or her. The terror isn't a monster or ghost—it's a situation of danger.

In order to pull off visual scares, they have to be, in fact, scary. This is where your hard work writing a scary script comes into play and where your actors pull off the job of bringing the scary elements alive on tape. This all comes with some practice and an eagle eye on behalf of you, the director.

Sound Scares

The visual portion of a movie is of utmost importance, but I'll tell you a big secret: Sound has a lot to do with the scare factor! Think about it, have you ever watched a scary movie that didn't have scary music in the background? No, of course not, and the reason is simple: The scary music is an auditory stimulus for your audience. The screams and dialogue of your actors are certainly important, but scary music and sound effects will have a great impact on the quality of your movie.

Windows Movie Maker allows you to keep your original camcorder track (whatever you record when you film your movie), but also you can add background music and special sound effects easily, many of which you can get free from the Internet. Because sound is such an important part of any movie, I have written a whole chapter just about using sound in Movie Maker. See Chapter 13 to learn more about creating a custom sound track.

How to ... Avoid the "Over Scare"

One problem that you have to watch out for with scary movies is what I like to call "over scare," which is really just overacting. It is trying to make something scary by overdoing the acting, which in most cases ends up silly and unbelievable. Have you ever watched a horror movie where the acting was so bad that the movie became more of a comedy than something scary? This is due to over scare, or overacting. To avoid this problem, simply don't over do it. When you are filming, you want the actors to play their parts well, but be wary of trying too hard to make things scary. Stick to your script and your ideas, and let the movie speak for itself.

The Element of Surprise

A major feature of any scary movie is the element of surprise. Think back to your favorite scary movie. What parts of the film scared you the most and made you jump out of your seat? More than likely, the answer is the element of surprise, which happens when something happens suddenly. There is an attack on one of the characters, or a cat jumps out at the viewer. The element of surprise is probably the scariest part of any movie, so as you are planning your movie, you'll need to spend some time thinking about this and how you can use the element of surprise to make your movie really terrifying.

Situational Tension

Another part of the scary movie that really enhances the scare factor is situational tension. This occurs when the audience believes that something scary is about to happen to one of the main characters. A character slowly opens an old house's creaky door and steps inside. As he or she walks down the hall, a spooky shadow appears on the wall, unknown to the character. The music begins to swell, and the audience bites their fingernails in anticipation of what is about to come.

While the element of surprise can certainly be used in situational tension, the point here is simply that you need to let the audience suffer a bit concerning what is about to happen. This brings the scare factor way up in your movie, making it fun to watch. As you are planning your movie, be sure to think about situational tension where you can build to a climax in different scenes of the scary movie.

Blood and Gore

Blood and gore are common parts of a horror movie, depending on the movie itself. Some scary movies use a lot of blood and gore to up the fright factor, while others depend more on the element of surprise and situational tension to make the movie scary. While you are free to use blood and gore, be advised that it can be overdone and it tends to lose its effectiveness rather quickly. Also, unless you are a genius with special effects, blood and gore effects can be difficult to create with believability. If you want to learn more, however, you might consider buying a book that explores movie effects and gives you tips on how amateur moviemakers can create them.

Plan Your Scary Movie

Planning a scary movie is really no different than planning any other movie. You'll need to start with a script and determine your story line. Depending on what you want to do, the script and the movie locations may be determined for you already. However, if you are creating something truly from scratch, you have a lot of planning and writing to do before you ever begin filming the first scene.

So, if you are sitting there staring at a blank piece of paper, how can you effectively plan your scary movie? The best approach is to break down the process into specific tasks so that it isn't overwhelming. Even if you are using your kids' Halloween video to make a fun scary movie, this process can be helpful so that you put together an effective film. The following sections discuss these steps to planning a scary movie:

1. Create summary statements.
2. Create a storyboard.
3. Write the script.

Create Summary Statements

One of the greatest problems when you start a project is really identifying what the movie is going to do. What is the goal? What's going to happen? You can help answer these questions with just a couple of summary statements. Grab a piece of paper and write something like this:

> A group of teenagers visit a haunted house. Inside, they find a witch who captures them and plans to use them to experiment with new potions. After being subjected to a few potions, the teens manage to escape by turning one of the potions back on the witch.

As you can see, these statements are not advertising statements. They tell, in a few sentences, exactly what is going to happen in the movie, from beginning to end. Once you write your statements (keep them short), tack this paper to the wall and use it to keep yourself focused on the "big picture" of your movie as you move forward.

Create a Storyboard

A storyboard is simply a grid that shows the different scenes of a movie. Basically, it shows what is going to happen in a scene-by-scene flow. You can do this with statements, or you can create a flowchart, which is the method I like to use. Try to limit the storyboard to a few sheets of paper. Then, when you are filming your movie, you can carry the storyboard around with you to keep you on track.

You can also use a storyboard to help you plan your Movie Maker special effects and audio. See Chapter 13 for a sample storyboard I've used to plan out some audio tracks for a birthday party movie.

Write the Script

The next task is simply to expand the storyboard and write the script for your movie. The script should be written on a scene-by-scene basis and should include movement information (called *blocking*) for the characters and their dialogue. Here's a sample:

JANE *(looking worried):* There's no way I'm going into that old house. Everyone knows the place is haunted!

JIM *(antagonistically):* I knew you would chicken out.

JANE *(grabbing Jim's arm to get his attention):* This is not a joke! A lot of strange things happen in that old house…

As you can see, the script outlines who is talking, what they are doing, and what they are saying. Use this basic approach, and keep the following tips in mind as you write:

- Keep dialogue brief and to the point. You are not writing a Shakespearean play, and long monologues simply are not believable (and they are boring).

- Strive for realistic dialogue. As you write a page or so, stop and read the lines out loud, and see how they sound to you. Many times, you'll want to back up and make some edits, because the way something looks on paper may not sound that great when it is read aloud.

- Remember that the script isn't a novel. Your viewers will be able to see what is happening, so don't fall into the trap of having your characters narrate all of the events and happenings. Let the action speak for itself.

- Be specific with blocking instructions. Try to envision what is going to happen in the movie and write it out. This will help your actors get things right more quickly.

- Don't fall in love with your script. A script is a blueprint, not the movie. In other words, use the script as a guide and be willing to change it as needed.

Film Your Scary Movie

Once all of your writing and planning work is done, you are ready to film your scary movie. Of course, depending on what you are doing, you'll want the actors to spend some time learning their lines and practicing. You can do this on a scene-by-scene basis, or you can rehearse the whole movie before you get started.

Once you are ready to record, use your storyboard and your script to guide you. However, I want to point out a big issue that you should get in your mind: When you use a camcorder, you often think of things in a linear fashion. In other words, you film what is happening at the moment, and the chronology creates the story (such as in the case of a birthday party). However, when you create a scary movie, or any other scripted movie, the chronology is part of the story, since you are not filming real action as it occurs.

Here's what all of that means: You don't have to film your movie in order; you need to think of the movie on a scene-by-scene basis instead of as one big picture. That said, using Movie Maker, you can create your clips and organize them into a chronological movie, but when you film, feel free to shoot the movie out of order. This may make things easier for you, since you can work on all of the scenes for one location and then move to another. In fact, this is how professional moviemakers work—they shoot the movie according to location, actor schedules, and other factors.

So get out of the habit of linear thinking and move to your storyboard. Then, shoot the movie in an order that is easy for you. Movie Maker enables you to shuffle the scenes around as needed, so shoot the movie in a scene-by-scene fashion. You'll have much less frustration if you do.

> **ROLL FILM** *What should you do if mistakes are made during a scene? No problem, just keep the film running and start over. Don't worry with backing up your camcorder take and filming over the bad scene. You can remove anything you don't like in Movie Maker anyway, so don't spend your filming time trying to edit on your camcorder. Use Movie Maker for that.*

Assemble Your Scary Movie in Movie Maker

Once your scary movie is filmed, it's time to go to Movie Maker and start assembling your movie. This is actually the fun (and easy) part of the process. The following sections walk you through the creation of your movie.

Import Your Video

The first thing you have to do is import your video into Movie Maker. Keep in mind that Movie Maker automatically creates clips for you, but you can adjust them as necessary. If you need help importing your video, see Appendix A for more information.

Create, Trim, and Combine Your Clips

The second task is to work with your clips. Get the clips trimmed up as needed, and you may even need to combine some of them. Use your storyboard to assemble the pieces of the movie into scene-by-scene chunks. You may even need to delete some clips that you don't want. If you need help with these tasks, see Appendix A.

Drag Clips to the Storyboard in Correct Order

Next, you actually assemble your movie on your storyboard and get the order correct. Again, think in terms of your original script and paper storyboard to create the actual movie storyboard. See Appendix A if you need extra help.

Create a Title Page and End Credits

It's easy to create a title page and end credits, which are nice touches. You can find out more about these elements in Chapter 10. Movie Maker can help you create these quickly, and you are free to create JPEG images for your title pages using an image-editing program such as Photoshop Elements. You can then import the images to your movie and drag them to the Storyboard. See Appendix A for more information.

Add Transitions and Effects

Windows Movie Maker contains basic transitions that you can put between your scenes. However, for your movie, transitions are ineffective except when the movie is going to a different physical location. For example, in my previous example of teens going to a haunted house, you can use a transition when the teens are leaving the haunted house, but as a general rule, I wouldn't use transitions between different scenes at the haunted house. This makes the movie look a bit choppy, so just because you can use transitions doesn't mean you should. Think carefully about the flow of the movie and use a critical eye.

One thing that you can do with Movie Maker that can enhance your scary movie is apply some effects to some of your scenes. In Movie Maker, under Edit Movie in the Movie Tasks pane, click the View Video Effects link. In the collections area, you'll see a listing of possible effects (see Figure 11-1). You can also get additional effects by purchasing and installing Microsoft Plus! Windows XP. You can download even more additional ones for free from www.microsoft.com/windowsxp/moviemaker.

FIGURE 11-1   Previewing movie effects

Not all of the effects will help with your scary movie, but there are some that can enhance certain scenes that you may wish to use. For example, Figure 11-2 shows a standard clip of my niece hanging upside-down from some monkey bars.

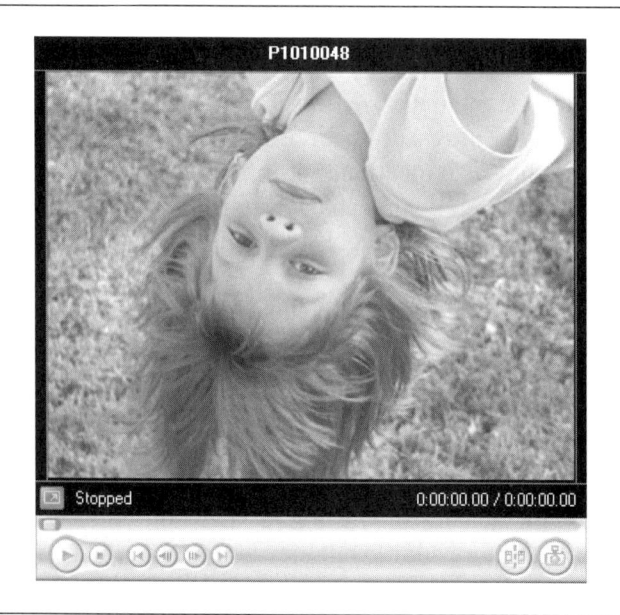

FIGURE 11-2   Here's a photo without any effects.

CHAPTER 11: Make a Scary Movie!

There's nothing scary here, of course, but let me show you what happens when I apply some different video effects to the scene. The following figures give you some examples, and again, you may not have all of these options if you don't have the Microsoft Plus! Windows XP software installed. However, the following images give you a good look at just how an effect can change the mood, tone, and look of a scene.

Use the Blur effect to make things a bit hazier and even spooky looking (see Figure 11-3).

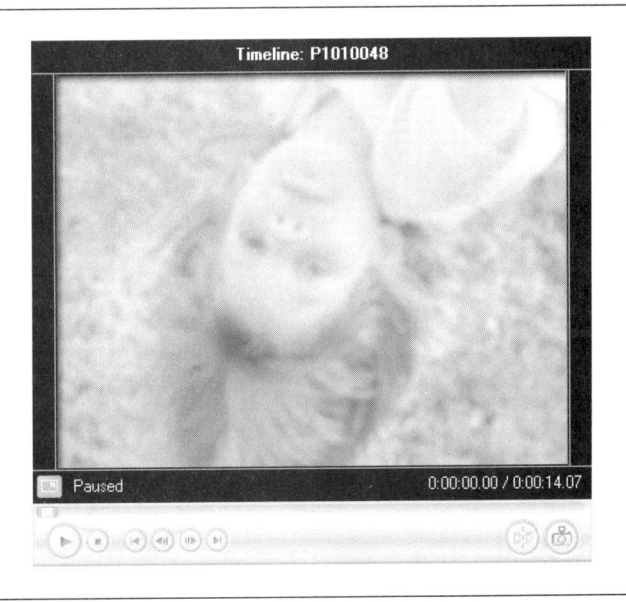

Use the Hue Spectrum effect to mix blues and reds into the film, which can give you a spooky look (see Figure 11-4).

The Plus! Color Warp effect also mixes in strong colors for odd and eerie effects (see Figure 11-5).

The Plus! Exotic Colors effect completely changes the look of the film (see Figure 11-6).

The Plus! Negative effect can be really effective (see Figure 11-7). It creates a negative film effect, which makes eyes glow and look really spooky!

The Plus! Texture effect can give shots an odd, textured sort of look (see Figure 11-8).

You'll also find some effect options to slow down or speed up the video. The slow-down effect can be great for slow motion during a quick action scene. As you can imagine, you have several options here to turn shots into something more interesting. You can even decrease or increase the brightness of film for added interest using the effects.

FIGURE 11-3   Blur effect

FIGURE 11-4 Hue Spectrum effect

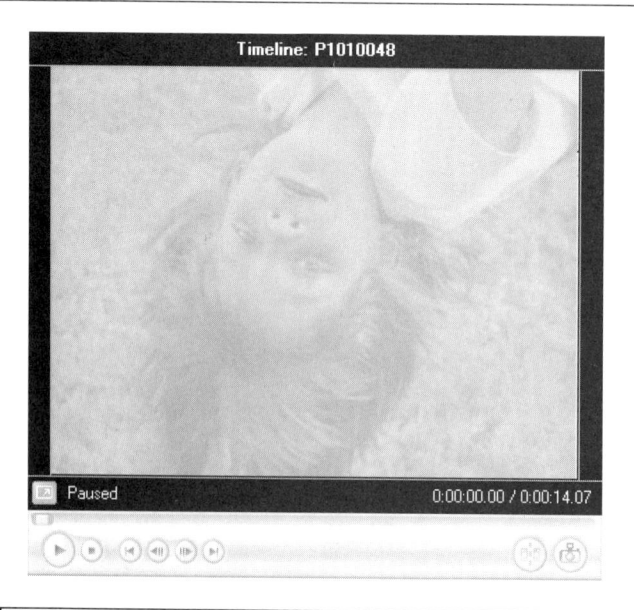

FIGURE 11-5 Plus! Color Warp effect

CHAPTER 11: Make a Scary Movie! **193**

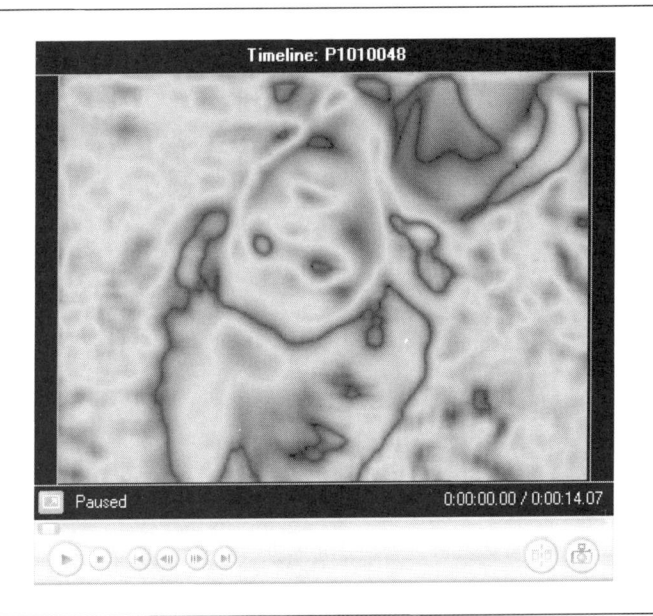

FIGURE 11-6 Plus! Exotic Colors effect

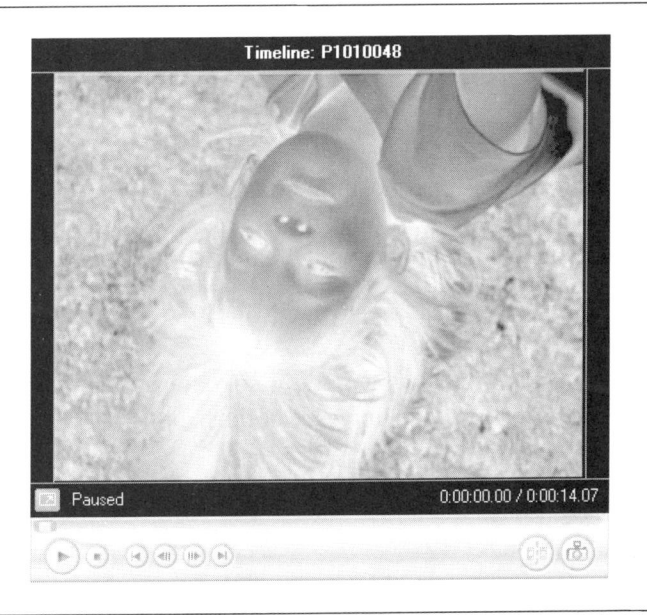

FIGURE 11-7 Plus! Negative effect

FIGURE 11-8 Plus! Texture effect

To use a video effect, all you have to do is simply drag it to the desired clip. Then, press Play in the monitor window to see how it looks. If you don't like the effect, just click Edit | Remove Effect.

Add Your Sound Track

As I mentioned earlier, one of the most important parts of your movie is the sound track, so you'll certainly want to spend some time working on it. See Chapter 13, which tells you all you need to know about creating effective sound tracks.

Save Your Movie

Movie Maker gives you several saving options so you can save the movie in a way that is useful to you. Chapter 14 explores all of those options.

More Great Ideas

Here are a few fun ideas to consider:

CHAPTER 11: Make a Scary Movie!

- Use your kids to make a fun and scary movie, and then have their friends over to watch it. Not only is this fun, but it will be a great keepsake, as well.

- Don't forget about scary-movie spoofs using your existing video. They can be a lot of fun, so get creative!

- Making movies can be a great family project. What else are you going to do a on a rainy Saturday?

Chapter 12

Step Back in Time and Create Movies That Look Like the Old Days

How to…

- Make an old movie
- Use Movie Maker to add old effects

My first introduction to home video came when I was around six years old. My parents had one of those old Super 8 silent video cameras. As best I can remember, my mother splurged and bought it when she was going to Hawaii to meet my dad, who was on furlough from the Vietnam War.

That old camera followed us, as a family, around for years, and we still have an old Super 8 projector in the closet on which we watch those old silent reel-to-reel movies from time to time. Ah, nostalgia.

Of course, in today's digital age, we have come a long way. Even the lowest-end camcorders produce great results, but what if you want one of your movies to look old? What if you want it to look *really* old, like a black-and-white, aged, silent film? Well, you can, and in this chapter, you'll see just how to have some fun with your modern movies by making them look old!

What You'll Need

All you need for this project is Movie Maker 2 and some movie footage you want to work with.

Why Old Movies Are Fun (and Why You Should Make One)

If you are reading this chapter and thinking, "This is sort of strange. Why would I want to make a movie look old?" then you have asked the right question. In truth, there is no benefit of making a movie look old except for some added effects. In other words, making a movie look like it was filmed in the old days is simply a fun way to play around with Movie Maker and have some fun with your existing video.

However, let me contradict myself—there's another benefit. Old movies can also be a great exercise for you, the movie producer, since there are a number of ways they can be fun to use. Just consider these ideas as you move forward:

CHAPTER 12: Step Back in Time and Create Movies That Look Like the Old Days

- Have some friends get together and create a movie script that is supposed to be from the old days. You'll need to choose your time period, dress in costume, and ensure that the props around you are in period. Remember, old movies are silent movies (if you want), so you'll need to think carefully about your silent script. This is a fun way to stretch your imagination and create something really neat.

- One of the great ways in which you can use old movies is to spoof some event. Gather that family reunion footage or holiday footage and make it look like it took place in 1920. This can be a fun way to create a memorable and fun spoof that you can share with friends and family.

- You can also turn a portion of a movie into an old-looking clip for some special effect. Let's say you are creating a video genealogy of your family. You have someone act out Uncle Claude, who came to America in 1890. You can then take that acted clip and make it look old, but you don't have to apply the effects to the other clips in your movie. As you can see, you can apply the old effect to certain clips or even photos that you import without having to change your entire movie.

Understand Old-Movie Basics

Before you grab a movie clip and make it look old, there are a few quick basics of old movies that you should know to make your movie look realistic. First, really old movies are silent, of course. So, one of the first things you may want to do to make your movie look old is remove the sound track in Movie Maker. I'll show you how to do that in the next section, but keep in mind that this is an exercise in creativity. You can bend the history rules a bit and keep the sound track if you want, so the choice is up to you. The point to remember is that old movies really should be silent for full effect. You can even add dialogue cards into your movie, as the old movies used to do.

Next, old movies were filmed in black and white. A major trick in making a movie look old is to simply turn it into a black-and-white movie. Again, no problem, because Movie Maker can do this for you with just a few mouse clicks.

However, if you really want your movie to look old, you can add some yellowing effects and even film-noise effects. The end result is a movie that looks sort of old and beat up—and, once again, Movie Maker can do this for you rather easily.

So, are you ready to get started? Then grab a movie, warm up Windows XP, and let's step back in time!

Make Your Old Movie

Making a movie look old simply involves a series of steps where you apply certain techniques in Movie Maker. The following sections walk you through these techniques, after which you'll be an old-movie pro. It's a good idea to take this book to your computer, then simply read along and perform the procedures in Movie Maker. In a few minutes, you'll have an old-looking movie clip!

Import Your Movie

The first thing you need to do is import the movie clip that you want to work with into Movie Maker. Spend some time cleaning up the clip, such as trimming it or doing any other tidying that you might need to do. See Appendix A for more details about these common and simple tasks.

Remove the Movie Sound Track

As mentioned previously, old movies had no sound, of course, but you may want to keep the sound in your movie and bend the rules of time a bit. That's fine, so if you don't want to remove the movie sound track, just skip to the next section.

But if you do want to cut the sound from your clip, start by knowing that the movie sound track refers to the original sound that you captured with your camcorder. This includes dialogue, any background noise, music, and so forth. When you import your movie, Movie Maker splits the video from the audio so you can work with them separately and, in this case, remove the original sound track all together.

Follow these steps to remove the movie sound track:

1. In Movie Maker, drag your clips to the storyboard in the desired order. If you are working with only one clip, then just drag it to the storyboard.

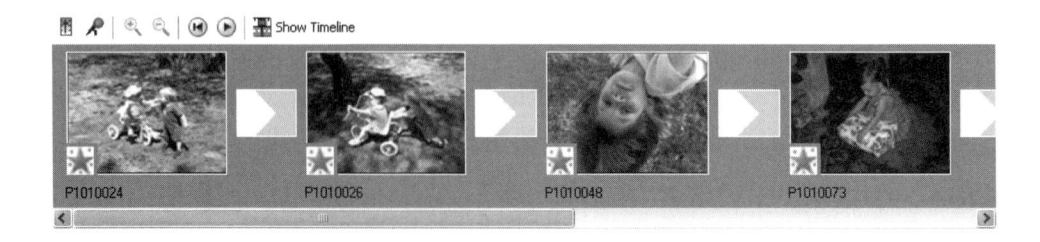

2. Click the Show Timeline button.

CHAPTER 12: Step Back in Time and Create Movies That Look Like the Old Days   201

3. On the Timeline, click the Audio/Music button. You'll see the movie's sound track as a block on the Timeline.

4. Right-click the soundtrack and click Delete. That's it—your movie soundtrack is gone!

Turn the Movie to Black and White

Your next task is to turn the movie to black and white. You do this on a clip-by-clip basis, which puts you in the driver's seat. In reality, turning a clip to black and white is done by simply applying an effect, and the following steps show you how:

1. Go to Storyboard view and, in the Movie Tasks pane, click the View Video Effects link.

2. Scroll through the video effects and find the one called Grayscale.

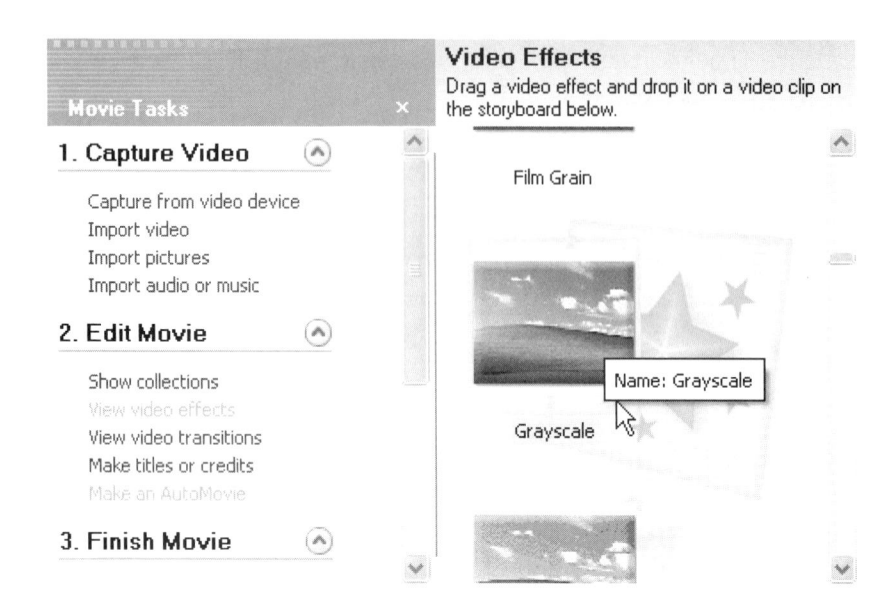

3. Drag the Grayscale effect to the Effects well on the desired clip (it's the star in the lower-left corner of the clip on the storyboard). The clip turns into a grayscale clip.

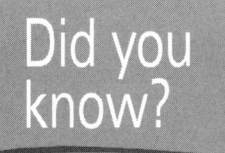

CHAPTER 12: Step Back in Time and Create Movies That Look Like the Old Days

Did you know?

Other Sound Options

It's important to think outside of the box when you work with sound on your movie. Aside from simply removing the original movie sound track, you can also add narration to the movie clip, or put in some old scratchy music, which also can be a cool effect. You can even do a combination of these. Since working with sound provides you with several different options, I've devoted Chapter 13 solely to working with sound. So, check out that chapter to learn about additional options before you make any final decisions.

Add Aging Effects

You can use Movie Maker to add a few different levels of aging effects to your movie. These effects provide video noise that resembles the kinds of screen anomalies you are likely to see when you watch an old movie. They are simple video effects that you apply in the same way you applied the grayscale effect.

You have three aging options:

- Film Age, Old
- Film Age, Older
- Film Age, Oldest

The first level applies some speckle effects to the film (see Figure 12-1).

The second level of age effect provides speckle effects but also adds jumps in the film and film lines (see Figure 12-2).

The last age-effect option turns the film to black and white and makes it very jumpy with a lot of film noise (see Figure 12-3). This effect is cool, but it makes the video sort of difficult to see. Use this if you really want the film to look very old, but as a general rule, the first two film options work a bit better.

To use the effect, just click View Video Effects in the Movie Tasks pane, and then drag the desired effect to your clip. Don't forget to click Play in the monitor area

FIGURE 12-1 Film Age, Old

to see the effect in action with your clip. Don't like what you see? Just right-click the Effects Well on the clip, click Delete Effects to remove them, and then experiment with other effects.

FIGURE 12-2 Film Age, Older

CHAPTER 12: Step Back in Time and Create Movies That Look Like the Old Days **205**

FIGURE 12-3 Film Age, Oldest

Create Cue Cards Between Clips

You can easily create titles for your movies, as explored in Chapter 10, but you also create title cue cards that you drag to the storyboard between each clip. This creates those narration cards that you sometimes see in old movies. This is a lot of fun and a great way to enhance your movie, and the cool thing is you can also add the old film effects to the cue card as well so that everything looks seamless in the movie. Just follow these steps:

1. In Movie Maker, select the clip on the storyboard in front of which you want to display a cue card.

2. In the Movie Tasks pane under Edit Movie, click Make Titles Or Credits.

3. In the title window, click the Add Title Before The Selected Clip On The Storyboard link.

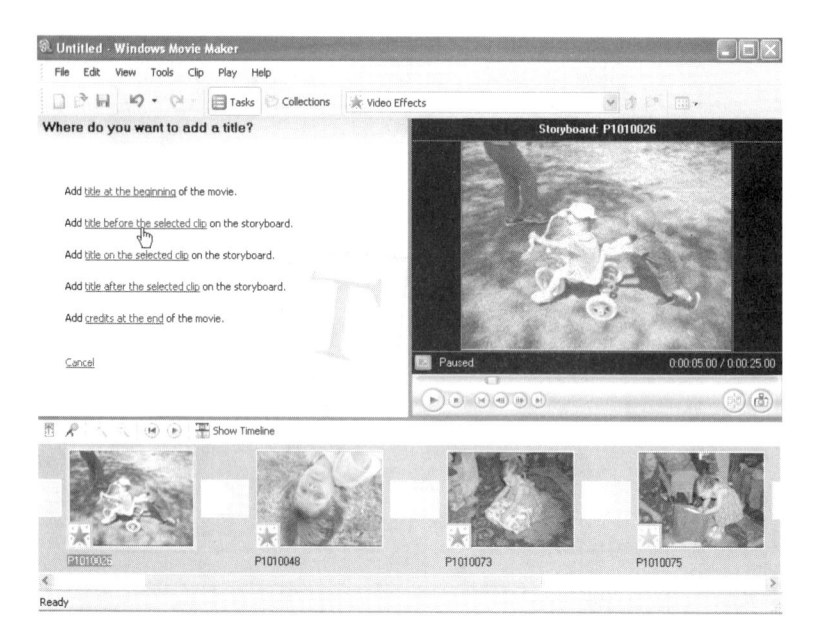

4. Enter the text for the title, which will serve as your cue card. Remember to keep it short and easy to read.

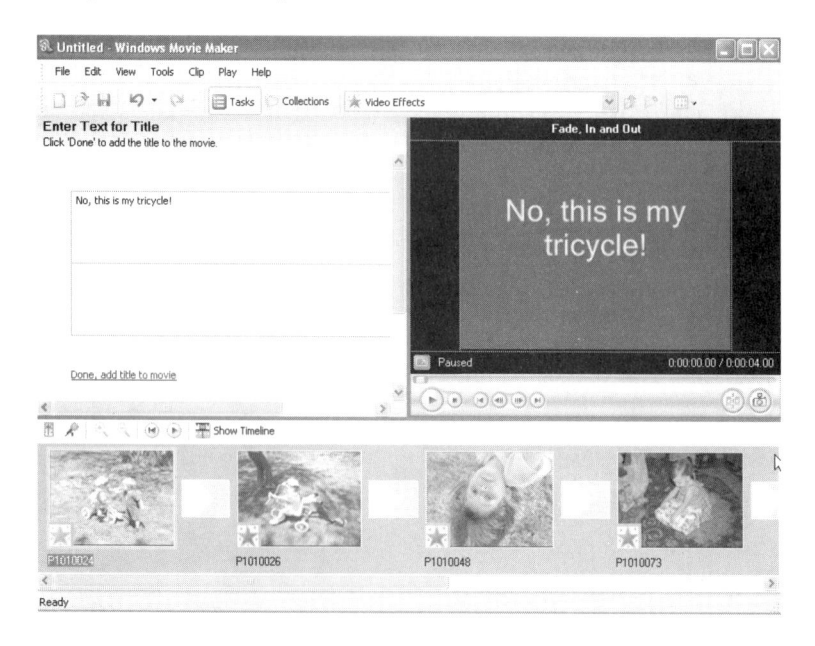

5. Click Done, Add Title To Movie. The cue card now appears in front of the clip.

6. Now, add the same old-age effects you used with your movie clip, and you end up with an old-looking cue card!

Save and Use Your Movie

Once you have made your old movie, you are ready to save it and use it in a way that works for you. See Chapter 14 for all the pertinent details.

More Great Ideas

Here are a few fun ideas to consider:

- Have your kids dress up like the olden days and make a fun movie. This a great project for a rainy day!
- Make a spoof of your last family get-together. Don't forget to include funny cue cards!
- Add some old music to your movie to get a really fun effect. See Chapter 13 to learn more!

Chapter 13

Build a Custom Video Sound Track

How to...

- Plan sound tracks
- Mute original sound tracks
- Make custom sound tracks with dialogue, background music, and other sound effects

If you stop and think about it, sound has a lot to do with movies. We tend to think of movies as a "visual" experience, but when was the last time you went to see a movie that did not have background music and special sound effects, not to mention dialogue from the actors? In truth, often we do not pay direct attention to the sound in a movie. We are caught up in the whole movie-going experience. The last time you saw an exciting car chase at the theater, you didn't think about the swelling music in the background, but it did add greatly to your whole experience watching the movie.

The good news is Windows Movie Maker allows you to add to the whole experience of watching *your* movies. If you made the birthday or wedding video that we explored in Chapter 10, or the scary movie in Chapter 11, you quickly discovered that you need a good sound track to make those movies all they can be. In this chapter, you'll see just how to create a sound track for any Movie Maker film that you want to create.

What You'll Need

For this project, you'll need Microsoft Windows Movie Maker 2. If your system has Microsoft Movie Maker 1, visit www.microsoft.com/windowsxp for more information about downloading Movie Maker 2. You'll also need some wedding/birthday video and/or photos.

Know the Basics: Sound Tracks 101

Before we get into Movie Maker and start creating your sound track, you should take a few moments and read this section to get an overall perspective of sound tracks and how they work. Don't worry, I'm not going to ramble on for pages and pages about sound track philosophy or anything like that, but you'll need to get a few concepts in your mind about how Movie Maker handles sound tracks and how you should use them.

Sound and Movie Maker

A sound track should always go along with the actual video sequence of events. In Movie Maker, you have the option to simply use the sound track from your original video clips, which Movie Maker calls the "video sound track." For example, let's say that you videotape a wedding ceremony. Since you have recorded the actual ceremony, you'll want the original movie track included in your wedding video. That's easy, since Movie Maker automatically imports it along with the video. In this case, you'll leave your video clips in the correct order, and the sound track will simply play along with them.

However, you may have video where you want to lose the sound track all together. Let's say you took some great video at a family reunion. The original video sound track has all of the standard background noise you might expect to find at a family reunion. However, you want to get rid of that video sound track and record narration for the movie. No problem—Movie Maker will enable you to do that.

Or, you may have a video sound track that you want to keep but you also want to interject some narration here and there. Or, maybe you want to add some background music. No problem, these tasks are easy with Movie Maker.

Now, if you have made a real film, such as a scary movie in Chapter 11, you'll want to use the actor dialogue, add some background music for effect, and you may even need to throw in some sound effects. Once again, you can use Movie Maker to put all of these items together in your movie with just a little work.

It is important to realize that Movie Maker looks at music and sound just as it does video—after all, they are all digital files, and Movie Maker doesn't care what you use in your movie. The task is completely up to you, once you understand how to put all of these items in your movie.

How You Should Use Sound in Your Movie

As you just read, Movie Maker gives you quite a bit of flexibility with sound. So, how should you use sound in your movie? What are the do's and don'ts of using sound? Well, there are a few rules you should keep in mind to ensure that you get quality sound in your movie:

- **The Rule of Simplicity** You have several different options with Movie Maker, but remember to keep it simple. You can use the original video sound track, or you can add your own narration, background music, and even special sound effects. However, just because you can doesn't mean you should. Sound tracks can easily get overcrowded and "junky," if you will, so it is important to think carefully about what you're doing. Just like Movie Maker transitions, too much variety tends to overcrowd the sound track, and an overcrowded sound track will really get on people's nerves and detract from the movie.

- **The Rule of Enhancement** Watching a movie is a visual and auditory experience. However, the visual portion of the movie should always be in the foreground, while background music and other effects should enhance the visual effect and the dialogue or narration (if you use them). In other words, don't get sound happy! Make sure that any sound you use backs up—not detracts from—the visual part of the movie. This is where your critical eye (and ear!) will make all the difference in your final movie project.

- **The Rule of Combinations** To use a simile, a sound track is a lot like an outfit: The different pieces of the outfit have to look right together in order for you to look good in the outfit. The same is true for movie sound tracks. The combinations of items that you use must match up with what's happening in the video. For example, if you wanted to add background music to a wedding reception, something classical and elegant will most likely be a better choice than your favorite rock-and-roll hit (unless the wedding has a rock-and-roll theme—hey, stranger things have happened). The point is simply this: The items on your sound track must fit together naturally. The background music and narration must go along with the theme of the video and overall mood of the event. Let common sense dictate which sound features work in your movie and which ones do not.

- **The Rule of Storytelling** A final point to remember is that a movie is a story. A movie, regardless of the kind of movie, is designed to tell the viewer about something. As such, the sound track needs to aid in that story and enhance it. As you work on movies, it is really easy to get bogged down in the details of the matter, but be sure you always keep that "storytelling umbrella" above your head. Let the overall big picture guide your decisions in all that you do.

Now that we have taken a look at some preliminary issues, let's get started! In the following sections, you'll see just how to plan your sound track and use the sound track creation features that Movie Maker gives you.

Plan Your Sound Track

Planning is one of those things we never like to do, but as you have seen in previous chapters, it is probably one of the most important steps in movie creation. After all, with the right plans, you can see the movie you want come to life. Without good planning, you usually end up with a movie that doesn't look the way you want, and you say things like, "Oh, I wish I had…"

Let's avoid that from the very start by planning a bit first. Just as you had to plan out the video portion of your movie, you really need to plan out exactly what you want to do with the sound track before you move forward. Depending on what you want to do, a sound track may be made up of several items all working together. Like building a house, you need a plan to work from; otherwise, things will get confusing in a hurry, so please don't skip over this section!

Okay, the easiest way to plan your sound track is to think about the overall goal of your movie and what you want to accomplish. Think about the theme of the movie, the style, and how you want the sound track to enhance the visual part of your movie. If you are creating a wedding video, you may think in terms of "classy" and "beautiful." In this case, you may wish to include the original video track, along with some added music playing softly in the background for effect. If you are creating a child's birthday video, you may want to include the original movie sound track but also mix in some narration so you can point out funny things that happened. And you may want to include some fun, kid-friendly music in the background during certain parts of the movie to liven it up.

If you are creating an actual acted movie (such as a scary movie; see Chapter 11), you'll want to include dialogue, of course, but you'll also want to think carefully about adding in scary music and even some sound effects (screaming, groaning noises, and so on) in just the right places.

As you can see, depending on your movie, you may have many different things to think about, and it is important to plan all of those items before you move forward.

Did you know?

But I want only the original sound track!

If you are reading this chapter and starting to get worried, don't. Maybe you want to use only the original video sound track from your camcorder. Maybe you have filmed a wedding ceremony and you want to remember it exactly as it looked and sounded without any tampering. That is certainly no crime, and there are plenty of examples of video that you should not tamper with in order to keep them as true memories of the times.

So, if you only want to use the original video sound track without any additions or changes, what do you need to do? Nothing, that's what! When you imported your video, the original video sound track was imported with the video clips. When you drag those clips to the storyboard, the original sound track is automatically included. If it's the original sound track that you want and nothing more, then your work here is already done automatically by Movie Maker!

So, how should you plan your movie sound track? The easiest way is to create a storyboard for it. A storyboard is simply a sketch you make on a piece of paper that outlines what you want to do. It contains the different clips you have placed on the Movie Maker storyboard, and you simply add notes about what sound effects, background music, narration, and so forth goes where. You can then use this storyboard as a working guide in order to keep things straight in Movie Maker as you are assembling your movie.

Figure 13-1 shows you a sample of a storyboard that I created for the birthday video that I made in Chapter 10. As you can see in Figure 13-1, I created boxes with quick notes to tell me what is on each clip in Movie Maker (and in order), and then I created sound notes beside each clip to help me keep everything straight. As you can see, in some parts of the storyboard, I have several different sound items running at once. This is why the storyboard can be really helpful—otherwise, your sound track can turn to chaos in Movie Maker, because the different sound elements can get really confusing when you start putting them together.

You can use Figure 13-1 as a model, but this is not an exact science. Just create the storyboard in a way that makes sense to you. After all, it is just a blueprint to help you get to your final product.

> **TIP** *It is really important that you keep the overall movie in mind as you make your storyboard. As you are adding in sound track pieces, try to visualize and imagine how the movie will look and sound. Then, ask yourself if the storyboard is really giving you the end product that you want. Now is the time to experiment and make changes—on paper—before you start working in Movie Maker.*

Mute the Original Movie Sound Track

As I mentioned earlier, Movie Maker automatically imports your movie track along with your movie clips. Once you assemble your movie clips on Movie Maker's storyboard, the movie track is already embedded into the movie. If this is what you want, then there is nothing else for you to do.

However, what if this is *not* what you want. What if you took some great video at a family reunion, but there is a bunch of muffled background noise due to all of the talking? What if you want to lose that movie track altogether and simply provide narration, or even music without any narration? In this case, what you want to do is mute the movie sound track. You can't actually remove the movie sound track, because it is interlaced with your video, but you can mute it and simply replace it with something else so that the original movie sound track isn't heard.

CHAPTER 13: Build a Custom Video Sound Track

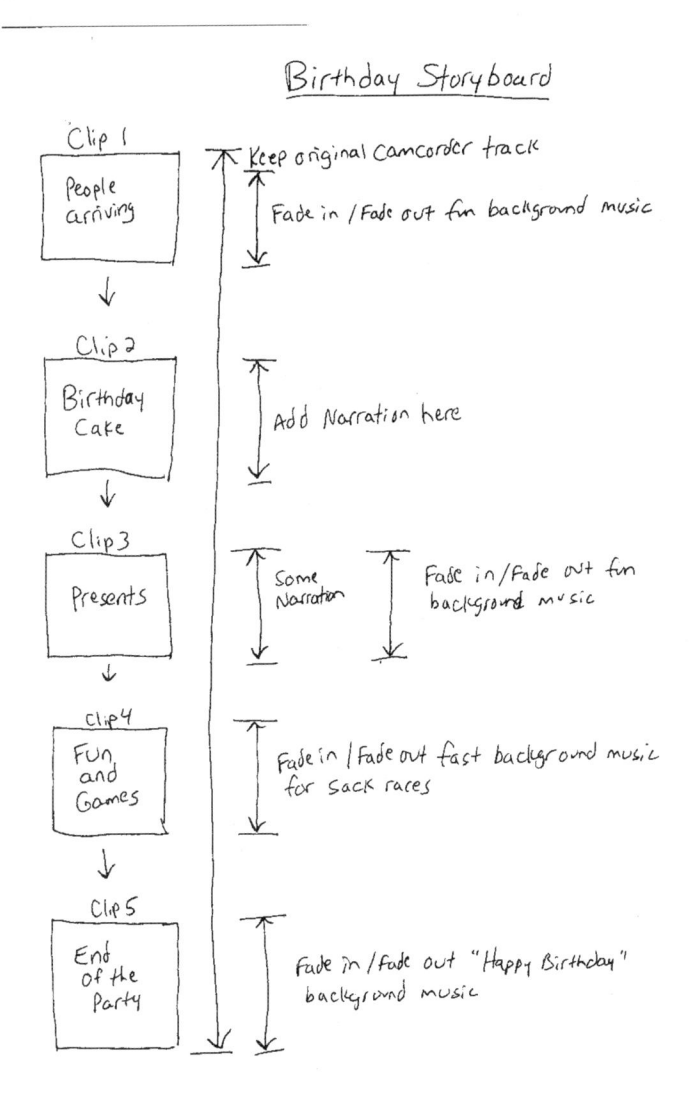

Birthday Storyboard

- **Clip 1 — People arriving**
  - Keep original camcorder track
  - Fade in/Fade out fun background music

- **Clip 2 — Birthday Cake**
  - Add Narration here

- **Clip 3 — Presents**
  - Some Narration
  - Fade in/Fade out fun background music

- **Clip 4 — Fun and Games**
  - Fade in/Fade out fast background music for sack races

- **Clip 5 — End of the Party**
  - Fade in/Fade out "Happy Birthday" background music

FIGURE 13-1 Create your own storyboard to outline your sound items before you start working in Movie Maker.

You can mute any existing movie sound track by muting each individual clip in your movie. Since you work with movies on a clip-by-clip basis, you can't mute the entire movie sound track at once; you have to mute the clips one at a time.

To mute an audio clip, you'll need to access Timeline view. First, open Movie Maker and open the desired project. On the Storyboard, in the bottom portion of the interface, click the Show Timeline button (see Figure 13-2).

Once you click Show Timeline, the Storyboard view changes to Timeline view (see Figure 13-3).

To mute the audio track for an individual clip, you have two different options (that do the same thing):

- Click the clip on the Timeline to select it, and then click Clip | Audio | Mute.

Or

- Click the plus sign (+) next to Video to expand it. As shown in Figure 13-4, you can see your transition areas and an existing video sound track. To mute the sound track for a clip, just right-click it and click Mute.

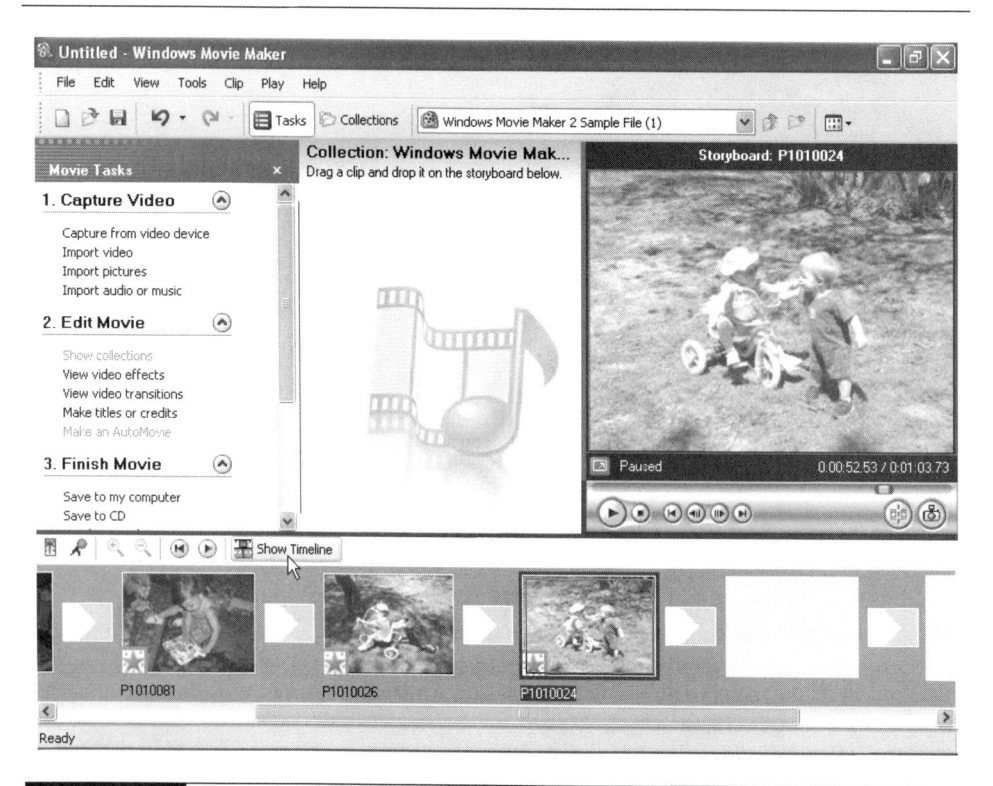

FIGURE 13-2 Click the Show Timeline button.

CHAPTER 13: Build a Custom Video Sound Track 217

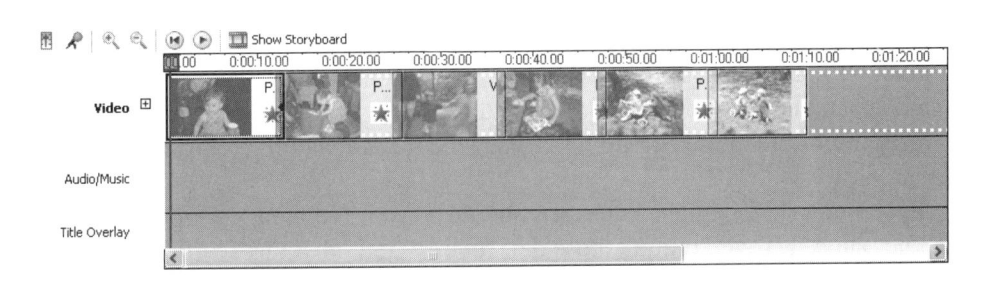

FIGURE 13-3 Timeline view

At this point, the original audio track is muted on the desired clip. Repeat this process to mute the audio track on other clips as desired.

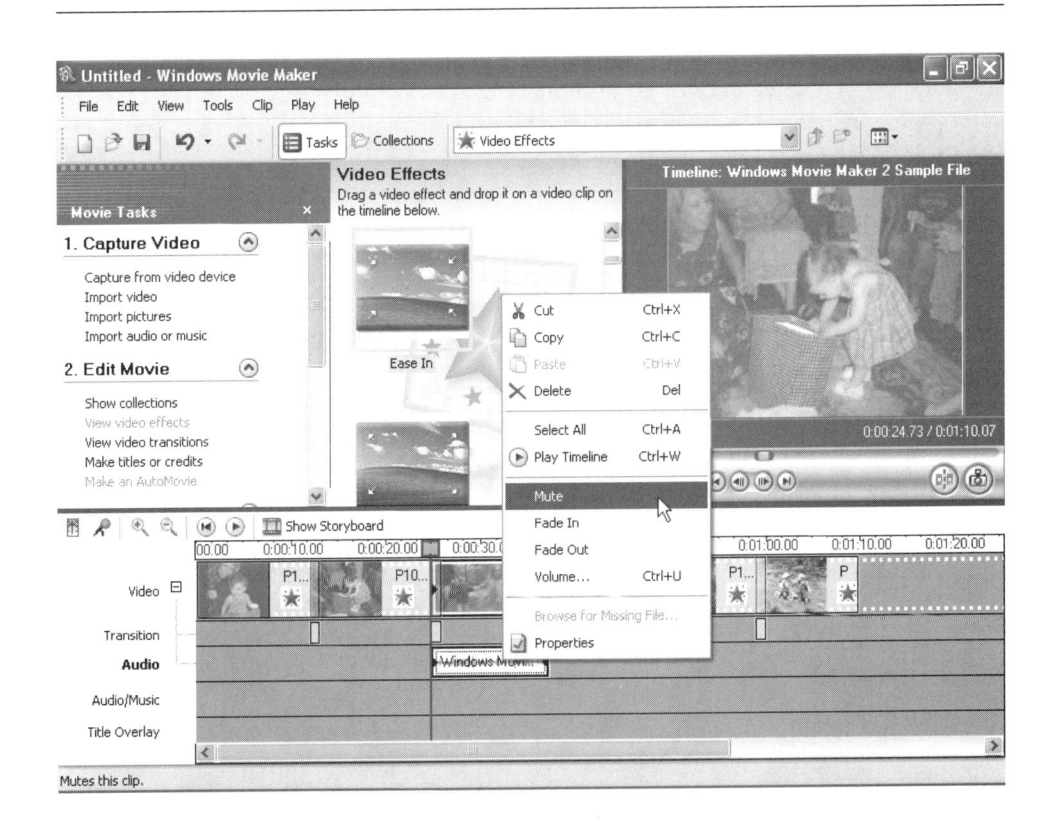

FIGURE 13-4 Right-click the sound track and click Mute in Expanded view.

Record Dialogue

In order to record dialogue, your computer will have to be outfitted with a microphone, of course, and in Movie Maker, you record narration on a track-by-track basis, or you simply start at the beginning of your movie and play it, recording narration as you like.

First things first, though: You really should consider creating a script to read for your narration. This will prevent those dull "umms" and "ahs" that so often accompany unscripted speech. Think carefully about what you want to say, make it interesting, and write it down before you get started. Refer to the storyboard that you sketched to help you with the narration.

To record your narration, get your microphone ready, open Movie Maker, open the desired movie, and go to Timeline view. Click the microphone button, as shown in Figure 13-5.

This action changes the upper portion of the interface to a narration feature, as you can see in Figure 13-6. First, notice the microphone input slider. Talk into your microphone and watch the indicator bar. You want your voice input to peak out in the upper green area but not go into the red. You can adjust the volume of your microphone by using the slider bar. Keep talking and adjust the slider bar until the narration falls primarily in the green range.

Next, click the Show More Options link. You'll see a few additional options, as shown in Figure 13-7. Here's what they mean:

- **Narration Captured**   The time elapsed for the current audio narration in hours, minutes, and seconds. Since you haven't captured any narration yet, the values are set to zero.

- **Time Available**   The available amount of time for audio narration when you use the Limit Narration To Available Free Space On Audio/Music Track option.

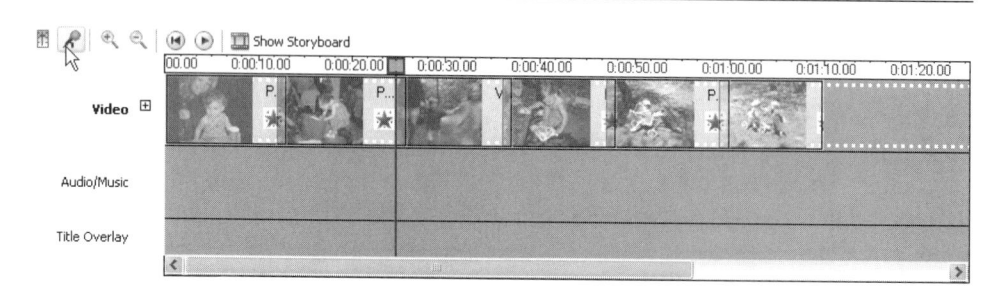

FIGURE 13-5   Click the microphone button to begin recording dialogue.

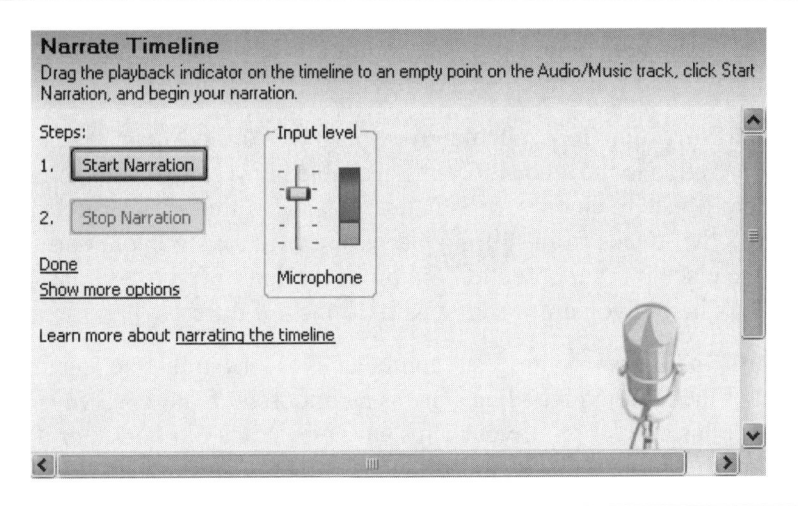

FIGURE 13-6 The narration area

- **Audio Device** The audio device (your sound card) that is used for capturing. You don't need to do anything here unless you have multiple sound cards on your computer and need to select an alternate.

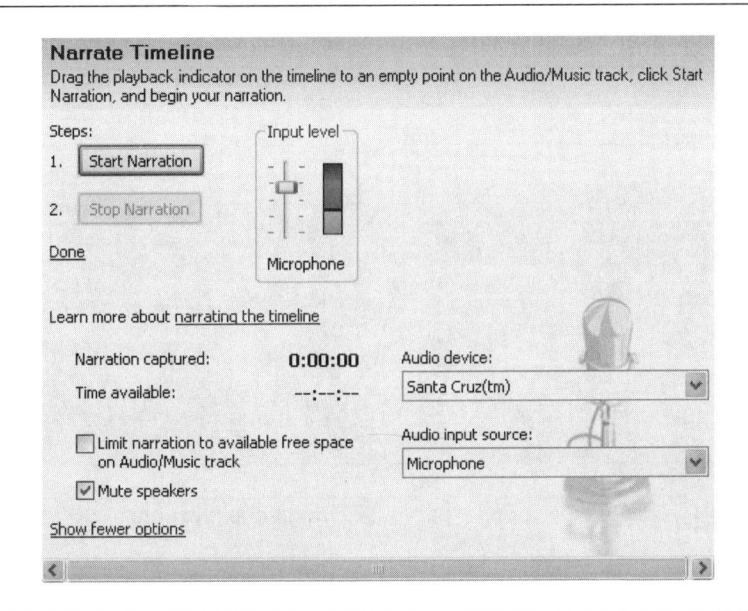

FIGURE 13-7 More narration options

- **Audio Input Source** The microphone you are using. You don't need to do anything here unless you have multiple microphones connected to your computer and want to select a different one.

- **Limit Narration To Available Free Space On Audio/Music Track** Limits the narration to the amount of time available between two audio clips on the Audio/Music track on your Timeline. Basically, this option offers a way to keep other tracks from shifting places and to make sure your narration fits in the place it is supposed to. You probably don't need to use this option, but it's here if you are working with a bunch of different narration clips.

- **Mute Speakers** Mutes your computer speakers so that no sound comes out of them during recoding. This is an important feature, so you should select this check box. If your clips have original audio tracks, or if you are using background music, those sounds will play during narration recording, which you don't want. You don't want any Windows sounds coming through during narration either, so be sure to select this option.

Once you are ready to record your narration, go back to the Timeline and drag the positioning bar to the beginning of the desired clip (see Figure 13-8). Keep in mind that you can drag the bar to the beginning of your movie and simply narrate the whole movie at one time, if you like.

Then, position your microphone, take a deep breath, and click the Record Narration button. Movie Maker begins playing your movie and recording your narration, as you can see in Figure 13-9. When you are done, click the Stop Narration button.

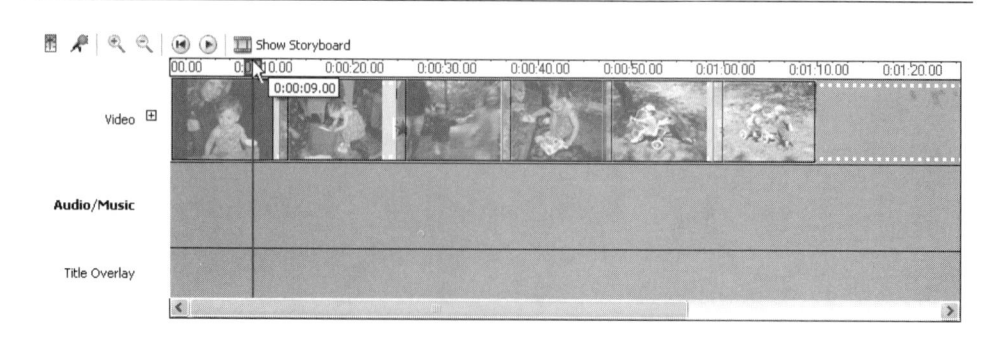

FIGURE 13-8   Drag the positioning bar to the correct clip location.

CHAPTER 13: Build a Custom Video Sound Track 221

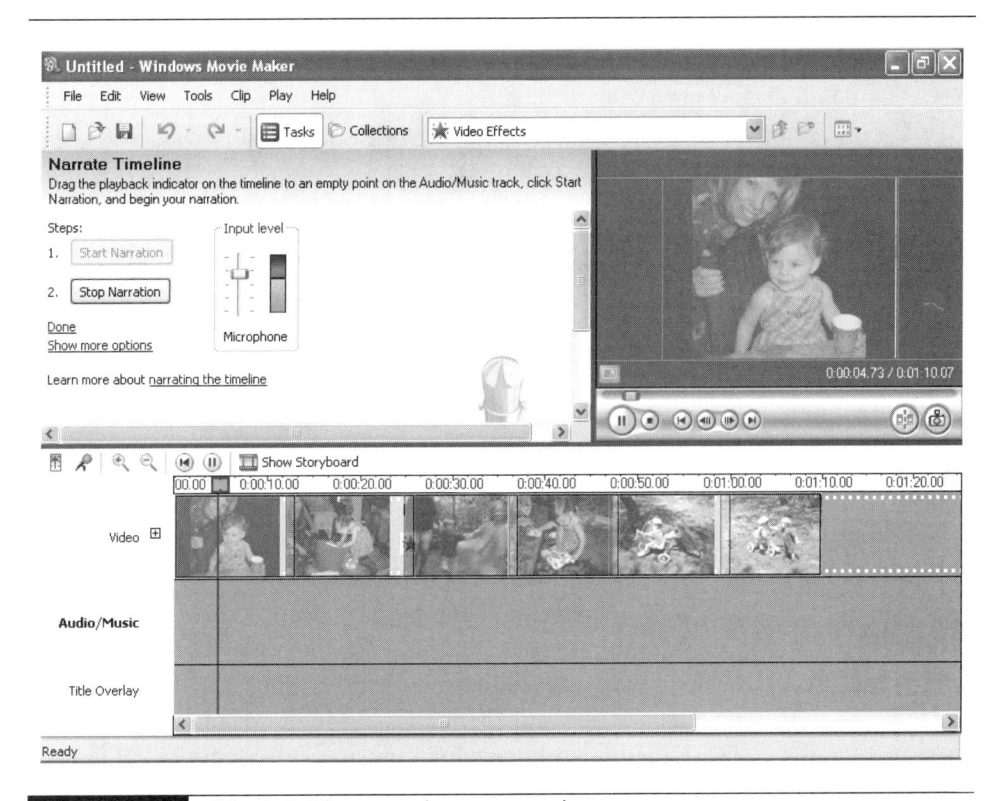

FIGURE 13-9 Movie Maker records your narration.

Then you'll be able to save the movie (a .WMA file), and Movie Maker will then import it to your Timeline, as shown in Figure 13-10.

Once you are done, repeat this process to add narration to any additional clips. Here are two more important notes on recording narration:

- Listen carefully to your narration to make sure that the quality is good and the narration falls in the right place. You can drag the narration blocks on the Timeline to move them around, if needed. To hear the narration played back when you play your movie, remember to clear the Mute Speakers check box in the Narrate Timeline window.

- You can have your clip fade in and out, and you can adjust the volume by simply right-clicking the clip and choosing the desired option.

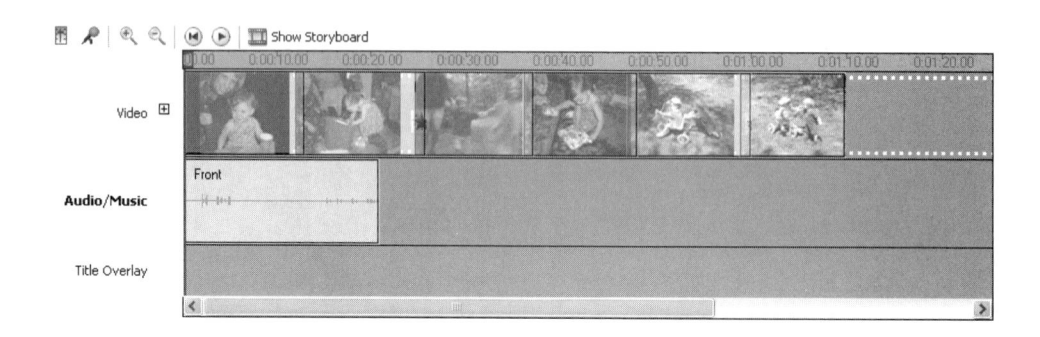

FIGURE 13-10 Your narration is imported to the Timeline.

Use Background Music

Adding background music to your movie is easy. When you add background music, you import a music file, just as you would a video file. Movie Maker automatically looks in your Windows Media Player library for a music file to import, so it is a good idea to import music to your Windows Media Library before proceeding (see Chapter 1).

When you import background music, you can adjust the volume so that it doesn't override your narration or original audio sound track from your camcorder. To use background music, follow these steps:

1. Go to Storyboard view to return to the Movie Tasks pane.

2. On the Movie Tasks pane, under Video Tasks, click Import Audio Or Music. This opens a standard Open window, where you can look for songs in Windows Media Player.

CHAPTER 13: Build a Custom Video Sound Track 223

3. Select a song and click Import.
4. Go back to Timeline view, and then simply drag the song from the clips area to the Audio/Music well.

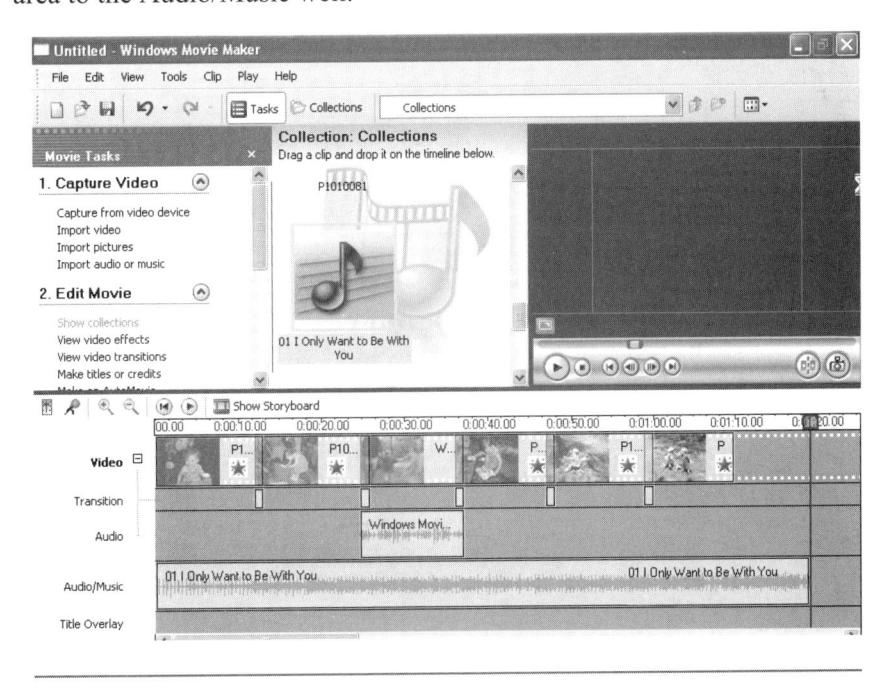

5. Drag the music clip as needed so that it fills in the desired space on the Timeline.

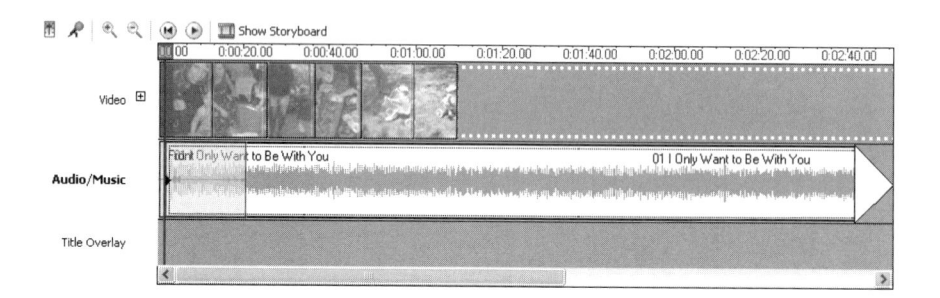

6. If you want the music to fade in or fade out, right-click the song and choose that option.

7. If the background music is too loud (or soft), right-click the music on the Timeline and click Volume. You can then adjust the volume.

TIP *Naturally, if you have narration and music running at the same time, you'll have to play around a bit with the volume of each to get the right balance.*

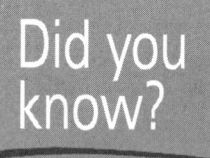

Did you know?

About Copyright...

Naturally, some of the sounds—such as music and even sound effects, which are explored in the next section—you use in your movie are copyrighted by other people. So, what copyright rules apply to you? Here's the deal: You can use music and sound effects in your movie, and you can share that movie with friends and family, but you can't sell your movie to other people if you are using copyrighted material without permission from the copyright owner. For home use, you're good to go, but if you are trying to make a movie to sell to other people, your music and sound effects must all be original.

Have Fun with Other Sound Effects

Movie Maker can work with any sound files (standard music and sound files, such as MP3s), so you are free to import all kinds of music, sound effects, or anything you like! Check out these sites to find some additional sound effects:

- **www.microsoft.com/windowsxp/moviemaker/downloads/create.asp** Get the free Movie Maker fun pack from Microsoft. It contains a bunch of extras, including some fun sound effects you can add to your movies.

- **www.sounddogs.coms** You can get your hands on loads of sound effect files here. There are even a bunch of haunted house effects, which will work great with your scary movie project from Chapter 11.

More Great Ideas

As you might imagine, you can do all kinds of things with Movie Maker sound tracks. Here are a few ideas for you:

- Add your favorite music to an anniversary video. Is the music old and on tape or vinyl? No problem! See Chapter 19 to learn how to digitize old cassettes and records with Windows XP.

- Get a bunch of sound effects and make a funny spoof of a family event. You can even add funny titles and effects!

- Record your children singing in Windows Movie Maker, then make a video of them for your parents as a holiday gift.

Chapter 14
Put Your Movie on a CD for Cannes, and More!

How to...

- Save Movie Maker movies
- Use movies on a CD, on the Web, in e-mail, and more

You have worked feverishly hard to make a perfect movie. You have used some of the tips and tricks in Chapters 10 through 13, and now you have put the finishing touches on your movie. Great! So now what can you do with it? Well, that depends on what you *want* to do with it. Luckily, Windows Movie Maker can help you get your movie ready for just about anything. In fact, using Movie Maker, you can save the movie to your computer, save it to a CD, send it in an e-mail message, send it to the Web, or send it back to a digital video (DV) camcorder and watch on your TV. There are lots of great options to meet your needs, and Movie Maker does all of the work for you. In this chapter, you'll see just how to do each of these things with your prized movie.

What You'll Need

For this project, you'll need Windows Movie Maker, a movie that you have created previously, and some CD-R discs. If you want to send a movie over e-mail or put it on a web site, you'll need Internet access. To find out more about downloading Movie Maker 2, see Appendix A.

Decide What to Do with Your Movie

Decisions, decisions. They seem to be a constant part of life, and doing things with your computer is no exception. But hey, decisions simply mean that you have options, which is always nice, and using Movie Maker, you have several different options concerning saving your movie. First of all, it is important to note that you can save a movie while you are creating it. This option saves the movie as a Movie Maker "project," which is what Movie Maker actually uses; this essentially means that only Movie Maker can open and use the file. That doesn't help you much when you want to share your movie with other people, so what you must do is save your movie in a more universal format.

As you might imagine, of the different save options you have, the quality of your movie will vary. Saving your movie to a CD so that others can watch it saves your movie with the best quality settings, but saving your movie so that you can e-mail it requires that Movie Maker shrink it a bit so that your e-mail recipient doesn't grow old before the movie is downloaded. With all of that said, you'll need to decide how you want to use your movie. Keep in mind that you can keep your movie project file and save it over and over again for different purposes, so the choice you make today concerning the saving of your movie is not a one-time decision. For example, you might save your movie for e-mail purposes now, but tomorrow you can simply go back to your movie project and save it for CD burning. That's good news, because you are not locked into one kind of format.

However, there is one negative caveat with Movie Maker, which I also rant about in Appendix A. Movie Maker does not support common movie file formats other than Windows' own internal file format. Forgetting the tech-speak, here's the deal: You must use Windows Media Player to watch the movie—all other media players need not apply. In other words, you can't save your movie as an AVI file so that any brand of media player can view it. The people with whom you share your movie must watch it in Media Player, and there is no direct workaround for this frustration.

So, before you move forward, decide how you want to use your movie for the moment. Then open Windows Movie Maker, and open the desired movie project. In this chapter, we'll explore the different ways you can save movies using Movie Maker. I'll use the birthday movie I created in Chapter 10, but you can pick any movie of your own that you want.

Save Your Movie to Your Computer

You can save your movie directly to a folder on your computer, where you can then watch the movie using Windows Media Player. The good news about saving your movie this way is you are free to watch it, or you can burn it directly to a CD any time you want. As a rule of precaution, I suggest that you save your movie this way so that you have a copy of it, and you can also back it up using Windows Backup or put it on a CD for safe keeping. You can never have enough copies of your movie that you took so much care and time to create!

To save your movie to your computer, in the Movie Tasks pane, simply click the Save To My Computer link under Finish Movie (see Figure 14-1).

If you like, you can also click File | Save Movie File to open a wizard window, as shown in Figure 14-2. Just click the option you want. Basically, this is the same thing as clicking the option you want in the Movie Tasks pane, but this takes an extra step.

FIGURE 14-1 Click Save To My Computer to save your movie to your computer.

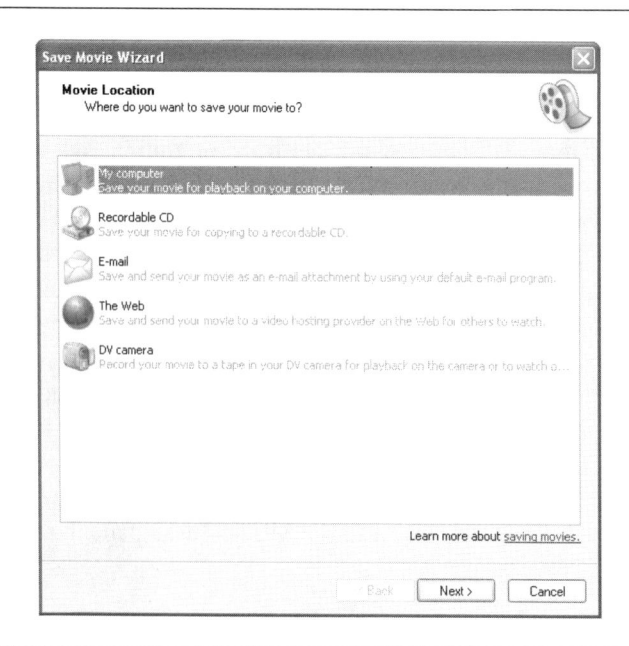

FIGURE 14-2 You can also use the selection window to choose how you want to save your movie.

Once you have chosen an option in the selection window, a wizard appears that guides you through the process of saving your movie. The following steps walk you through the wizard:

1. In the Saved Movie File window, enter a name for the movie (choose something friendly), and choose where you want to save it. Click the Browse button to pick a folder; you can save it directly to your desktop. Click Next when you're done.

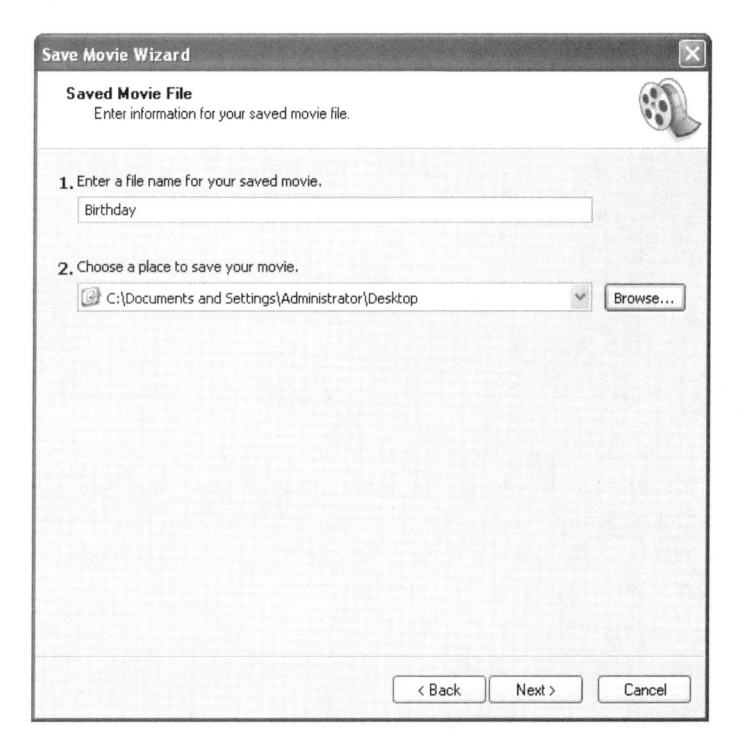

2. On the Movie Setting window, Movie Maker chooses the best-quality option to save your movie, by default. Notice the basic playback information about the movie at the bottom of the window as well as the size of the movie and how much disk space is available where you want to save it.

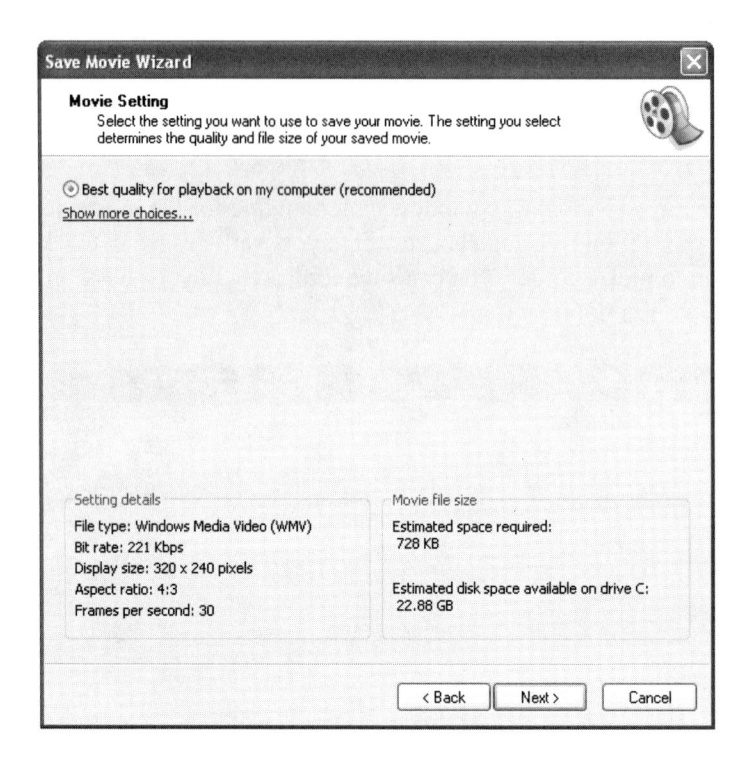

If you click the Show More Choices link, you can use the Movie Setting page that appears to specify the size of the file you want, and you can use the drop-down menu to customize how you want to save the movie. Generally, your best bet is to use the default setting because you probably want the highest quality available, considering the fact that you are saving locally to your computer.

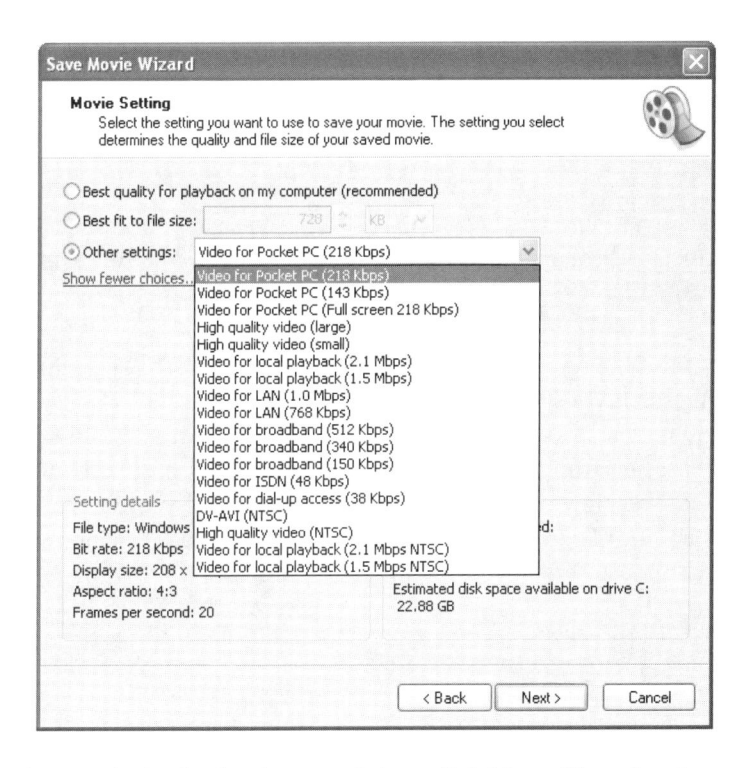

CHAPTER 14: Put Your Movie on a CD for Cannes, and More! **233**

3. Make any desired selections, and then click Next. The wizard saves your movie to the desired location.

Save Your Movie to a CD

One of the cool things you can do with your movie is save it to a CD. Actually, you can do this process over and over and create multiple CDs, which you can then share with your family and friends. Considering the inexpensive nature of CD-R discs these days, the option of saving to a CD is a great way to share those fun memories. Anyone with a computer that runs Windows Media Player can simply pop the CD into his or her CD drive and watch the movie. Combine this with the option to create custom CD labels (see Chapter 2) and you have a great birthday, anniversary, or other holiday gift for your friends and family!

To save your movie to a CD, start by inserting a CD-R disc into your computer's CD burner. Then just follow these steps:

1. In the Movie Tasks pane, click the Save To CD option under Finish Movie, or click File | Save Movie File and choose to save the movie to a CD.

Did you know?
Problems Saving Movies

If you get an error message when you are trying to save your movie to your computer, there is probably an easy (and likely) reason. The following list mentions some things that might be wrong and what you need to do:

- *The movie exceeds the FAT32 4GB file-size limit.* If your computer is using the FAT32 file system instead of the NTFS (NT File System) file system, you can't save movies that are larger than 4GB. Of course, that's a huge movie, but in case you run into this problem, you'll need to either scale your movie down a bit or convert your computer file system to NTFS. To learn more about NTFS, see the Windows Help and Support Center by clicking Start | Help.

- *Not enough free disk space available.* To save a movie, there must be enough free disk space available. In other words, if your movie is 2MB in size, there has to be a bit more than 2MB of free disk space to save the movie. If not, you'll have to free up some disk space on your computer by removing old files or uninstalling unnecessary applications.

- *Movie File Saving destination does not exist.* This simply means that you have typed in a saving path that does not exist, such as a folder name that you don't actually have. To fix this problem, start the saving process again, and use the Browse button to select a valid place on your computer to save your movie.

- *Source files for movie not found.* During the saving process, Movie Maker must be able to access your original files, such as imported pictures or video. If you have moved one of those items in the interim, you'll need to go back to Movie Maker and fix the problem. The missing media will appear with an X over it in the collections area. Just double-click the icon, and Movie Maker will help you relocate the missing movie item.

CHAPTER 14: Put Your Movie on a CD for Cannes, and More! 235

2. On the Saved Movie File window that appears, enter friendly names for the movie and for the CD. If you want them both to have the same name, that's fine. After you enter the names, click Next.

3. On the Movie Setting window, the default setting makes the movie fit on the CD, if possible. In other words, if the movie is too large, you may lose some quality settings so that the movie will fit on the CD. Most CD-R discs will hold about 700MB of data, so you can have a big movie still fit easily on the CD. If you want to click Show More Options (which is shown in the following illustration as Show Fewer Options; the option changes once you click it), you can also make some determinations of your own, but as a general rule, let Movie Maker do the work for you.

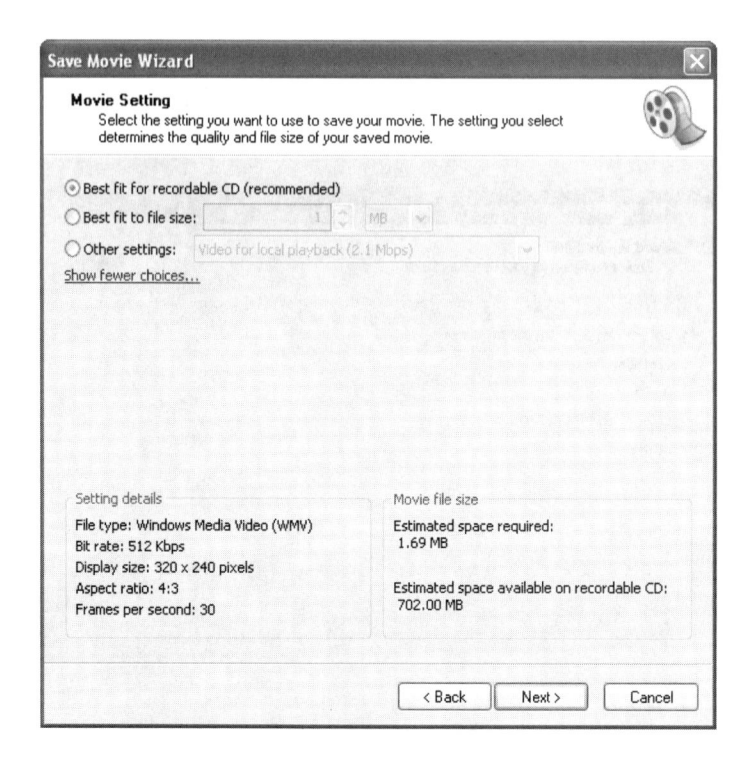

4. Click Next, and Movie Maker will burn your movie to the CD.

ROLL FILM *Movies are saved to a recordable CD by using Microsoft HighMAT (High-performance Media Access Technology) technology. A HighMAT CD can contain audio, video, and pictures. HighMAT-compatible consumer electronic devices recognize how the content is organized on the CD and enable users to play content using the displayed menus. The recordable CD can be played back on a computer as well.*

Send Your Movie Over E-Mail

I'll say this upfront: Movies are not really made to be sent over e-mail. Simply put, the files are usually too large. An average Movie Maker movie may be several hundred megabytes in size, and even with the tricks Movie Maker does to reduce file size, you can still end up with a really big file that will take a long time to download. That might be okay if your friends and family are all using broadband Internet connections (such as cable or DSL), but for the dial-up user, downloading big e-mails can be really painful. In order to send the movie over e-mail, Windows Movie

Maker will attempt to severely shrink the movie so that the quality is low and the actual movie display is really small. It's all about shrinking your resolution in order to get the low file size.

So does that mean you shouldn't use this option? No, not all, but it does mean that large movies with a bunch of clips, effects, and a soundtrack are not your best e-mail fodder. If you have a short movie containing some photos or a clip or two, then you can send it over e-mail. But again, as a general rule, e-mail is not your best transfer method for that movie you have spent several days creating.

If you want to e-mail a movie, Windows Movie Maker formats the movie and automatically attaches it to an e-mail message using your default e-mail program. Then, you simply type the recipient's e-mail address, a subject, and any message you want before sending the message.

You can also save your movie to your computer and manually attach it to an e-mail yourself, but this doesn't give you any direct file-management options (unless you manually selected them when you saved them to your computer).

So, to send a movie to an e-mail message, just follow these steps:

1. In the Movie Tasks pane, click the Send In E-Mail option under Finish Movie, or click File | Save Movie File and choose to save the movie in an e-mail message. Windows Movie Maker saves your movie and automatically attaches it to an e-mail message.

2. Enter the recipient's e-mail address, subject, and any message to send it.

TIP *This feature to save a movie in an e-mail message assumes you are using a local e-mail application, such as Microsoft Outlook or Outlook Express. You can't use this feature if you are using web mail, such as Hotmail or Yahoo!. However, you can still save the movie to your computer and manually attach it to an e-mail. Again, make sure you consider the size of the movie before you send it over e-mail. Most Internet Service Providers (ISPs) and web-mail servers have limits on the sizes of attachments you can send.*

How to ... Handle Movie Maker Sending Your Movie to the Wrong E-Mail Application

Movie Maker sends your e-mail to the default e-mail program on your Windows XP computer. However, what if you are not using the default program? In this case, you should change the default e-mail program so that your applications know what program you want to use. Follow these steps:

1. Click Start | Control Panel | Internet Options.
2. Click the Programs tab.
3. In the E-Mail box, the default e-mail program is displayed. To change it, simply choose the correct e-mail program (the one you actually use) and click OK.

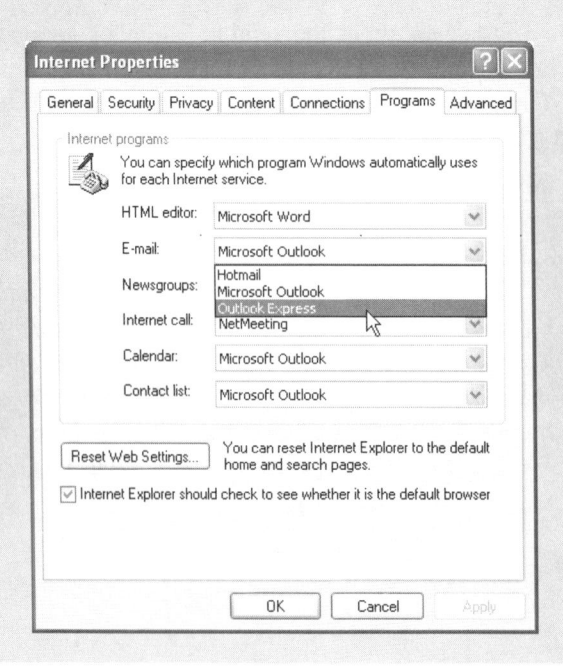

CHAPTER 14:   Put Your Movie on a CD for Cannes, and More!   239

Send Your Movie to the Web

In addition to saving your movie to your computer or sending it in an e-mail message, you can also send it to the Web. When you choose this option, the wizard formats your movie for Web viewing, allows you to connect to the Internet, and then uploads your movie to a third-party web server. Note that Microsoft doesn't provide web services, so you'll have to set up an account and pay the necessary fees so that you can show your movie on the Web. Once you upload your movie to the web server, the server will give you a web address that you can share with friends and family who can then watch your movie over the Internet. Fun!

To send your movie to the Web, just follow these steps:

1. In the Movie Tasks pane, click the Send In E-Mail option under Finish Movie, or click File | Save Movie File and choose to save the movie to the Web.

2. On the Saved Movie file page, enter a name for your movie and click Next.

3. In the Movie Setting window, choose the connection speed at which you want to save your movie. If some people who will watch your movie are using dial-up connections (and they probably are), choose the dial-up option. If all of your friends and family are on broadband connections, you can choose the ISDN or DSL option. You can also click Show More Choices to customize the connection speed. Remember, this setting applies to the people who will watch your movie—not to you. Make a selection and click Next.

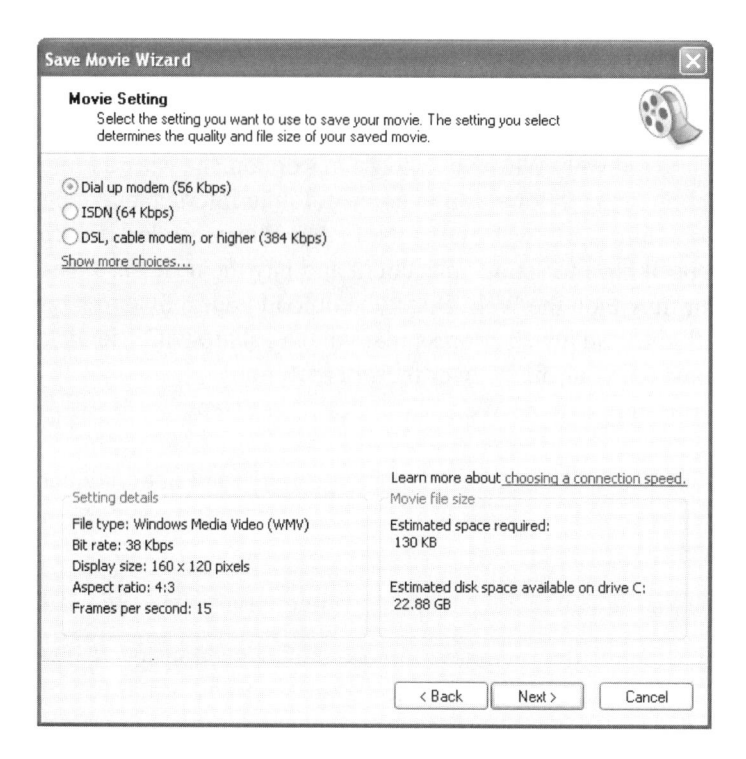

4. The wizard saves your movie and then attempts to connect to your ISP. Just follow the remaining wizard screens and enter the desired information.

Save Your Movie to a DV Camera

If you are using a DV camera, you can record your movie back to the camera, where you can then watch it on the camera or connect the camera to your TV. Sorry, this process does not work with analog camcorders.

To choose this option, first connect your DV camera to your IEEE 1394 card on your computer, and then turn on the camera. Then, on the Movie Tasks pane, click the Send To DV camera option under Finish Movie, or click File | Save Movie File and choose to save to a DV camera. The wizard will then start your camera's recording feature, and the movie will be recorded back to the DV camera (make sure you are not recording over something you want to keep!). Once the recording is finished, you can watch the movie on your DV camera or television.

CHAPTER 14: Put Your Movie on a CD for Cannes, and More!

More Great Ideas

Windows Movie Maker is lots of fun and gives you plenty of options to use your movie. Try these additional ideas:

- Use the Save To Web feature to save all kinds of videos to a web site where people can view them. This feature works great for business videos on your company's web site.

- One of the easiest ways to share your movie is to burn it to a CD and give it away. Remember to make a custom label for the CD (see Chapter 2)!

Part IV

Become a Digital Maniac!

Chapter 15

Monitor Your House with a Webcam

How to...

- Get your webcam set up and running
- Use Timershot to monitor your house
- View your webcam photos

Sure, no one likes to be spied on, but let's face it: Sometimes you wish you could see what the dog is up to when you're away for the day. Why is the refrigerator door always open, or what happens to the mail, or where does the dog hide your slippers? Aside from the family pet, you may want to see what your kids are doing when you're gone or what the uninvited houseguest is up to.

Privacy issues aside, there are numerous times when we would like to find out what is going on at home when we're away. Maybe you've thought of running your video camera for the day and checking things out, but that's not practical because of tape usage. You need a sensible way to get the information you want, without anyone (or the dog) knowing what you are up to. Look no further: A Microsoft PowerToy called Timershot can come to your rescue. Using a simple webcam, Timershot can automatically take pictures throughout the day and store them for you so you can really see what the family pet is up to when you're not home!

What You'll Need

For this project, you'll need a Microsoft PowerToy called Timershot, which is available for free download. You can get it at www.microsoft.com/windowsxp/pro/downloads/powertoys.asp. You'll also need a basic webcam. See the next section for details about these two items.

Get the Stuff You Need

In order to snap photos of your house, you need two items: the Timershot software and a webcam. First things first: You can use any basic webcam for this project—nothing fancy is needed. In case you haven't used one, a webcam is simply a small camera that can be used to transmit video to a friend or web site over the Internet. This simple device connects to your Windows XP computer through one of the computer's Universal Serial Bus (USB) ports. You can use a webcam with a number of different applications and for a number of different purposes, even for taking quick photos like this project will show you.

> **TIP** *Virtually all webcams sold today connect to computers through a USB port, so make sure your computer has an available USB port to which you can connect your webcam.*

You can get a webcam at most major department stores as well as any computer store. You can also get them online from such places as www.amazon.com, www.circuitcity.com, www.compusa.com, and so forth. Generally, webcams start around $35 and go up from there, depending on what you want. Keep in mind before you buy a webcam that you don't need one with a bunch of bells and whistles, unless you want to use it for other purposes besides taking pictures of your house.

The second thing you need for your project is the Timershot software from Microsoft. This software is a part of the free PowerToy collection, which is a group of utilities that Microsoft developed for Windows XP after releasing the operating system. All of the utilities are free, which is great news, so all you have to do is download the collection; alternatively, for you folks who use dial-up connections, you can download the utility individually (this way, you don't grow old waiting on the download).

Did you know? Get More Ports with USB Hubs

If you have several devices connected to your computer via USB ports, you may be running out of USB ports. No problem. The cool thing about USB is that it allows for numerous devices to connect to your computer without any fuss. What you need is a *USB hub,* a small device that connects to a USB port on your computer and contains several other used connections to which you can connect several other devices in a daisy-chain fashion. This cool and inexpensive way to attach more USB hubs to your computer gives you plenty of flexibility as you accumulate more and more USB devices over time. With a USB hub, you can rest assured that you always have room for your USB camera, a webcam, a second printer, a disk drive, a scanner, or anything else that you might need to connect to your computer. At any computer store, you can get a four-port USB hub (which will add four additional USB ports to your computer) for around $20.

To download and install the Timershot software, just follow these steps:

1. If necessary, start an Internet connection.

2. Open your web browser and go to www.microsoft.com/windowsxp/pro/downloads/powertoys.asp.

3. Scroll down the page until you find the webcam Timershot software. Click the Timershot.exe link to start the download.

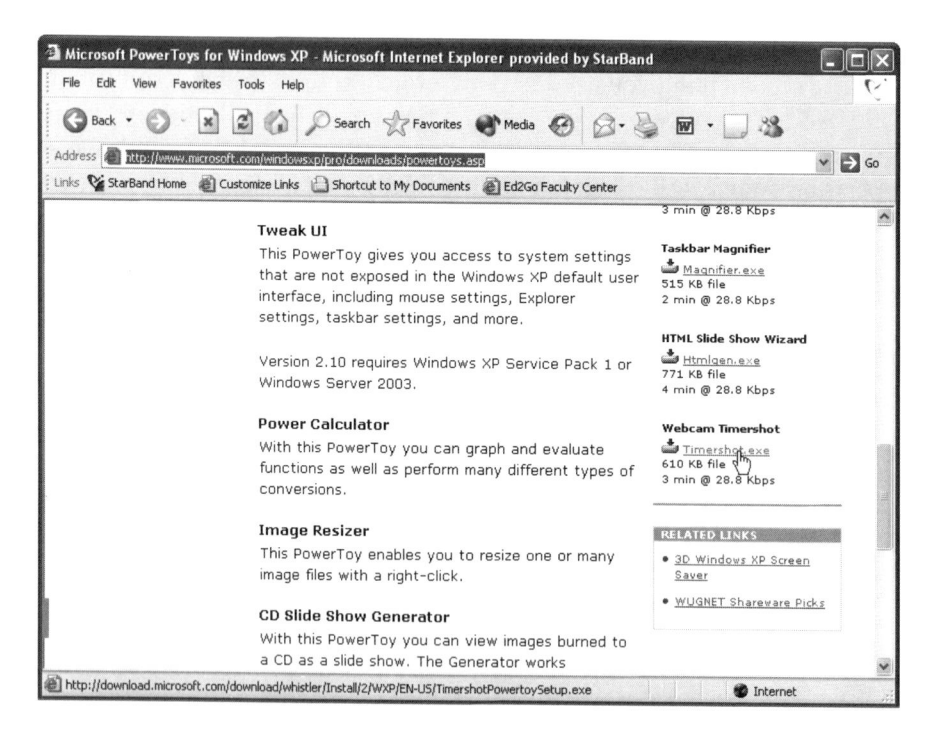

4. In the dialog box that appears, click the Open button. The software downloads to your computer, and an installation window appears. Follow the simple installation wizard instructions to install the software.

Understand How Timershot Works

Timershot is really just a simple utility that uses your webcam to take pictures at certain intervals. You can decide how often the webcam takes photos. Once the photos are taken, Timershot stores them in the My Pictures folder on your computer (or you can choose another folder) so you can review the photos at your leisure.

The photographing is completely silent, and webcams don't come with a flash or anything else that would alert someone that you are taking photos.

> **NOTE** *Timershot runs in the background on your computer, so the photos you are taking don't flash on the computer screen or anything like that.*

That's the good news. The bad news is that Timershot can work with only one webcam. If you are really enthusiastic and thinking about connecting webcams all over your house, you can forget it. You'll need a different computer for each webcam, even if you have multiple webcams connected to your computer. So unfortunately, you can't monitor several rooms in your house with different webcams.

So, as you're thinking about what you want to monitor, you'll have to decide where you want to put the webcam, considering where you can physically place it. The webcam has to be connected to your computer, so that may limit your location possibilities. You can use a USB hub with a long extension to give your webcam some extra cable length, but you may have to move your computer around to get the webcam where you need it. Obviously, monitoring the room where your computer resides is quite easy, but monitoring other parts of your house may require you to think a bit creatively. This is, of course, where a laptop computer comes in handy.

Set Up Timershot

To use your webcam and Timershot, your computer must be turned on, and the webcam software must be started. Once you have the webcam connected to your computer (follow the manufacturer's installation instructions, if necessary), you are ready to turn on Timershot and put it to work. You can open Timershot by clicking Start | All Programs | PowerToys for Windows XP | Timershot. The Timershot software appears, as you can see in Figure 15-1.

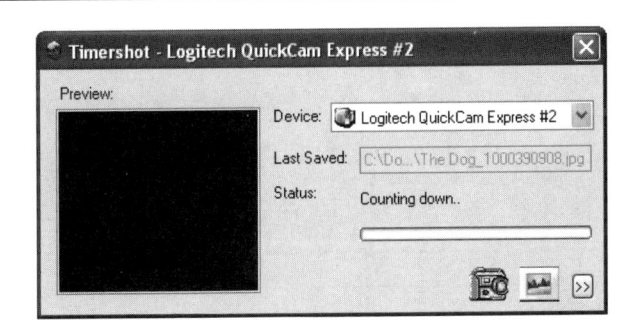

FIGURE 15-1 Starting webcam Timershot

First things first: Notice that the Timershot software has already found your webcam and is using it. However, if you have multiple webcams attached to your computer, use the drop-down menu to select the one you want to use. If Timershot doesn't see any webcams, then yours is not installed correctly. Refer to the webcam manufacturer's instructions for more information; you may need to install a device driver so that the webcam will work properly.

To set up the webcam, click the little double-arrow button found in the bottom-right corner of the dialog box in Figure 15-1. This will expand the Timershot dialog box so that you see all of the available options (see Figure 15-2).

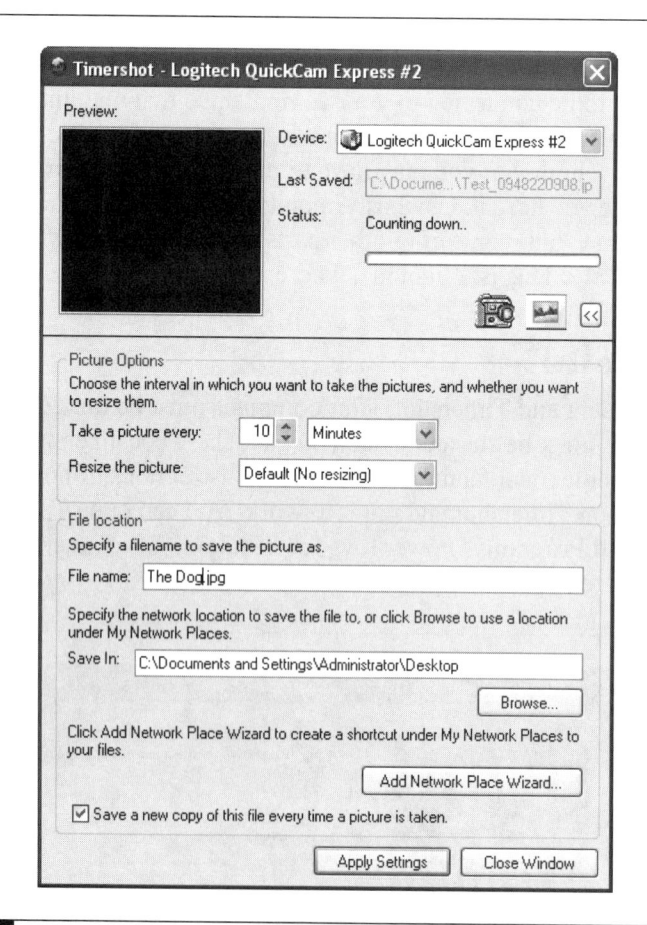

FIGURE 15-2   Selecting Timershot options

At first glance, the options seem fairly simple, but there are a few tricky details we need to talk about, so let's take a look at what you can do.

Frequency of Pictures

First of all, you can determine how often you want to take pictures and the size of those pictures. The default setting is to take photos every ten minutes, but you can change this to a few minutes, every few seconds, every few hours, or even every few days. The options here give you extreme flexibility so that you can have Timershot take photos whenever you want. Note, however, that you can't configure Timershot to take a photo at a specific time or on a specific day. In other words, the Timershot software doesn't give you a way to take a photo on Tuesday at 6:15 P.M. The software works on an interval basis—not an actual clock time. Bummer, but this is one of the limitations.

Photo Sizes

Concerning the size of the photos, you have four options:

- Default (no resizing occurs)
- Small (640×480)
- Medium (800×600)
- Large (1024×768)

So, what should you choose? That all depends on your needs, but consider this: Webcams aren't known for great resolution, so a large photo is going to give you a bigger picture, but not necessarily a clearer one. Also, the bigger the picture, the more storage space it consumes. For example, a typical Timershot photo under the Default size setting will take up around 13KB of storage space, while a larger one will take up around 50KB. So, unless you have a good reason for taking large photos, the Medium, Small, or even Default settings are fine for your surveillance work.

> **TIP** *The Timershot software saves all photos as JPEG files. There is no option to save photos as a different file type.*

File Location

The next section of the window addresses file location. You may be tempted to skip over this section because file locations always seem boring, but listen up—there are several important things here. First of all, you can provide a filename for the photo, which is My Pic by default. You can leave this name as it is, name it something else, or just clear the box altogether, in which case Windows will provide a numeric filename for you.

Where to Save

Next, you can determine where to save your photos. By default, the Timershot software puts them in My Pictures, which is found in My Documents. You can click the Browse button and choose a different location. I usually create a folder just for the photos so I can keep them organized and in one place. After all, you can end up with a lot of photos, so it may be easier just to keep them in your own custom folder. (Check out Chapter 5 to learn more about organizing photos.)

The second option you have, which is rather cool, allows you to save the photos to the Web each time they are taken. For example, let's say that an egg disappears from your refrigerator every day. You suspect that Fido, the pet canine, is the culprit, but you are not sure. You set up your laptop and webcam in the kitchen, and configure Timershot to take a photo of the fridge every three minutes, hoping to catch Fido on film. Although you can simply save all of the photos to your PC and review them when you get home, you may be able to send them to yourself if your computer has an always-on Internet connection. For example, if your company has an FTP account for you on their web server, you can simply have Timershot send a copy to the FTP site each time a photo is taken, and you can view the photos throughout the day at work. You can also set up an MSN Community account and have the photos stored there, or on some other site. Regardless, this feature enables you to see the photos from a remote location on the Web, which is really nice.

To configure this option, you'll create a Network Place with the help of a wizard. Click the Add Network Place button to get you started. The wizard will ask you to enter some Internet site information where Timershot can send the photos. If you want to set up an MSN Community site, just choose that option when the wizard appears.

The last check box you see at the bottom of the window is Save A New Copy Of This File Every Time A Picture Is Taken. This is one of the most important settings on the whole window. If you clear this check box, each new photo overwrites the old one. In other words, if you leave the Timershot to take a photo every ten minutes all day long and you provide a filename with this check box cleared, guess how many photos you'll have at the end of the day? Only one, and it will be the last photo taken before you get home! When this check box is cleared, the software keeps only one photo at a time, so each time the webcam takes a photo, Timershot overwrites the last one taken using the same filename.

Of course, this does not work well for surveillance work, so what can you do? The answer is simple. You absolutely *must* keep this check box enabled—otherwise, each new photo will overwrite the previous one. So, in a nutshell, if you want to save each picture every time, which you do if you are monitoring your house, leave the Save A New Copy Of This File Every Time A Picture Is Taken check box selected.

Once you have fixed all of the settings you want, click Apply Settings. The settings portion of the window will close, and you'll be left with the small Timershot dialog box. Notice that the software is already at work, and you'll see a Counting Down progress bar, which is counting down the number of minutes, seconds, hours, or whatever is needed to reach the deadline for the photo.

At this point, you can close the dialog box by clicking the red X. However, this doesn't close the application. Instead, the application minimizes to your Notification Area, where it continues running in the background and taking pictures. To see the last photo taken, right-click the icon in the Notification Area and click Open or Show Last Picture. If you right-click the icon and click Exit, the software will close, and Timershot will stop taking photos.

Review Your Photos

Once Timershot has been working for you, you are free to review your photos at any time. Keep in mind that you can review the photos, delete them, or do anything with them. After all, they are simply JPEG files.

To review your photos, simply browse to the location in which you told Timershot to store them. As you can see in Figure 15-3, I created a folder called Timershot and configured the software to put the photos in that folder.

As you are taking a look at your Timershot photos, it's a good idea to use certain Windows views so you can browse through the pictures more quickly and clearly. In the folder window, click the View button on the toolbar, then choose

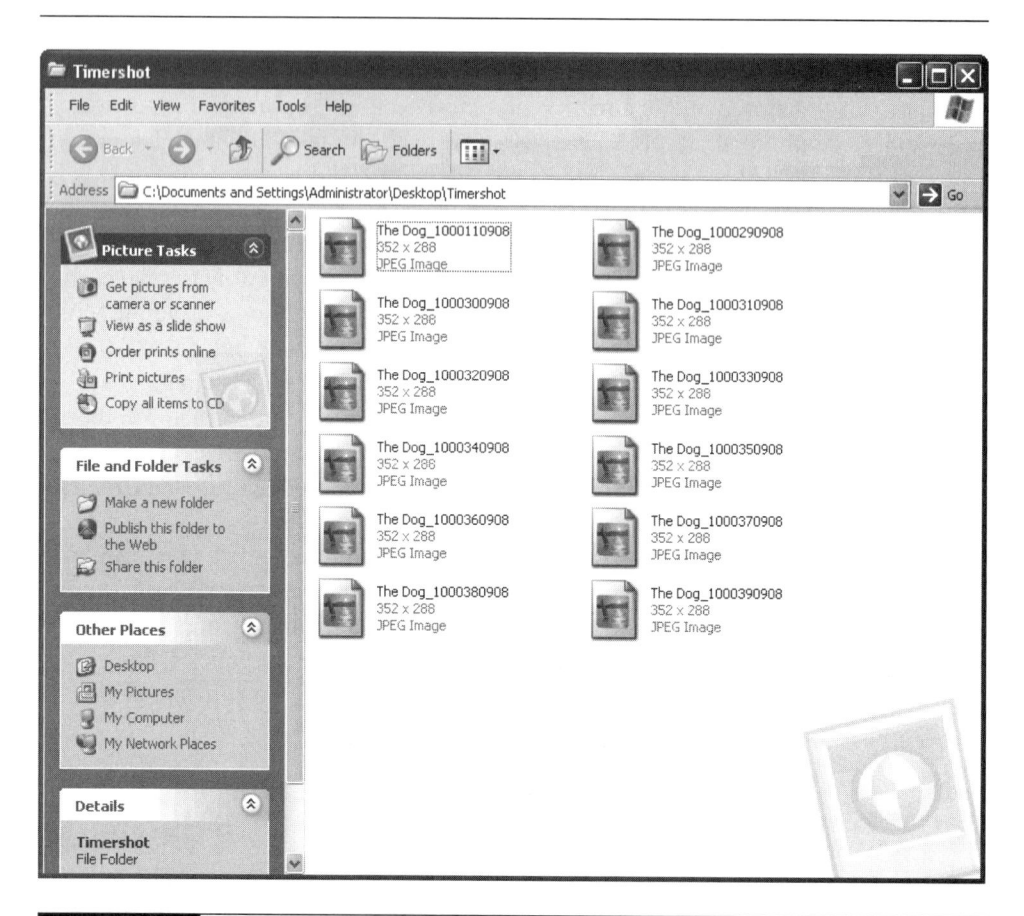

FIGURE 15-3 Timershot photos are stored in the location you choose.

either Filmstrip or Thumbnails. In Figure 15-4, I am using the Filmstrip view to take a look at my photos by easily clicking through them to see what has gone on while I was away.

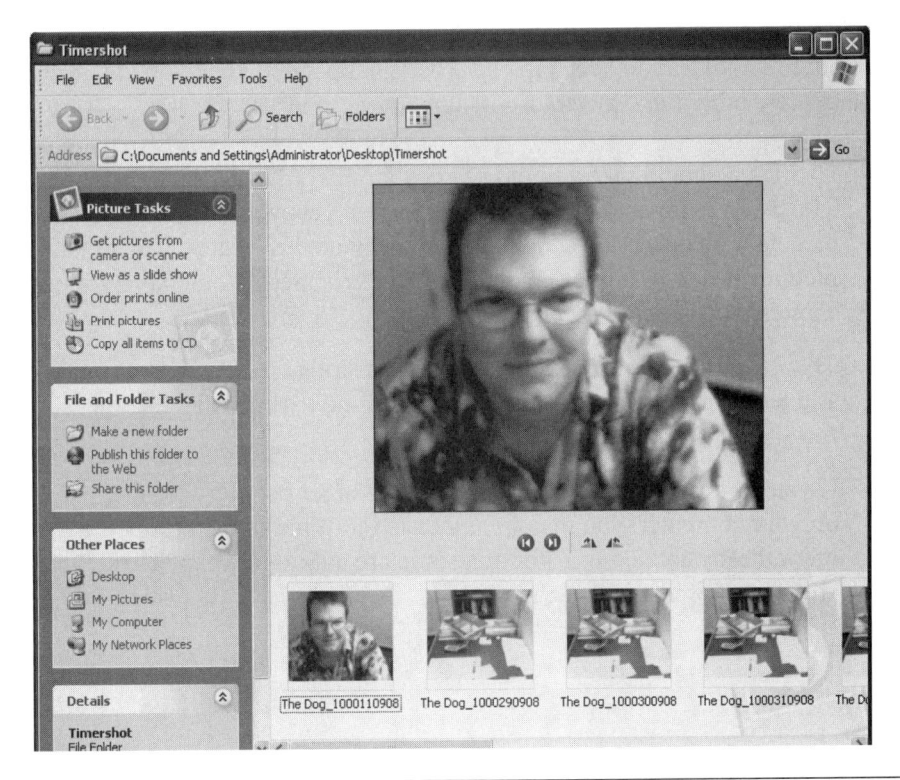

FIGURE 15-4 Use Filmstrip view for an easy look at your photos.

How to ... Manage All of Those Timershot Photos

If you are away for a day or two and you put Timershot to work, you may end up with several hundred photos. After reviewing them, you can easily delete all of the ones you don't want by individually right-clicking them and clicking Delete, or by choosing Edit | Select All and then Edit | Cut. You can also right-click a photo and print it, or do anything else you might do with a photo on Windows XP. See Chapters 5 and 6 to learn more about using photos in Windows XP.

More Great Ideas

Timershot is a cool way to keep tabs on what's happening when you are away, but there are a few other fun ways to use it. Try out these ideas:

- Use Timershot to take a photo of your family or kids. Just set up the Timershot to give you a few moments, then get everyone in front of the camera. Of course, a webcam doesn't provide the greatest way to take pictures because of poor resolution, but if you need a quick picture, Timershot can help you out.

- Try using Timershot at your next party. Just string up the webcam somewhere and let the Timershot take pictures from time to time. You may get some fun shots!

- If you are really interested in seeing what other people are doing on your computer, you may be interested in some of the products at www.thespystore.com. Although some are admittedly expensive, there are several products that can do all kinds of cool and interesting things.

Chapter 16

Use Your Vacation Video to Make a Video Screen Saver

How to...

- Gather your film footage
- Create a video screen saver

A few months back, my family went on a Caribbean cruise. It was great fun, especially watching my two young daughters play in the crystal-clear water for the first time. After we returned home, I took some of my digital photos and used photos from within Windows XP's My Pictures to flash photos across my computer screen when I'm not using it. This is a nice feature, but what if you could do something a bit more elaborate? What if you could take your vacation video and play it as a screen saver, complete with sound? Well, you can!

In this chapter, you'll see how to make a video screen saver. You'll do this quickly and easily with some helpful and free software you can download from Microsoft.com.

What You'll Need

For this project, you'll need Microsoft's Windows XP Video Screen Saver PowerToy, which is discussed next. You'll also need to round up the video you want to use for the screen saver; this is discussed in detail later in the chapter.

Get the Windows XP Video Screen Saver PowerToy

The Windows XP Video Screen Saver PowerToy is a cool little utility that allows you to play your movies as a screen saver on Windows XP. It's a software program that you install on Windows XP; after that, the PowerToy appears as a screen saver option you can select, just as you would select any other screen saver. The XP Video Screen Saver PowerToy is a free download from Microsoft.com, so you'll need to get it before you can move forward. Simply go to www.microsoft.com/windowsxp and, on the right side of the page, you'll see some different categories and links. Under Top Downloads, click the Amazing Windows XP Downloads link. This takes you to another page where you can choose the PowerToys Fun Pack. Click the link and choose to download the Partial Fun Pack 2: Video Screen Saver PowerToy that appears in the right column (see Figure 16-1).

TIP *You can go directly to the Windows XP Video Screen Saver PowerToy download page at www.microsoft.com/windowsxp/experiences/downloads/ create_powertoy.asp.*

CHAPTER 16: Use Your Vacation Video to Make a Video Screen Saver   259

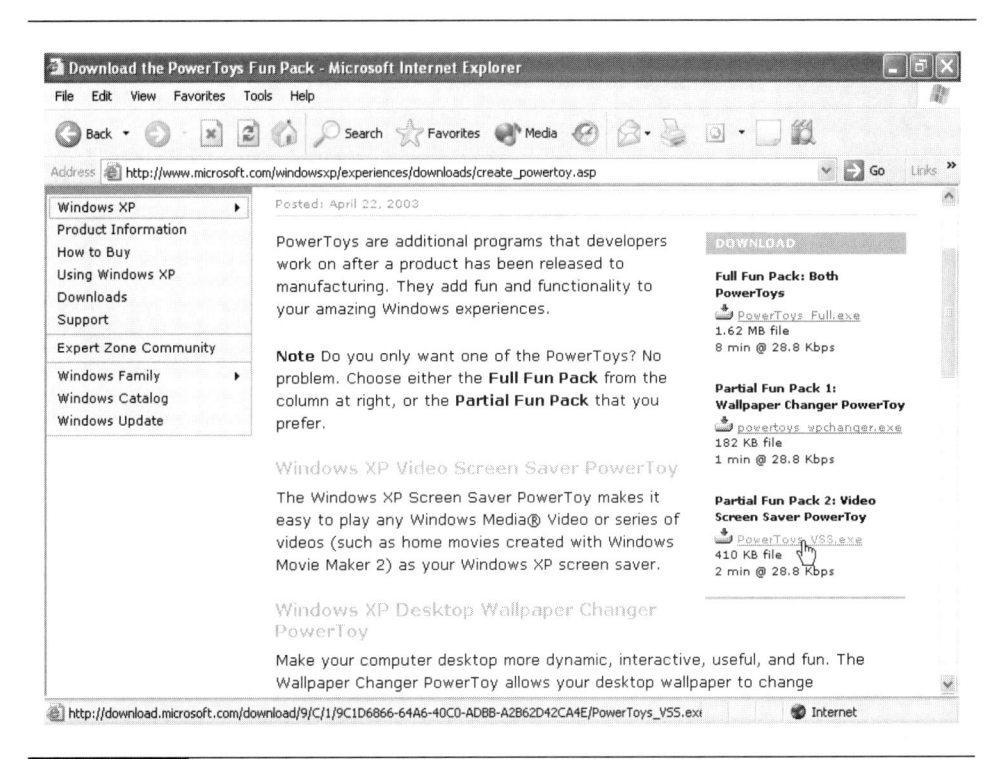

FIGURE 16-1   Downloading the Windows XP Video Screen Saver PowerToy

Click the PowerToys_Vss.exe link to start the download. You can choose to just save the download to your desktop for now. The download is 401KB in size, so it will take only a moment to download with a broadband connection, or up to a few minutes with a dial-up modem. Once the download is complete, you'll see a PowerToys download icon on your desktop. Just double-click the icon, and a setup wizard appears. Follow the wizard instructions to install the PowerToy. When setup is complete, you can open the Display Properties window (Start | Control Panel | Display Properties) and click the Screen Saver tab. As shown in Figure 16-2, the XP Video PowerToy is now a screen saver selection.

Choose a Video File Format

Before you get too happy about the Windows XP Video Screen Saver PowerToy, there are some limitations to the video that you can use. First of all, the PowerToy will play certain kinds of videos as screen savers, and it will also play playlists

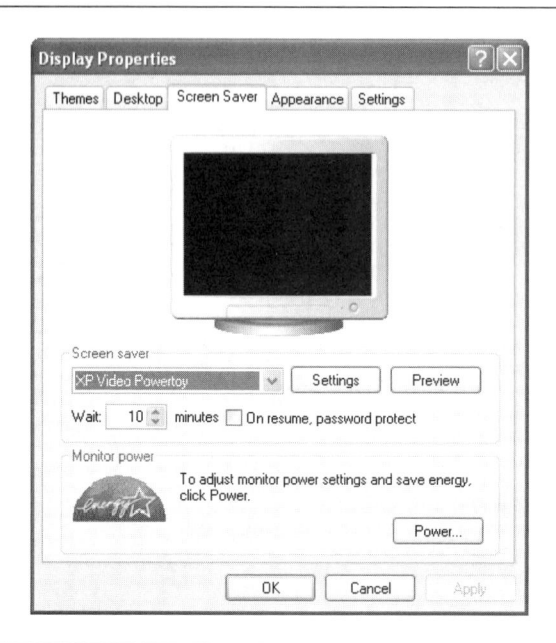

FIGURE 16-2 Access the Screen Saver tab to select your XP Video PowerToy.

from Windows Media Player. This means that you can create a playlist of videos and use the playlist to run the video. Naturally, this gives you a few cool options.

However, the XP Video Screen Saver PowerToy will not play just any kind of movie file. In fact, it is rather specific—it plays ASF, WMA, WMV, AVI, and WAV video files. This is a bit restrictive, especially if you are using some third-party software to create videos. However, there is some good news. First of all, this PowerToy can play videos that you create and save with Movie Maker. This is nice because you can create a video of your vacation for personal use but also use it as a screen saver without any additional work. The second piece of good news is that AVI is a standard video-file format, and most other video-editing programs will give you the option to save video as an AVI file. So, potentially you have a few issues to work around, but as a general rule, just remember either to use Movie Maker to edit your video or to make sure that, if you're using another video editor, video files are saved in the AVI format.

CHAPTER 16: Use Your Vacation Video to Make a Video Screen Saver

How to ... Combine Video Clips

You may have several video clips that you would like to use as video screen savers. The XP PowerToy allows you to choose only one video or other media file at a time, so you can't select multiple video files and have the XP PowerToys rotate through them for you. Thus, you're stuck with using only one file at a time. But wait! Keep in mind that you can use Windows Movie Maker to combine video clips by editing them and even using transitions to put them together. Then, when you save the movie to your computer, it'll be saved as a single movie with the .wma extension. You can use this single movie as your screen saver, which now contains all of the video clips combined! See Part III of this book to learn more about using Windows Movie Maker.

Set Up Your Video Screen Saver

Now that you have installed the XP Video PowerToy, you can set up your screen saver. This process requires only a few clicks, so just follow these steps:

1. Click Start | Control Panel | Display, or just right-click an empty area of your desktop and click Properties.

2. In the Display Properties dialog box, click the Screen Saver tab. In the Screen Saver drop-down menu, choose the XP Video Powertoy option, as shown in Figure 16-2.

3. Click the Settings button. The Windows XP Video Screensaver PowerToy Configuration window appears.

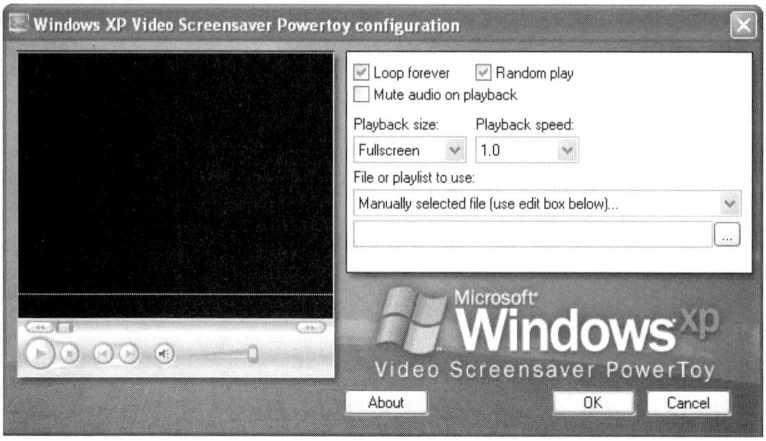

4. To choose your video for the screen saver, click the ellipsis (…) button. If you want to use a playlist, see the next section for details.

5. In the browse dialog box, locate the video you want to use, and then select the file and click the Open button. In this example, I want to use a vacation video that I created with Windows Movie Maker:

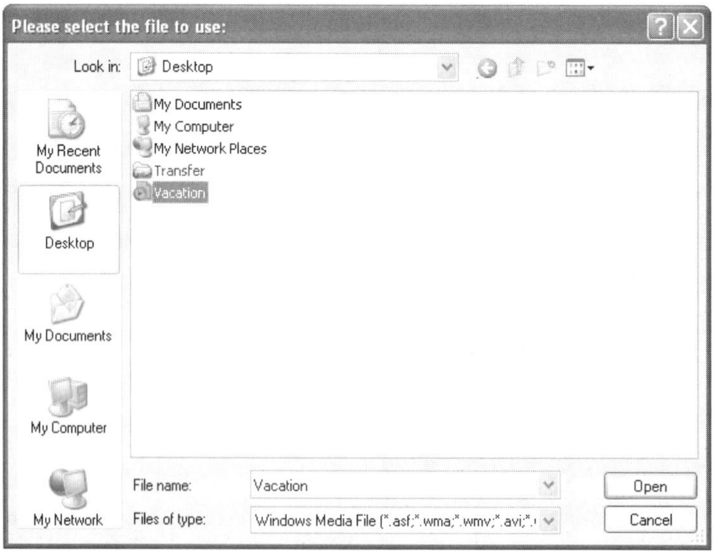

NOTE *The PowerToy will not allow you to choose a file that uses an unsupported file format.*

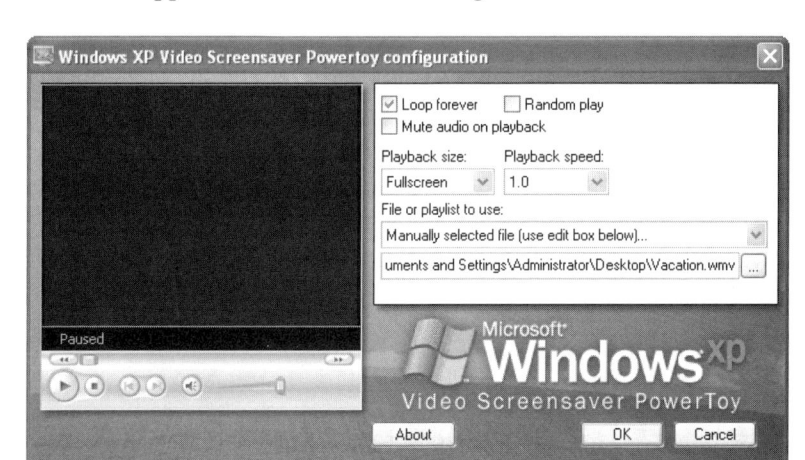

CHAPTER 16: Use Your Vacation Video to Make a Video Screen Saver 263

6. The video appears selected on the configuration window.

Note that you can choose a few helpful check box options at this point:

- **Loop Forever**   Plays the video over and over as long as the screen saver is active. You should select this option.

- **Random Play**   Plays portions of the video at random. Don't use this feature if you want the video to play in order.

- **Mute Audio On Playback**   Mutes the audio track so that you only see, not hear, the movie. By default, the audio track is played along with the movie. However, in terms of a screen saver, the movie sound track may get old after a while—especially if it wakes you up in the middle of the night!

7. Click OK. The video screen saver is now configured and will play. As with any screen saver, you can adjust the amount of idle time that you want to pass before the screen saver plays. Just use the Display tab to enter a time value.

8. Click OK on the Display Properties dialog box.

Use a Playlist As a Screen Saver

As I mentioned earlier, you can also use a playlist for a screen saver directly from Windows Media Player. This cool feature allows you to use a listing of moving clips, music, photos, or anything else you put on a playlist. To use the option, just return to the Windows XP Video Screensaver PowerToy Configuration window and choose a playlist from the File Or Playlist To Use drop-down menu. The list will show all playlists that exist in your Media Library. Note that if you choose a music playlist, you see only a visualization, if you have configured Media Player to use a visualization. See Chapter 4 to learn more about selecting visualizations in Media Player.

More Great Ideas

As you can see, the Windows XP Video Screen Saver PowerToy is a cool addition to your arsenal of fun things to do with Windows XP. Here are a few more ideas:

- Use the Video Screen Saver PowerToy to play any video you like—including vacation, birthday, anniversary, and holiday videos—for loads of fun.

- Consider creating a video in Movie Maker to use as your video screen saver. You'll be able to use transitions, effects, and a soundtrack, and see the whole movie as a screen saver. See Part III of this book to learn more about these features.

- Create a video screen saver and give it to friends and family on a CD. If your friends and family are using Windows XP, they can also download the video screen saver and use your movie on their computers!

Chapter 17

Wake Up to Windows XP: Turn Your Computer into an Alarm Clock

How to...

- Turn Windows XP into an alarm clock
- Create alarms
- Manage alarms

If you are like most of us, you have a love/hate relationship with your alarm clock. Sure, you love it because it keeps you from running late to work, but you hate it because…well, it wakes you up in the morning! Unfortunately, alarm clocks are just a part of life. They keep us on track, help us stay organized, and generally keep our lives in order.

However, how would you like an alarm clock that can not only wake you up in the morning, but also can sound an alarm during certain times of the day or the week—something to remind you to take your medicine, put the cat out, pay your bills, or anything else you need a reminder for? Well, look no further. Using Windows XP Plus! Alarm Clock, you can turn your computer into an alarm clock! Awake in the morning to the dreamy sounds of any song you choose from your Windows Media Player Media Library, and configure any number of alarms you want for any purpose throughout the day. It's more than an alarm clock—it's practically a personal assistant!

What You'll Need

For this project, you'll need Microsoft Plus! Digital Media Edition, which can be purchased for $20 or less at most computer stores or online computer stores, such as www.amazon.com or www.compusa.com. See Chapter 2 to learn more about getting and installing this software.

Start the Alarm Clock

You can start the Plus! Alarm Clock by clicking Start | All Programs | Plus! Digital Media Edition | Plus! Alarm Clock. You may also be able to access it from Start | All Programs | Accessories | Entertainment | Plus! Alarm Clock. The Plus! Alarm Clock appears on your desktop with a friendly welcome screen (see Figure 17-1). This screen just tells you what you can do with Alarm Clock. It will come to life every time you start Alarm Clock, so if you don't want to see this window again, click the Do Not Show This Welcome Page Again check box.

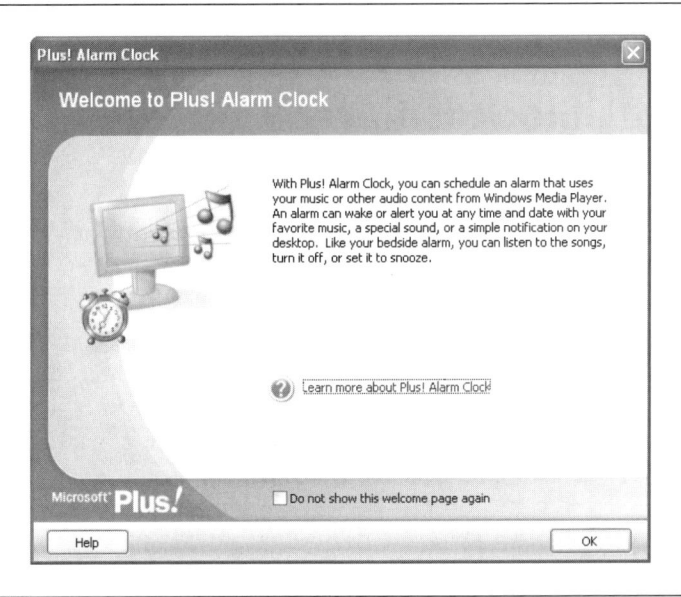

CHAPTER 17: Wake Up to Windows XP: Turn Your Computer into an Alarm Clock

FIGURE 17-1 Launching Plus! Alarm Clock

Once you click OK to close the welcome page, you see the Alarm Clock interface (see Figure 17-2). On its own, the basic interface isn't too exciting, and as you can see, the Alarm Clock doesn't do anything until you set up an alarm. The next section shows you how to do that.

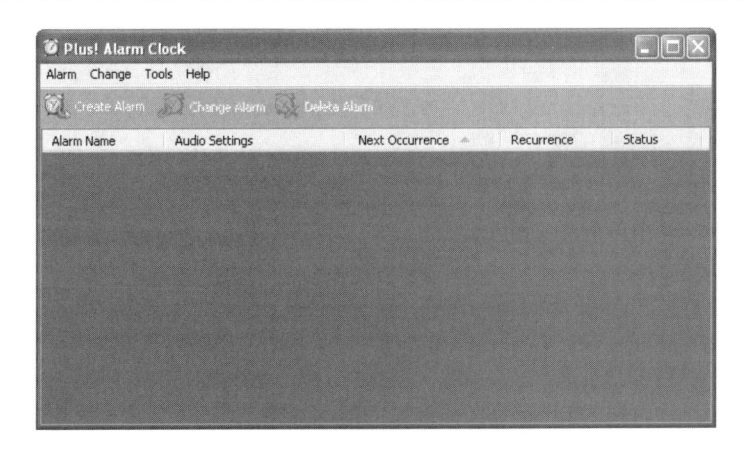

FIGURE 17-2 The Alarm Clock interface

How to ... Make Sure Your Computer's Clock Is Correct

Hey, do you like waking up at 3:00 A.M.? No, I'm sure you don't, but that is exactly what can happen if your computer's clock is not correct. Plus! Alarm Clock is really just a piece of software that sets off alarms when you tell it to. As such, it is not an actual clock on which you set the time. Instead, Alarm Clock uses Windows XP's existing clock to determine when it should go off. So, if XP's clock is wrong, your alarms will sound at the wrong time also.

Don't worry, you can easily check your Windows XP clock to make sure it is accurate. To do so, just follow these steps:

1. Click Start | Control Panel.

2. In Control Panel, double-click Date And Time.

3. On the Date And Time tab, make sure the date and time are correct. If they're not, simply change them and click OK when you're done.

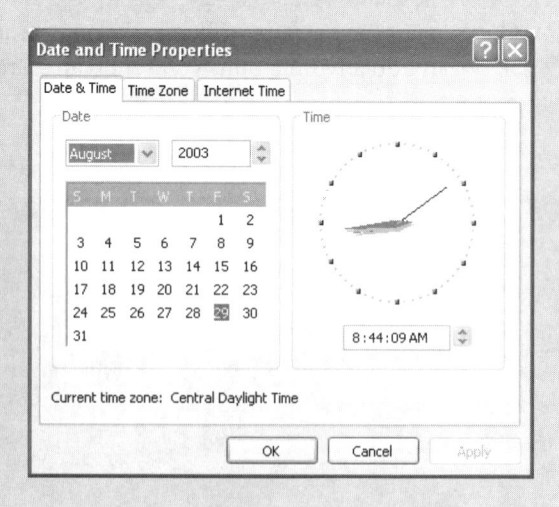

Create a Wake-Up Alarm

With the help of a wizard that Plus! Alarm Clock provides, you can easily create an alarm for your alarm clock. So, decide when you want your alarm to sound, then just follow these steps:

1. On the Alarm Clock window, click the Create Alarm button. The Create New Alarm Wizard appears.

2. On the first wizard screen, give the alarm a recognizable name—something that has meaning to you. Since you are creating a wake-up alarm, just type **Wake Up** in the Name Of Alarm dialog box.

3. In the same wizard window, set the days and time the alarm should sound. To set a daily alarm, for example, choose Daily from the Set This Alarm To Occur list on the left side of the window, then choose the time and days when you want the alarm to sound. In the following example, the alarm is set to sound every weekday at 6:00 A.M. Once you have made your selections, click Next.

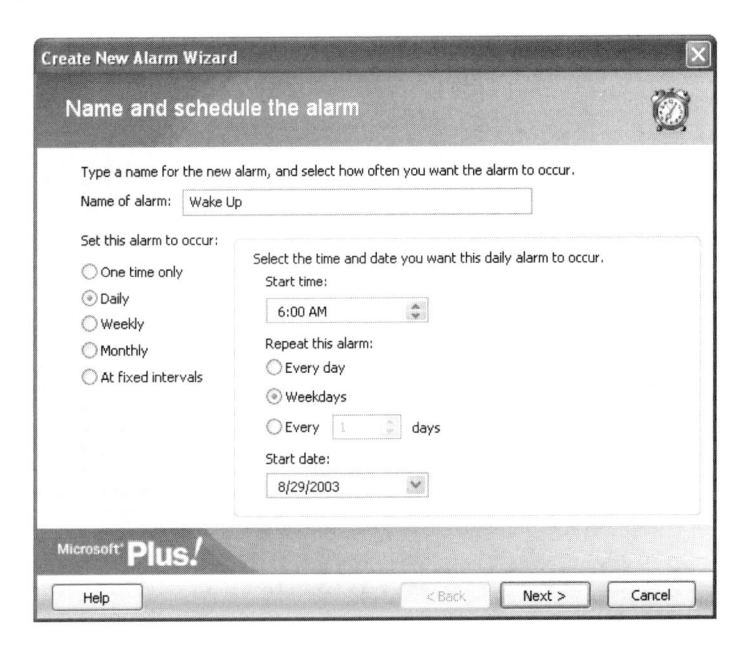

4. On the next wizard screen, choose what music or sound you want to use for the alarm. You can pick anything that is stored in your Windows Media Player

Media Library. Use the drop-down menu to choose an album, playlist, songs by artist, and so forth. Then, click the selection in the main box to see the songs you can choose from. Once you choose the song, you can click the Volume button to adjust the volume (you don't want it blasting you out of bed), and you can click Preview to hear a preview of the song and the volume. When you like what you hear, click Next.

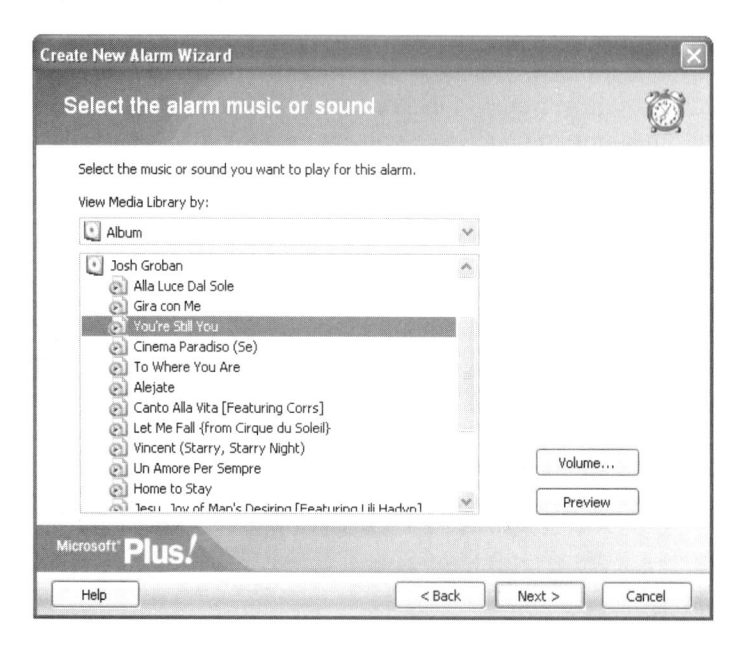

   5. The final wizard page gives you an alarm summary—the time and dates as well as the music that will be played. Click Finish.

> **TIP**
>
> *So what happens if, after picking a song or album from Windows Media Player for your alarm, you delete the song or album? Will the alarm still sound? Yes, indeed: If Alarm Clock can't find the song in the Media Library, it just uses a default alarm sound. This way, you are sure to hear an alarm, one way or another.*

Create a Weekly or Monthly Alarm

Aside from your daily wake-up alarm, you can create alarms that occur at certain times on a weekly or monthly basis, or on an interval basis. These options give you an easy way to create alarms that occur whenever you need them to. This way, you

CHAPTER 17: Wake Up to Windows XP: Turn Your Computer into an Alarm Clock

can remind yourself of a doctor's appointment or a task that you have to complete every week or every month.

To create these alarms, follow these steps:

1. Open Plus! Alarm Clock and click the Create Alarm button.

2. On the first wizard screen, you can choose Weekly, Monthly, or At Fixed Intervals. For example, in Figure 17-3, I am creating an alarm that sounds every Monday, Wednesday, and Thursday at 9:28 A.M. Since I have a conference call at 9:30 A.M. on those days, the alarm—which I'm calling Conference Call—gives me a two-minute reminder notice of the upcoming call.

3. The alarm is configured to run every week, but I could change it so that it occurs every other week, every third week, and so on, using the Repeat This Alarm option.

If you need a monthly alarm, such as a reminder to attend a meeting, choose the Monthly radio button. You can set the time, date, and the months that you want the alarm to sound on a yearly basis. It's a great way to remember anything that you have to do once a month—like pay the rent!

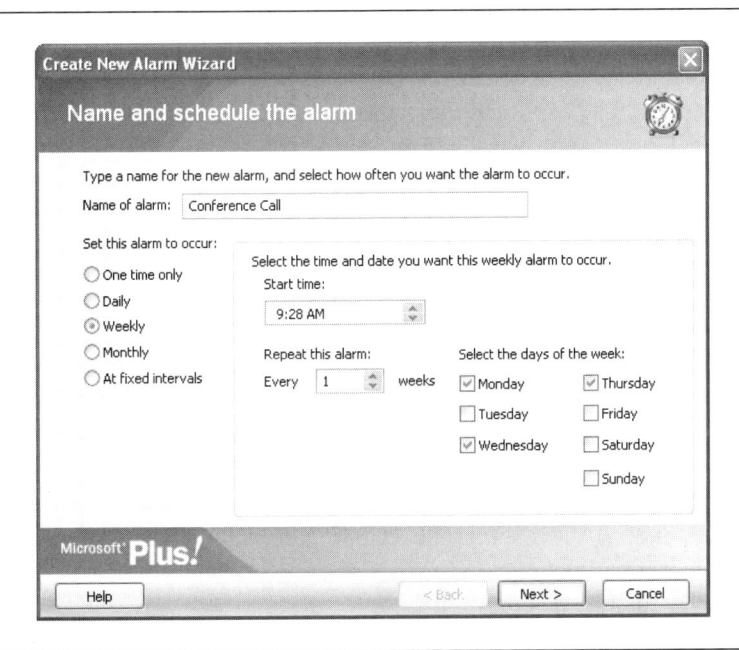

FIGURE 17-3 Setting a weekly alarm

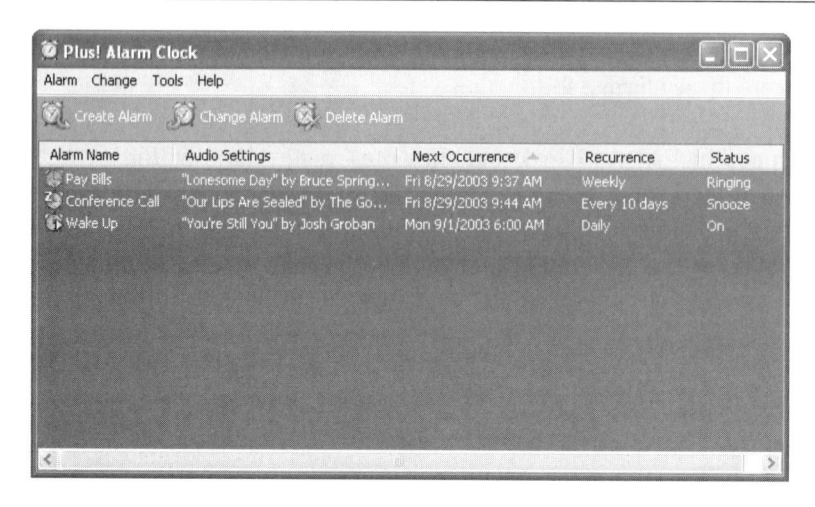

FIGURE 17-4 Using the At Fixed Intervals alarm option

Finally, there's the At Fixed Intervals option, which gives you extreme flexibility. With this option, you can set a time for the alarm, a date, and then tell the alarm to repeat every certain number of days (see Figure 17-4). This alarm is great for an event that happens every certain number of days, but not necessarily on the same day of the week.

As you can see, you can create just about any kind of alarm you might possibly need using the Create New Alarm Wizard options!

Manage Alarms

Once you have your alarms set to run, you can take a look at the Alarm Clock interface and see what is going on with each alarm. As you can see in Figure 17-5, one alarm is currently ringing, one is on snooze, and one is scheduled.

When an alarm rings, what happens? Well, you hear the alarm, of course, but you also get a little dialog box that appears on your screen (see Figure 17-6). You can use this dialog box to turn off the alarm, change it (which just opens the wizard again), or click Snooze.

If you click Snooze, the alarm is silenced for a period of seven minutes by default, and then the alarm will play again, just as it would on a bedside clock. The good news is you can change the length of time for the snooze easily. Just click Tools | Options and, on the Alarm tab (see Figure 17-7), change the snooze interval and click OK.

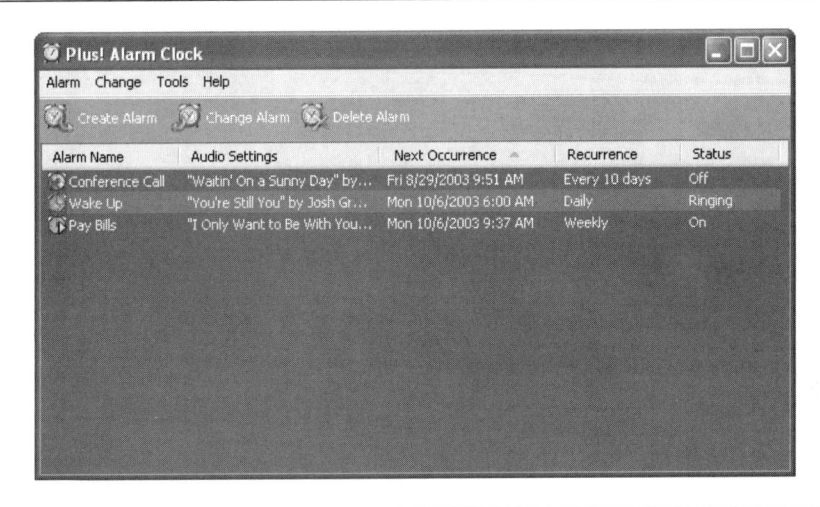

CHAPTER 17: Wake Up to Windows XP: Turn Your Computer into an Alarm Clock 273

FIGURE 17-5 Use the Alarm Clock interface to see what your alarms are currently doing.

Change, Delete, or Turn Off an Alarm

Let's face it: Life changes a lot and, thus, you may need to change your alarms from time to time, or you may even need to scrub an alarm completely. No problem. Plus! Alarm Clock gives you total control. Here are your quick and easy options:

- To change an alarm, select the alarm on the Alarm Clock interface and click the Change Alarm button. This opens the same wizard that you used when you created the alarm, and you can simply make changes as needed. Feel free to change the alarm times/dates and even the music as you like.

FIGURE 17-6 Use this dialog box to manage an alarm.

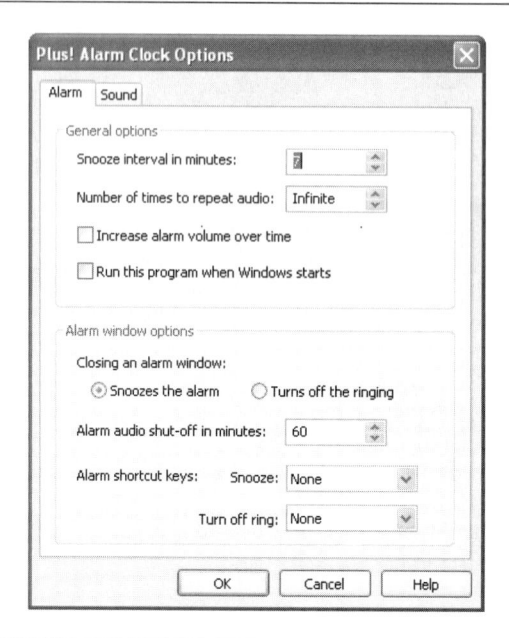

FIGURE 17-7 Setting alarm options on the Alarm tab

- To completely delete an alarm, select the alarm on the Alarm Clock interface and click the Delete Alarm button.

- You can also turn an alarm off without deleting it. For example, let's say you are going on vacation for a week and you don't want your Conference Call alarms blaring out at the neighborhood while you are gone. To avoid this, just select the alarm on the Alarm Clock interface and click Tools | Turn Off. The alarm is temporarily turned off, but not deleted. When you are ready to use the alarm again, just select it and click Tools | Turn On.

Use Cool and Cruel Options

Plus! Alarm Clock gives you some extra options you may want to employ, and you can change some basic ways that Alarm Clock behaves. You can access these options by clicking Tools | Options.

On the Alarm tab (see Figure 17-7), you can change the snooze interval, as discussed earlier, but you can also do some cool and cruel things here. As for cool options, you can:

CHAPTER 17: Wake Up to Windows XP: Turn Your Computer into an Alarm Clock

- **Have your songs play in an infinite loop.** This simply means that your alarm song can play over and over as needed. You should leave the Infinite setting as it is.

- **Run this program when Windows starts.** Alarm Clock has to be running in order for your alarms to function (it can stay minimized as an icon in your Notification Area), but what happens if you have to restart your computer? By default, you will have to manually restart Alarm Clock so that it will work. Save yourself the hassle and select the Run This Program When Windows Starts check box. This will tell Alarm Clock to start automatically whenever you have to restart Windows.

- **Snooze or turn off an alarm when you close the alarm window.** When you close an alarm dialog box, you can choose to have the alarm automatically snooze or turn off. I suggest that you use the Turn Off The Ringing radio button so that all you have to do is close the alarm window to turn off the alarm.

- **Have the alarm shut off after a specified period of time.** By default, your alarm will play the same song over and over for 60 minutes if you don't turn it off. After 60 minutes of no input from you, the alarm will turn itself off. This feature is good should an alarm occur when you are not home. You can change the 60-minute audio shutoff value to whatever you want.

- **Configure keyboard shortcuts.** Make it easy on yourself: Set keyboard shortcuts so you can just press a keystroke combination to turn off the alarm.

And now for the cruel option. Notice the Increase Alarm Volume Over Time check box. This option gives you a little time to turn off the alarm, but if you don't, the music will get louder, and louder, and louder! This feature is great for those of us who have trouble getting out of bed, but beware: It can drive your spouse, kids, dog, and anyone else in your house crazy with the blaring music. It's a cruel wake-up option but can be really helpful if you are a sleepyhead.

On the Sound tab, shown in Figure 17-8, there are a couple of quick options you might like. First, if Alarm Clock can't find the alarm audio it needs to sound, it will use its own default alarm. You can change that if you want by clicking the Browse button. Another cool option on this page is the chime. You can have Windows XP chime every hour if you like, much like you would hear from a grandfather clock. Just click the No Hourly Chime radio button, and a default chime sound will play; you can change this chime by clicking the Browse button. Finally, you can also adjust volume as well as date and time controls from here by clicking their respective buttons.

FIGURE 17-8   Setting options on the Sound tab

More Great Ideas

The Plus! Alarm Clock is just that—a cool alarm clock feature. As such, it doesn't do anything but play alarms, but here are few quick ideas for using it:

- Configure a monthly alarm that reminds you to pay your bills.

- Use a different song for each alarm. You'll begin to differentiate the alarms by the songs you choose and know what the alarm is for without looking at your screen.

- Use weekly or monthly alarms to remind you of upcoming appointments, such as doctor's visits, school events, work events, and so forth. Make Alarm Clock work more like a personal assistant who reminds you of upcoming events!

Chapter 18

Turn Your Computer into a Jukebox (and Back Again)

How to...

- Turn Windows XP into a jukebox
- Configure jukebox security, features, and more!

I love those old jukeboxes you see at city diners, pizza parlors, old ice cream shops, and places like that. I remember being a kid and getting to play a jukebox and standing there, staring through the plastic window, wondering how the machine kept track of all those records. Sadly, the days of vinyl record jukeboxes are basically gone, left to nostalgia for those of us who are old enough to really remember them.

However, the need for jukeboxes has not changed. Think about this: Your teenage son is having a party and wants to use the computer to play music for it. It's a great idea because of the playlists you can create in Windows Media Player, but the idea of a bunch of teenagers clicking around your computer is enough to give you the willies.

Relax. With Party Mode for Windows Media Player, a Microsoft Plus! Digital Media Edition software, you can turn your computer into a jukebox that safely protects your personal files and applications while letting the music play all night long.

What You'll Need

For this project, you'll need Microsoft Plus! Digital Media Edition, which can be purchased for about $20 at most computer stores or online computer stores, or downloaded for free if you have a broadband Internet connection. See Chapter 2 for more details about getting and installing this software.

What Is Party Mode for Windows Media Player?

Party Mode for Windows Media Player is actually a skin. If you took a look at Chapter 4, you are familiar with the concept of skins, but if not, a skin is simply an interface overlay of sorts. Using skins, you can change the way Media Player looks. The Party Mode feature is just another skin, but the difference is that the skin takes up the entire Windows XP desktop and essentially turns the whole Windows XP interface into a skin. In other words, you can't access your Start menu or other programs or files when Party Mode is in use.

So, why use Party Mode? The main reason, of course, is security. With Party Mode, you can turn your PC into a digital jukebox so that the computer can play music at a party. Guests can even access the interface and choose songs from playlists that you create beforehand, and leave you little notes about the party. It's a fun way to bring music to a party and allow party-goers to choose the songs they want while keeping your computer locked from any tampering. Sound like a good deal? It is! And Party Mode is really simple to set up, and fun and easy to use...

Get Ready to Use Party Mode

Before you start using Party Mode, there are two things you need to do. First of all, go into Windows Media Player and create one or more playlists for your party. Be sure to think carefully about the kind of party that you're having and choose appropriate songs for your playlists. Try to think of songs your guests are likely to enjoy. You can check out Chapter 1 for some steps to create playlists, but as you are creating them, keep the following ideas in mind:

- Give the playlists fun but descriptive names. If you use several playlists, this will help your guests find what they need more quickly.

- If you decide to use several playlists, try to group songs according to type. For example, you might have a party where you have a '70s hits playlist, an '80s hits playlist, and a '90s hits playlist. Or you could create playlists by genre, such as pop, rock, country, rap, and so on. In short, make the songs easy for your guests to locate.

- Playlists are rather versatile and, essentially, can be of any length, so if you like, just make one long playlist that guests can scroll through. However, consider putting some order to the list. Group songs according to genre, date, slow/fast tunes, and so forth. Again, try to make the playlist quick and easy for party-goers to find what they want.

- Guests can access anything in your Media Library from Party Mode, if you let them. In other words, you can't limit them to accessing only one playlist: If something is in your Media Library, they can get to it, so make sure there is nothing private in your Media Library that you don't want other people to see if you give guests access to the Media Library. You'll see how to choose this option in the "Set Up Party Mode" section later in this chapter.

Your second task, which is a very important one, concerns security. As mentioned earlier, Party Mode allows people to play songs from your computer but not access your personal files or anything else on your computer. Well, that may not be *entirely* true depending on your current computer setup. Here's what I mean: Basically, Party Mode runs on top of Windows XP. When you want to leave Party Mode, the software takes you to the Windows Welcome screen, where you can log back on. This is Party Mode's approach to security—you have to log in with your username and password to get into the actual computer system. This is also where the big security hole can come in if you are not careful. Windows XP allows you to use blank passwords. Simply put, when Windows XP boots and displays the Welcome screen, all you have to do is click your username icon to log on. This is a nice and easy feature for people like you and me who have computers but aren't particularly worried about security. You may have several accounts on your computer—your account, a kid's account, and so forth. The problem is this: If all of your accounts are not password-protected, a party guest can choose to exit Party Mode and simply click a user account icon on the Welcome screen. Since you don't have any passwords configured, the party-goer gets logged on to your system!

You may think, "Well, so what? I don't have any private information on my computer anyway." That may be true, but do you want some twelve-year-old logging on to your computer and deleting your C: drive, or maybe the folder that contains the novel you have been writing for the past 12 years? Do you want someone uninstalling your printer, CD-ROM, or other device? I thought not. As you can see, there are a number of reasons why you wouldn't want someone else fooling around with Windows XP.

So, here's the bad news: If you can go to the Welcome screen and click any account icon to log on without providing a password, then your computer is not secure when you use Party Mode. The good news is that you can remedy the situation easily and quickly, and here's how you do it:

1. Log on to Windows XP with an administrator account, or an account that has administrative privileges. You must be an administrator to make password changes to other accounts on your computer. If those statements have completely baffled you and you think, "But, I have only one account that I know of," then you are using an administrator account. Just log on as you would normally.

2. Click Start | Control Panel | User Accounts.

3. Take a look at the following example of the User Accounts window. Notice that under "or pick an account to change," you can see what accounts are password-protected. For example, my Administrator and Remote accounts are password-protected. The Guest account is turned off, so that's no problem, but I have an account for my daughter, Mattie, which is not password-protected. Here is my security hole. If any party guest exits Party Mode and goes to the Welcome screen, all he or she has to do is click the Mattie account icon to get logged on to my system.

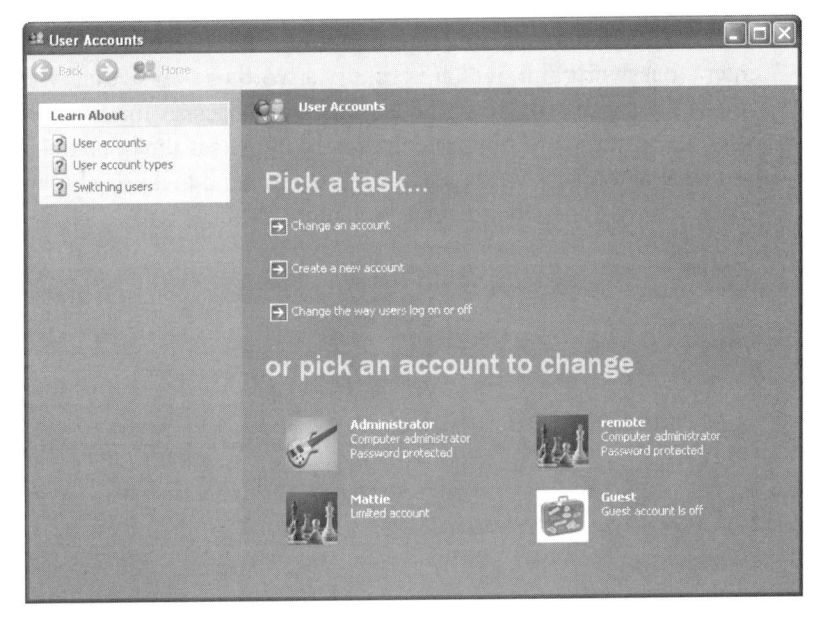

CHAPTER 18:   Turn Your Computer into a Jukebox (and Back Again)

4. If all of your accounts are password-protected, then you having nothing to worry about. Click the red X in the upper-right corner to close the User Accounts window. If not, click the account that doesn't have a password so you can change it.

5. In the window that appears, click Create A Password.

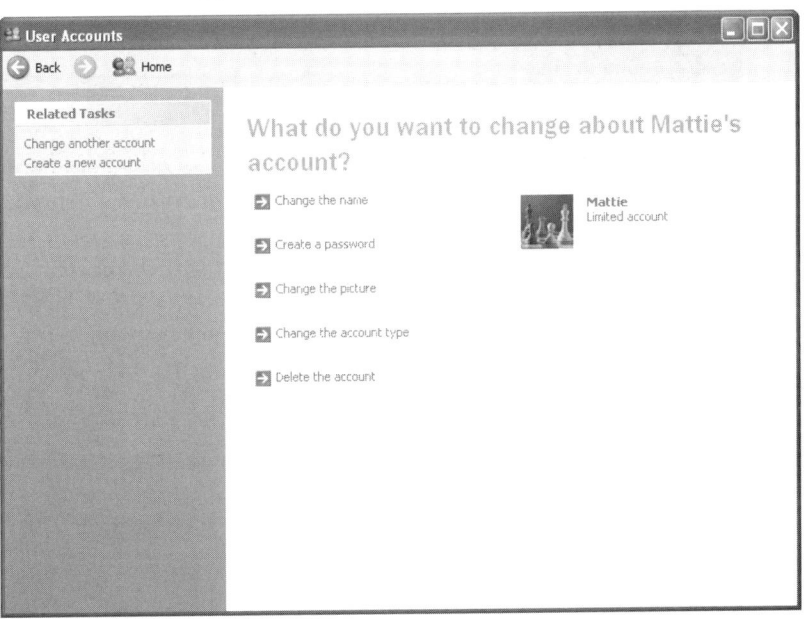

6. In the window that appears, type and retype the password. You can also enter a password hint, which is simply a word or phrase that will remind you of the password. However, anyone who accesses the Welcome screen can see the password hint, which greatly increases the odds that someone will be able to guess your password. I recommend that you skip this feature. When you're done, click Create Account.

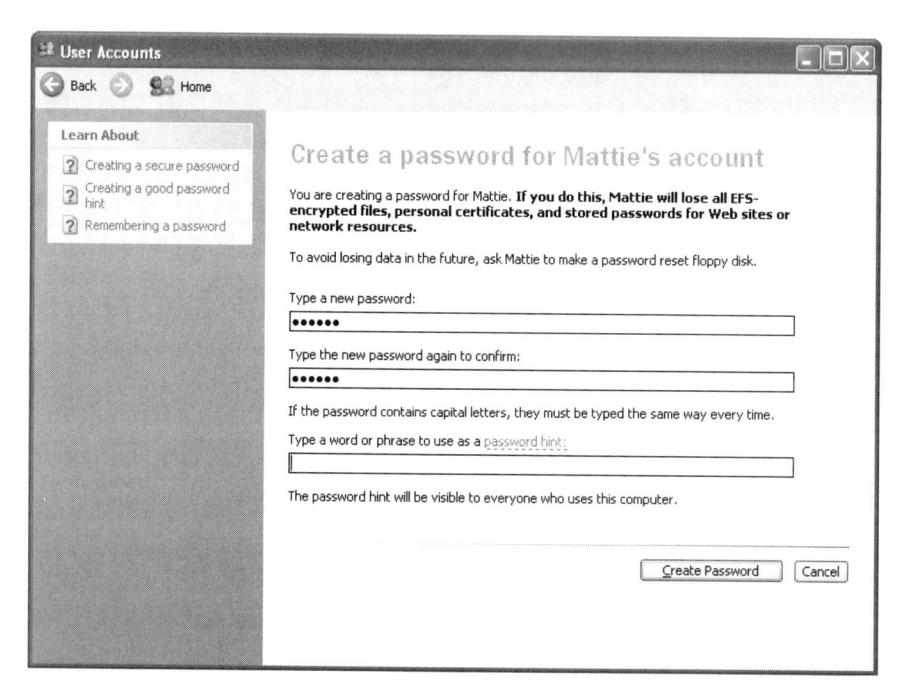

7. Now you are back to the Change Account window. You can click the Back button to return to the main screen, where you can click another account to change, or just click the red X in the upper-right corner when you are done.

CAUTION *Every account on your computer must be password-protected, otherwise your computer has a gaping security hole. Be safe rather than sorry! Also, if you are wondering what makes a good password, see the "Did You Know? What Makes a Great Password" sidebar.*

Did you know?

What Makes a Great Password

When you create passwords, there is always one major problem: You want to make the password too difficult for someone else to guess but easy enough for you to remember. Often, consolidating those two goals isn't easy, so if you are scratching your head, wondering what makes a great password, here are some do's and don'ts:

- Don't use your telephone number.

- Don't use your kids' names, pets' names, any portion of your address, or anything concerning your work. If it is obvious to you, it will be obvious to someone else.

- Don't use any words that are commonly associated with you. For example, if everyone knows you go to the Rocky Mountains every year for vacation, don't use "Rockies" for your password.

- Do make the password at least six characters long. Longer passwords are tougher passwords.

- Do use a combination of letters and numbers. "Sailboat479" is much more difficult for someone to guess than simply "Sailboat."

- Passwords are case-sensitive, so use case to your advantage. For example, "SaiLBoaT479" is a much more complex password than "Sailboat479." Remember, you are trying to keep anyone from guessing your password, so make it count.

Finally, don't write down your password and leave it lying around on your computer desk. If you are worried about forgetting the password, then write it down and store it in a safe place where no one can get to it.

Set Up Party Mode

Now that you have the preliminary security tasks out of the way, it's time to set up the Party Mode features. Make sure you have installed Microsoft Plus! Digital Media Edition, then just click Start | All Programs | Microsoft Plus! Digital Media Edition | Plus! Party Mode for Windows Media Player. You can also access the software by clicking Start | All Programs | Accessories | Entertainment | Plus! Party Mode for Windows Media Player. Either way, the Party Mode software begins, and you see a welcome screen, as shown in Figure 18-1.

The welcome screen just tells you what Party Mode does, and it will appear each time you start Party Mode. You can just click OK here, but if you don't want to see this welcome screen again, click the Do Not Show This Welcome Page Again check box, and it won't bother you any more.

When you click OK, the Specify Your Party Mode Settings window appears. Party Mode contains only one screen that you configure (see Figure 18-2), and then you start your party. There are several options you can choose, and we'll review them in this section so you can get your party started.

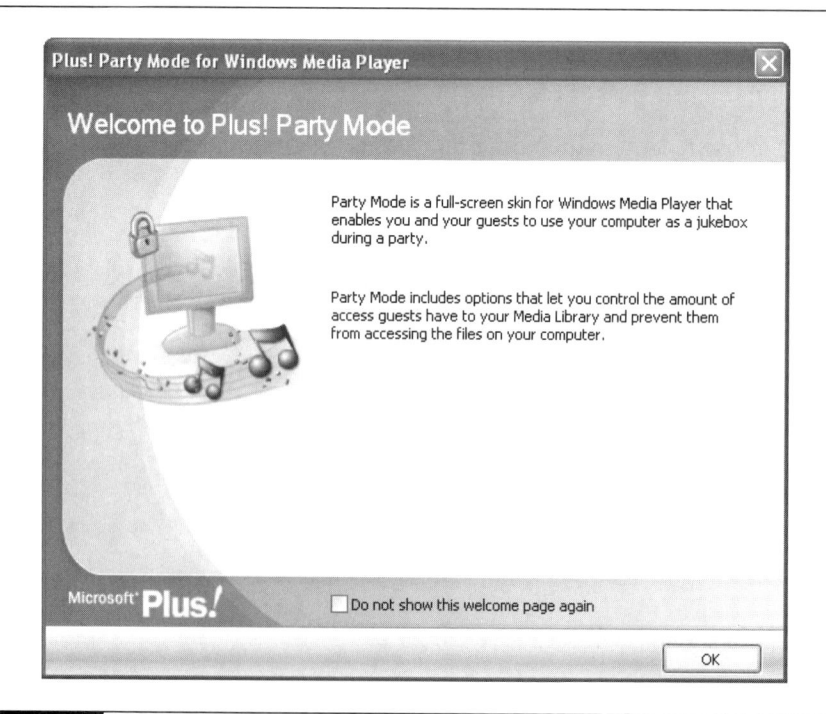

FIGURE 18-1 Welcome to Plus! Party Mode for Windows Media Player

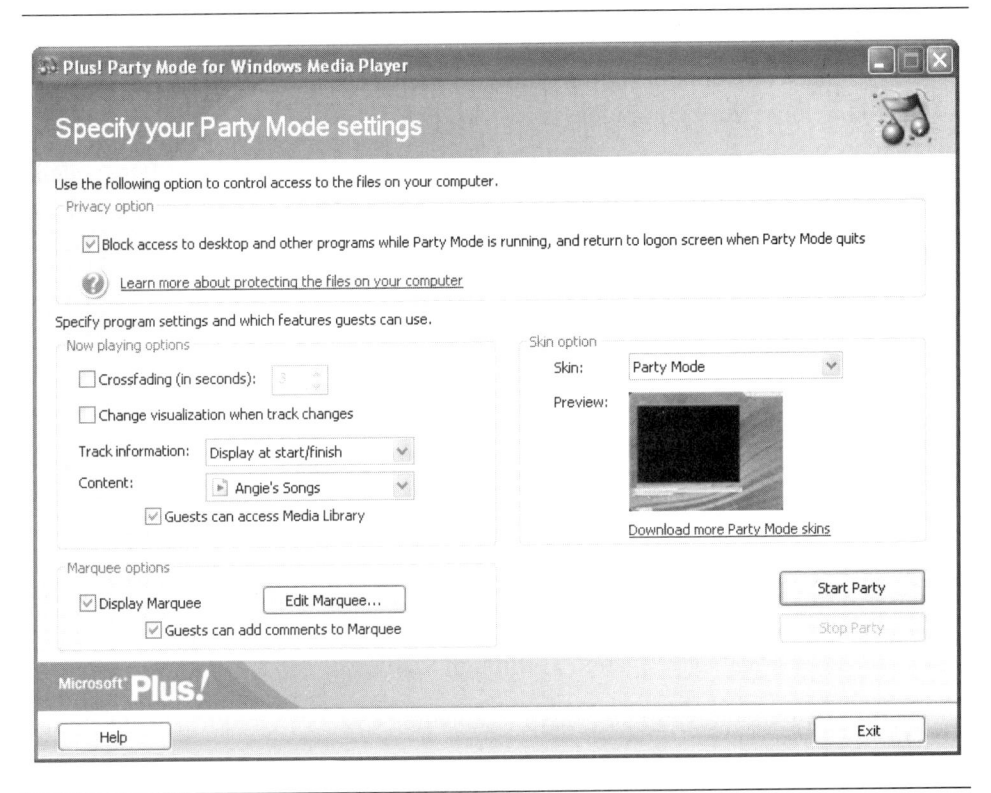

CHAPTER 18: Turn Your Computer into a Jukebox (and Back Again)   **285**

FIGURE 18-2   Use the options on this screen to get your party started.

Privacy Option

In the Privacy Option section of this page, you see a check box that, if selected, protects your personal files and brings you to the welcome screen when you leave Party Mode. This is what we talked about in the previous section of this chapter, and you should certainly use this privacy feature. When you click the check box, a dialog box appears, telling you to review the security features and potential security holes. You can click OK to this message and simply review the previous section, which tells you all about the security features. However, Party Mode uses some very cool security features, including the following:

- Guests cannot close Party Mode.

- Guests cannot start other programs or change content within your Media Library.

- Guests cannot access your computer's hard disk or connected networks.
- If a guest attempts to start another program, or if an error occurs, Party Mode locks your computer.
- Party Mode also disables the autorun capability for CDs and DVDs, which prevents guests from starting any applications from CDs.
- Party Mode restricts Start menu and keyboard access to prevent other programs or system events from overriding Party Mode. Party Mode does not accept the following Windows shortcut keys:
  - ALT+ENTER
  - ALT+ESC
  - ALT+SPACEBAR
  - ALT+TAB
  - CTRL+ESC
  - F1, F2, F3, F5, F6, F7, and F11 through F24
  - All Windows logo key +*key* combinations, except Windows logo key+L
  - The Browser, Sleep, Mail, and My Computer keys on natural keyboards

With the knowledge of these features, now you can rest easy. However, make sure you follow the instructions in the previous section about password-protecting all of your accounts. That way, just in case someone gets out of Party Mode, the welcome screen will stop him from logging on to Windows XP.

Now Playing Options

Party Mode supports a few helpful Now Playing options, which you can also learn more about in Chapter 4. First, you can use cross-fading, which fades one song into the next so that there is no silence during the party. A setting of three seconds works nicely. Also, you can choose to change the visualization automatically every time the track changes, which also gives some variety to Party Mode.

Next, the Track Information drop-down menu allows Media Player to display the track name and artist when a song starts and when it is ending (much like a music video), not at all, or during the entire playback of the song. Figure 18-3 shows you a Party Mode sample, where the track information is displayed.

FIGURE 18-3 You can configure the track information to appear when a song is played.

The next option is the Content drop-down menu. The content for the party comes from the Media Player Library. You can choose a specific playlist, or use the All Music setting so that users can pick different songs from your Media Library. If you want guests to be able to access the Media Library, click the Guests Can Access Media Library check box; this will let guests roam around your Media Library and choose the songs they want. If you don't select this check box and you select a specific playlist, then the single playlist is all that will be available to guests. Some people allow guests to use their Media Library, while others create one long playlist of songs and block guests out of the rest of the Media Library. The choice is completely up to you, but think carefully about letting people access everything in Media Library.

Marquee Options

You can choose to use a marquee, which simply scrolls text across the top of your computer screen. This is a fun way to put a personal message on Media Player.

If you want to use this feature, simply click the Display Marquee check box and click Edit Marquee. In the dialog box that appears, enter the text that you want on your marquee (see Figure 18-4).

> **TIP** *Watch your spelling! There is no spell checker in Party Mode.*

Notice that you can put a lot of information on the marquee that will scroll across your screen—you can use whole paragraphs, if you like. However, the marquee is more fun and readable if you keep your information short and simple. For example, you might put, "Welcome to my party! Visit the snack table for some great desserts." Or you can put instructions, such as "Welcome to my party! Click a song on the playlist to hear it." Anyway, the point is you can put welcome messages or instructions as you want, but be careful of overdoing it. No one wants to try to read an entire book scrolling across the marquee.

Also, you can allow guests to add items to the marquee. This can be a fun way for guests to add their own comments and so forth. Just click the Guests Can Add Comments To Marquee check box to enable this option.

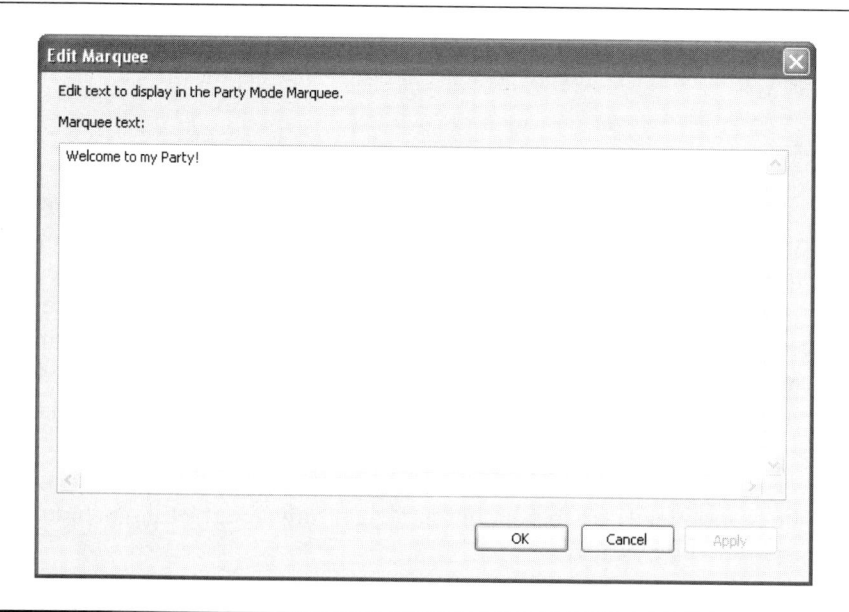

FIGURE 18-4   Using a fun marquee

Skin Option

Under Skin Option, you can choose from a short list of Party Mode skins. You have a few various options, such as the default Windows XP skin (it has a blue border like most other things in Windows XP), Plasma, Butterflies (see Figure 18-5), and so forth. Just use the drop-down menu to select the skin you want.

You can also download more skins. Click the Download More Party Mode Skins link to access the Microsoft web site, where you can check out some more party skins that are available for free download. Some of them are over 2MB in size, so if you are using a modem, downloading will take several minutes. Figure 18-6 shows the Terminator 3 skin that is available for download for Party Mode.

> **NOTE** *Other skins for Media Player, such as you might download from another web site, will not work for Party Mode. The skin has to be specifically made for Party Mode in order for it to work.*

FIGURE 18-5 The Butterflies Party Mode skin

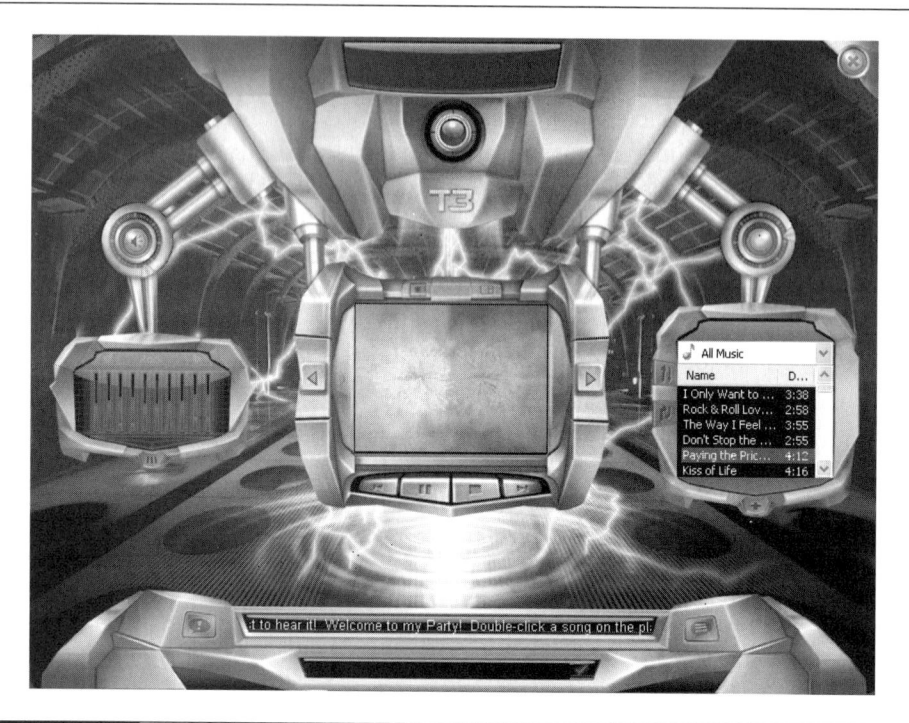

FIGURE 18-6 You can download additional Party Mode skins, such as this Terminator 3 skin.

When you have all of your settings configured, all you have to do is click Start Party.

Use Party Mode

All right, now it's time to party! When you click Start Party on the Specify Your Party Mode Settings window, Party Mode begins, and your screen turns to the Party Mode skin that you have selected. What you see there depends on the skin and the options you chose when you were setting up your party. For the most part, the controls are basically the same as those that you see when using Windows Media Player, but Figure 18-7 offers a quick look at the default Party Mode skin.

- **Exit** Takes you to the Welcome Screen, if you have chosen to use the Privacy option.

- **View/Hide Playlist** Shows the playlist on the screen, or hides it. If you have allowed users to access your Media Library, they can use the drop-down menu here to select other playlists available.

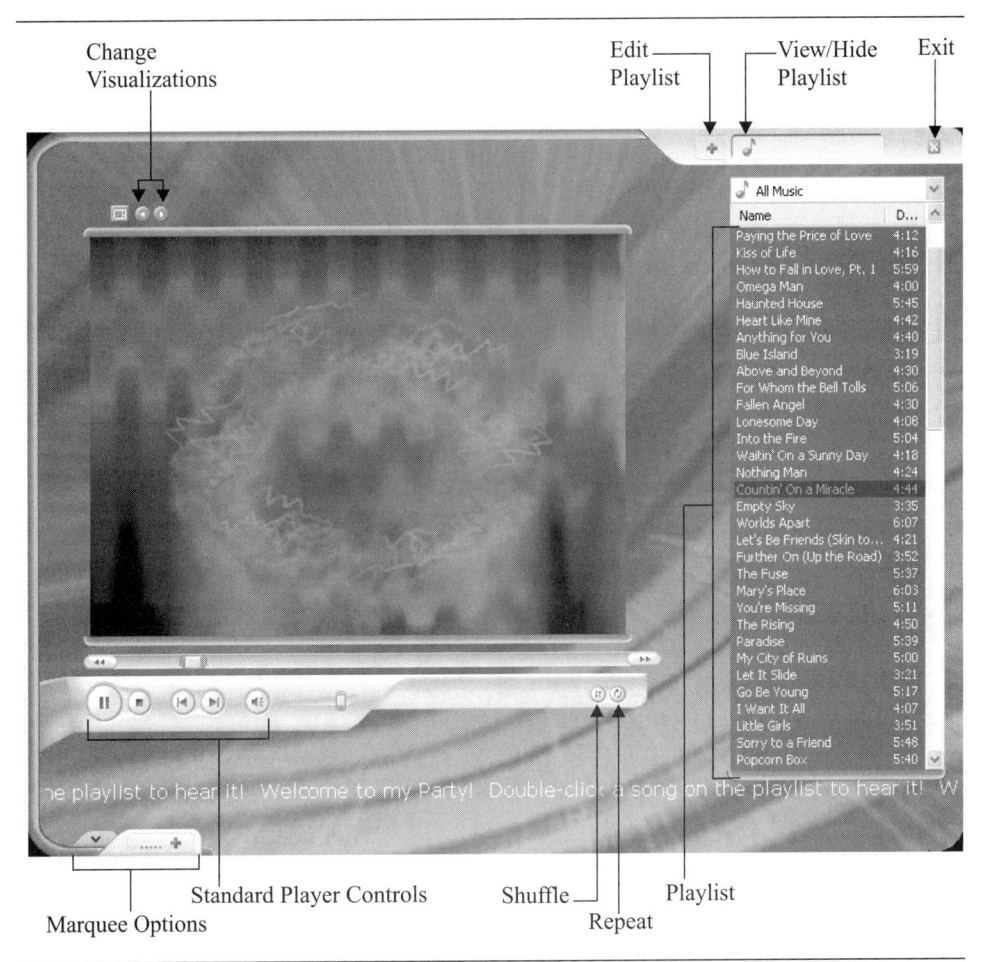

CHAPTER 18: Turn Your Computer into a Jukebox (and Back Again) 291

FIGURE 18-7 The Party Mode options

- **Edit Playlist** Enables users to make changes to the playlist, if you have allowed users to access the Media Library.
- **Playlist** Users can find the song they want here and double-click to hear it.
- **Repeat** Repeats the current song.
- **Shuffle** Plays songs on the playlist at random.
- **Standard Player Controls** Include Pause, Stop, Go Forward, Go Backward, and Volume buttons.

- **Marquee Options** Enables users to turn the marquee on or off or add their own comments, if you allowed this option.

- **Change Visualization** Users can click these buttons to choose a different visualization.

As you can see, the controls are pretty simple. Keep in mind that your interface may look different than the one in Figure 18-7, depending on the skin and the options you selected. As you can see in Figure 18-8, the Nature skin looks quite a bit different, but the controls all do the same things as those in the default skin. As with Windows Media Player, you can hover over a button and a text box appears, telling you what the controls do.

FIGURE 18-8   Nature Party Mode skin

Stop the Party

Like all good things in life, the party must come to an end at some point. How can you stop the party? Here's what you do:

- If you didn't use the Privacy Option, just click the Exit button in Party Mode. This will take you back to your desktop and Specify Your Party Mode Settings window. Click the Stop Party button. A message appears, asking you to confirm that the party is over (see Figure 18-9). Click Yes to stop the party.

- If you used the Privacy Option, click the Exit button in Party Mode. You are taken to the Windows welcome screen. Click your user account and enter your password, and you'll end up back at your desktop and the Specify Your Party Mode Settings window (see Figure 18-9). Click the Stop Party button, and then click Yes in the message window that appears.

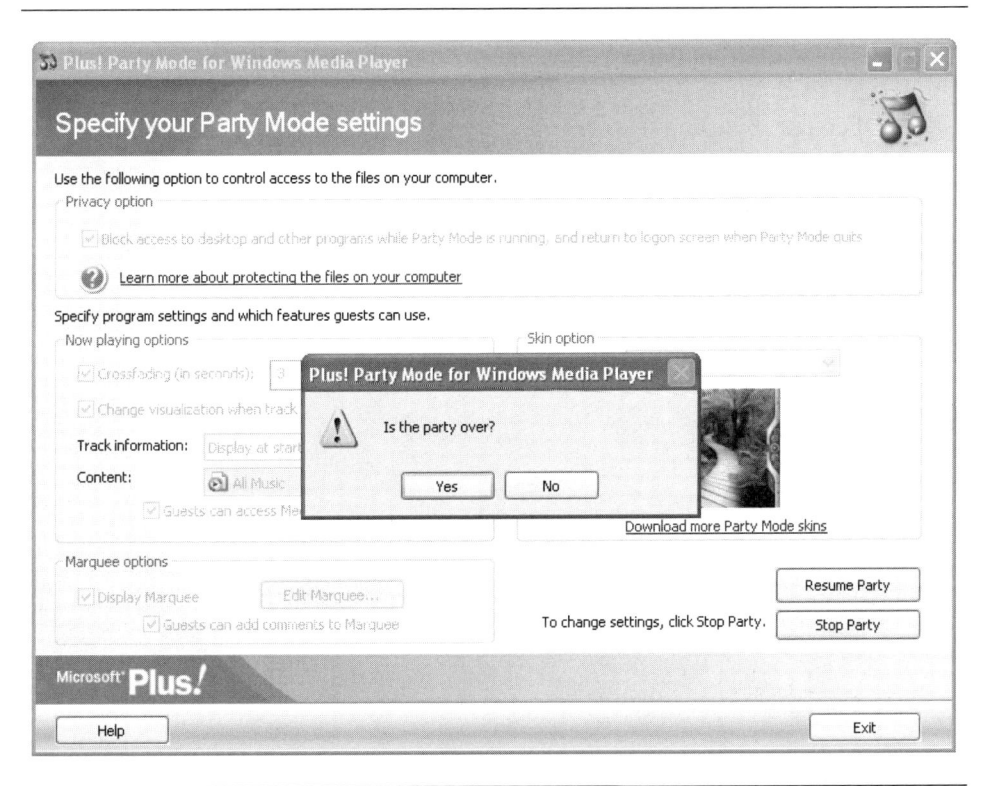

FIGURE 18-9 To stop your party, click Stop Party, and then click Yes in this message window.

Next, click the Exit button to close the Party Mode software. A dialog box appears, asking if you want to save your settings. If you do, click Yes, and you'll see the same settings the next time you open Party Mode.

More Great Ideas

Party Mode is loads of fun! Try these additional ideas:

- Put personal messages to some of your guests on the marquee. If you are using Party Mode for a birthday party, don't forget to put up a happy birthday message.

- Keep in mind that you can edit the songs on your playlist as well as the song titles on the playlist. Consider making a few personal changes, such as "Bill's favorite song."

- If you want the party to be automatic, keep in mind that you can choose the playlist you want but not allow guests access to the playlist at all. This will have Party Mode run automatically without anyone choosing different songs. Of course, by using this feature you may lose some of the fun of the party, but you may have reasons for doing so!

Chapter 19
Digitize Your Old Cassettes, 8-Tracks, and Records

How to...

- Connect your audio device to your Windows XP computer
- Digitize and save your music to Windows Media Player

Okay, I can admit it. I'm over thirty. And in my downstairs closet, hidden far, far away in the corner, is a collection of my favorite '80s groups, including Prince, Madonna, the Go-Gos, Bon Jovi, and many others. My seven-year-old daughter was looking through them just a few weeks ago and remarked, "Why did they all dress so weird and have such weird hair?" Ah, the passing of time.

In my collection, I have a lot of old cassettes as well as a bunch of old records. I loved them all, but let's face it, technology has left them behind. I don't even have a record player any more, and I can't stand listening to cassettes. Sure, you can try to rebuy some of those old favorites that are now on CD, but many of the artists I liked years ago are longer "in business," and that last cassette or record is all that remains.

This is where Microsoft Plus! Digital Media Edition comes to the rescue. Digital Media Edition has a little utility called Plus! Analog Recorder. This little recorder allows you to connect your stereo, record player, or even reel-to-reel player to your Windows XP computer, and then record all of the analog data into Windows XP! From that point, the Analog Recorder can clean it up, and then you are free to use it as a digital file. Sound cool? It is, and in this chapter, I'll walk you through the project of saving your old music to your computer.

What You'll Need

For this project, you'll need Microsoft Plus! Digital Media Edition, which can be purchased for about $20 at most computer stores or online computer stores, or downloaded for free if you have a broadband Internet connection. See Chapter 2 for more details about getting and installing this software.

Connect Your Player to Your Computer

The most difficult part of using the Analog Recorder is really just getting your record player, cassette player, 8-track player, or whatever audio device you want to use hooked up to your computer. Once the device is connected to your Windows XP computer, the Analog Recorder can detect it and "listen" to the device, recording the cassettes or records that you play. So, your main task is to get the device connected, and this section is organized to make that as easy as possible.

Check Out the Hardware Requirements

When you connect a device to your computer and expect your computer to interact with it, you are working with hardware. The main task with any computer and any device is to get the device connected to the computer so that the computer software (such as Analog Recorder) can recognize it and use the actual hardware. Sounds simple enough, but of course, there are certain requirements that must be met.

First, the record player, stereo, cassette player, or whatever you want to connect has to have a line-out port. This port, which is typically found on the back of the unit, allows you to connect cables that send the analog signal to something else. Check on the back of the unit and refer to your owner's manual if necessary to see if your device has a line-out port so that you can connect it to your computer.

If you are sending a line-out from the device, guess what your computer must have? That's right, a line-in port. The line-in port is found on the computer's sound card on the back of the computer. Turn your computer around and check it out. The place where you connect your speakers and microphone should have another port that is a line-in port. Again, check your computer documentation for details. What if you don't have a line-out and line-in port? Sorry, I'm afraid you must have these items in order to move forward.

To connect a stereo receiver, a record player, or a reel-to-reel or cassette player, you'll need the right connection cables. Table 19-1 tells you what you need.

If all of this sounds like gibberish to you, here's an easy trick. Write down what you need using the following table, and take a quick trip over to an electronics store such as RadioShack, CompUSA, or Best Buy, hand the clerk your piece f paper, and say, "Help me, please." The items listed are standard connection components

Analog Audio Device	Hardware Requirements
Stereo receiver	Use one of the following connector options: A Y stereo adapter cable with a pair of RCA-style, left- and right-channel connectors (male) and a single line-in, 1/8-inch (3.5mm) mini connector. A stereo hookup cable with two pairs of RCA-style, left- and right-channel connectors (male), and an audio adapter with a pair of RCA-style, left- and right-channel connectors (female), and a single line-in, 1/8-inch (3.5mm) mini connector.
Record player	Use a preamplifier, which increases the record player's signal to the proper line-out specification for the line-in port on your computer's sound card. To meet this preamplifier requirement, you must connect your record player to a stereo receiver or a phono preamplifier unit, and then connect the receiver or preamplifier unit to your sound card.

TABLE 19-1 Hardware Requirements for Analog Audio Devices

Analog Audio Device	Hardware Requirements
Cassette or reel-to-reel player	Use one of the following connector options: A Y stereo adapter cable with a pair of RCA-style, left- and right-channel connectors (male) and a single line-in, 1/8-inch (3.5mm) mini connector. A stereo hookup cable with two pairs of RCA-style, left- and right-channel connectors (male), and an audio adapter with a pair of RCA-style, left- and right-channel connectors (female), and a single line-in, 1/8-inch (3.5mm) mini connector.

TABLE 19-1 Hardware Requirements for Analog Audio Devices *(continued)*

that you should be able to get your hands on without having to order them from the North Pole. If you prefer to shop online, you can also find these items at sites such as www.amazon.com, www.tigerdirect.com, and other general electronics sites.

Connect a Stereo

If you are connecting your stereo or, in truth, even your VCR to your computer, you have one of two ways to connect it, using the information from Table 19-1. First, keep in mind that stereos have two line-out ports. This gives you the left- and right-speaker sound as an out port. However, your computer has only one line-in port. So, you need to do a bit of fancy cable footwork to make it happen.

In order to connect your stereo to your computer, take a look at Figure 19-1. You have an option to connect with either a single Y cable (top) or a stereo cable

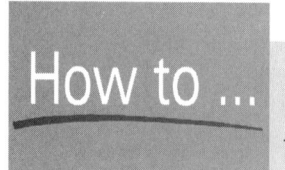

How to ... Connect Your VCR to Your Computer

A VCR has two line-out ports: One carries video and one carries audio, and you have probably used them in numerous occasions to connect the VCR directly to your television. However, what if you have a music video and want to record the music to Windows XP? No problem, just connect the line-out audio to your line-in port on your computer, and you're all set. Of course, you do not get stereo quality due to the single line, but you can still record the music, clean it up in Windows XP, and enjoy it anyway.

CHAPTER 19: Digitize Your Old Cassettes, 8-Tracks, and Records

Connection using a single "Y" cable.

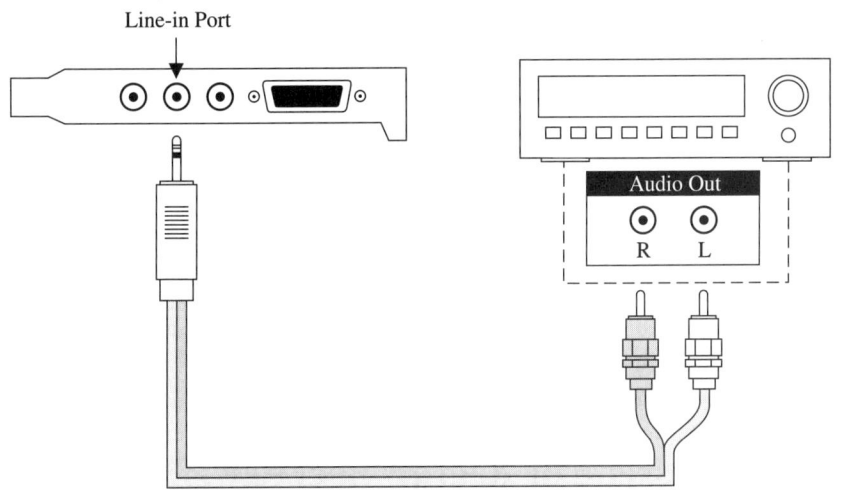

Connection using a stereo cable and adapter.

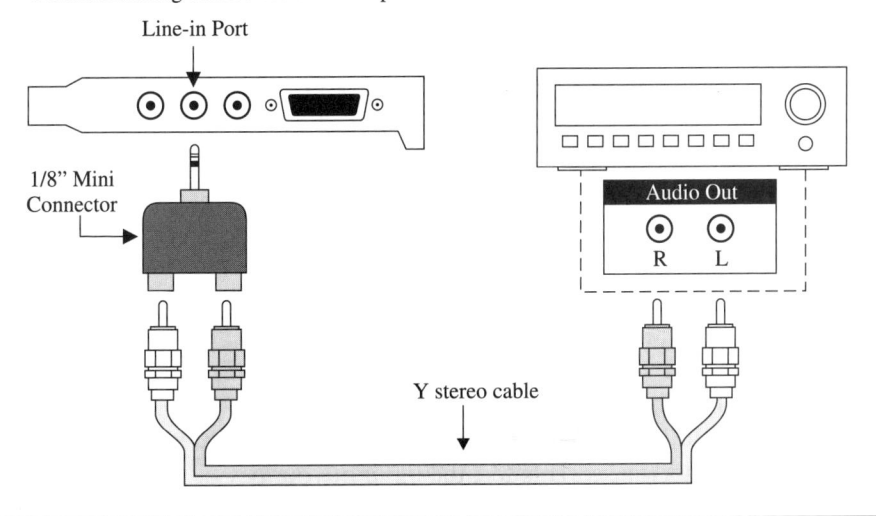

FIGURE 19-1 You can connect your stereo to your computer using a Y cable (top) or an adapter (bottom).

and adapter (bottom). As you can see, the goal in both configurations is to get the dual-line stereo feed down to one line for your computer.

If you are starting to fret that this is getting too technical, don't worry. Again, these connection cables are readily available at nearly all electronics stores. Often, this kind of connection-cable hula hoop is needed to connect different kinds of stereo components, so you are not doing anything weird or strange. You can even take this book along with you to the electronics store and show them Figure 19-1, and they should be able to set you up with what you need.

Once you have your cables, just hook them up as shown in Figure 19-1, and you're all set. Skip to the "Digitize Your Music" section.

Connect a Record Player

To connect your record player to your computer, it must be connected to an amplifier or, more simply, a stereo unit. The way to do this is to connect the record player to the stereo, select the record player as the output option on the stereo, and then connect the stereo to your computer in the same configuration as shown in Figure 19-1. Obviously, you must have a stereo that supports a record player hookup. Once you're done, skip to the "Record Your Music" section.

Connect a Cassette or Reel-to-Reel Player

Your cassette or reel-to-reel player must have line-out ports, which may also be called tape-out or line-level ports on the player. Then, make the exact same kind of connection as shown in Figure 19-1. Note that some tape players and reel-to-reel players do not provide line-out ports, in which case you have to use a stereo that provides this kind of output. Otherwise, the connection to the computer is exactly the same.

Digitize Your Music

Once you get your stereo or component connected to your computer, the rest of the process is rather easy. However, the simple Analog Recorder does give you quite a few important options for managing the audio that you record. In this section, you'll see just how to use those options.

First things first: Insert the tape or get the record ready that you want to play. The Analog Recorder will want to test the input of your device before you actually start recording. To get started with the Analog Recorder, click Start | All Programs | Plus! Digital Media Edition | Plus! Analog Recorder. The Analog Recorder appears (see Figure 19-2), and you can select some options to learn more about connecting your device to your computer or about recording and management options. We'll explore those as we move forward, so go ahead and get started by clicking Next here, and then just follow the rest of this chapter to record and work with your music.

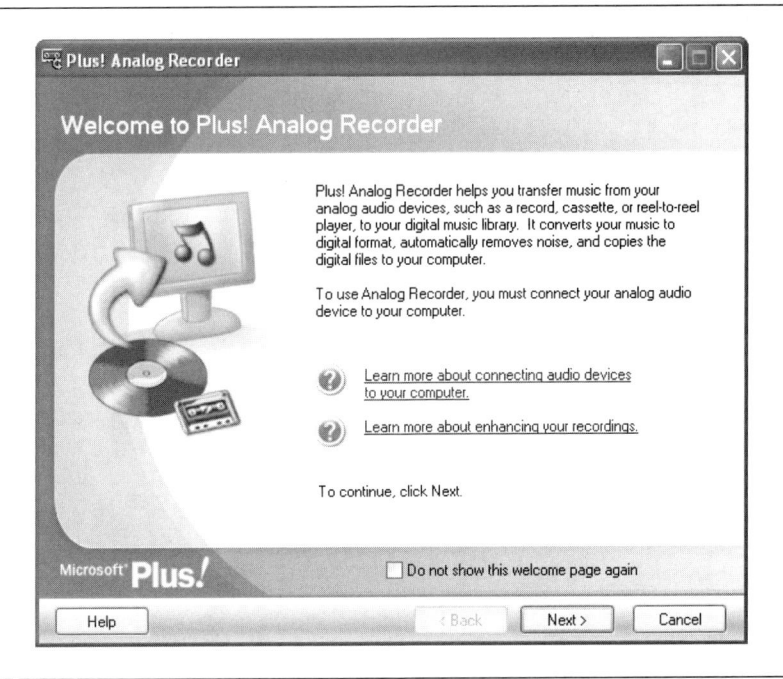

FIGURE 19-2   The Plus! Analog Recorder

Test Your Input

The next wizard screen gives you a place to test your input (see Figure 19-3). Start your tape or record and a portion of generally loud music, then use the drop-down menu to select the input option, which should be Line In. Next, click the Test option to test the input. The Analog Recorder will test your input to see if it is loud enough. If you get a message telling you that Analog Recorder has detected only a faint signal, you need to:

1. Ensure that your equipment is connected properly and that you are connected to the line-in port on your sound card. If you continue to have problems, you can try using the microphone input and see if that works.
2. Turn up the volume on your stereo or device.
3. Turn up the Volume slider bar on the wizard screen.
4. Run the test again.

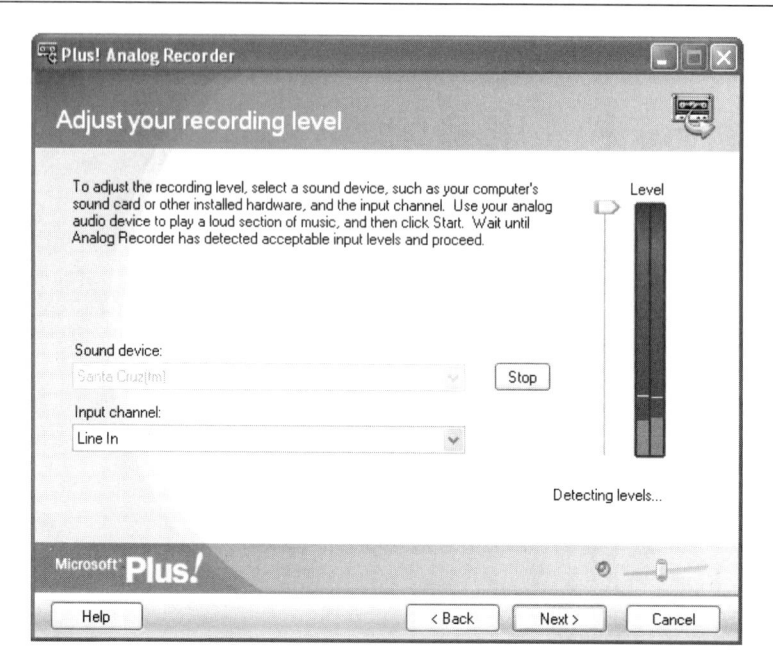

FIGURE 19-3 Testing the audio input level

Once you run a successful test, the Analog Recorder will stop testing, and you'll see a message on the wizard screen telling you that an acceptable level of audio was detected. You can now move forward with the wizard, so click Next.

Record Your Music

Now you are ready to record your music. On the Record Your Music page of the wizard, you see Record, Pause, and Stop buttons (see Figure 19-4). When you are ready, press play on your stereo or other device, then click the Record button on the wizard screen. At this point, all you have to do is sit back and wait until you are finished recording the music. You can record the entire tape or record at one time. If you need to stop and turn over the record or cassette, just click the Pause button on the wizard screen, flip the tape or record, and click Pause again to resume recording.

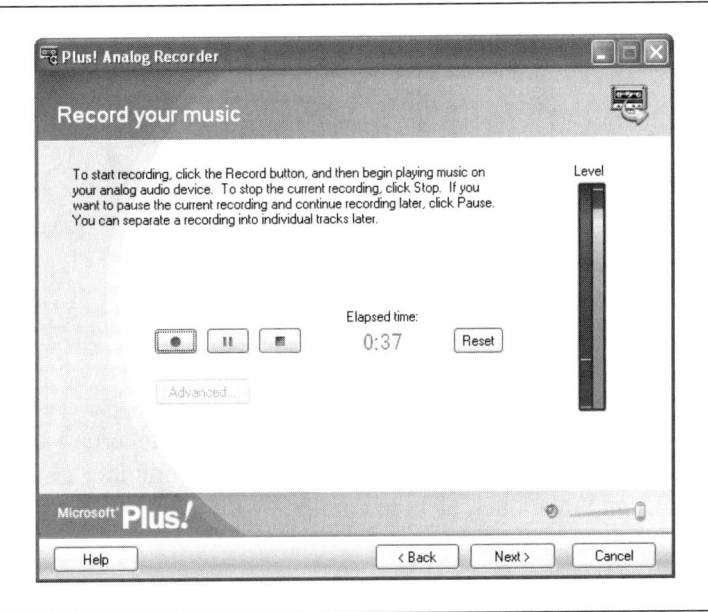

FIGURE 19-4 Recording your music

Now, what if you want some—but not all—songs from a cassette or record? You can do one of two things:

- Use the Pause button on the wizard screen to edit out the songs you don't want as your cassette or record continues playing.

- Record everything and use the wizard to edit it later, which we explore in the "Review, Modify, and Delete Tracks" section.

Once the recording is complete, you'll notice that the Advanced button on this page becomes active. If you click it, the Advanced Recording Options window opens (see Figure 19-5). The Automatically Detect And Split Tracks check box, which is selected by default, allows the Analog Recorder to try to determine where the track breaks occur; it looks for the silence gap between songs and determines the track break from that point. You should leave this option selected, because it is a

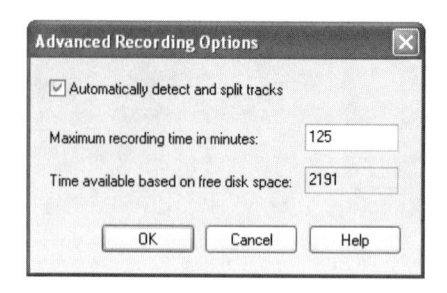

FIGURE 19-5 Advanced recording options

big help to you. You also see the amount of time you have recorded and the total amount of available time on the disk, according to your computer's available disk space. Click OK, and then click Next to continue with the wizard.

Review, Modify, and Delete Tracks

The next wizard screen, Review And Name Your Tracks, is a bit misnamed, because you perform other important tasks here, including splitting tracks, combining tracks, or deleting unwanted tracks.

Name and Review Tracks

The Analog Recorder simply records what it hears, so it has no idea about the names of your songs. So, you can simply walk through your recording and give the tracks actual names. This will make using the tracks easier later on.

To name a track, just select it in the track list on the left of the wizard screen (see Figure 19-6). Then, in the right portion of the window, type a new track name, the artist, the album name, and the genre. You don't have to type all of the information—you can type just the name, if you like. After you enter this information, it is a good idea to click the Play button and listen to the track, just to make sure everything recorded OK. Continue this process for each track until you have all of your tracks named.

Delete Tracks

As mentioned earlier, you can edit out tracks as you are recording by using the Pause button on the wizard's Record Your Music page. If you didn't do that, don't fear—you can delete the tracks you don't want now. Just locate the track and click Play on the wizard screen to make certain that it is the one you want to delete. If you are sure, just click the Delete button. Click Yes to the confirmation message that appears, and the track disappears from your track list.

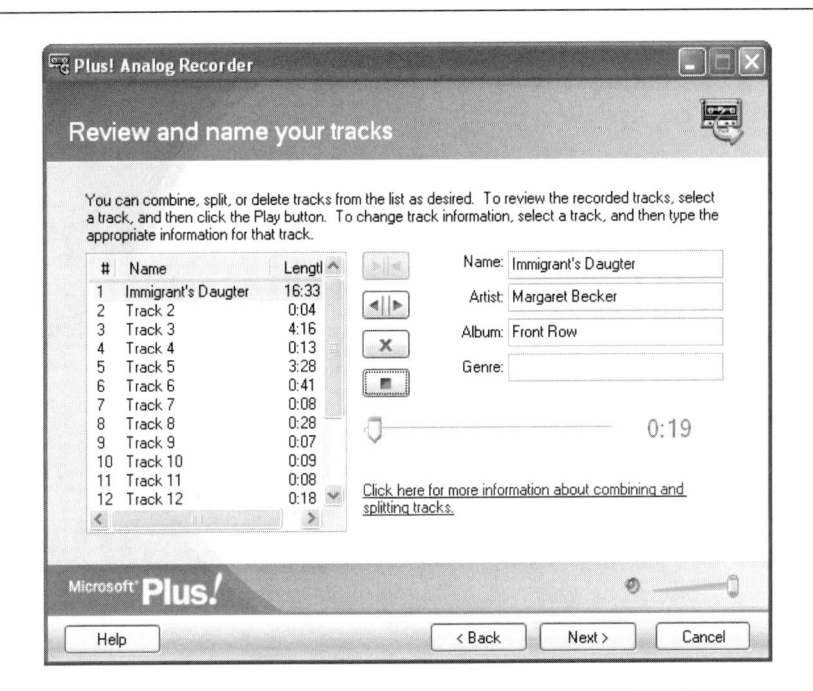

CHAPTER 19: Digitize Your Old Cassettes, 8-Tracks, and Records   305

FIGURE 19-6   Select a track and type your naming information for it.

CAUTION   *Be careful! There is no Undo option within the wizard, so if you delete a track accidentally, you'll have to go back and re-record.*

Split Tracks

The Analog Recorder does a good job of splitting tracks on normal records and cassettes. However, sometimes it makes a mistake. Or, what if you are recording a live concert that has talking and clapping? These kinds of recordings really confuse Analog Recorder so you'll have to help it out. If you refer to Figure 19-6, you'll see that some of my tracks are long and some are very short (Track 2 is only four seconds!). This occurred because I recorded a music concert from a VHS tape. In order to clean everything up and remove the extra stuff, I'll have to split some tracks and remove the extra noise I don't want.

Again, don't worry—the process is easy. Just do this:

1. Select the track in question and click Play. Listen to the track until you reach the point where you want to split it.

2. Click the Stop button.

3. Click the Split Track button (see Figure 19-7). The track is split in two, and now you can name and work with the new track.

4. Repeat this process as needed for other tracks.

Combine Tracks

In the same way that you can split tracks, you can combine a track or two. Again, this is especially true if you are recoding a concert, as the Analog Recorder may inadvertently split a track that should be one. No problem, you can fix it easily, and here's how:

1. Hold down the CTRL key on your keyboard and then, in the track list, select the two tracks that need to be combined.

2. Click the Combine Selected Tracks button (see Figure 19-8).

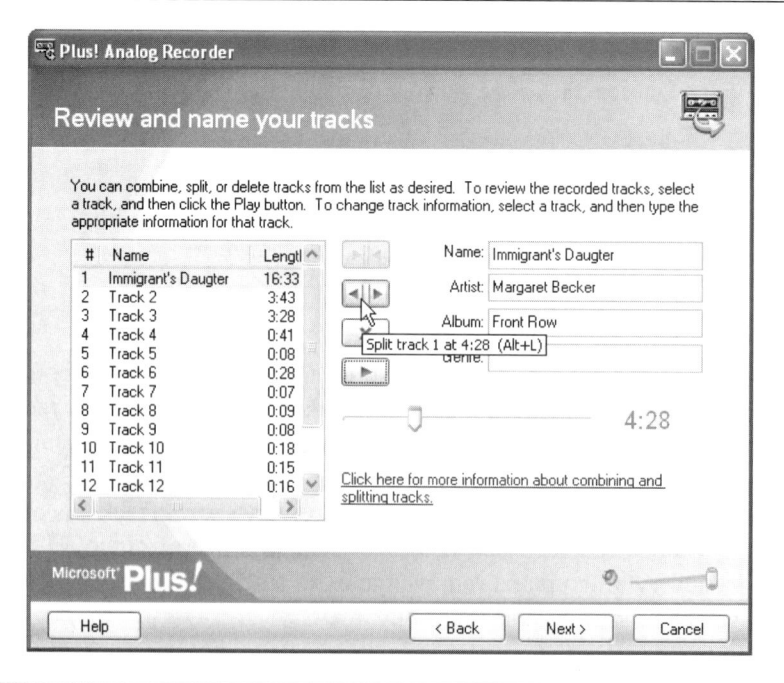

FIGURE 19-7 Stop playing the music where you want to split the track and press the Split Track button.

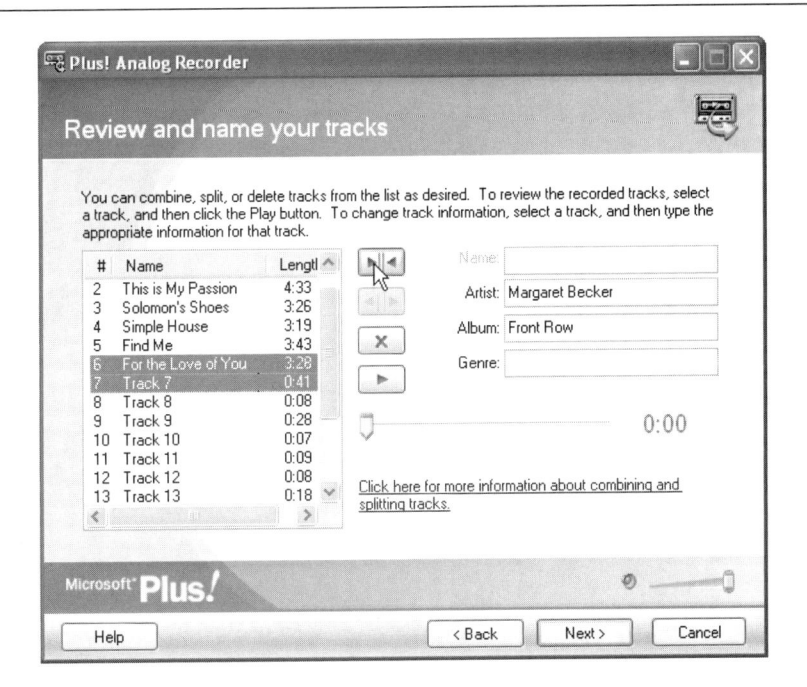

FIGURE 19-8 Click the Combine button to combine two selected tracks.

As you can see, the Analog Recorder's split and combine options enable you to do just about any editing you need with your music! Spend some time now cleaning everything up, and you'll be really happy with your recording later.

Once you are done with all of your editing, click Next to continue.

Clean Tracks

Analog tapes and records are notorious for pops and hissing sounds, which are caused basically by nature of analog media itself as well as by scratches and imperfections on the tape or record. Analog Recorder can place a couple of filters over your tracks to try to remove—or at least greatly diminish—those imperfections. I strongly recommend that you use these filters, since they can really help your recording.

To do so, just click the Reduce Pops and Reduce Hiss check boxes on the Clean Your Tracks wizard screen (see Figure 19-9). Then, select a track and click Play to hear how well the Analog Recorder has cleaned it up. When you're done cleaning, click Next to continue.

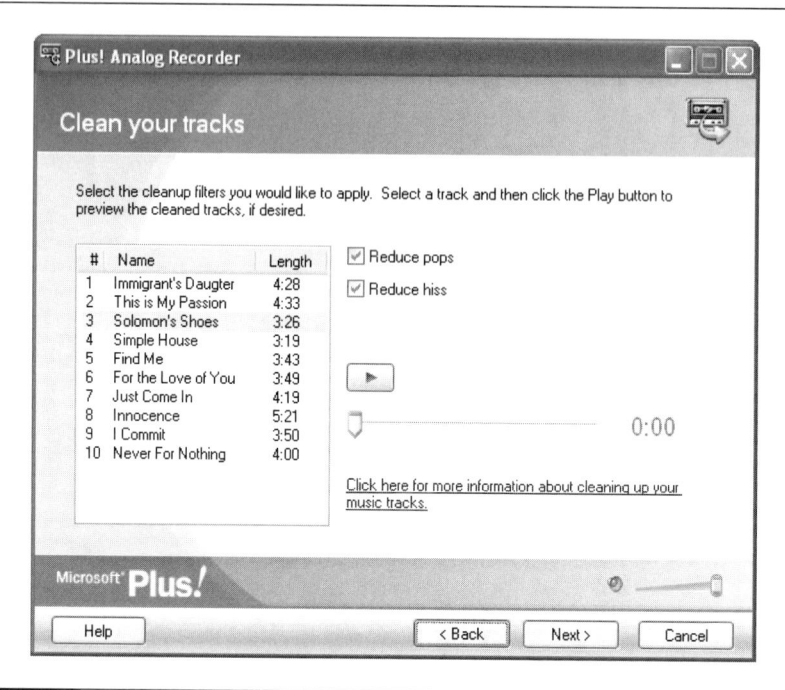

FIGURE 19-9 Cleaning up your tracks

Set Content Protection Options

After you clean up your tracks and click Next, a Content Protection Options pop-up box appears (see Figure 19-10). This window enables you to copy-protect music so that it can be played on your computer or a portable device. Or, you can choose not to copy-protect music, which will allow you more ways to work with it. You must select the check box concerning illegal distribution.

Here's the skinny: You don't have to copy-protect the music but, by law, you cannot give it away to other people or make CDs of the music and sell it. Okay, enough said on that issue. Click the option you want and click OK to close the window.

Select Quality Settings and Save Tracks

The next wizard window, Select Settings And Save Tracks, enables you to save your tracks and choose quality settings (see Figure 19-11). By default, the music is saved in your My Music folder, and that location is fine. However, you can choose a different location just by clicking the Change button. You can also click the Advanced button to specify some additional information about what data is

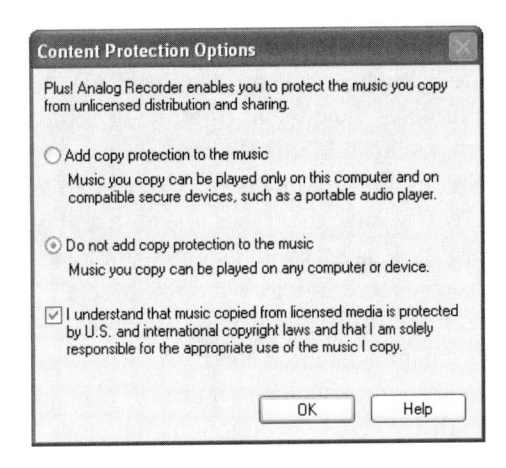

CHAPTER 19: Digitize Your Old Cassettes, 8-Tracks, and Records   309

FIGURE 19-10   Copy-protection options

saved with your track (such as the artist). You don't really need to change anything here, so I suggest you just skip over it.

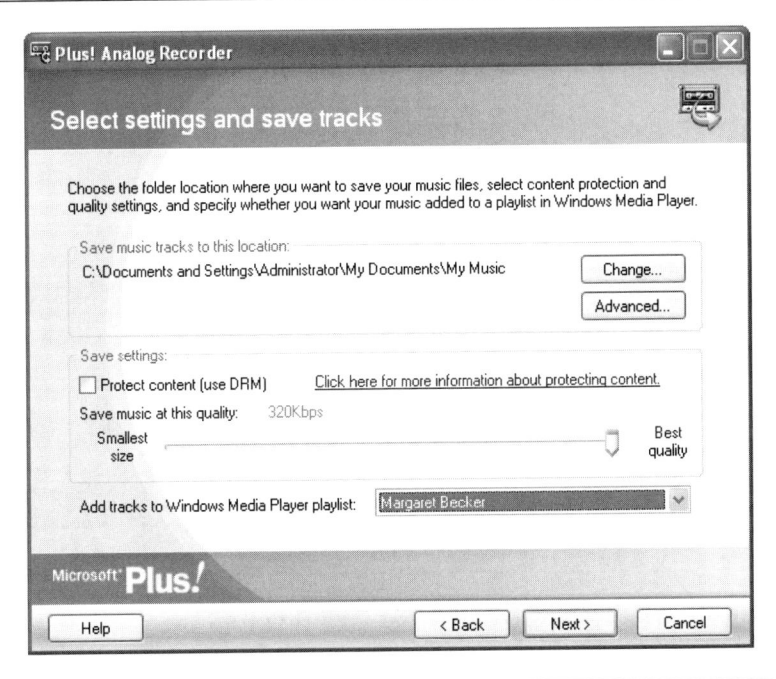

FIGURE 19-11   Choosing your saving options

You can also adjust the quality settings slider bar. For now, I suggest that you save your music at the highest-quality setting. This will give you the best playback and use with your recorded music. You can also use the Protect Content check box, if you like, which protects the content from being copied, just like any other content-protected file in Windows Media Player.

The final cool feature on this window is Add Tracks To Windows Media Player Playlist, which enables you to have the tracks added to a playlist in Windows Media Player automatically. This saves you some work later, so I actually created a playlist specifically for my recording in Windows Media Player beforehand. See Chapter 1 to learn more about using playlists in Windows Media Player. When you are done with this wizard page, just click Next.

Now, the wizard saves your music (see Figure 19-12). Notice that the music is saved as a WMA file so that you can listen to it in Windows Media Player. Saving may take a little time, depending on how much data you recorded. Once the saving process is complete, you can open Windows Media Player and listen to your newly digitized music!

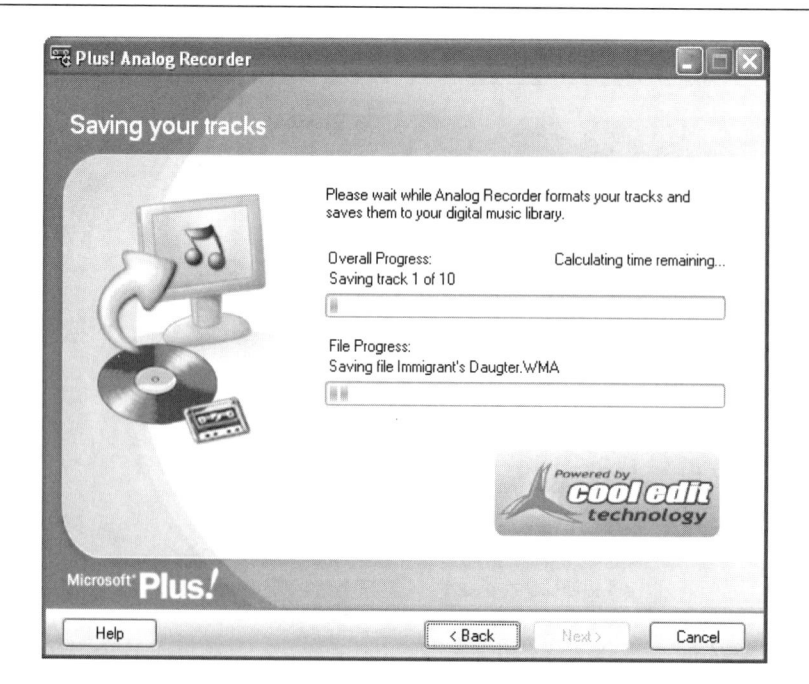

FIGURE 19-12   The wizard saves your music as a WMA file.

More Great Ideas

Analog Recorder is one of Microsoft's best-kept secrets! Try these additional ideas:

- Record your old music, and use Windows Media Player to listen to it and create new playlists. You can work with your new tracks just as you would any other song in Media Player.

- Create a music CD of your newly recorded music so that you can listen to it while you are on the go. See Chapter 1 for details!

Appendix A: Get to Know Windows Movie Maker 2

How to…

- Get connected with Movie Maker
- Learn the Movie Maker interface
- Use and manage movie clips

Windows Movie Maker 2 is a fun, free utility included with Windows XP (or available for download if you need the latest version), but before you can start using it, you'll need to get your bearings and know how to move around and do a few things in Movie Maker. Also, you'll need to know how to import video data and even still pictures that you might want to use, so this appendix will help get your feet on solid ground with Movie Maker. Then, you can go back to Part III of this book and do those fun Movie Maker projects.

What You'll Need

For this appendix, you'll need Windows Movie Maker 2 (which can be downloaded for free from www.microsoft.com/windowsxp/moviemaker), some video you want to get into Movie Maker, and some digital photos.

What Movie Maker 2 Can Do for You

If you are like me, you tend to make a lot of videos. There's everything from Aunt Ruth's birthday party to little Johnny's latest shenanigans. You may also have piles of still pictures lying around—most of them not even in albums. Windows Movie Maker is designed to help you both manage and edit your home videos and pictures. You can use Movie Maker to organize the data, edit it, save it, and even share it with others over the Internet. In short, it gives you a way to manage those precious moments electronically and reduce the clutter around your house.

One of the greatest benefits of Windows Movie Maker is that you can take analog video (such as your typical camcorder or VHS tape), import it into your computer, and then manage it electronically. "So what?" you might ask. The great thing about this feature is the *fault tolerance*—once the video (and even pictures) are stored electronically, you can create multiple copies of them. If your computer has a CD/DVD burner (Read/Write CD-ROM), you can store your movies on CD/DVD for safekeeping. Windows Millenium Edition (Windows Me) enables you to make copies safely and easily of your life captured on film to ensure that nothing happens to those memories in the future.

APPENDIX A: Get to Know Windows Movie Maker 2

Another great feature of Movie Maker is editing. In any given videotaping session, you are likely to have a lot of dull spots. Consider this personal example: Our daughter was born a few years ago, and in my excitement, I took miles of videotape at the hospital. A few weeks after the commotion of the new birth, we sat down to watch the hospital video. We saw heartwarming moments and memories we never want to lose, but we were also faced with hours of boring footage. Not wanting to miss anything, we filmed *everything*. Although everything seemed important at the time, in retrospect, I don't need to see hours of myself saying: "Here we are, waiting for the baby…"

With Windows Movie Maker, it's easy to cut away the boring sections of video and keep the good stuff. This ability makes watching your movies more interesting and entertaining—and shorter. Also, the editing feature can help reduce the amount of storage space, and you can even join together unrelated clips of video.

Finally, you can have lots of fun with Movie Maker. Create your own home movies and edit in transitions, voice, background music, and much more. Once you get your hands on the software, you'll see that Movie Maker is simple and fun to use, and you'll be all set to do the great projects in Part III of this book.

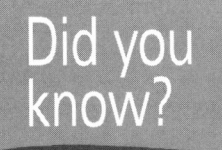

Did you know?

What's Not So Great About Windows Movie Maker

Believe me, I'm not completely enraptured with Windows Movie Maker. So for all of you skeptics and otherwise curious readers who want to know what's not so great about Windows Movie Maker, I'll give you my two cents in this section.

First, Windows Movie Maker is a free application included with your XP system— this should indicate to you that video-editing software is not Microsoft's main focus, and Movie Maker is, in fact, a *basic* video-editing package. It is not an advanced application. I've used other video-editing software from other vendors that was much, much better, so I don't mind telling you up front that if you are really interested in getting into movie editing and production, you want to look for a different software package that will really give you the power and tools that you need. However, Windows Movie Maker is free and readily available; if you have basic video-editing needs, Movie Maker will work just fine. Overall, the software is very intuitive and easy to use, as you will discover in this appendix.

> There is one caveat regarding Windows Movie Maker: When you create movies in Movie Maker, you are forced to save them in Windows Media Video (WMV) file format. You do not have the option to use other standard video formats, such as AVI or MPEG, even though Windows Movie Maker can read these types of files. The point here is that you will need a Windows computer that has Windows Media Player installed to be able to play Movie Maker files. That may not be a big deal, but if you want to play the video on a system that does not have Windows Media Player, such as a Macintosh, you may have some compatibility problems.

Get Ready to Use Windows Movie Maker

If you read like I do, you may be tempted to skip over this section and get to the fun stuff, but I encourage you to read this section carefully to avoid a bunch of headaches and sorrow later on. Windows Movie Maker is a great tool, but in order to make it work, you have to spend a little time inspecting the hardware requirements. The trick, of course, is to get your analog or digital video and/or pictures inside your computer and to Windows Movie Maker.

First of all, let's consider the basic system requirements that you need in order to run Windows Movie Maker:

- **Pentium 600 MHz or equivalent** If you're using Windows XP on an older processor that is limping along, I'm afraid it won't have the power that Movie Maker needs to process graphics and sound.

- **128MB of RAM** You need a minimum of 128MB of RAM for Windows Movie Maker to function properly. If you want to function well, you should have more RAM than 64MB.

- **Up to 2GB of storage space** Movie files use a lot of storage space. Make sure your computer has plenty of room to store the movies that you create.

- **A video card or video capture device**

- **A sound card or sound capture device**

> **TIP** *Windows Movie Maker will look for and expect to find both a video card and a sound card or other capture device. If it doesn't, you'll receive a message telling you that your computer does not meet the Movie Maker requirements. In this case, you'll need to do some hardware upgrading to your computer.*

Get Video into Windows Movie Maker

Now that you know the basic requirements, let's spend a moment talking about getting video and pictures into your computer. First, if you are using a digital camera or camcorder, you're not going to have any problems at all. Because the media is already digital, you simply connect your camera or camcorder into your computer and follow the manufacturer's instructions for saving the digital content to your hard disk.

For the best performance, your computer needs an IEEE 1394 card so that you can import movies from a digital camcorder into your computer (this is especially important if you'll be using any streaming-media devices). This type of card provides fast transfer from the camcorder to the computer and is highly recommended by Microsoft. You will need to do a little investigative work to determine whether your computer has this card, if your digital camcorder supports it, and if this transfer card is right for you. Refer to your computer and camcorder documentation for more information. You can purchase IEEE 1394 cards at most computer stores. Most major video-card manufacturers make these cards, although they are not standard hardware on most computers.

Windows Movie Maker can recognize all kinds of graphics files, from AVI and MPEG to basic web files such as JPEG and GIF. Once the files are loaded and saved onto your hard disk, you can use Windows Movie Maker to import and begin working with them.

But what about still pictures or analog video? What about a song you have written that you want to use as background music? Once you move out of the native digital arena, you must use *capture devices* to move the analog information into your computer, where it is converted to digital information and saved. In order to do that, you need a capture device that can import the data into your computer. These capture devices are video cards with video- and audio-input ports and sound cards with audio-input ports (they have the same kind of connections that, typically, you would find on the back of a VCR). By connecting your analog camcorder or VCR to a video card, you can receive the analog data from the camcorder or VCR and convert it to a digital format for use on your computer. In the same manner, your sound card can convert music and voice data from an analog device into a digital format that can be used on your computer.

You may have a video card and a sound card already that supports this process. If not, you can purchase new cards at your local computer store. They're not terribly expensive (generally anywhere from $100 to $200), but do make sure they are compatible with Windows XP—check the Windows XP web site (www.microsoft.com/windowsxp) for continually updated information about compatible hardware.

Also, if you previously owned one of these cards under Windows 98/Me/2000, you may need to download new drivers from the card's manufacturer for it to work correctly with Windows XP. Check the manufacturer's web site to see if there is an update.

NOTE *If you decide to buy a new card, make sure you know what kind of slot—usually either PCI or AGP—is available in your computer for the card. Refer to your computer's documentation for more information about available ports.*

Once you connect your analog device to the capture devices, you can start the video on the analog device and then use Windows Movie Maker to view and capture it—in a perfect world, anyway. Unfortunately, depending on your hardware, you can experience problems. Because of the variety of hardware available, it is impossible to solve all potential problems here, but I can give you a big tip that might save you some headaches. Usually, the capture device will ship with a CD-ROM containing the card's drivers and a program or two to help you capture video. Use the card's capture program and save the video in a common file format, such as AVI or MPG. You can then import the file into Movie Maker and begin your work from there. (See the upcoming "Record and Import Video" section for information about importing.)

TIP *Check out your capture device's instructions. Most capture devices tell you exactly how to connect the analog device to the card and capture video—and most even provide the cables you'll need to do so.*

CAUTION *Many capture devices save video files in their own default format, which may include compression that Windows XP does not support. When you start to save video using the card's program, make sure you are saving it in a format that Windows Movie Maker supports.*

Check Out the Movie Maker Interface

Before you get started using Movie Maker, take a few moments to familiarize yourself with the interface (see Figure A-1). Fortunately, the Movie Maker interface follows the typical Windows program interface, so it's not completely foreign to you. You can find Windows Movie Maker by clicking Start | All Programs | Windows Movie Maker.

APPENDIX A: Get to Know Windows Movie Maker 2   319

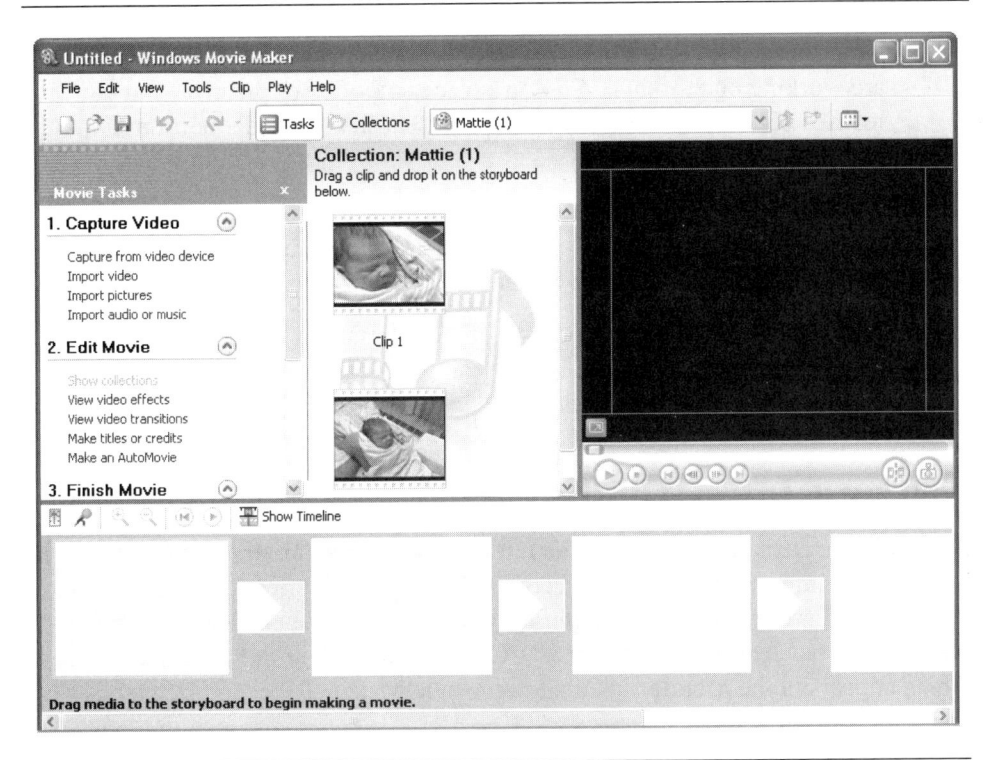

FIGURE A-1   You see a basic interface when you open Movie Maker for the first time.

There are four major parts to the Windows Movie Maker interface:

- **Toolbars**   At the top of the interface, you see the Windows Movie Maker toolbars. You first see the menu options, such as File, Edit, View, Clip, and so on. The menu options contain typical Windows menu features plus those that are specific to Windows Movie Maker. You will also see the standard toolbar, under the menus, which presents typical toolbar options. Finally, you will see a third toolbar called the Collections/Locations Toolbar, which is used to manage the video collections you are working on at the moment. *Collections* are simply file folders used to hold portions of video or pictures—a simple way to organize your files.

- **Tasks area** The middle-left side of the interface is called the Tasks area, which is used to view and manage collections of data and view clips that you are working on currently. *Clips* are pieces of video or pictures, and you'll learn about those in a moment. Clips appear in the middle portion of the interface.

- **Monitor** The middle-right side of the interface is called the Monitor. When you are working with video or still shots, the picture appears here. You also have standard Start and Stop buttons (along with others) to view video.

- **Workspace** The bottom portion of the interface is called the Workspace, which you use to edit video and/or combine still shots. You'll learn how to use the Workspace later in this appendix.

Record and Import Video

Now that you have taken a look at the interface setup, you are ready to begin recording or importing video. You record video if you are streaming it live into your computer. For example, with your digital camcorder, analog camcorder, or other device (such as a DVD Player or VCR), you can begin the streaming process, which appears in the Monitor in Windows Movie Maker. To record the video as it appears, just follow these steps:

1. Begin playing the video from the desired device into your computer.
2. Click Start | Programs | Windows Movie Maker to open the interface. You will see the video appear on the Monitor.
3. Click File | Capture Video.
4. In the window that appears (in which you can change the default recording options), make sure the Create Clips check box is selected, and then click the Record button. The video is recorded by Windows Movie Maker, as shown in Figure A-2. Notice that clips are being created and appear in the Collections area.
5. When you have finished recording, click File | Stop Capture.
6. Press the Save button on the toolbar, or click the File menu and then click Save Project As. The Save As window appears. By default, the project is saved in the My Videos folder found in My Documents. You can select an alternative location if you want. The file is saved as a Windows Movie file (.mswmm).

APPENDIX A: Get to Know Windows Movie Maker 2 **321**

FIGURE A-2 Video is recorded and broken into clips for easy management.

Aside from recording video, you can also import multimedia files—both video and audio (as well as still pictures). In many cases, you will choose to use the Import feature simply because you can work with previously saved files. To import a file that has been previously saved, just follow these steps:

1. In Windows Movie Maker, click File | Import Into Collections. The Import File window opens (see Figure A-3).

2. By default, the import feature looks in My Videos for a file to import, so you may have to navigate to another location on your computer where the file is stored. Windows Movie Maker looks for all kinds of media files; just select the one you want and click Open. Notice that there is a Create Clips For Video Files check box. You should leave this check box selected.

3. Click the Import button. The file is imported into Windows Movie Maker. You can now work with it or save it as a project.

NOTE *When you import a file, the actual source file that you choose to import is not moved from its current location. Windows Movie Maker imports and uses the data but does not change the location of the existing source file. You are then free to use the source file for other purposes as needed.*

A

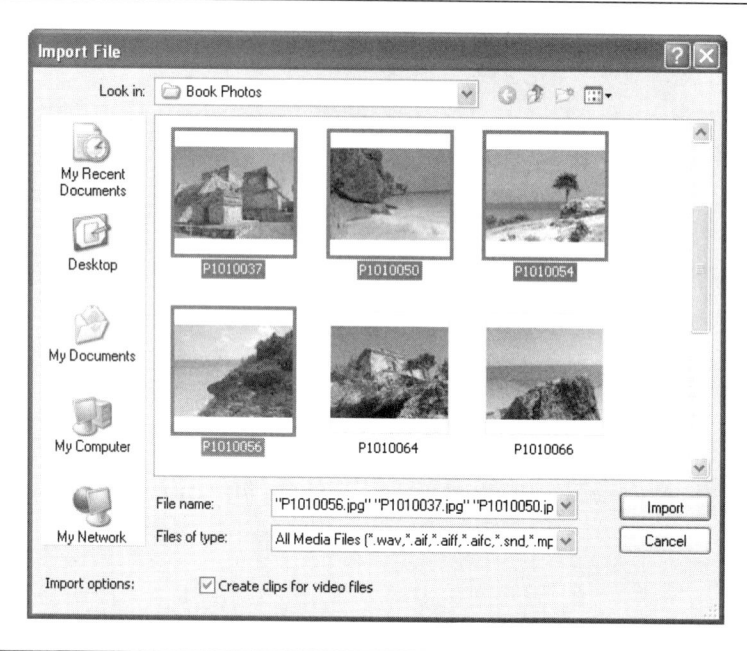

FIGURE A-3 Use the Import File window to browse for the files you want to import.

Work with Collections and Clips

As previously noted, collections are basically folders that contain clips of video or audio data. Collections provide a way for you to organize and save those clips as a project. Whenever you record or import media, Windows Movie Maker creates clips by default. Windows XP examines the video stream and attempts to segment it when the picture sequence changes.

For example, I imported some video of a birthday party. One portion of the video contained the cake and presents, while the next showed the kids playing outside. Windows XP broke the two sequences into two different clips, which I can manage and use. This doesn't always work perfectly, but it does work well enough so that Windows Movie Maker can help you manage and edit your video more easily.

If you right-click any collection, you can delete the collection (which deletes all of the clips that belong to it), rename it, or import or record more clips into it. Remember, collections are just folder structures that enable you to organize clips, so do what works best for you to keep your data organized in a suitable manner.

NOTE *You can create collections within collections.*

Make Movies

Now that you know how to record or import data and how to manage collections and clips, it's time to turn our attention to making movies. Using Windows Movie Maker, you record or import the clips you want to use, organize them into collections, edit them as desired, and then save the project.

Let's begin by editing video or still-shot clips. Keep in mind that you can combine video and still shots into one collection and blend them together as desired. You can also import background music and narrate a movie by recording your voice. The following sections show you how to perform these basic tasks, and you can learn more about specific features and options in Part III of this book.

Split Clips

As mentioned, Windows Movie Maker creates clips for you. However, you may need to split those clips into more manageable pieces. You can perform this function by using the Split command. The following steps show you how:

1. Select the clip that you want to split in the Collections area.

2. In the Monitor area, click the Play button.

3. When the clip reaches the point at which you want to split it, click the Split Clip button in the Monitor area. You can also click the Clip Menu and click Split, or simply press CTRL+SHIFT+S on your keyboard. In the Collections area, the clip is split in two—the first part of the clip retains its original name, while the second clip contains the original name followed by "(1)" (see Figure A-4). You can change the name as desired.

Combine Clips

Just as you can split a clip into two or more clips, you can also combine clips as needed. If you want to combine two or more clips, just follow these steps:

1. In the Collections area, select the clips that you want. Simply select the first clip, hold down the SHIFT key, and select the remaining clips that you want to combine.

2. Click the Clip menu, and then click Combine. The clips are combined using the first clip's name.

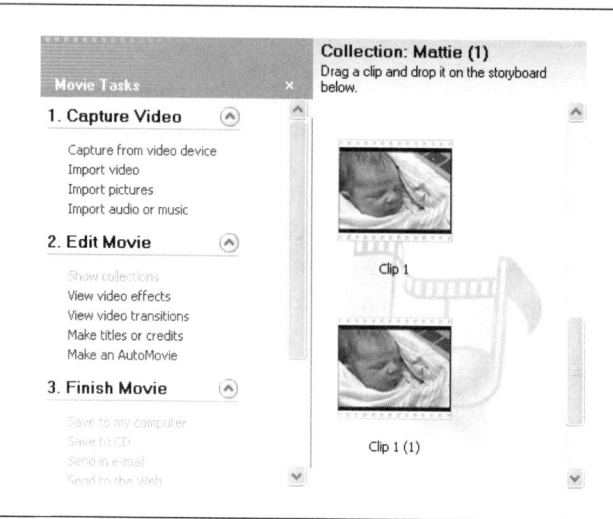

FIGURE A-4   Split a clip to break it into two manageable pieces.

Get Familiar with the Workspace

The Workspace, at the bottom of the interface, is the area where you edit and assemble movies (see Figure A-5). If you examine the interface, you see a few buttons on the top left of the area that correspond to areas in the Workspace. You can access volume controls, narration options, zoom controls, play and rewind buttons, and a button that you click to toggle between Timeline view and Storyboard view.

Create a Storyboard

You can use the Workspace to create a storyboard or to sequence your clips together. To do so, drag clips onto the Workspace area to create the storyboard. Begin by dragging the first clip in your movie to the video area of the Workspace. Once in position, you see the first frame of the video displayed in the box. If you change to Timeline view, you can see how much time is consumed by the click. By using the Timeline, you can connect pieces of clips together while keeping a watch over the

FIGURE A-5   Use the Workspace to assemble your movie.

FIGURE A-6 Drag clips and photos to the storyboard in Storyboard view.

time frame of the whole movie. However, you will probably find that the Storyboard view is initially easier to use when you are assembling your movie (see Figure A-6).

The Zoom In and Zoom Out buttons let you see more detail concerning the Timeline (click the Timeline button to switch to Timeline view). While zoomed out, the storyboard is displayed in increments of ten seconds. You can zoom in and out more to see the clips in whatever time measure you want.

Remember, feel free to mix video and still shots together on the storyboard. By default, imported still shots are given five seconds of time on a storyboard. You can change that value on the timeline by simply grabbing the edge of a photo and dragging to increase its duration on the timeline, as shown in Figure A-7.

Trim Clips

As you are working with clips in the storyboard, you will notice areas of your video that you want to cut out, or trim. These are often dead spots in the video where not much is happening. For example, let's say you have been videotaping your dog. Your dog does this great trick, but to capture the trick, you end up filming a boring minute or two waiting for the dog to do his trick. Now you want to lose the dead time when you create the movie. No problem—just trim off the excess.

In reality, the trim feature is very powerful because it gives you a fine level of control over your clips. You can use the Timeline feature in the Workspace and

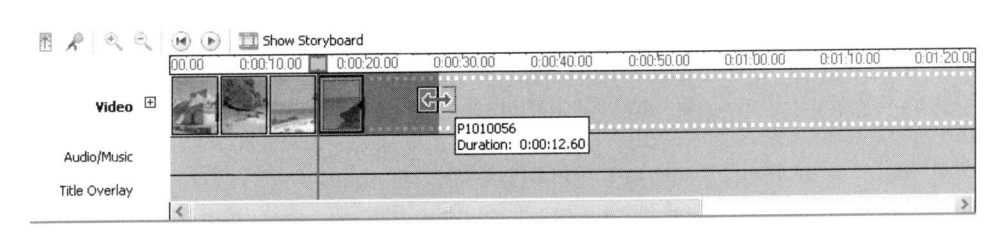

FIGURE A-7 Drag still shots to increase the time interval.

trim away seconds of a clip that you do not want to use. There are two ways to trim clips, and here's the first:

1. In the Workspace, select the clip you want to trim. The first frame of the clip appears in the Monitor.

2. The trimming process *keeps* the portion of videotape that you trim and discards the rest. That seems a little confusing, but think of it as trimming a piece of paper. You trim away the pieces you don't want in order to keep the primary piece. With the trim feature, you set beginning and end trim points, and everything outside of the area is trimmed away. To begin trimming, click Play in the Monitor.

3. Watch the clip until it reaches the place where you want to begin trimming. Click the Clip menu, and then click Set Start Trim Point. (Remember, anything previous to the beginning trim point will be discarded.)

4. When the clip reaches the point where you want to stop trimming, click Clip, and then click Set End Trim Point. All video outside of the trim area is cut away.

5. If you don't want to keep the trim points, just click the Clip menu and click Clear Trim Points.

NOTE *As you can probably guess, the trim feature is very useful—but a little confusing at first. Spend a few moments playing with it until you get the hang of how it works.*

Add Audio Files to Your Movies

Once you have placed clips on the storyboard, and trimmed and transitioned them as desired, you can add audio to your movie. For example, you can add narration, background music, or even additional background noise. In short, if it's an audio file, you can add it to your movie.

You may think, "What about the audio on my existing video?" For example, let's say you tape a family reunion. Everyone is talking and laughing, but you want to add soft background music to the movie. Can you add the music without ruining the original audio? Absolutely! Windows Movie Maker gives you several great options for your sound track, and you find out more about them in Chapter 13. In fact, you can learn all about using effects, using transitions, saving movies, and creating your movie projects in Part III of this book!

Appendix B

More Inexpensive and Fun Digital Software

If trying all of the projects in this book has whetted your appetite for even more, never fear: There are plenty of additional cool tools and utilities from third-party vendors that you can grab and use, and many are listed in the following table. Most of these tools allow you a free trial download for about a month, and most are under $50 if you decide to buy. You can get all of ese tools at www.download.com— just search for the tool's name to find it. Have fun!

Tool	What You Can Do with It	What It Costs
PC Inspector Smart Recovery 4.0	Recover deleted photos from any digital camera	Free
Ashampoo AudioCenter 1.0	Extract, convert, burn, and repair audio files	Free trial, $50 to purchase
eZediaMX 3.0.6	Create all kinds of digital media, text, and even virtual reality	Free trial, $239 purchase
PhotoTalk Deluxe 1.0	Organize your digital photo albums	Free trial, $25 to purchase
Media Jukebox 8.0.399	Play, manage, and use audio content	Free trial, $25 to buy
J. River Media Center 9.1	Turn your PC into a media and entertainment center	Free trial, $40 to buy
iView Media 1.2	Play, view, and convert all kinds of digital files	Free trial, $30 to buy
Media Digitalizer 1.0	Convert LPs and tapes to digital format	Free trial, $25 to buy
Anokee PLUS Wizard Edition 4.0	Manage and cross-reference multimedia files on your computer	Free trial, $60 to buy
AudioBANK 2003 1.1	Browse music on your computer by looking at album cover art	Free trial, $30 to buy
Image Vault 1.0	Archive, manage, and keep secure your photo images	Free trial, $20 to buy
Acoustica 3.0	Import CD tracks, make custom CD tracks, and burn CDs	Free trial, $29 to buy
Digital Photo Librarian Image Editor	Manage and edit your digital photos quickly and easily	Free
Preclick Digital Photo Software 2.0	Manage and edit photos	Free trial, $20 to buy
Digital Photo Album 1.0.1.6	Create photo albums for the Web	Free
Digital Photo Resizer	Resize a group of photos at one time	Free trial, $10 to buy
MemoriesOnTV 4.0.6	Create a DVD or VCD of your photos for viewing on a TV	Free trial, $40 to buy
PhoTags 2.0	Add labels and tags to your photos for organizational purposes	Free trial, $20 to buy
ArcSoft Fun House 1.0	Combine photos into one for funny effects and more	Free trial, $36 to buy
ScreensaverMaker 2.0	Make custom screen savers	Free trial, $60 to buy

Index

A

Acrobat Reader files, 76
Advanced Recording Options window, 303–304
Advanced slide show options, 137–138
aging effects, 203–205
Alarm Clock feature, 266–276
    changing alarms, 273
    computer clock and, 268
    cool and cruel options, 274–275
    deleting alarms, 274
    ideas for using, 276
    managing alarms, 272–275
    setting alarms, 269–272
    starting, 266–267
    turning off alarms, 274
    wake-up alarms, 269–270
    weekly or monthly alarms, 270–272

albums. *See* photo albums
analog audio devices, 296–300
    connection process for, 298–300
    hardware requirements for, 297–298
Analog Recorder, 296–311
    cleaning tracks in, 307–308
    combining tracks in, 306–307
    Content Protection Options, 308, 309
    deleting tracks in, 304, 305
    device connections and, 296–300
    ideas for using, 311
    naming tracks in, 304, 305
    quality settings, 308–310
    recording music in, 302–304
    reviewing tracks in, 304
    saving tracks in, 308–310
    splitting tracks in, 305–306
    starting, 300
    testing input in, 301–302

analog video, capture devices, 317–318
animating titles, 172–173
audio CDs, 15–16
    burning your own, 15–18
    ideas for creating, 39
    jewel case inserts for, 37–38
    personalized labels for, 19, 22–36
    ripping songs from, 8–12
audio tracks
    cleaning, 307–308
    combining, 306–307
    deleting, 304, 305
    naming, 304, 305
    reviewing, 304
    splitting, 305–306
    See also sound tracks
Auto Volume Leveling feature, 59
AVI file format, 260

B

Background Image Settings dialog box, 30–32
background images
    CD labels and, 29–33
    desktop and, 84
    photo editing of, 34
    title pages and, 158
background music
    movies and, 179, 222–224
    photo stories and, 146–147, 159
    See also music

Backup or Restore Wizard, 88–92
backups
    digital photo, 87–96
    online, 92–96
    types of, 90
    Windows XP utility for, 87–92
birthday videos, 166–179
    assembling, 174–175
    importing video and photos for, 168–169
    organizing footage for, 169–170
    preparing to create, 166–168
    special effects in, 178–179
    title pages for, 170–174, 175
    transitions added to, 176–178
bitmap files, 78
black and white effect, 201–202
blocking, 187
Blur effect, 191
BMP files, 78
broadband connections, 44
burning CDs, 5, 15–18
    audio, 17–18
    movie, 233, 235–236

C

camera software, 131
capture devices, 317–318
case-sensitive passwords, 283

Index

cassette player connections
    description of, 300
    hardware requirements for, 298
CD labels, 22–39
    backgrounds for, 29–34
    choosing CDs or playlists for, 24–25
    ideas for creating, 39
    jewel case inserts and, 37–38
    launching the label maker, 24
    materials required for, 22–23
    planning considerations for, 23–24
    previewing, 28–29, 30, 33
    printing, 34–36
    problems with duplicating, 27
    process of designing, 27–34
    templates for, 25–27
    text for, 28–29
CD Music discs, 16
CD-R discs, 16
CD-RW discs, 16
CDs
    burning your own, 5, 15–18
    jewel case inserts for, 37–38
    movies saved to, 233, 235–236, 241
    personalized labels for, 19, 22–36
    ripping songs from, 8–12
    slide shows on, 140–141
    types of, 15–17
    See also custom CDs
CD Slide Show Generator, 141

clips, 320, 322
    combining, 261, 323
    splitting, 323, 324
    trimming, 325–326
clock, computer
    checking accuracy of, 268
    See also Plus! Alarm Clock
collections, 319, 322
color chooser, 58
Color Warp effect, 191
combining
    audio tracks, 306–307
    video clips, 261, 323
computers
    checking the clock in, 268
    connecting analog devices to, 296–300
    saving movies to, 229–233
Content Protection Options, Analog Recorder, 308, 309
Copy Music tab, 7–8
copy-protected music, 7, 159, 308, 309
copyright issues, 224
Create New Alarm Wizard, 269–270, 271
credits, movie, 189
cross-fading feature, 59
cue cards, 205–207
custom CDs, 4–19
    burning, 15–18
    downloading songs for, 12

ideas for creating, 19
jewel case inserts for, 37–38
organizing playlists for, 13–15
personalized labels for, 19, 22–36
planning considerations for, 4–6
requirements for making, 4
ripping songs for, 6–12

D

data CDs, 16
Date and Time Properties dialog box, 268
deleting/removing
    alarms, 274
    audio tracks, 304, 305
    photos from slide shows, 134
    visualizations, 63
designing CD labels, 27–34
    backgrounds, 29–34
    text, 28–29
desktop backgrounds, 84
Details view, 82
dialogue, movie
    recording, 218–222
    writing, 187
dial-up connections, 44
differential backups, 90

digital cameras
    saving movies to, 240
    software included with, 131
digital media software, 328
digital photos, 74–97
    albums of, 118–126
    backing up, 87–92
    contact sheets of, 109
    culling for slide shows, 130–132, 133
    desktop background from, 84
    editing, 34, 83, 113–115, 170
    e-mailing, 113–114
    file types for, 74–78
    folder structure for, 85–87
    ideas for working with, 96–97
    importing into Movie Maker, 168–169
    managing, 82–84
    naming, 78–79
    online storage of, 92–96
    ordering prints of, 108–112
    organizing, 85–87
    photo stories of, 144–161
    previewing, 82–83
    printing, 83, 100–101, 106–108, 115–116, 119–120
    publishing on the Web, 112
    resizing, 83–84
    resolution of, 103–105
    right-clicking on, 82
    rotating, 84

slide shows of, 84–85, 128–142
used in videos, 167
viewing, 79–85
webcams and, 251
digitizing music, 300–310
cleaning tracks, 307–308
combining tracks, 306–307
content-protection options, 308
deleting tracks, 304, 305
naming tracks, 304, 305
quality settings, 308–310
recording music, 302–304
reviewing tracks, 304
saving tracks, 308–310
splitting tracks, 305–306
testing your input, 301–302
disk space, 234
document files, 76
downloading
digital media software, 328
HTML Slide Show Wizard, 128–129
skins, 66–67
songs, 12
Timershot software, 248
Video Screen Saver, 258–259
visualizations, 62
dpi (dots per inch), 105
DV cameras, saving movies to, 240

E

editing
digital photos, 34, 83, 113–115, 170
video clips, 323–324
effects in movies, 178–179
element of surprise, 185
ellipses (...) button, 262
e-mail
default program for, 238
media link for, 59
movies sent via, 236–237
photos sent via, 113–114
sharing slide shows via, 140–141
Exotic Colors effect, 191, 193

F

FAT32 file system, 234
fault tolerance, 314
Featured Stations list, 43
file formats, 75–77
movie files, 229, 260
picture files, 77–78
file location, 251–252
file types, 74–77

Film Age effects, 203–205
film footage
    gathering for movies, 167
    importing into Movie Maker, 168–169, 188–189, 200
    organizing, 169–170
    See also movies; videos
filming scary movies, 188
Filmstrip view, 81, 138, 254–255
finding Internet radio stations, 45–47, 48
FlipAlbum software, 125
folders
    camera software and, 131
    photo files and, 79, 85–87
    saving movies to, 229–233
    subfolders and, 86–87
Font dialog box, 29
FotoSlate software, 120–124
Fullscreen option, 139

G

GIF files, 78
GlobeDesk web site, 95, 96
graphic equalizer, 59
Grayscale effect, 201–202

H

Halloween movies, 183
headset microphones, 146
HighMAT CDs, 17
home monitoring, 246
    frequency of pictures for, 251
    great ideas for, 256
    items required for, 246–248
    reviewing photos from, 253–255
    system setup for, 249–253
horror movies. *See* scary movies
HTML (Hypertext Markup Language), 129–130
HTML Slide Show Wizard, 128–130, 132–139
    downloading, 128–129
    explained, 129–130
    options, 134–139
    removing photos, 134
    selecting photos, 132–133
Hue Spectrum effect, 191, 192

I

iBackup web site, 96
icons
    digital photos as, 81
    files represented by, 75

Index   335

Icons option, View menu, 81
IEEE 1394 cards, 317
ImageStation web site, 95
importing into Movie Maker
    music, 222–224
    photos, 168–169
    title pages, 175
    videos, 168–169, 188–189, 200, 317, 321–322
incremental backups, 90
inkjet printers, 101–102
Internet
    broadband connections to, 44
    downloading songs from, 12
    publishing photos on, 112
    storing photos on, 92–96
    See also World Wide Web
Internet Properties dialog box, 238
Internet radio, 42–52
    broadband connections and, 44
    finding stations on, 45–47, 48
    ideas for using, 51–52
    interface for, 42–44
    listening to, 47, 49–50
    My Stations list, 50–51, 52
    requirements for, 42
Internet Service Providers (ISPs), 237
IrFanview utility, 114–115

J

JAlbum software, 125
jewel case inserts, 37–38
JPEG files, 76, 77–78
jukebox feature. *See* Party Mode

L

labels. *See* CD labels
laser printers, 101–102
List view, 82
lossy files, 78

M

managing
    alarms, 272–275
    digital photos, 82–84
    webcam photos, 255
Marquee options, Party Mode, 287–288
Media Library, 12, 279
Media Link For E-Mail feature, 59

Media Player. *See* Windows Media Player
Microphone Test window, 152
microphones
    movie dialogue recording with, 218
    photo story recording with, 146, 152
Microsoft Outlook, 237
Microsoft Plus! Digital Media Edition, 22
    Alarm Clock, 266–276
    Analog Recorder, 296–311
    CD Label Maker, 22–23
    movie transitions, 176
    Party Mode, 278
    Photo Story, 144–145
    plug-ins, 68
    skins, 66
    Speaker Enhancement, 69–70
    special effects, 178, 189, 191
    visualizations, 62
Microsoft Word files, 76
Monitor, Movie Maker, 320
monthly alarms, 270–272
movies, 166–179, 228–241
    aging effects for, 203–205
    assembling, 174–175, 188–194
    background music in, 222–224
    birthday or wedding, 166–179
    black and white, 201–202
    burning to CDs, 233, 235–236, 241
    capturing, 317–318
    credits for, 189
    cue cards in, 205–207
    deciding how to use, 228–229
    dialogue recording for, 218–222
    filming, 188
    gathering film and photos for, 167
    ideas for creating, 179, 194–195, 207
    identifying goals for, 166–167
    importing into Movie Maker, 168–169, 188–189, 200, 317, 321–322
    narration in, 179, 184, 218–222
    old-looking, 198–207
    organizing footage for, 169–170
    planning, 167–169, 185–187, 212–214
    recording, 320–321
    requirements for, 166
    saving, 194, 207, 228–241
    scary, 182–195
    screen savers from, 258–264
    sending via e-mail, 236–237
    sound tracks for, 184, 194, 200–201, 210–225, 326

Index

special effects in, 178–179, 189–194, 201–205
storyboards for, 174–175, 186–187, 189
summary statements for, 186
title page for, 170–174, 189
transitions added to, 176–178, 189
uploading to the Web, 239–240, 241
writing scripts for, 187
See also Windows Movie Maker 2

music
Alarm Clock feature and, 269–270
copy-protected, 7, 159, 308, 309
copyright issues and, 224
digitizing, 300–310
downloading from the Internet, 12
importing into Movie Maker, 222–224
movies and, 179, 184, 222–224
organizing into playlists, 13–15, 279
photo stories and, 146–147, 159
recording from analog sources, 302–304
ripping from CDs, 4, 6–12
See also songs

music CDs. *See* audio CDs

muting sound tracks, 214, 216–217, 263
My Stations list, 43, 50–51, 52
MyDocsOnline web site, 95
MyPublisher web site, 125, 126

N

naming
audio tracks, 304, 305
photo files, 78–79

narrating movies
old movies, 203
recording process for, 218–222
scary movies, 184
wedding or birthday movies, 179

narrating photo stories
basic rules for, 151
considerations for, 145–146
recording process for, 152–154
script writing tips for, 146

Negative effect, 191, 193
normal backups, 90
Normal mode, Media Player, 64
Now Playing area (Media Player), 54–61
color chooser, 58
cross-fading feature, 59

graphic equalizer, 59, 60
illustrated, 55
Media Link For E-Mail, 59
options and controls, 55–57
Party Mode options, 286–287
play speed settings, 59
Quiet Mode, 60
SRS WOW Effects, 60
Video Settings, 61
volume leveling feature, 59
NTFS file system, 234

O

old movies, 198–207
    aging effects, 203–205
    basics of, 199
    benefits of, 198
    black and white effect, 201–202
    ideas for, 198–199, 207
    importing clips for, 200
    saving and using, 207
    sound track of, 200–201, 203
    steps for making, 200–207
    title cue cards in, 205–207
online storage, 92–96
    safety of, 93
    web sites providing, 94–96

organizing
    digital photos, 85–87
    footage for movies, 169–170
    songs into playlists, 13–15
Outlook Express program, 237

P

panning feature, 154–155, 157
paper, photo-quality, 102–103
Party Mode (Media Player), 278–294
    explained, 278–279
    ideas for using, 279, 294
    interface options, 290–292
    Marquee options, 287–288
    Now Playing options, 286–287
    Privacy option, 285–286
    security issues, 279–283
    setting up, 284–290
    Skin option, 289–290
    starting, 290–292
    stopping, 293–294
    welcome screen, 284
passwords
    creating, 281–282
    do's and don'ts, 283
PDD files, 77

Index 339

PDF files, 76
personal CDs. *See* custom CDs
photo albums, 118–126
    electronic, 125
    ideas for creating, 126
    manually creating, 118–120
    photo books and, 124–126
    printing photos for, 119–120
    software for creating, 120–124
photo books, 124–126
photo printers, 101–102
Photo Printing Wizard, 106–108, 109, 119
photo stories, 144–161
    Advanced Options for, 154–155
    background music for, 146–147, 159
    choosing photos for, 145, 148
    creating, 147–161
    display time of photos in, 151, 156, 159
    ideas for producing, 161
    narrating photos in, 145–146, 151, 152–154
    non-narrated photos in, 151, 156
    organizing photos for, 149–150
    panning feature for, 154–155, 157
    previewing, 160
    quality settings for, 160, 161
    recording, 150–157
    saving, 160, 161
    sharing, 161
    software for producing, 144–145, 147–148
    title page for, 157–158
    writing scripts for, 146
    See also slide shows
Photo Story Wizard, 147–148
photo-processing centers, 113
photo-quality paper, 102–103
photos, digital. *See* digital photos
Photoshop, 34
Photoshop Album, 80, 125
Photoshop Elements, 34, 77
picture size options, 135–137
pixels, 103–104, 105
play speed settings, 59
playlists
    adding audio tracks to, 310
    organizing songs into, 13–15
    Party Mode feature and, 279, 290–291
    screen savers and, 264
plug-ins, 68–69
Plus! Alarm Clock, 266–276
    computer clock and, 268
    cool and cruel options, 274–275

ideas for using, 276
managing alarms, 272–275
setting alarms, 269–272
starting, 266–267
Plus! Analog Recorder, 296–311
    device connections and, 296–300
    digitizing music with, 300–310
    ideas for using, 311
Plus! CD Label Maker, 24–38
    CD label creation, 24–36
    jewel case creation, 37–38
    starting, 23, 24
Plus! Color Warp effect, 191, 192
Plus! Exotic Colors effect, 191, 193
Plus! Negative effect, 191, 193
Plus! Speaker Enhancement feature, 69–70
Plus! Texture effect, 191, 194
PowerToys
    CD Slide Show Generator, 141
    HTML Slide Show Wizard, 128
    Timershot, 246, 247
    Video Screen Saver, 258–259
Premium Services, Media Player, 67–68
previewing
    CD labels, 28–29, 30, 33
    digital photos, 82–83
photo stories, 160
slide shows, 138
printers, 101–102
printing
    CD labels, 34–36
    contact sheets, 109
    digital photos, 83, 100–101, 106–108, 115–116, 119–120
    paper quality and, 102–103
    resolution and, 103–105
    tips and ideas for, 115–116
prints of photos
    online ordering of, 108–112
    photo-processing centers and, 113
    web sites providing, 109
PrintShop program, 120
Privacy option, Party Mode, 285–286, 293
publishing digital photos, 112

Q

quality settings
    for analog recording, 308–310
    for photo stories, 160, 161
Quiet Mode, Media Player, 60

R

Radio Tuner
- finding stations with, 45–47, 48
- interface features, 42–44
- My Stations list, 50–51, 52
- *See also* Internet radio

ReaGallery Pro software, 125

Recently Played Stations feature, 43, 51

record player connections
- description of, 300
- hardware requirements for, 297

recording analog music, 296–311
- device connections for, 296–300
- digitization process and, 300–310
- *See also* Analog Recorder

recording movie dialogue, 218–222
- important points about, 221
- Movie Maker options for, 218–220

recording photo stories, 150–157
- Advanced Options and, 154–155
- basic rules for, 151
- narration, 152–154

recording video, 320–321

reel-to-reel player connections
- description of, 300
- hardware requirements for, 298

resizing digital photos, 83–84

resolution
- photo, 103–105
- printer, 102, 105

right-clicking
- on digital photos, 82–84
- on sound tracks, 216–217

ripping songs, 4, 6–12

rotating digital photos, 84

S

Save Movie Wizard, 231–233, 235–236, 240

saving audio tracks, 308–310

saving movies, 194, 207, 228–241
- to CDs, 233, 235–236
- to computers, 229–233
- to DV cameras, 240
- to e-mail messages, 236–238
- options for, 229, 230
- problems with, 234
- to the Web, 239–240, 241

saving photo stories, 160, 161

saving slide shows, 135

saving webcam photos, 252–253

scary movies, 182–195
- assembling, 188–194
- filming, 188
- ideas for, 194–195
- overacting in, 184
- planning, 185–187
- sound track for, 184, 194
- storyboards for, 186–187
- title page and credits for, 189
- transitions and effects in, 189–194
- types of scares in, 183–185
- varieties of, 182–183
- visual scares in, 183–184
- writing scripts for, 187

screen savers
- playlists and, 264
- video, 258–264

scripts
- for photo stories, 146
- for scary movies, 187

searching for Internet radio stations, 45–47, 48

security issues
- Party Mode feature and, 279–282
- password creation and, 283

sharing
- photo stories, 161
- slide shows, 140–141

Simple slide show option, 137
situational tension in movies, 185
Skin mode, Media Player, 64
Skin option, Party Mode, 289–290
skins, 64–67
- getting additional, 66–67
- Party Mode feature, 278, 289–290, 292
- steps for choosing, 64–66

Slide Show view, 137
slide shows, 128–142
- adding images to, 132–133
- CD Slide Show Generator and, 141
- choosing options for, 134–139
- creating, 130–139
- culling photos for, 130–132, 133
- Full Screen option for, 139
- HTML Slide Show Wizard and, 128–130, 132–139
- ideas for producing, 142
- picture size options for, 135–137
- Previews option for, 138
- removing photos from, 134
- saving, 135
- sharing, 140–141
- types of, 137–138
- viewing, 139–140
- Windows XP feature for, 84–85
- *See also* photo stories

software
- digital camera, 131
- photo album, 120–124, 125

Index

songs
- third-party, 328
- webcam, 246–256

songs
- copyright issues and, 224
- downloading from the Internet, 12
- importing into Movie Maker, 222–224
- organizing into playlists, 13–15, 279
- photo stories and, 146–147, 158–159
- ripping from CDs, 4, 6–12
- *See also* music

sound effects
- Alarm Clock and, 269–270
- copyright issues and, 224
- web resources for, 225

Sound Hardware Test Wizard, 152

sound tracks, 210–225, 326
- basics of, 210–212
- copyright rules and, 224
- ideas for creating, 225
- music used in, 222–224
- muting, 214, 216–217, 263
- old movies and, 200–201
- original video sound and, 211, 213, 214
- planning, 212–214
- recording dialogue for, 218–222
- rules for using, 211–212
- scary movies and, 184, 194
- sound effects and, 225
- storyboards for, 214, 215
- wedding/birthday movies and, 179
- *See also* audio tracks

Speaker Enhancement feature, 69–70

special effects
- old movies and, 201–205
- scary movies and, 189–194
- wedding/birthday movies and, 178–179

splitting
- audio tracks, 305–306
- video clips, 323, 324

spoofs of scary movies, 183

SRS WOW Effects, 60

stereo receiver connections
- description of, 298–299
- hardware requirements for, 297

storage, online, 92–96

stories. *See* photo stories

Storyboard mode (Movie Maker), 174–175, 324–325

storyboards
- creating, 324–325
- scary movies and, 186–187, 189
- sound tracks and, 214, 215
- wedding/birthday movies and, 174–175

streaming media, 44

Streamload web site, 95
subfolders, 86–87
surround sound, 60

T

Tasks area, Movie Maker, 320
templates for CD labels, 25–27
text files, 76
text for CD labels, 28–29
Texture effect, 191, 194
third-party software, 328
3-D Album software, 125
Thumbnails view, 80, 81
TIF (or TIFF) files, 78
Tiles option, 81
Timeline view, 216, 217
Timershot software, 246–256
    downloading, 248
    explained, 248–249
    file locations, 251–252
    ideas for using, 256
    installing, 248
    managing photos, 255
    photo size options, 251
    picture frequency options, 251
    saving photos, 252–253
    setting up, 249–253
    viewing photos, 253–255
    See also webcams
title pages
    for movies, 170–174, 175, 189, 205
    for photo stories, 157–158
toolbars, Movie Maker, 319
tracks. *See* audio tracks; sound tracks
transitions
    in scary movies, 189–194
    in wedding and birthday movies, 176–178
trimming clips, 325–326

U

USB hubs, 247
USB ports, 246, 247
User Accounts window, 280–282

V

VCR connections, 298
Video Screen Saver, 258–264
    downloading, 258–259
    file formats and, 259–260
    ideas for using, 264
    installing, 259
    muting audio, 263
    playlists and, 264
    setting up, 261–263

Video Settings, Media Player, 61
videos
    capture devices for, 317–318
    importing into Movie Maker, 168–169, 188–189, 200, 317, 321–322
    recording in Movie Maker, 320–321
    screen savers created from, 258–264
    sound tracks from, 211, 213, 326
    working with clips from, 189, 322, 323–326
    See also movies; Windows Movie Maker 2
View menu, 81–82
viewing
    digital photos, 79–85
    slide shows, 139–140
    webcam photos, 253–255
visual scares, 183–184
visualizations, 61–63
    getting additional, 62
    modifying behavior of, 62–63
    removing, 63

W

wake-up alarm, 269–270
Web Publishing Wizard, 112
web sites
    online storage on, 94–96
    photo printing via, 109
    saving movies to, 239–240, 241
    sharing slide shows on, 141
    sound effects from, 225
    See also World Wide Web
webcams, 246–256
    ideas for using, 256
    managing photos from, 255
    saving photos taken by, 252–253
    setting up software for, 249–253
    USB connections and, 246, 247
    viewing photos from, 253–255
    where to purchase, 247
    See also Timershot software
wedding videos, 166–179
    assembling, 174–175
    importing video and photos for, 168–169
    organizing footage for, 169–170
    preparing to create, 166–168
    special effects in, 178–179
    title pages for, 170–174, 175
    transitions added to, 176–178
weekly alarms, 270–272
Windows Backup utility, 87–92
    installing, 87–88
    steps for using, 88–92
Windows Media Player, 4–5, 54–70
    color chooser, 58
    Copy Music tab, 7–8

cross-fading feature, 59
current version of, 5
customization options, 54–70
graphic equalizer, 59, 60
Media Library, 12
Media Link For E-Mail, 59
Movie Player files and, 229, 316
Now Playing area, 54–61
Party Mode for, 278–294
play speed settings, 59
playlist creation, 13–15
plug-ins, 68–69
Plus! Speaker Enhancement, 69–70
Premium Services, 67–68
Quiet Mode, 60
Radio Tuner interface, 42–44
ripping songs to, 6–12
skins, 64–67, 289
SRS WOW effects, 60
Video Settings, 61
visualizations, 61–63
volume leveling feature, 59
Windows Media Video (WMV) format, 316
Windows Movie Maker 2, 166, 314–326
 assembling movies in, 174–175, 188–194
 background music in, 222–224
 capturing analog video in, 317–318
 clips in, 320, 322, 323–324
 collections in, 319, 322
 combining video clips in, 261
 dialogue recorded in, 218–222
 digital photos used in, 168–169
 downloading from Microsoft, 166, 314
 file format limitations of, 229, 316
 fun pack extras for, 225
 ideas for using, 179
 importing videos into, 168–169, 188–189, 200, 317, 321–322
 interface for, 318–320
 making movies with, 323–326
 muting audio tracks in, 214, 216–217, 263
 overview of features in, 314–315
 recording video in, 320–321
 saving movies in, 194, 207, 228–241
 sending movies via e-mail with, 236–238
 sound tracks in, 184, 194, 200–201, 210–225
 special effects in, 178–179, 189–194, 201–205
 storyboards, 174–175, 324–325
 system requirements for, 316

title page feature, 170–174
transition options, 176–178, 189
uploading movies to the Web with, 239–240
Workspace, 320, 324
See also movies
Windows Photo Printing Wizard, 106–108, 109
Windows XP PowerToys
    CD Slide Show Generator, 141
    HTML Slide Show Wizard, 128
    Timershot, 246, 247
    Video Screen Saver, 258–259
WMA files, 261, 310
WMV files, 316
word-processing files, 76
Workspace, Movie Maker, 320, 324
World Wide Web
    broadband connections to, 44
    downloading songs from, 12
    Internet radio and, 42–52
    publishing photos on, 112
    sending movies to, 239–240, 241
    sharing slide shows via, 141
    storing photos on, 92–96
    See also Internet; web sites
writing scripts
    for photo stories, 146
    for scary movies, 187

X

XDrive web site, 94–95

Z

zip code, radio search by, 46–47

INTERNATIONAL CONTACT INFORMATION

AUSTRALIA
McGraw-Hill Book Company
Australia Pty. Ltd.
TEL +61-2-9900-1800
FAX +61-2-9878-8881
http://www.mcgraw-hill.com.au
books-it_sydney@mcgraw-hill.com

CANADA
McGraw-Hill Ryerson Ltd.
TEL +905-430-5000
FAX +905-430-5020
http://www.mcgraw-hill.ca

**GREECE, MIDDLE EAST, & AFRICA
(Excluding South Africa)**
McGraw-Hill Hellas
TEL +30-210-6560-990
TEL +30-210-6560-993
TEL +30-210-6560-994
FAX +30-210-6545-525

MEXICO (Also serving Latin America)
McGraw-Hill Interamericana Editores
S.A. de C.V.
TEL +525-1500-5108
FAX +525-117-1589
http://www.mcgraw-hill.com.mx
carlos_ruiz@mcgraw-hill.com

SINGAPORE (Serving Asia)
McGraw-Hill Book Company
TEL +65-6863-1580
FAX +65-6862-3354
http://www.mcgraw-hill.com.sg
mghasia@mcgraw-hill.com

SOUTH AFRICA
McGraw-Hill South Africa
TEL +27-11-622-7512
FAX +27-11-622-9045
robyn_swanepoel@mcgraw-hill.com

SPAIN
McGraw-Hill/
Interamericana de España, S.A.U.
TEL +34-91-180-3000
FAX +34-91-372-8513
http://www.mcgraw-hill.es
professional@mcgraw-hill.es

**UNITED KINGDOM, NORTHERN,
EASTERN, & CENTRAL EUROPE**
McGraw-Hill Education Europe
TEL +44-1-628-502500
FAX +44-1-628-770224
http://www.mcgraw-hill.co.uk
emea_queries@mcgraw-hill.com

ALL OTHER INQUIRIES Contact:
McGraw-Hill/Osborne
TEL +1-510-420-7700
FAX +1-510-420-7703
http://www.osborne.com
omg_international@mcgraw-hill.com

[Sound Off!

Visit us at **www.osborne.com/bookregistration** and let us know what you thought of this book. While you're online you'll have the opportunity to register for newsletters and special offers from McGraw-Hill/Osborne.

We want to hear from you!

[Sneak Peek

Visit us today at **www.betabooks.com** and see what's coming from McGraw-Hill/Osborne tomorrow!

Based on the successful software paradigm, Bet@Books™ allows computing professionals to view partial and sometimes complete text versions of selected titles online. Bet@Books™ viewing is free, invites comments and feedback, and allows you to "test drive" books in progress on the subjects that interest you the most.

OSBORNE DELIVERS RESULTS!]

OSBORNE
www.osborne.com

Know How

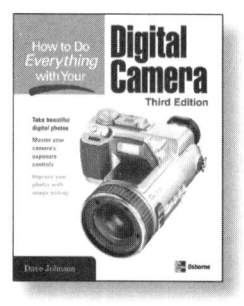

How to Do Everything with Your Digital Camera
Third Edition
ISBN: 0-07-223081-9

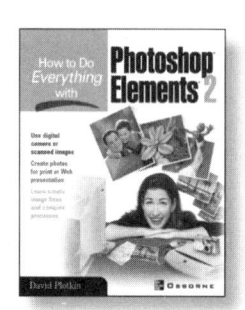

How to Do Everything with Photoshop Elements 2
ISBN: 0-07-222638-2

How to Do Everything with Photoshop CS
ISBN: 0-07-223143-2
4-color

How to Do Everything with Your Sony CLIÉ
Second Edition
ISBN: 0-07-223074-6

How to Do Everything with Macromedia Contribute
0-07-222892-X

How to Do Everything with Your eBay Business
0-07-222948-9

How to Do Everything with Illustrator CS
ISBN: 0-07-223092-4
4-color

How to Do Everything with Your iPod
ISBN: 0-07-222700-1

How to Do Everything with Your iMac,
Third Edition
ISBN: 0-07-213172-1

How to Do Everything with Your iPAQ Pocket P
Second Edition
ISBN: 0-07-222950-0

OSBORNE DELIVERS RESULTS!

McGraw Hill Osborne
www.osborne.com